Satomi Ikezawa

TRANSLATED AND ADAPTED BY
William Flanagan

LETTERED BY
Michaelis/Carpelis Design

LONDON

Published in the United Kingdom by Tanoshimi in 2007

1 3 5 7 9 10 8 6 4 2

First published in Japan in 2003 by Kodansha Ltd., Tokyo

Published by arrangement with Kodansha Ltd., Tokyo and with Del Rey,
an imprint of Random House Inc., New York

Tanoshimi
Random House, 20 Vauxhall Bridge Road,
London, SW1V 2SA

www.tanoshimi.tv
www.randomhouse.co.uk

Addresses for companies within The Random House Group Limited can be found at:
www.randomhouse.co.uk/offices.htm

The Random House Group Limited Reg. No. 954009

A CIP catalogue record for this book is available from the British Library

ISBN 9780099506560

The Random House Group Limited makes every effort to ensure that the papers used in its books are made
from trees that have been legally sourced from well-managed and credibly certified forests. Our paper
procurement policy can be found at: www.randomhouse.co.uk/paper.htm

Printed and bound in Germany by GGP Media GmbH, Pößneck

Translator and adaptor — William Flanagan
Lettering — Michaelis/Carpelis Design

Contents

Honorifics

Throughout the Tanoshimi Manga books, you will find Japanese honorifics left intact in the translations. For those not familiar with how the Japanese use honorifics, and more importantly, how they differ from English honorifics, we present this brief overview.

Politeness has always been a critical facet of Japanese culture. Ever since the feudal era, when Japan was a highly stratified society, use of honorifics—which can be defined as polite speech that indicates relationship or status—has played an essential role in the Japanese language. When addressing someone in Japanese, an honorific usually takes the form of a suffix attached to one's name (example: 'Asuna-san'), or as a title at the end of one's name or in place of the name itself (example: 'Negi-sensei,' or simply 'Sensei!').

Honorifics can be expressions of respect or endearment. In the context of manga and anime, honorifics give insight into the nature of the relationship between characters. Many translations into English leave out these important honorifics, and therefore distort the 'feel' of the original Japanese. Because Japanese honorifics contain nuances that English honorifics lack, it is our policy at Tanoshimi not to translate them. Here, instead, is a guide to some of the honorifics you may encounter in Tanoshimi Manga.

-san: This is the most common honorific, and is equivalent to Mr., Miss, Ms., Mrs., etc. It is the all-purpose honorific and can be used in any situation where politeness is required.

-sama: This is one level higher than '-san.' It is used to confer great respect.

-dono: This comes from the word 'tono,' which means 'lord.' It is an even higher level than '-sama,' and confers utmost respect.

-kun: This suffix is used at the end of boys' names to express familiarity or endearment. It is also sometimes used by men among friends, or when addressing someone younger or of a lower station.

-chan: This is used to express endearment, mostly towards girls. It is also used for little boys, pets, and even among lovers. It gives a sense of childish cuteness.

Bozu: This is an informal way to refer to a boy, similar to the English term "kid".

Sempai: This title suggests that the addressee is one's 'senior' in a group or organization. It is most often used in a school setting, where underclassmen refer to their upperclassmen as 'sempai.' It can also be used in the workplace, such as when a newer employee addresses an employee who has seniority in the company.

Kohai: This is the opposite of 'sempai,' and is used towards underclassmen in school or newcomers in the workplace. It connotes that the addressee is of lower station.

Sensei: Literally meaning 'one who has come before,' this title is used for teachers, doctors, or masters of any profession or art.

[blank]: Usually forgotten in these lists, but perhaps the most significant difference between Japanese and English. The lack of honorific means that the speaker has permission to address the person in a very intimate way. Usually, only family, spouses, or very close friends have this kind of permission. Known as *yobisute*, it can be gratifying when someone who has earned the intimacy starts to call one by one's name without an honorific. But when that intimacy hasn't been earned, it can also be very insulting.

A Note from the Author

It's been almost a year since the first
volume came out (in Japan), and now,
finally, Volume 2 is on sale! During the
time that I wasn't feeling well and when
I was on vacation, many of you readers
were kind enough to send me letters
with queries and well-wishes! I'm sorry
if I worried you. Thanks to you all, I'm
feeling much better now! Thank you
everyone!!

OTHELLO
オセロ。

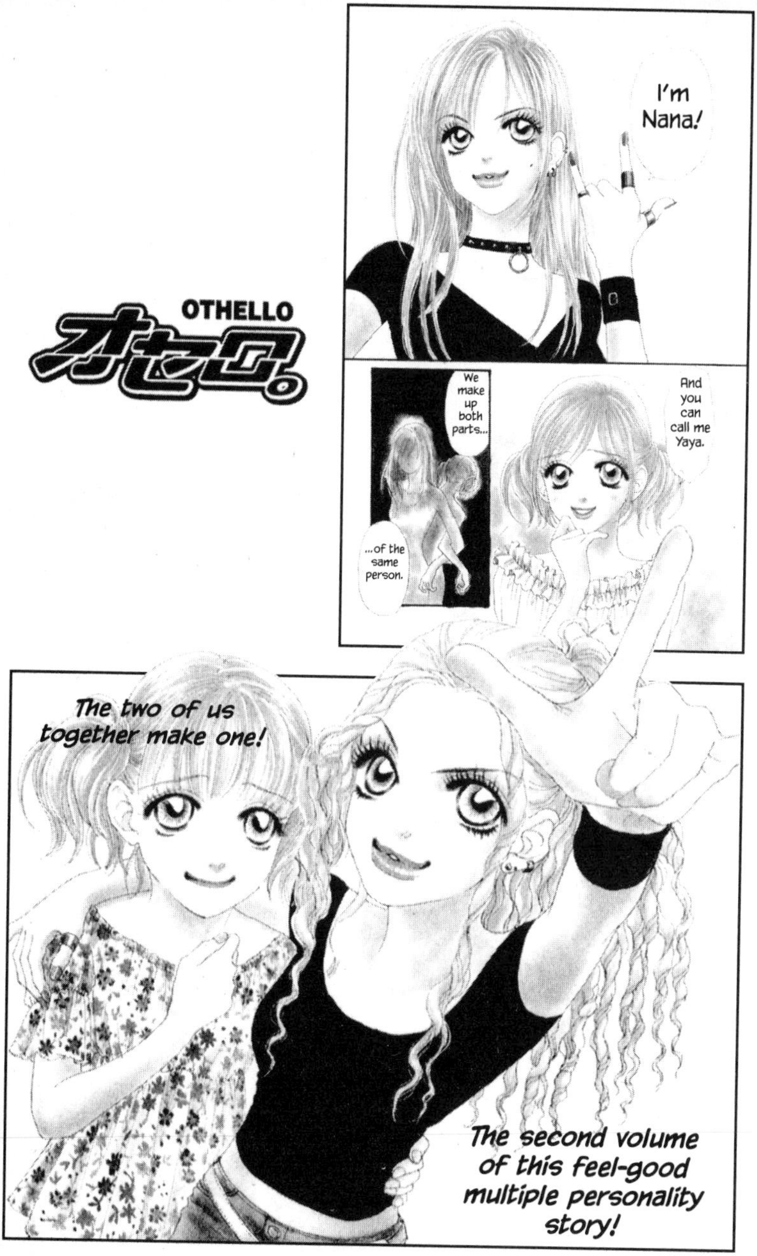
I'm Nana!
And you can call me Yaya.
We make up both parts...
...of the same person.
The two of us together make one!
The second volume of this feel-good multiple personality story!

OTHELLO オセロ。

Satomi Ikezawa

2

Chapter 5

A Void of Time

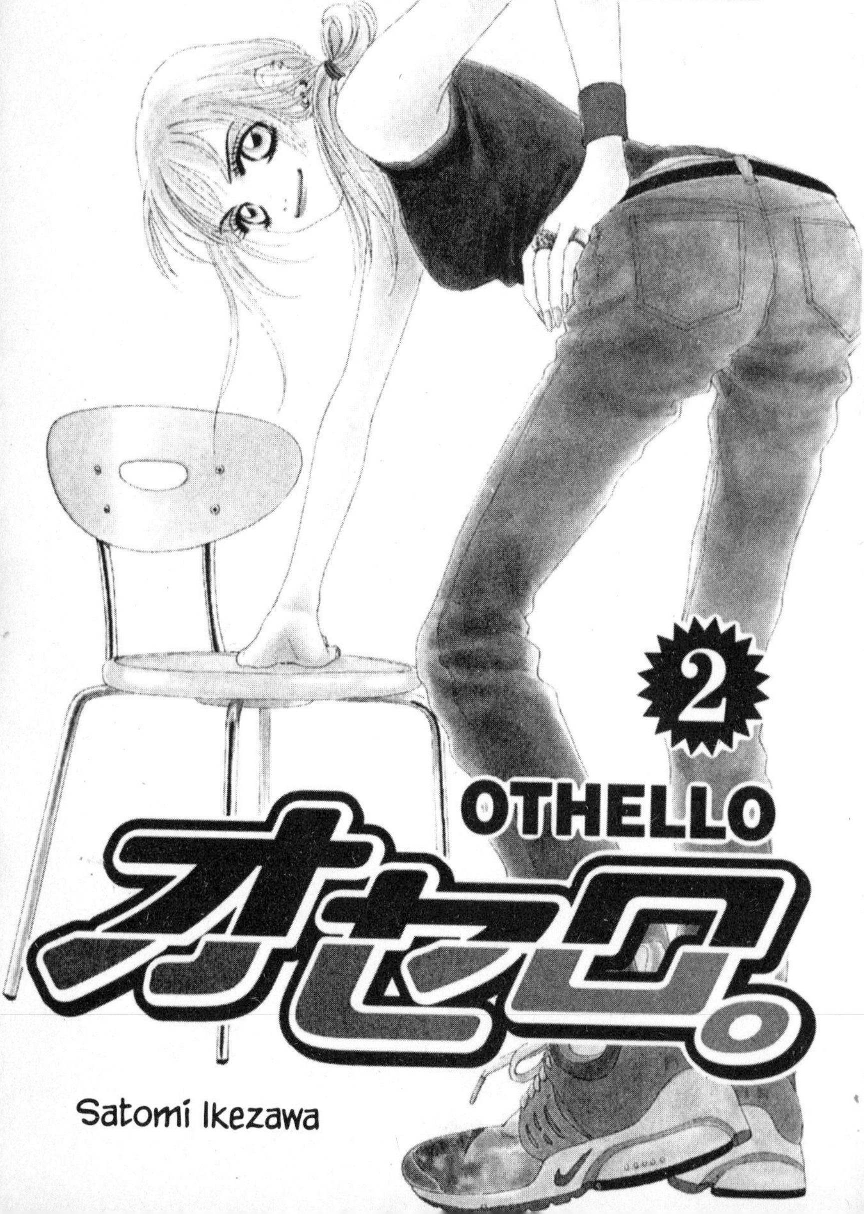
2
OTHELLO
オセロ。
Satomi Ikezawa

OTHELLO

オセロ。

MOTOR
CITY
BODY

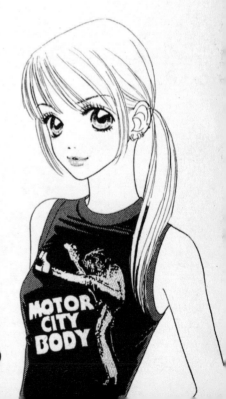

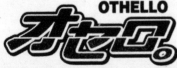

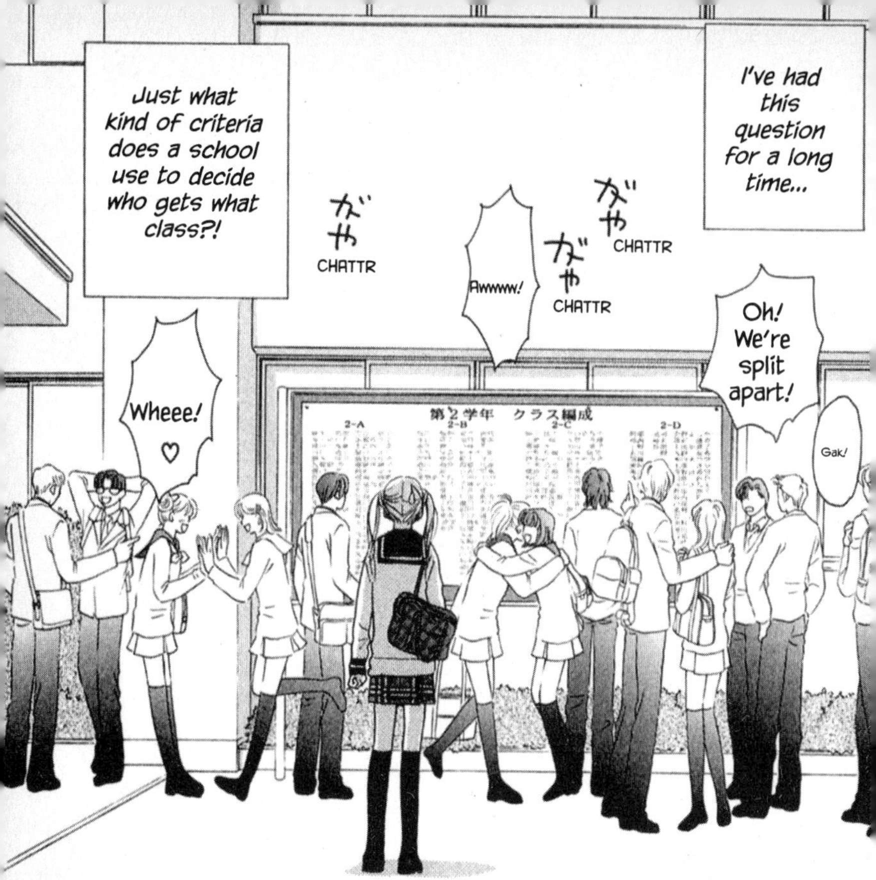

I've had this question for a long time...
Just what kind of criteria does a school use to decide who gets what class?!
Oh! We're split apart!
Gak!
ガヤ CHATTR
ガヤ CHATTR
Awwww!
ガヤ CHATTR
Wheee! ♡
第2学年 クラス編成
2-A
2-B
2-C
2-D

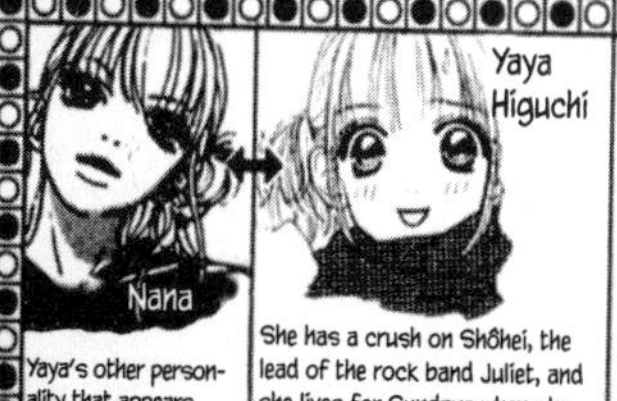

Nana
Yaya's other personality that appears when she sees a reflection of herself.
Yaya Higuchi
She has a crush on Shôhei, the lead of the rock band Juliet, and she lives for Sundays when she can join other fans in cosplay in Harajuku.
Seri & Moe
"Friends" from Yaya's class.
Moriyama
The guy Yaya is beginning to really like. Nana kissed him during a concert.
Shôhei
Yaya's ideal man.

Nana's on a rampage, and Yaya doesn't know!!

オセロ。

The Story Thus Far

Sixteen-year-old Yaya Higuchi's "friends" have been making fun of her with words like, "Yaya the cry-ya! Yaya the misfi-ya!" But Yaya has no idea that within her is a completely different personality that goes by the name of Nana.

During Spring Break, Yaya's class goes on an End of the School Year party, and just as Yaya and the handsome Moriyama find themselves in the right mood, Yaya's "friends," Seri and Moe, decide to play a prank on her. They throw Yaya's lunch that she painstakingly made for the three of them into the pond. She caught a glimpse of her shocked face reflected on the surface of the pond and changed into Nana. Seri and Moe met justice when they sank into the pond.

Now Yaya hopes to be put into a different class from Seri and Moe, but she wants to be in the same class as Moriyama. With that wish in mind, Yaya heads into the new school year.

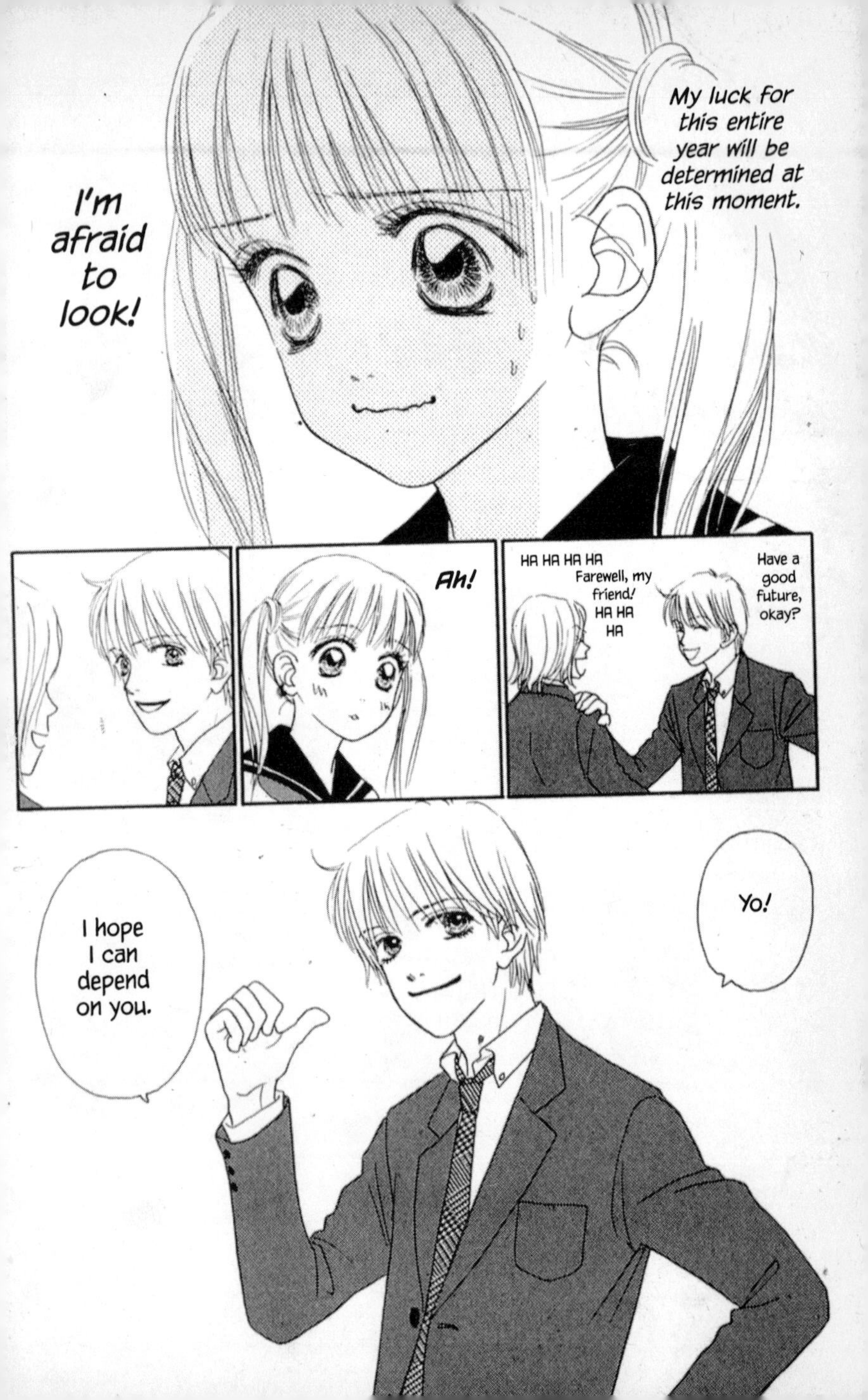
My luck for this entire year will be determined at this moment.
I'm afraid to look!
Have a good future, okay?
HA HA HA HA
Farewell, my friend! HA HA HA
Ah!
Yo!
I hope I can depend on you.

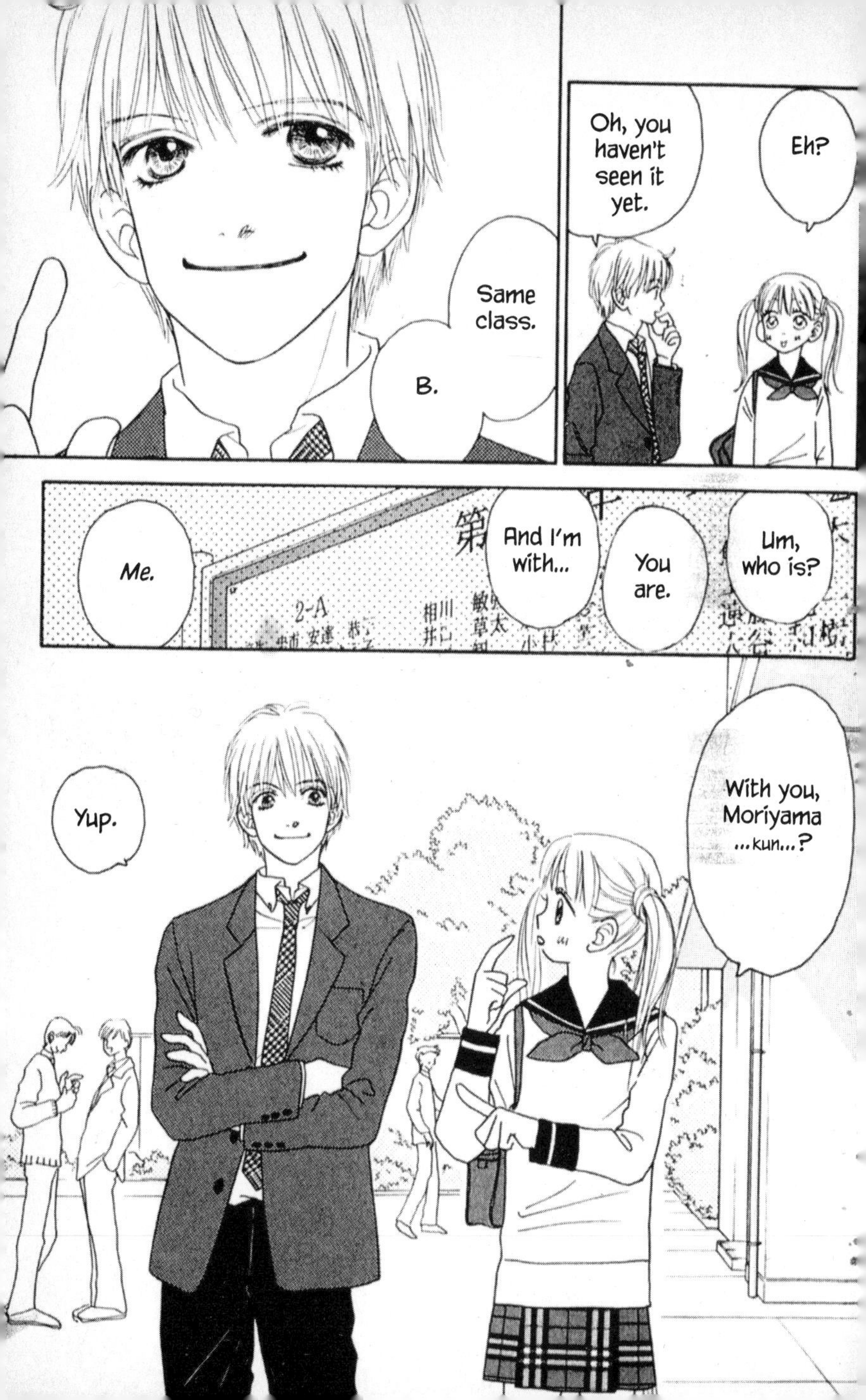
Eh?
Oh, you haven't seen it yet.
Same class.
B.
Um, who is?
You are.
And I'm with...
Me.
With you, Moriyama ...kun...?
Yup.

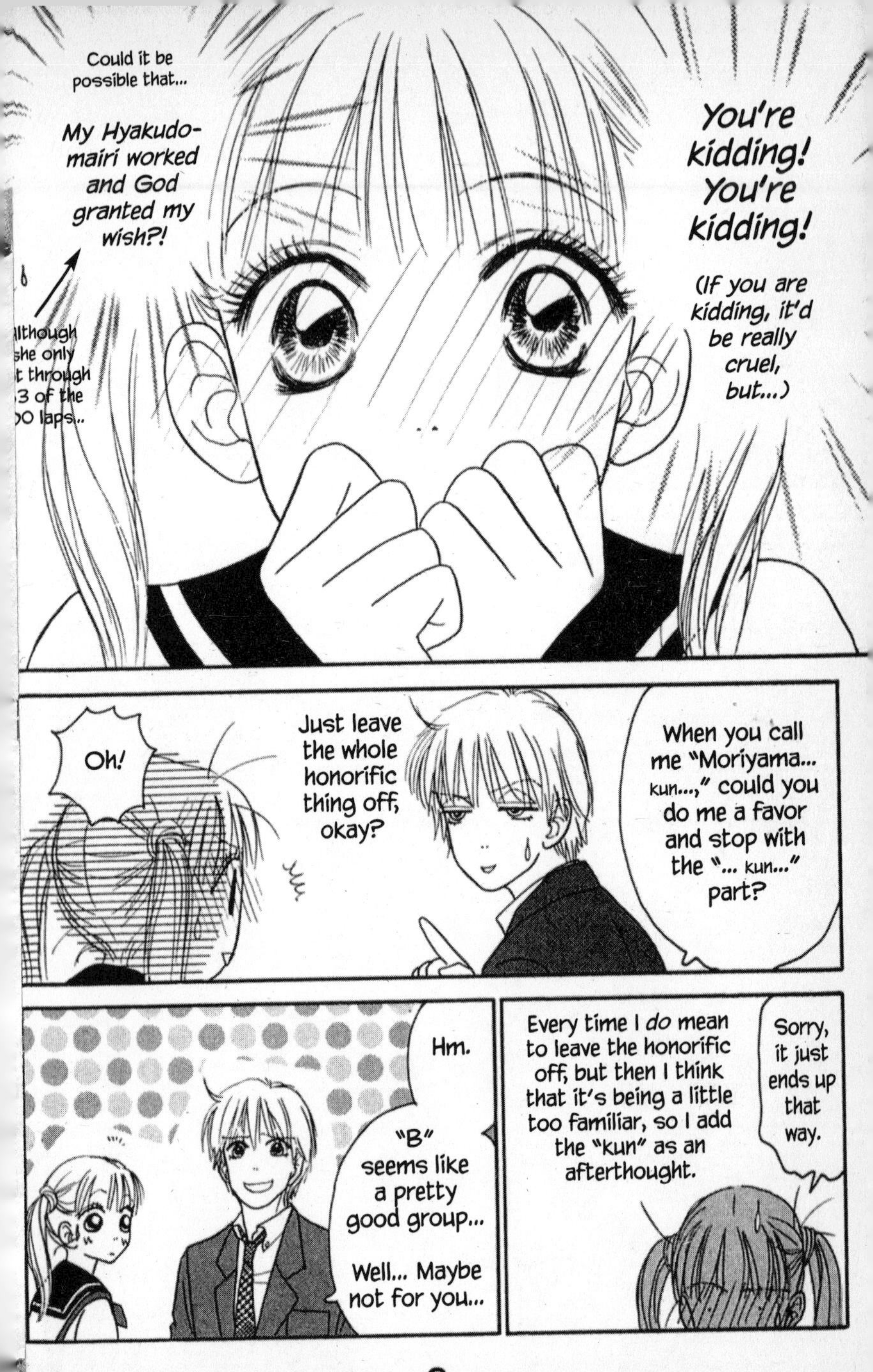

You're kidding! You're kidding!
(If you are kidding, it'd be really cruel, but...)
Could it be possible that...
My Hyakudo-mairi worked and God granted my wish?!
lthough she only t through 3 of the 0 laps..
When you call me "Moriyama... kun...," could you do me a favor and stop with the "... kun..." part?
Just leave the whole honorific thing off, okay?
Oh!
Sorry, it just ends up that way.
Every time I *do* mean to leave the honorific off, but then I think that it's being a little too familiar, so I add the "kun" as an afterthought.
Hm.
"B" seems like a pretty good group...
Well... Maybe not for you...

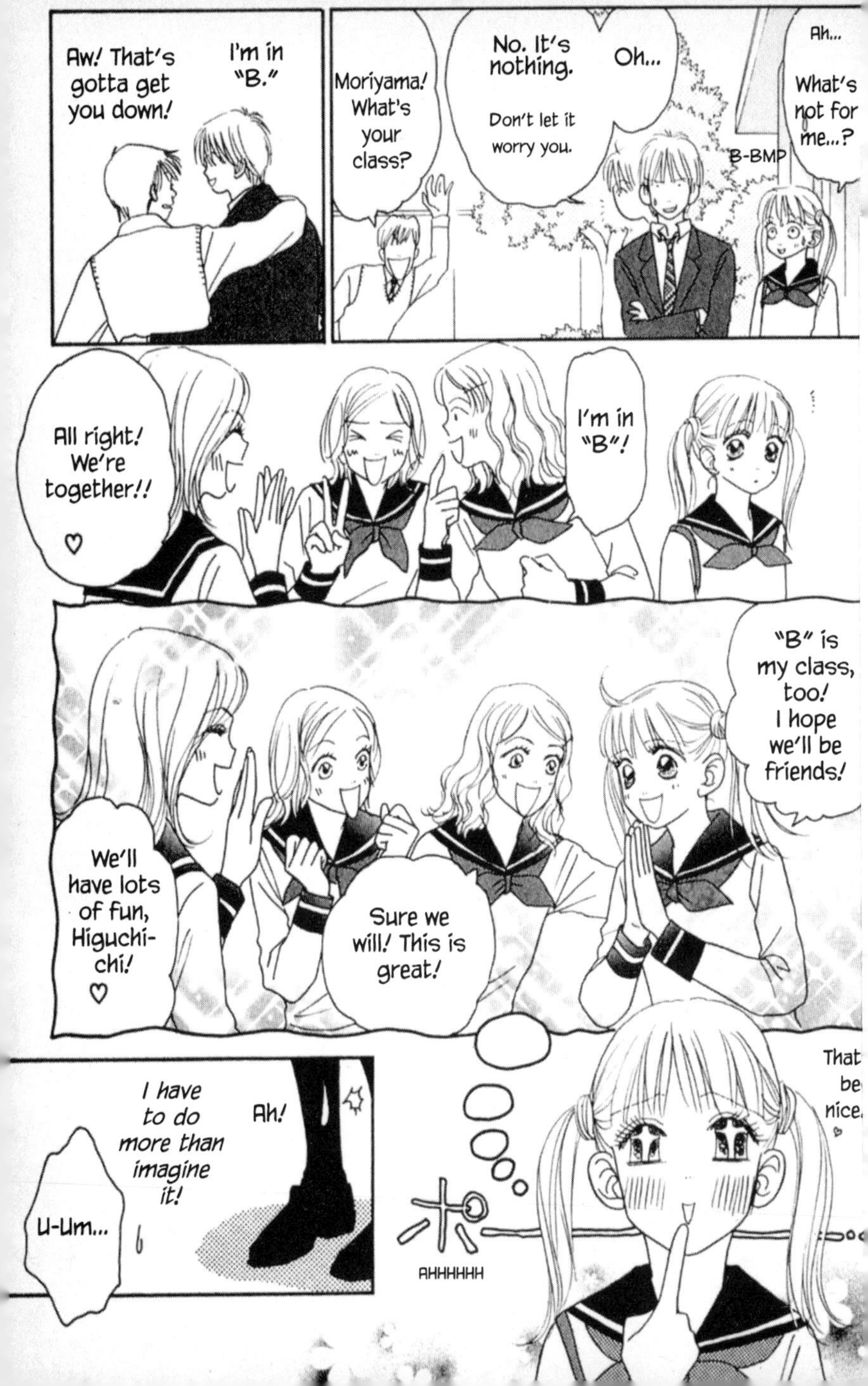
Ah...
What's not for me...?
B-BMP
Oh...
No. It's nothing.
Don't let it worry you.
Moriyama! What's your class?
I'm in "B."
Aw! That's gotta get you down!
I'm in "B"!
All right! We're together!! ♡
"B" is my class, too! I hope we'll be friends!
Sure we will! This is great!
We'll have lots of fun, Higuchi-chi! ♡
That be nice.
AHHHHHH
Ah!
I have to do more than imagine it!
U-Um...

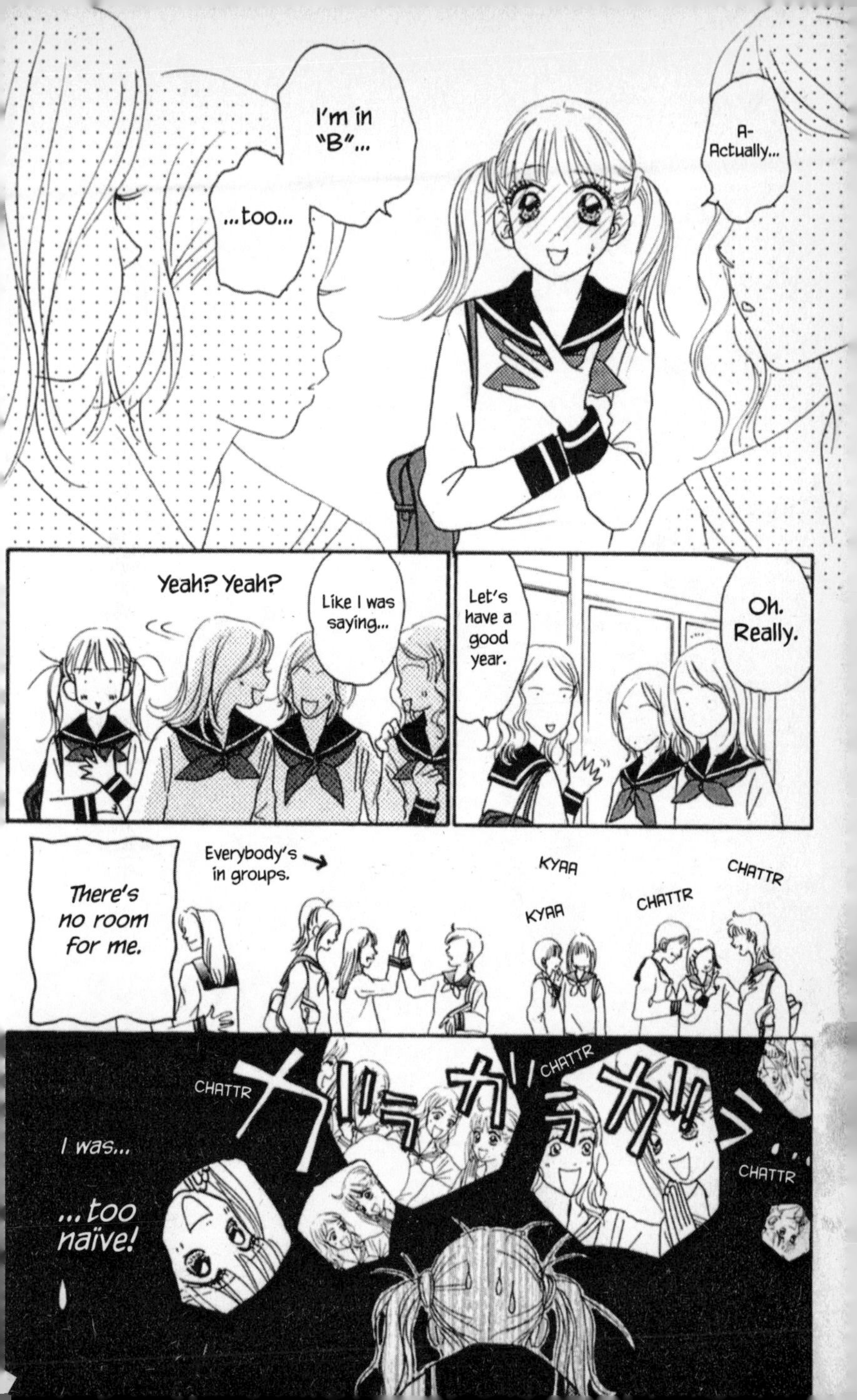

A-
Actually...
I'm in
"B"...
...too...
Oh.
Really.
Let's
have a
good
year.
Like I was
saying...
Yeah? Yeah?
CHATTR
CHATTR
KYAA
KYAA
Everybody's
in groups.
There's
no room
for me.
CHATTR
CHATTR
CHATTR
I was...
...too
naïve!

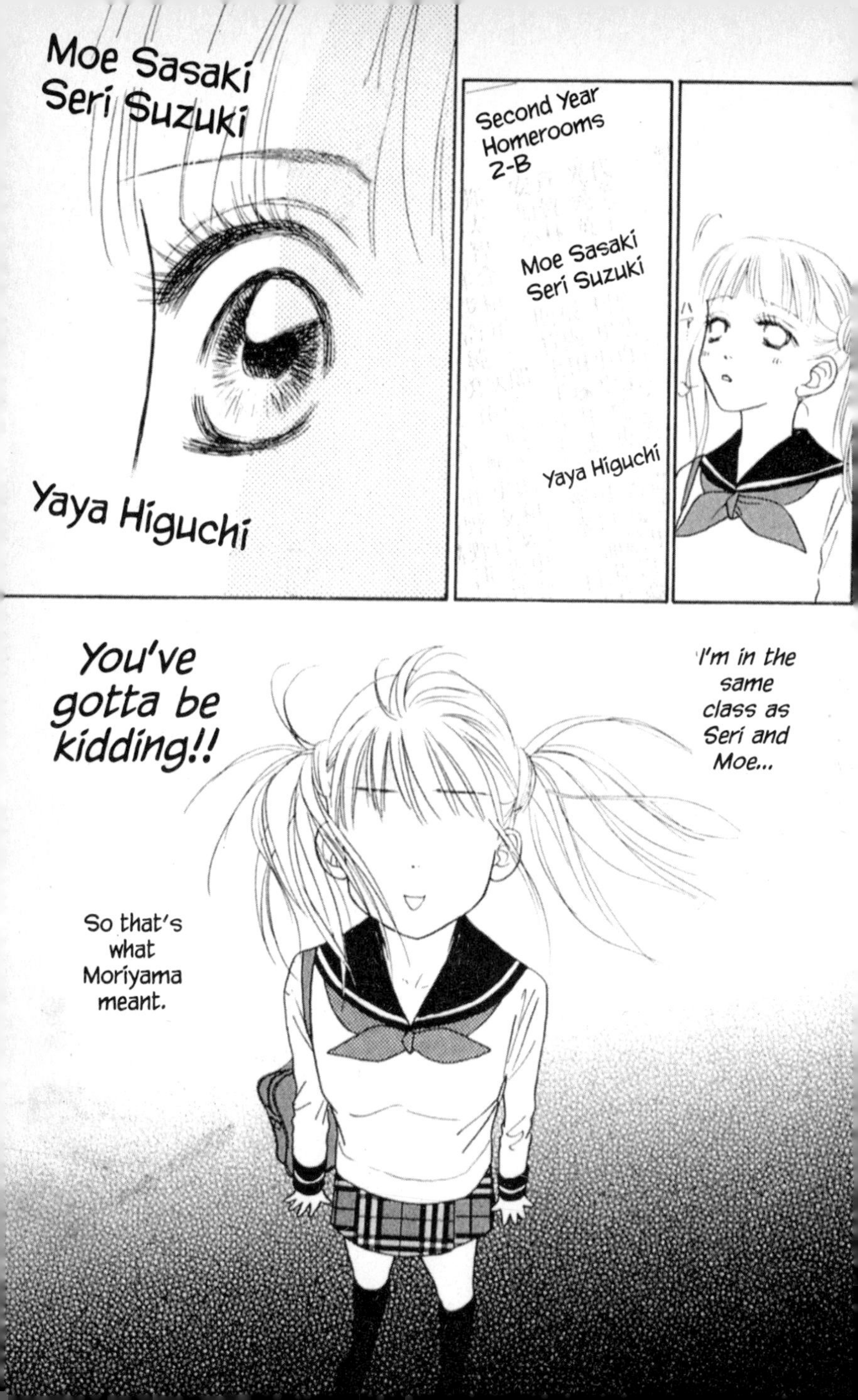

Second Year Homerooms 2-B
Moe Sasaki Seri Suzuki
Yaya Higuchi
Moe Sasaki Seri Suzuki
Yaya Higuchi
I'm in the same class as Seri and Moe...
You've gotta be kidding!!
So that's what Moriyama meant.

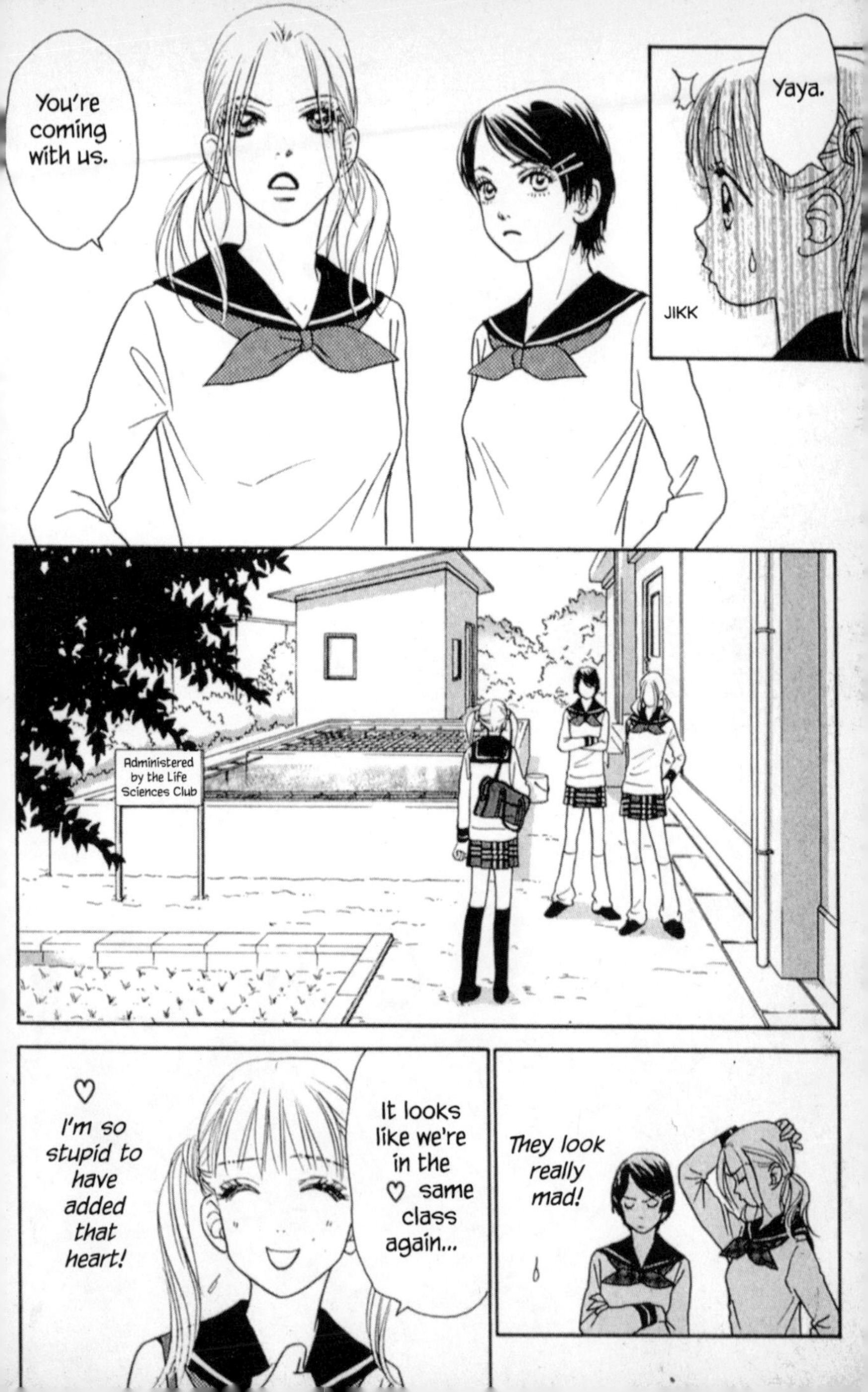
Yaya.
JIKK
You're coming with us.
Administered by the Life Sciences Club
They look really mad!
It looks like we're in the ♡ same class again...
♡ I'm so stupid to have added that heart!

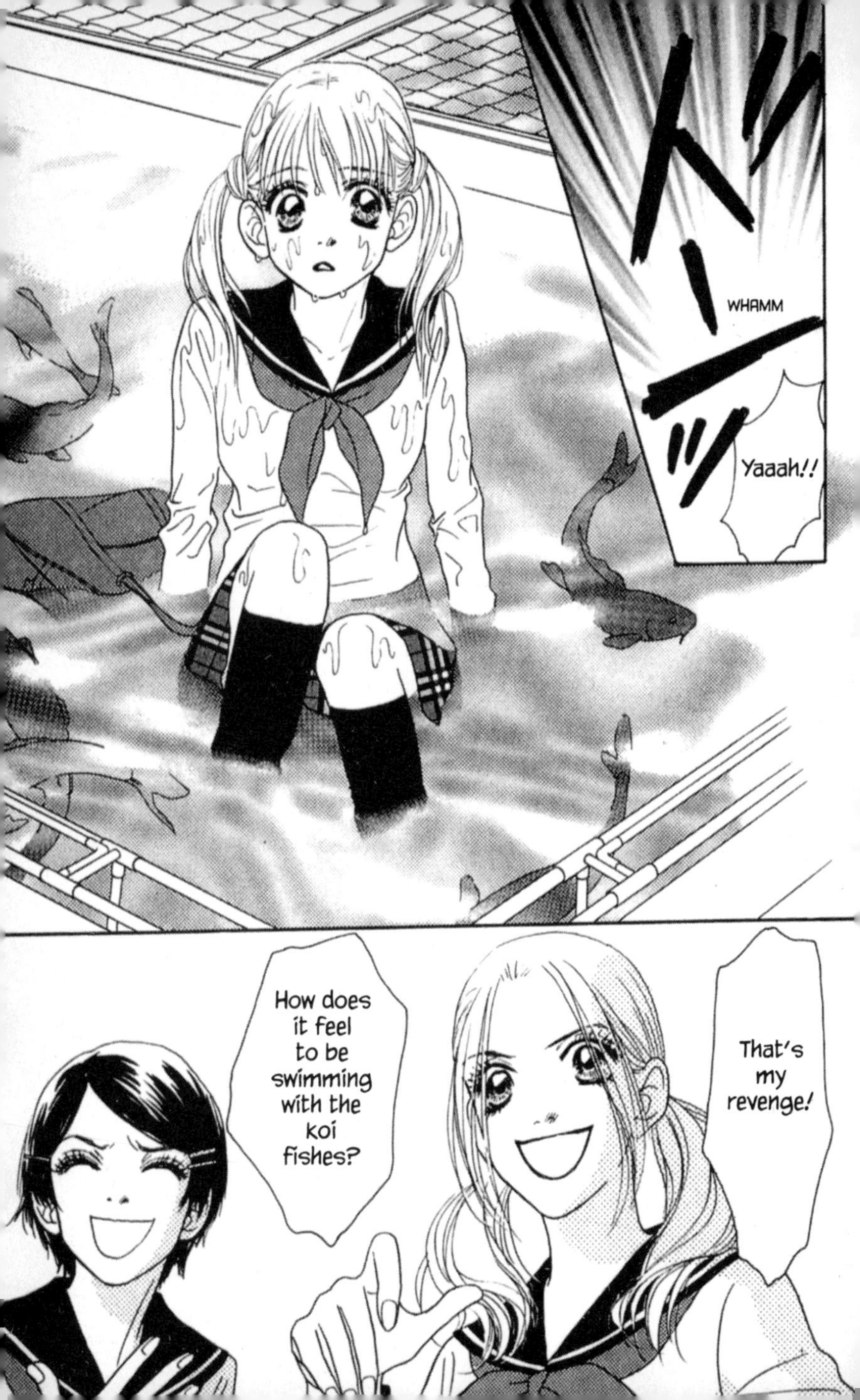
WHAMM
Yaaah!!
That's my revenge!
How does it feel to be swimming with the koi fishes?

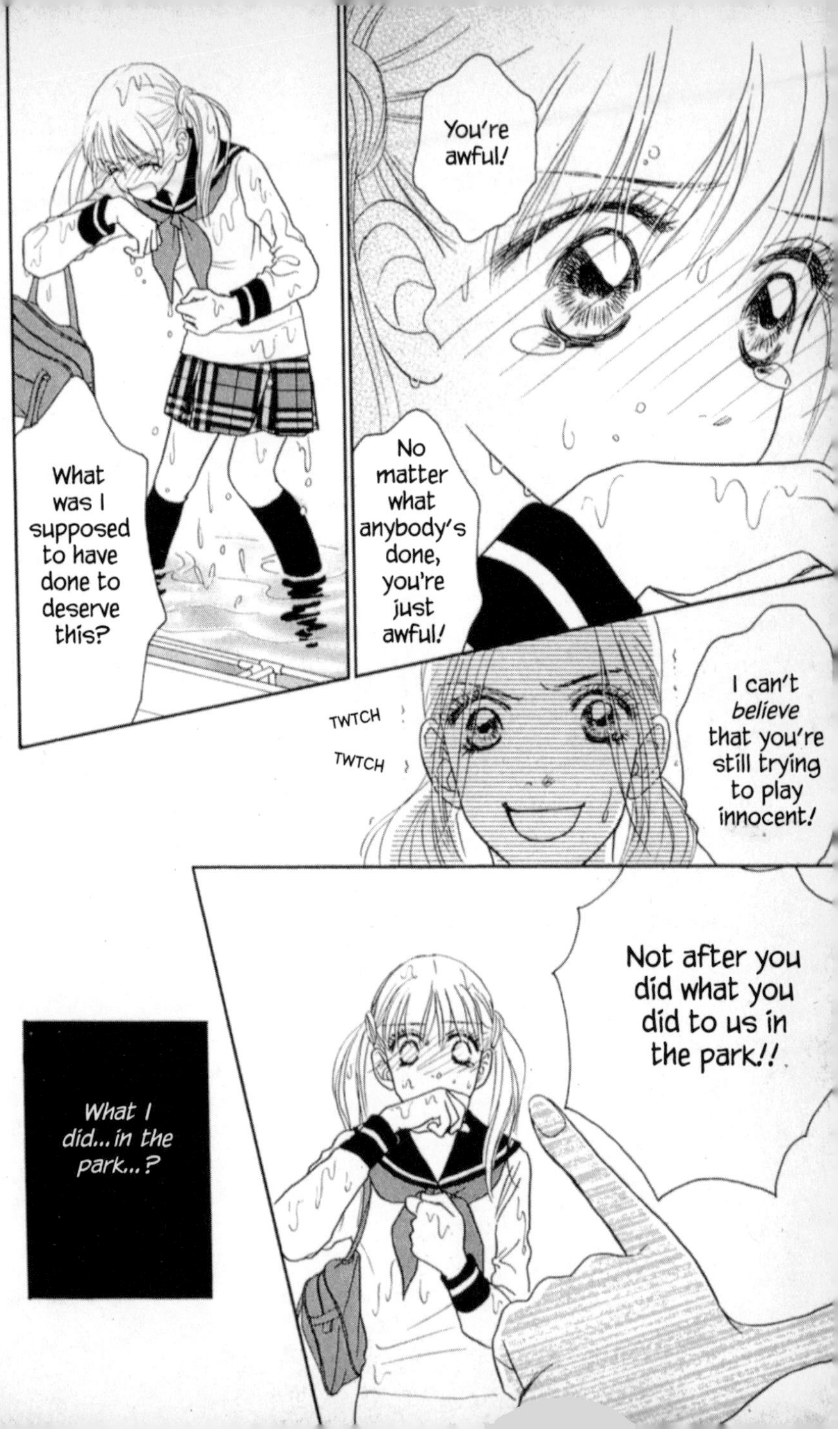
You're awful!
No matter what anybody's done, you're just awful!
What was I supposed to have done to deserve this?
I can't *believe* that you're still trying to play innocent!
TWTCH
TWTCH
Not after you did what you did to us in the park!!
What I did... in the park...?

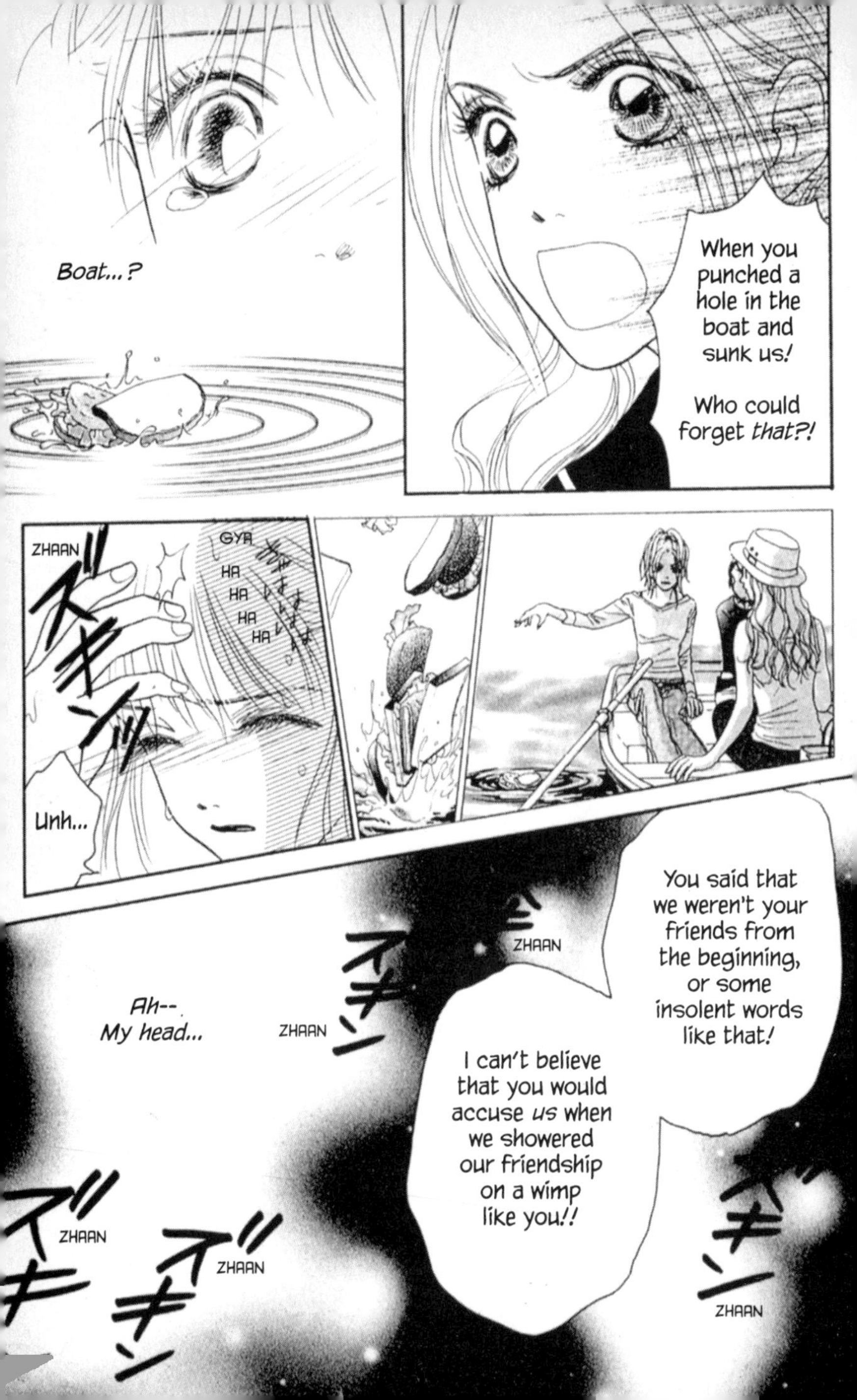
When you punched a hole in the boat and sunk us!
Who could forget that?!
Boat...?
ZHAAN
GYA
HA
HA
HA
HA
Unh...
You said that we weren't your friends from the beginning, or some insolent words like that!
I can't believe that you would accuse us when we showered our friendship on a wimp like you!!
ZHAAN
ZHAAN
Ah-- My head...
ZHAAN
ZHAAN
ZHAAN

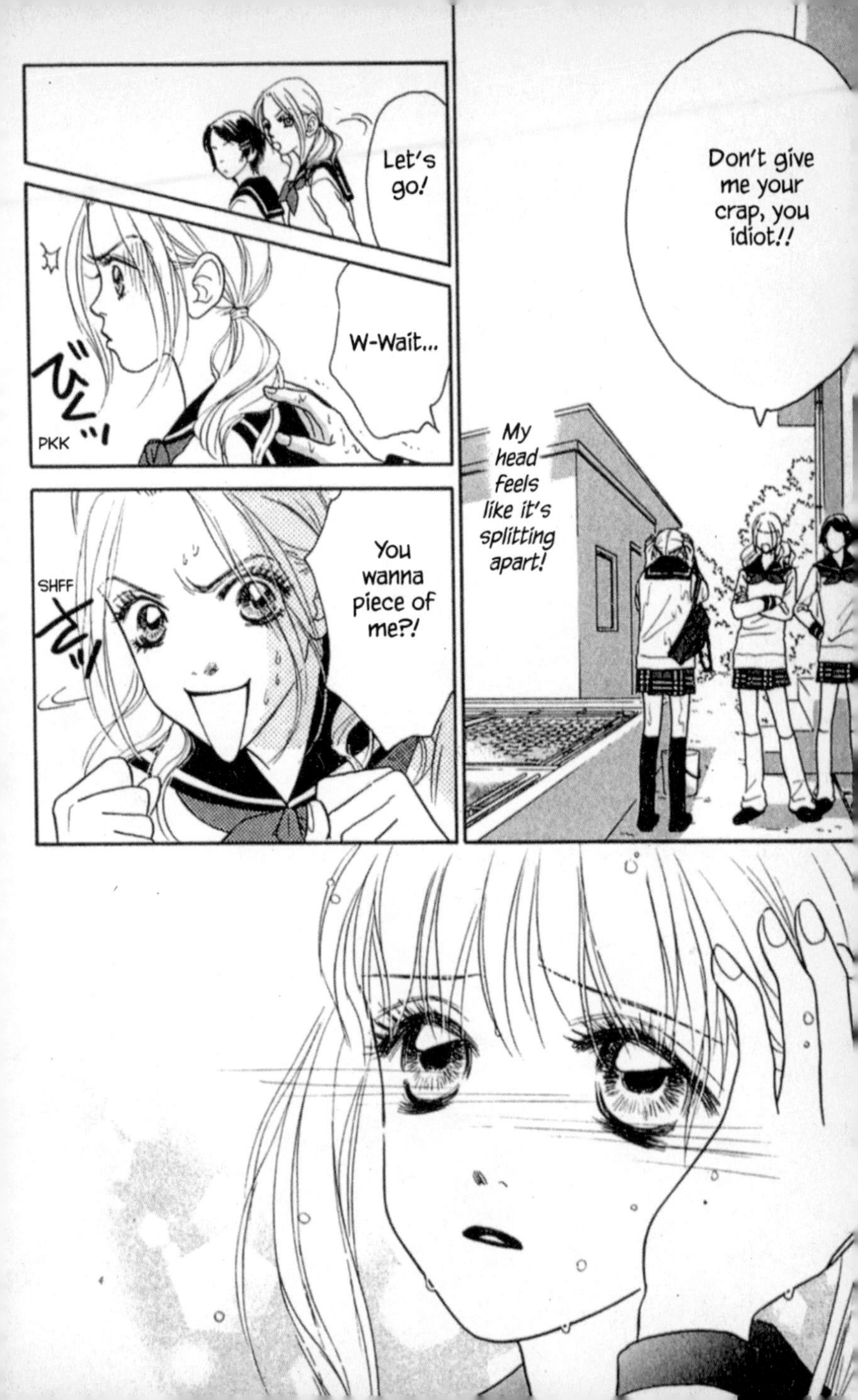

Don't give me your crap, you idiot!!
My head feels like it's splitting apart!
Let's go!
W-Wait...
PKK
You wanna piece of me?!
SHFF

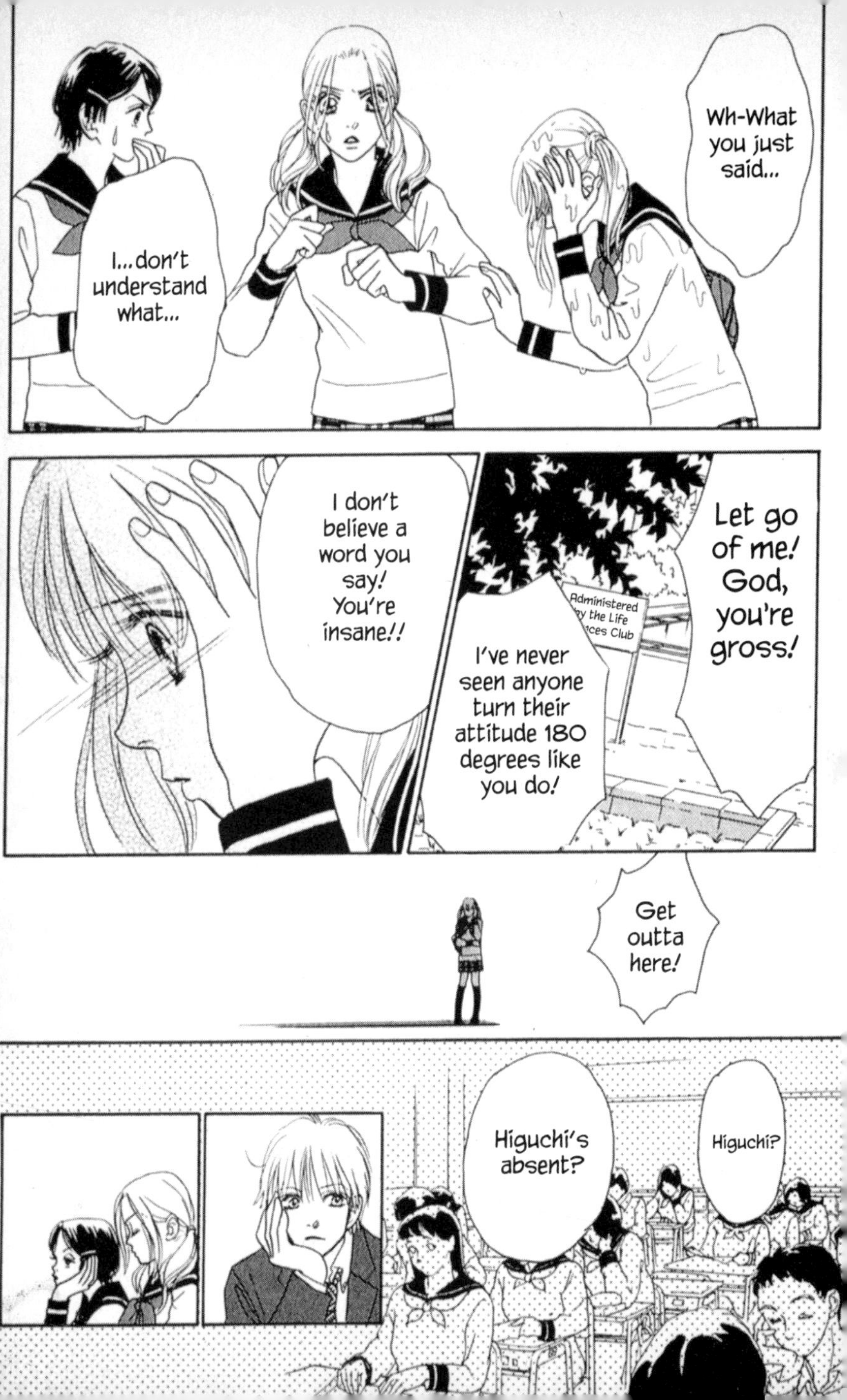
Wh-What you just said...
I...don't understand what...
Let go of me! God, you're gross!
Administered
I've never seen anyone turn their attitude 180 degrees like you do!
I don't believe a word you say! You're insane!!
Get outta here!
Higuchi?
Higuchi's absent?

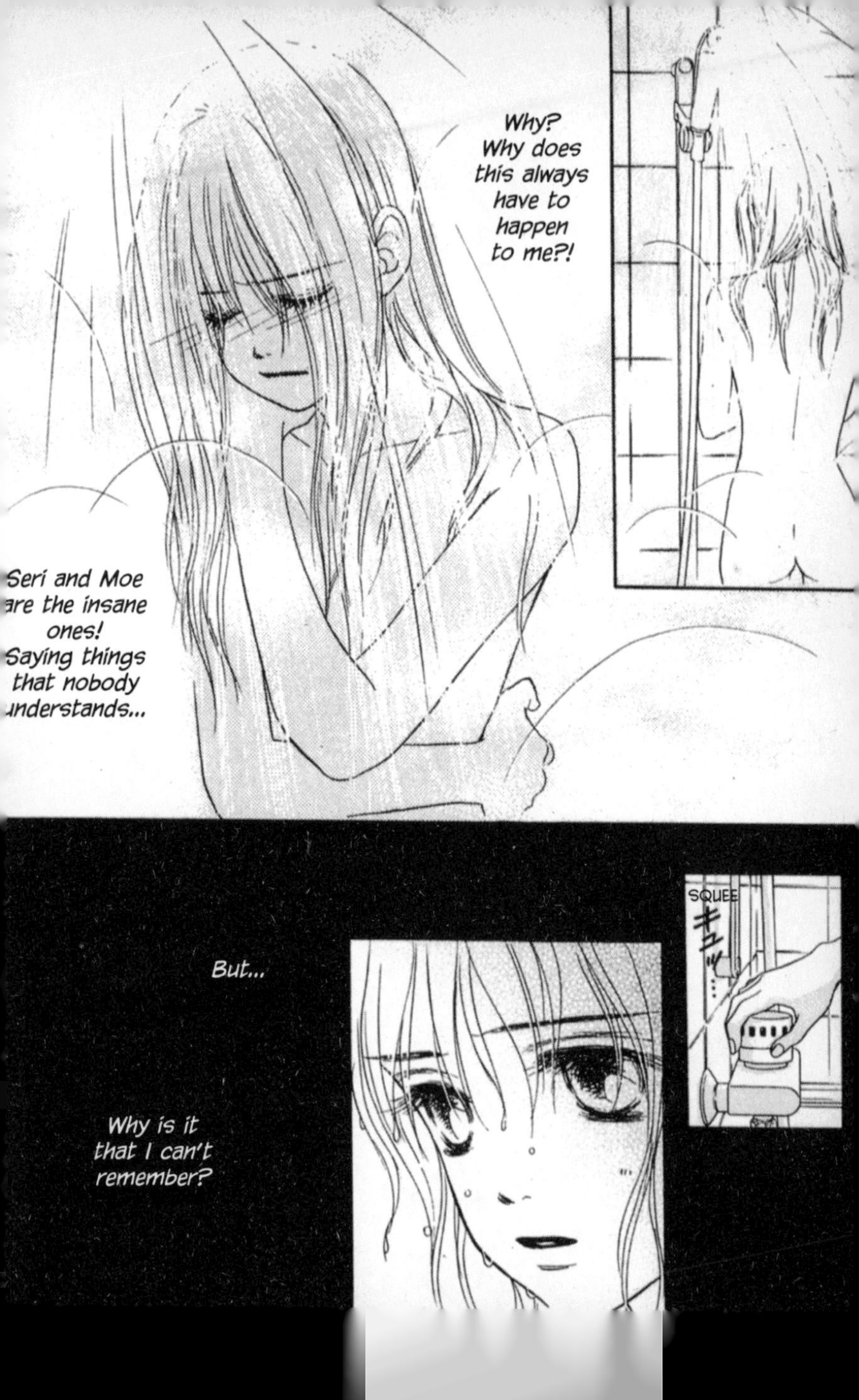
Why?
Why does this always have to happen to me?!
Seri and Moe are the insane ones! Saying things that nobody understands...
SQUEE
But...
Why is it that I can't remember?

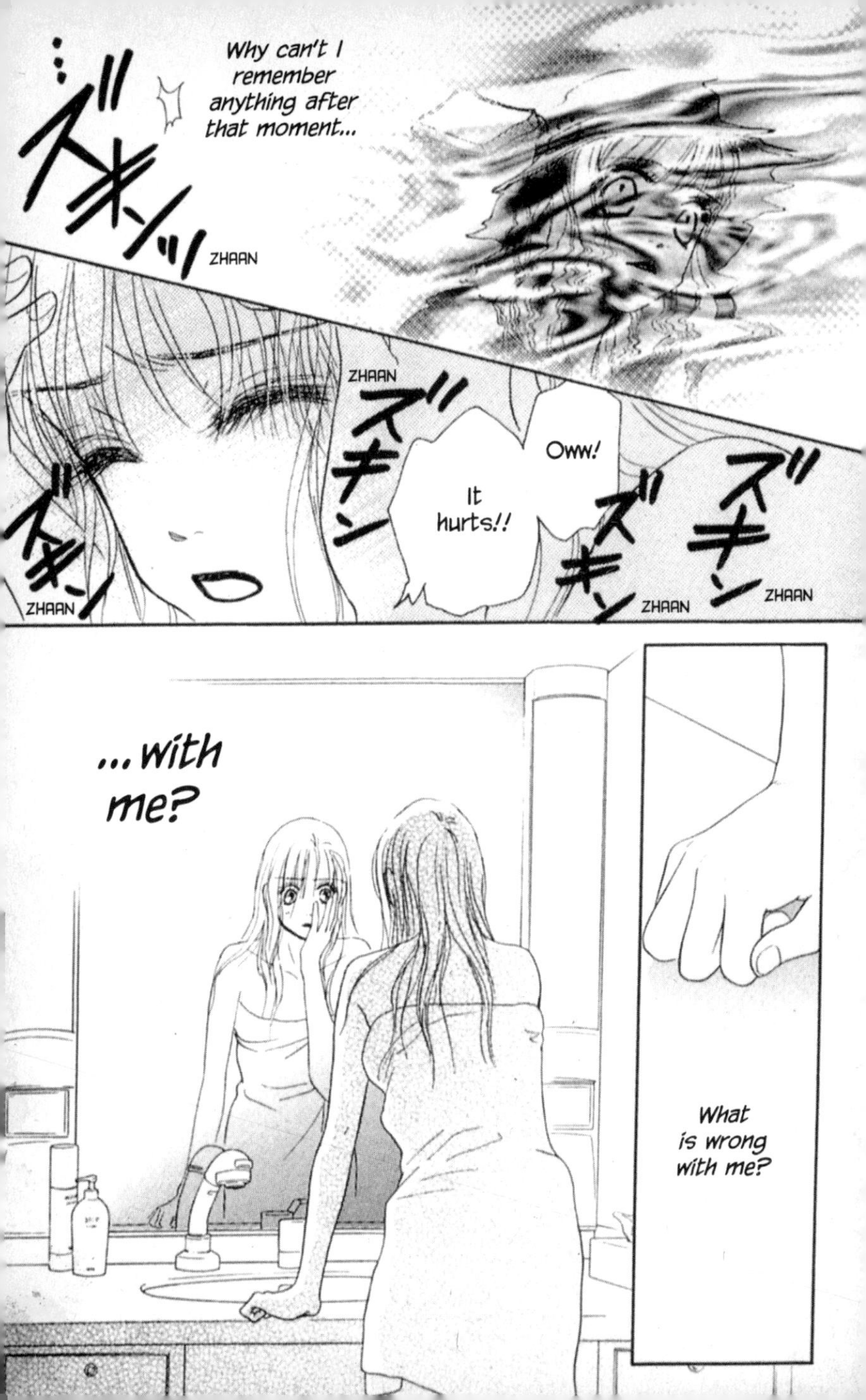
Why can't I remember anything after that moment...
ZHAAN
ZHAAN
ZHAAN
Oww!
It hurts!!
ZHAAN
ZHAAN
What is wrong with me?
...with me?

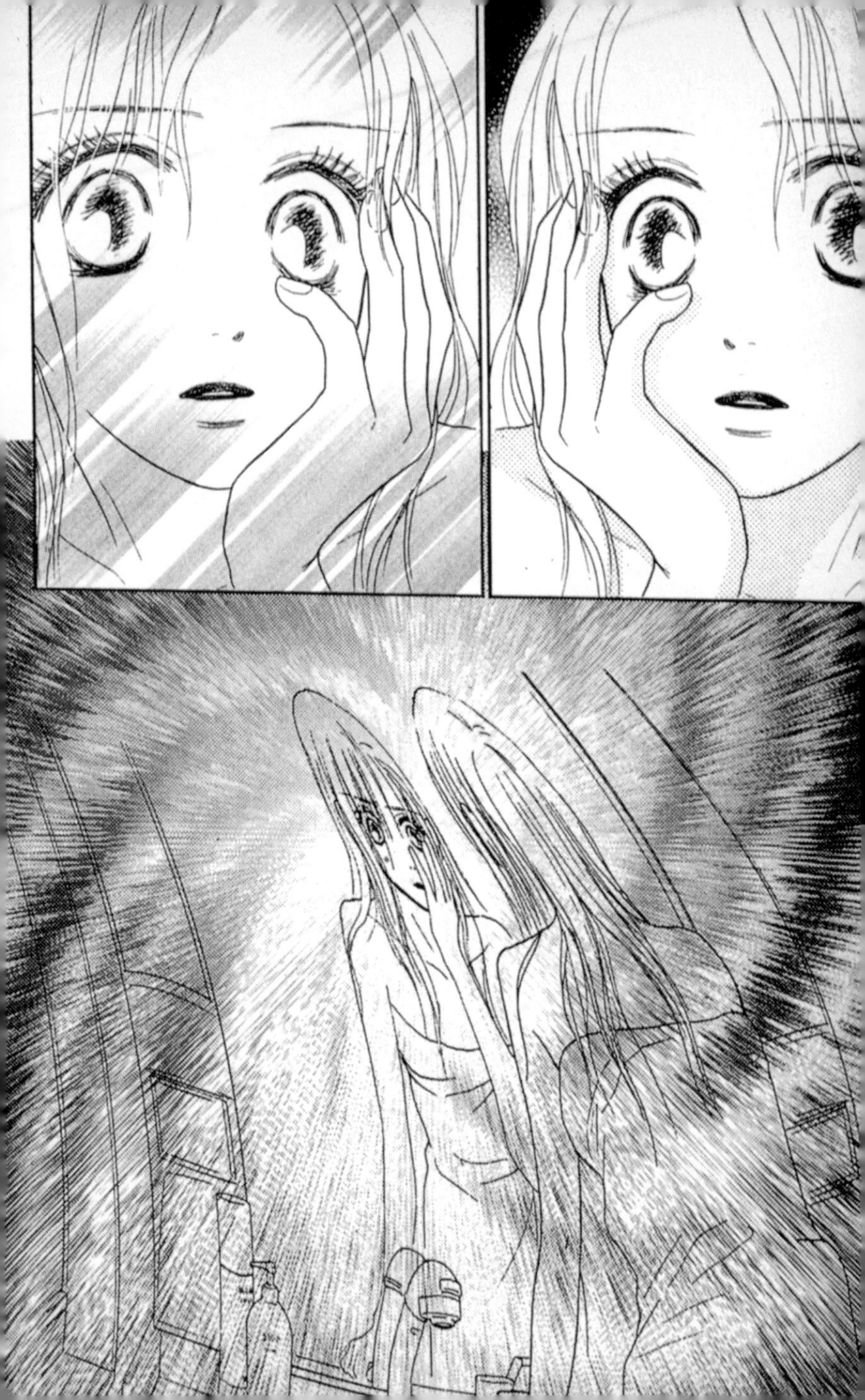

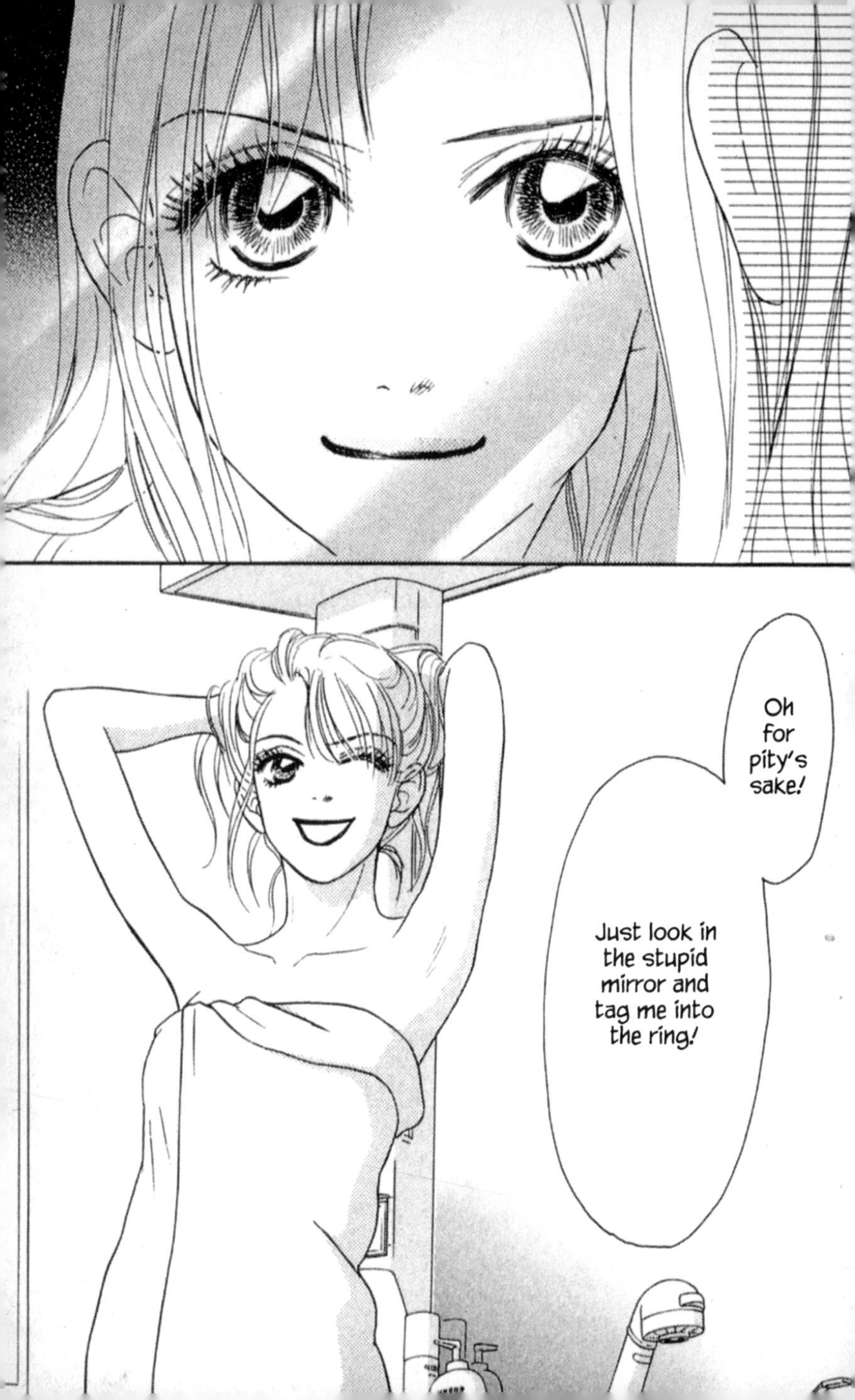
Oh for pity's sake!
Just look in the stupid mirror and tag me into the ring!

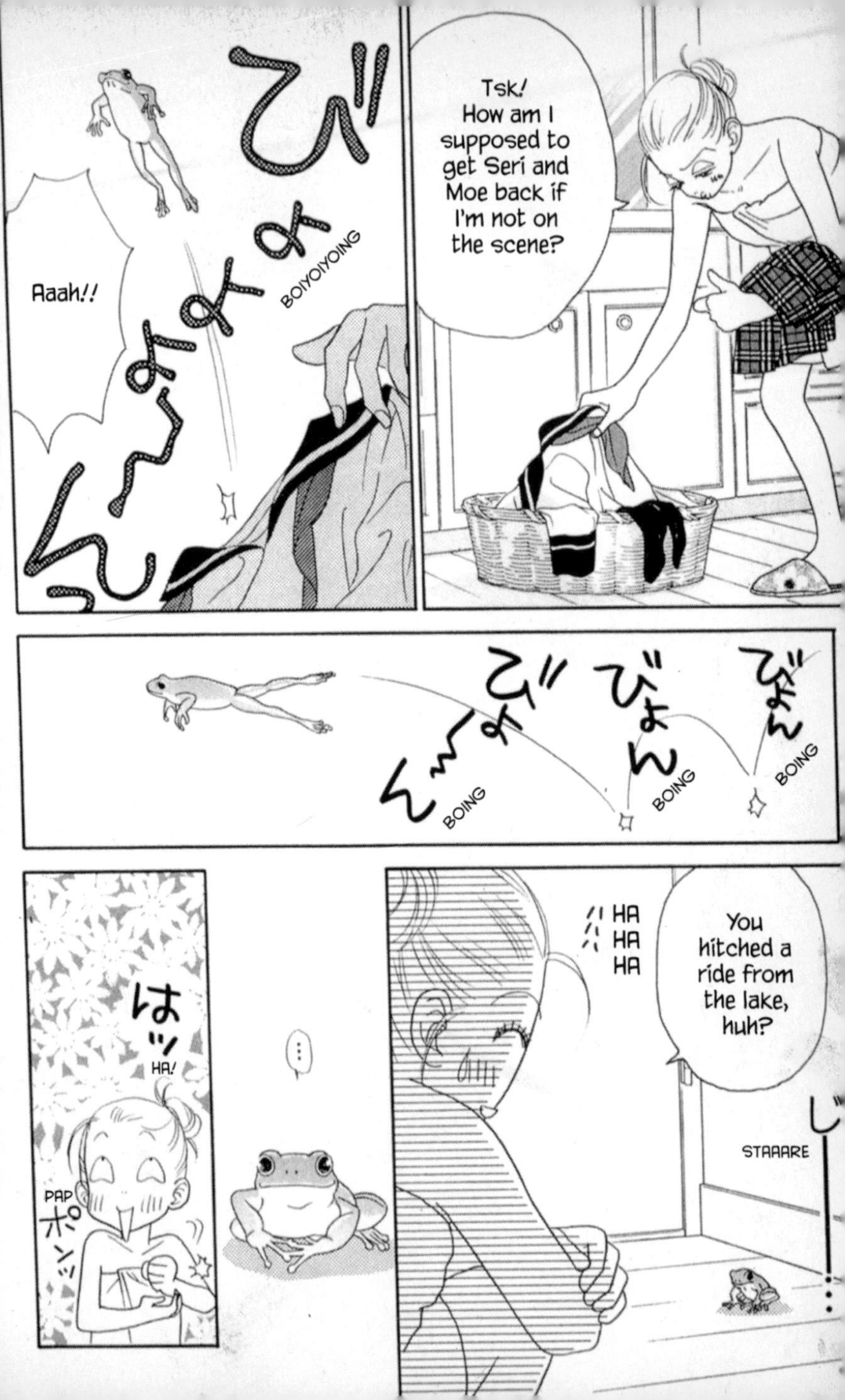

Tsk! How am I supposed to get Seri and Moe back if I'm not on the scene?
BOIYOIYOING
Aaah!!
びょん
BOING
びょん
BOING
BOING
You hitched a ride from the lake, huh?
HA HA HA
じー
STAAARE
...
はッ
HA!
ポンッ
PAP

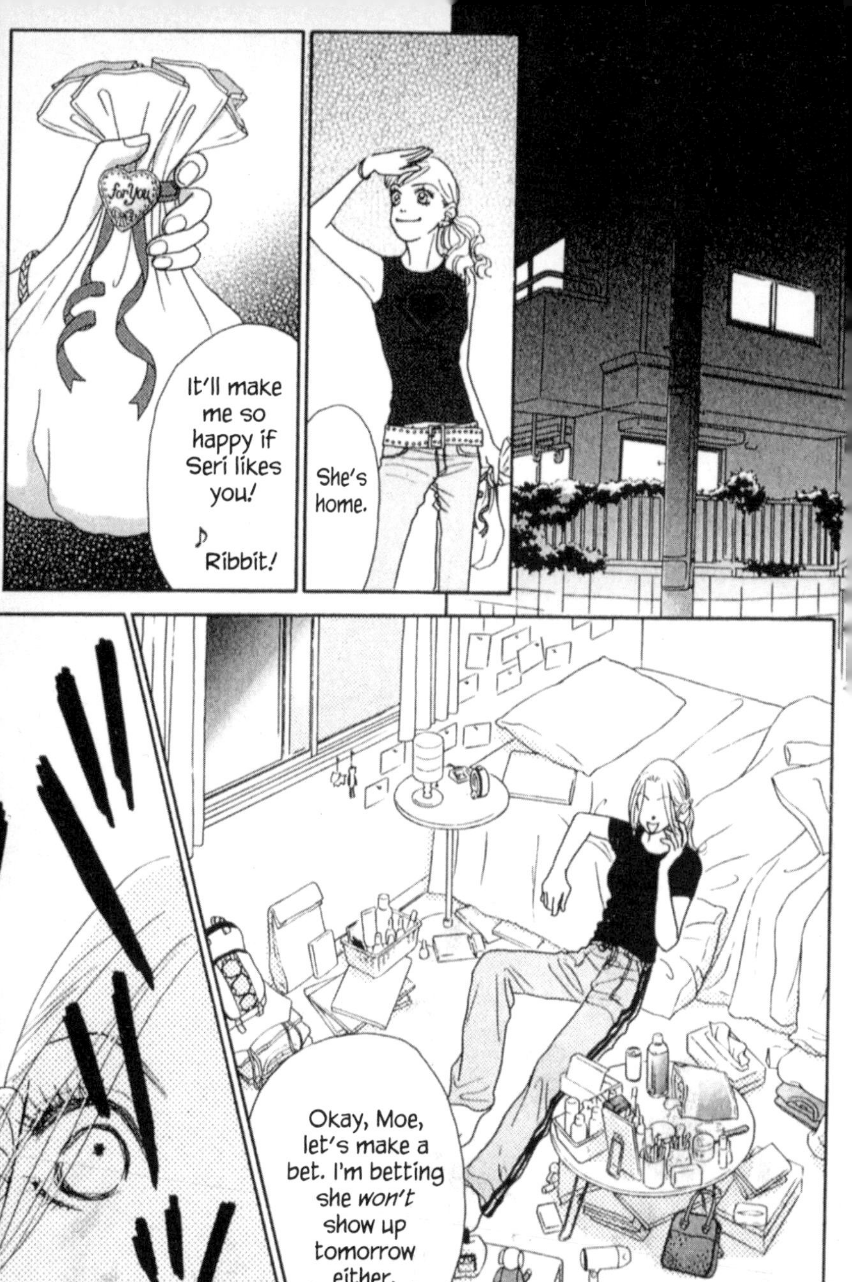
She's home.
It'll make me so happy if Seri likes you!
♪ Ribbit!
Okay, Moe, let's make a bet. I'm betting she *won't* show up tomorrow either.
RIIPPT

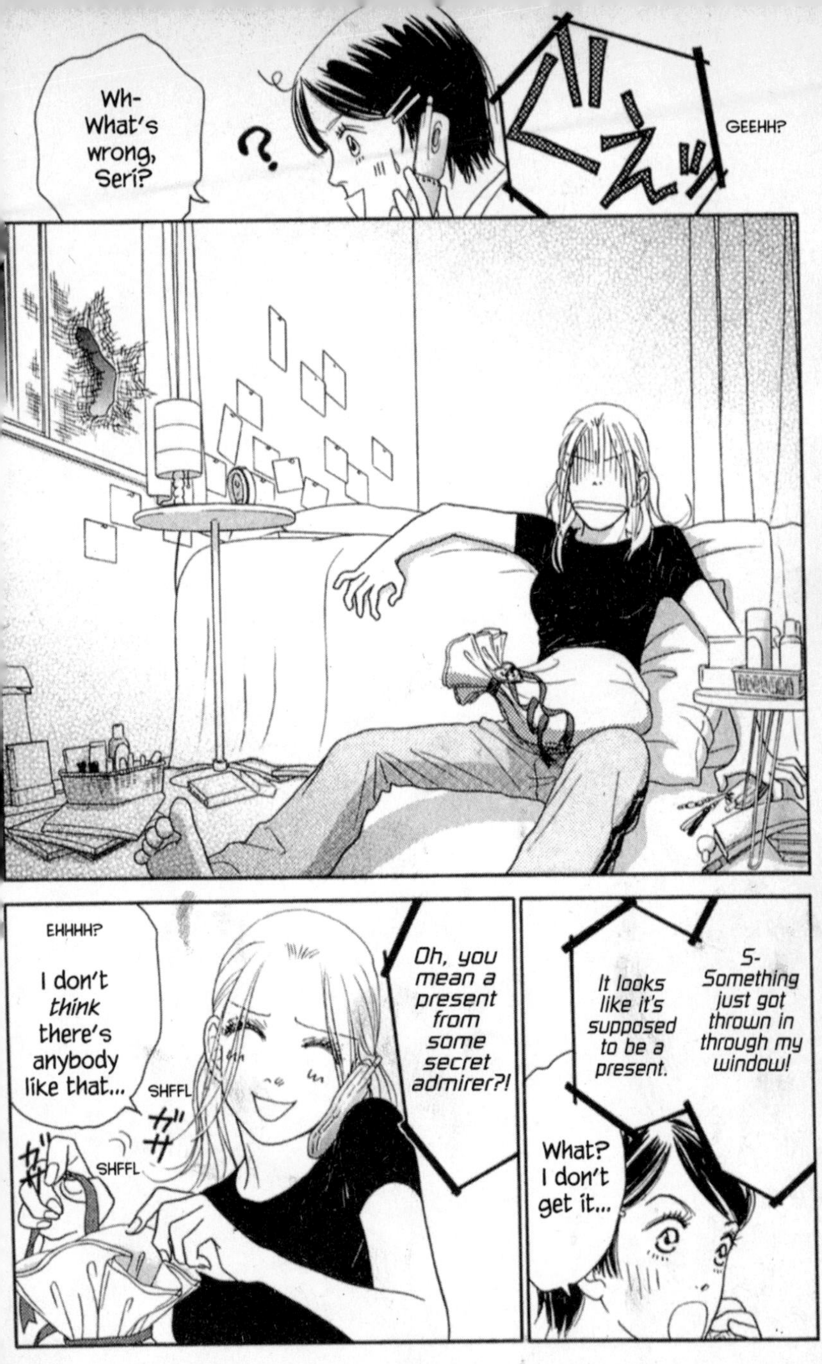
GEEHH?
Wh- What's wrong, Seri?
S- Something just got thrown in through my window!
It looks like it's supposed to be a present.
What? I don't get it...
Oh, you mean a present from some secret admirer?!
EHHHH?
I don't *think* there's anybody like that...
SHFFL
SHFFL

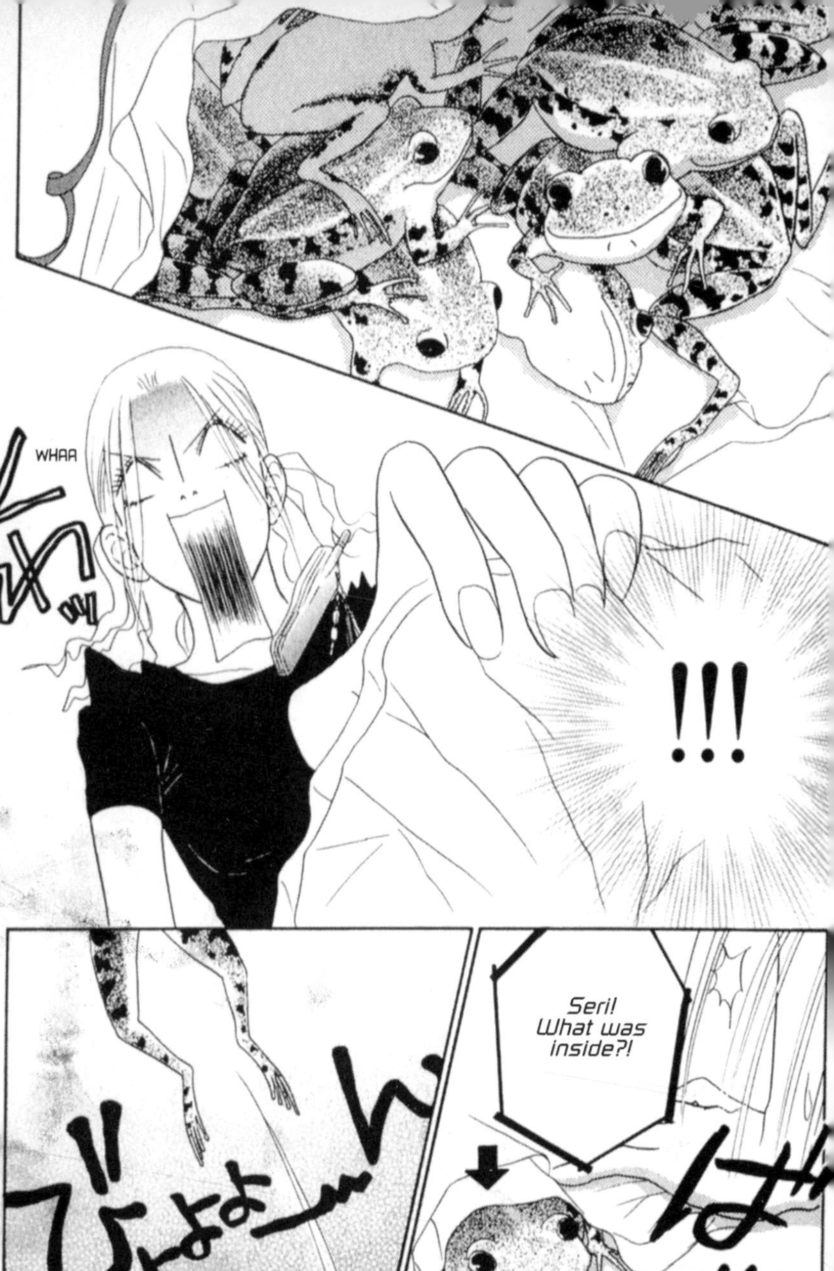
!!!
WHAA
Seri! What was inside?!
WHMP
BOYIINNG

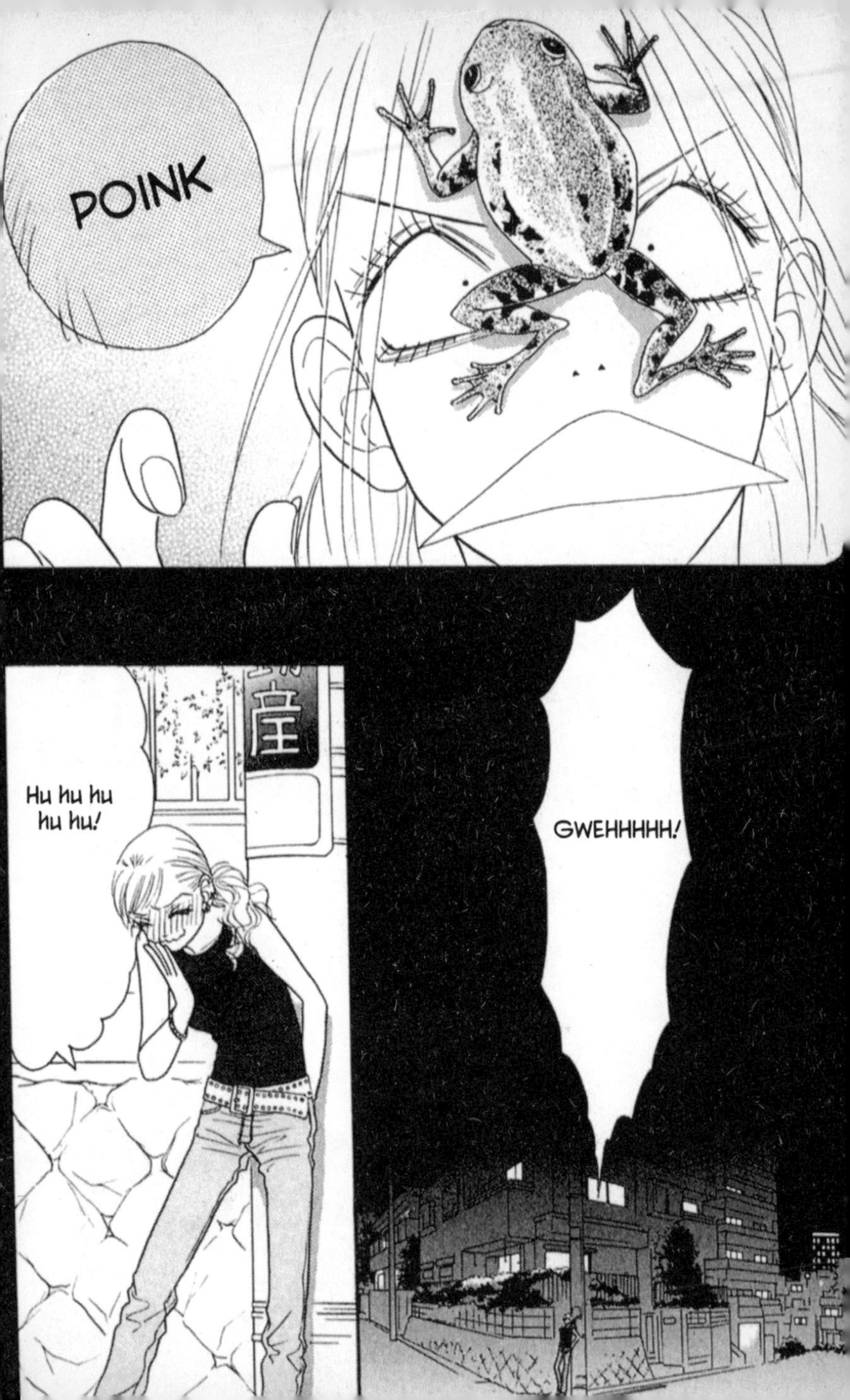
POINK
GWEHHHHH!
Hu hu hu
hu hu!

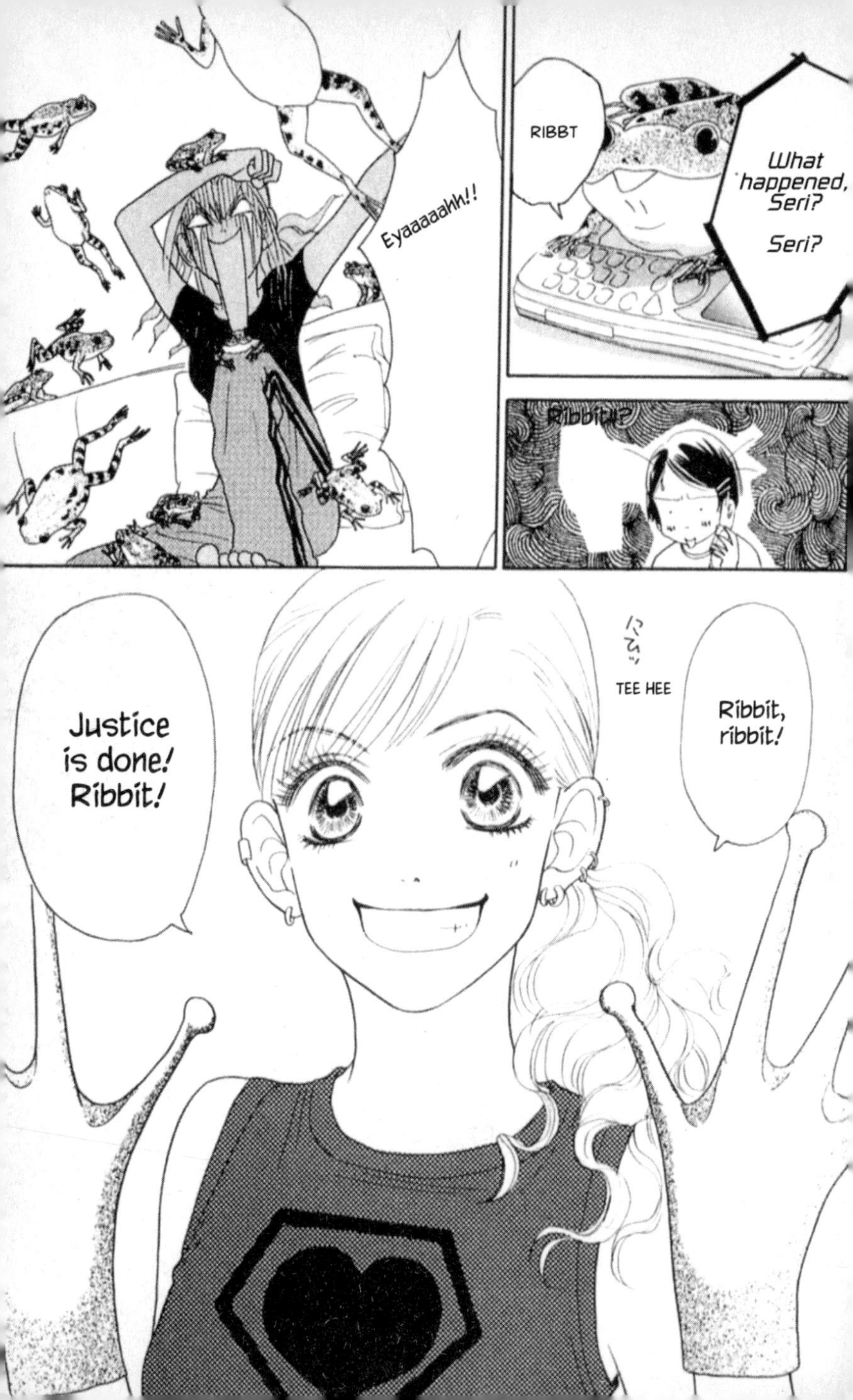
RIBBT
What happened, Seri?
Seri?
Ribbit!?
Eyaaaaahh!!
Ribbit, ribbit!
TEE HEE
Justice is done! Ribbit!

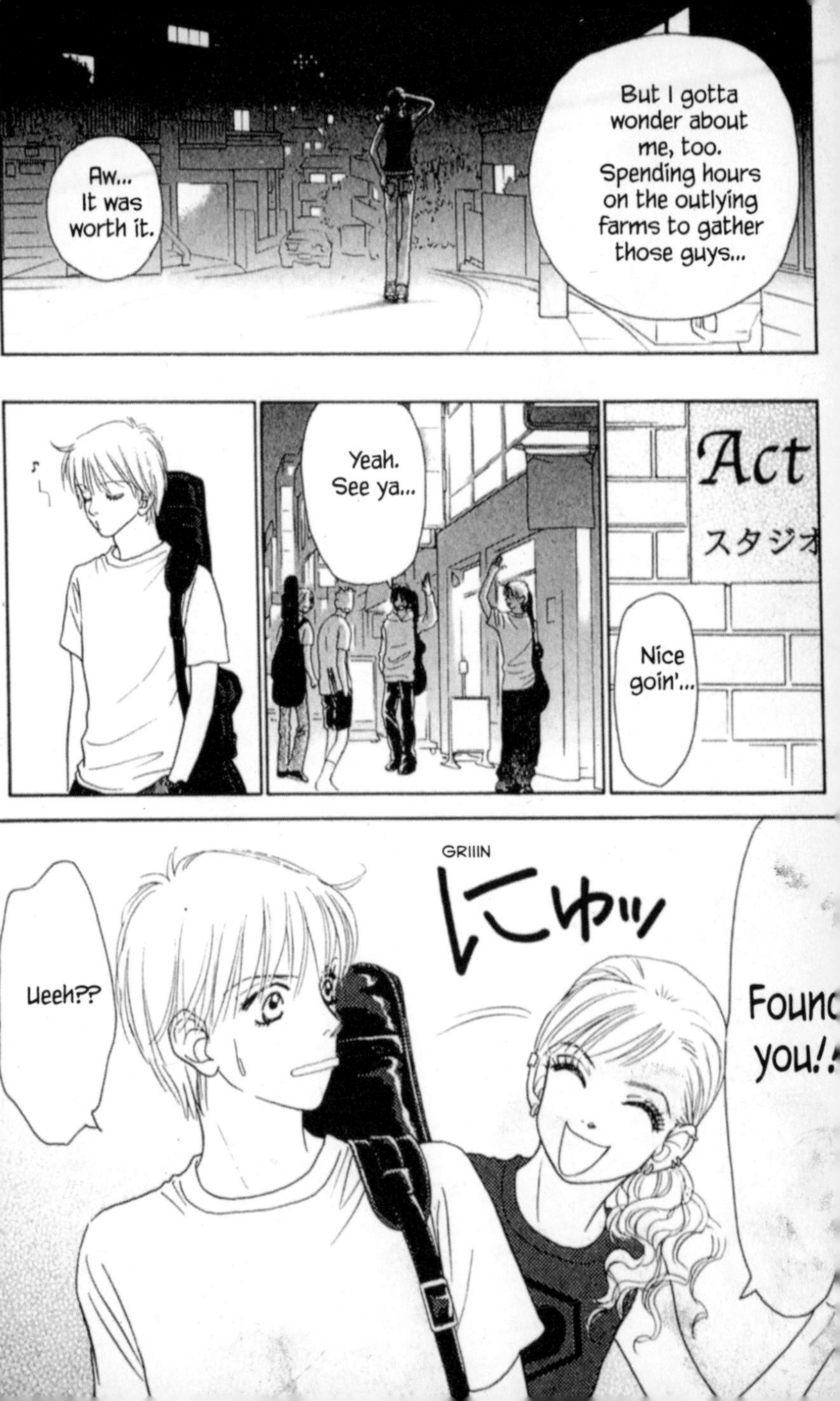

But I gotta wonder about me, too. Spending hours on the outlying farms to gather those guys...
Aw... It was worth it.
Act
スタジオ
Nice goin'...
Yeah. See ya...
Foun
you!
GRIIIN
にゅッ
Ueeh??

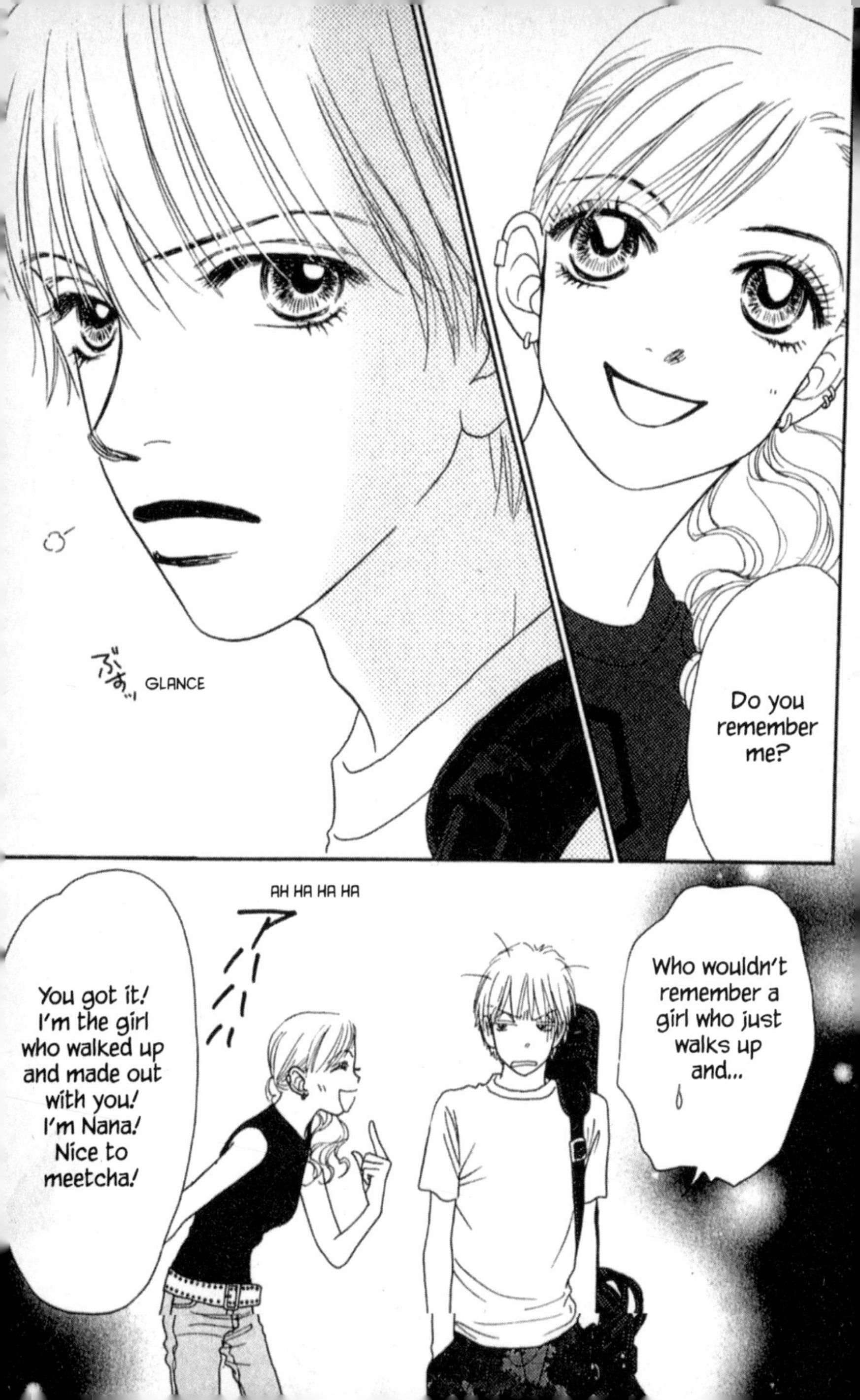
Do you remember me?
GLANCE
Who wouldn't remember a girl who just walks up and...
AH HA HA HA
You got it! I'm the girl who walked up and made out with you! I'm Nana! Nice to meetcha!

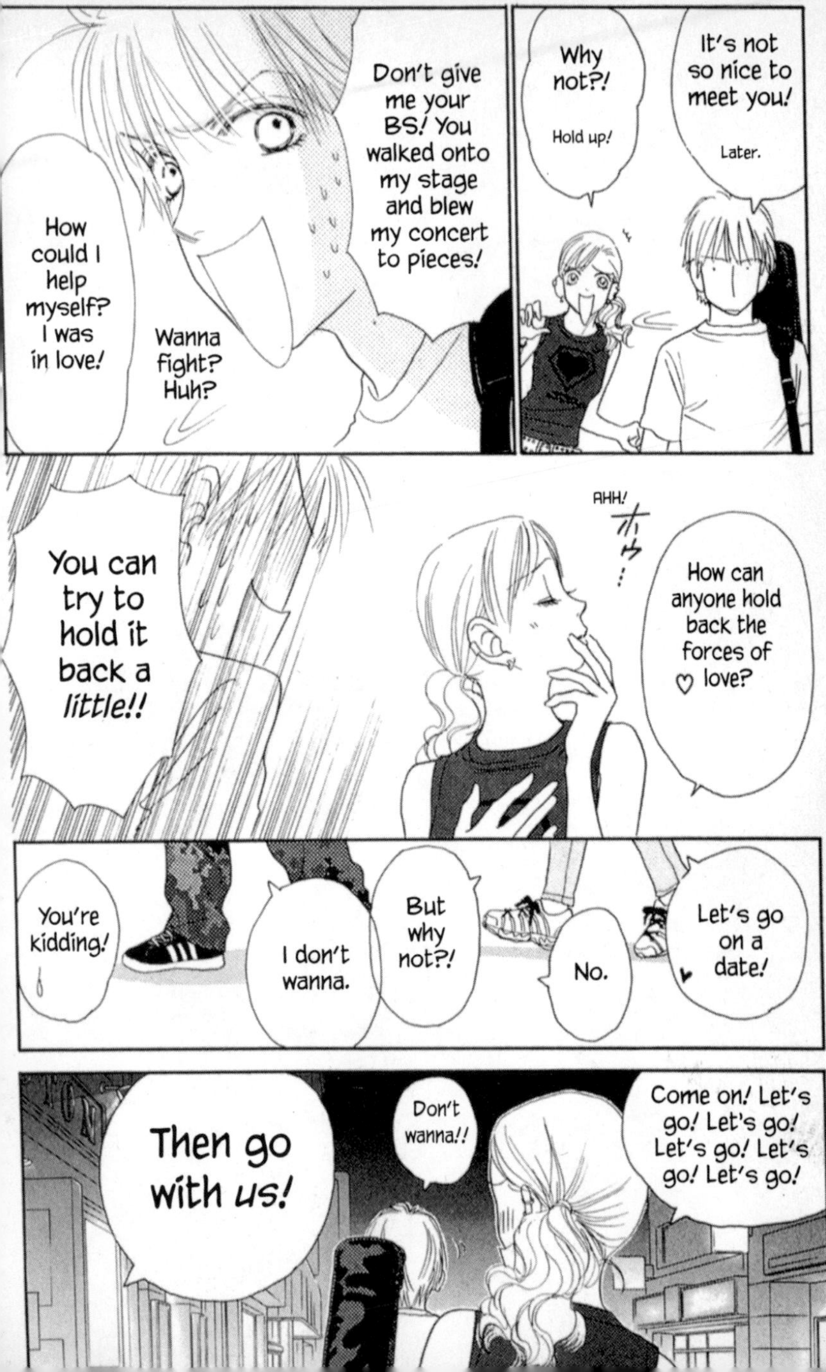
It's not so nice to meet you!
Later.
Why not?!
Hold up!
Don't give me your BS! You walked onto my stage and blew my concert to pieces!
Wanna fight? Huh?
How could I help myself? I was in love!
AHH!
How can anyone hold back the forces of ♡ love?
You can try to hold it back a *little*!!
Let's go on a date! ♥
No.
But why not?!
I don't wanna.
You're kidding!
Come on! Let's go! Let's go! Let's go! Let's go! Let's go!
Don't wanna!!
Then go with *us*!

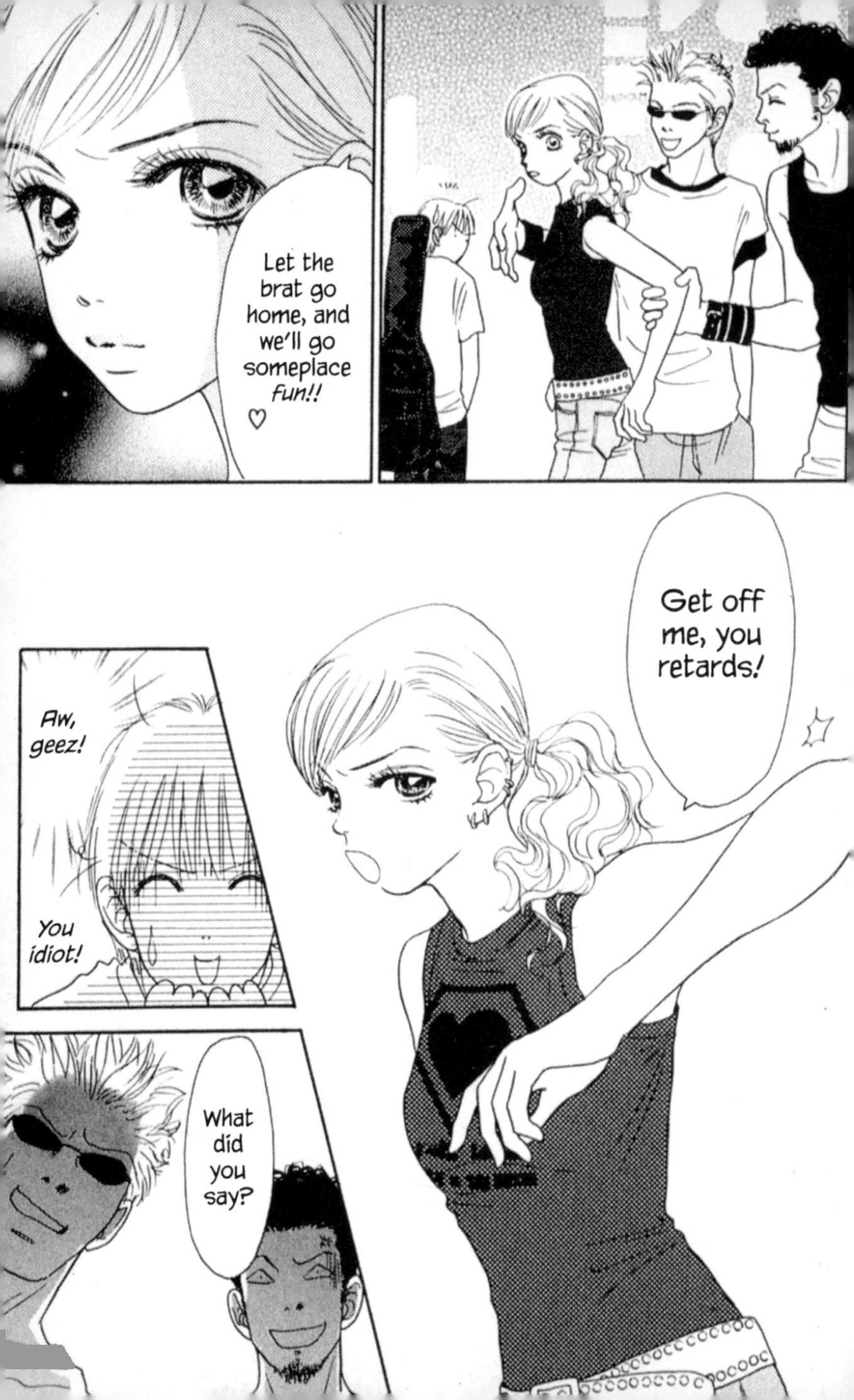
Let the brat go home, and we'll go someplace fun!! ♡
Get off me, you retards!
Aw, geez!
You idiot!
What did you say?

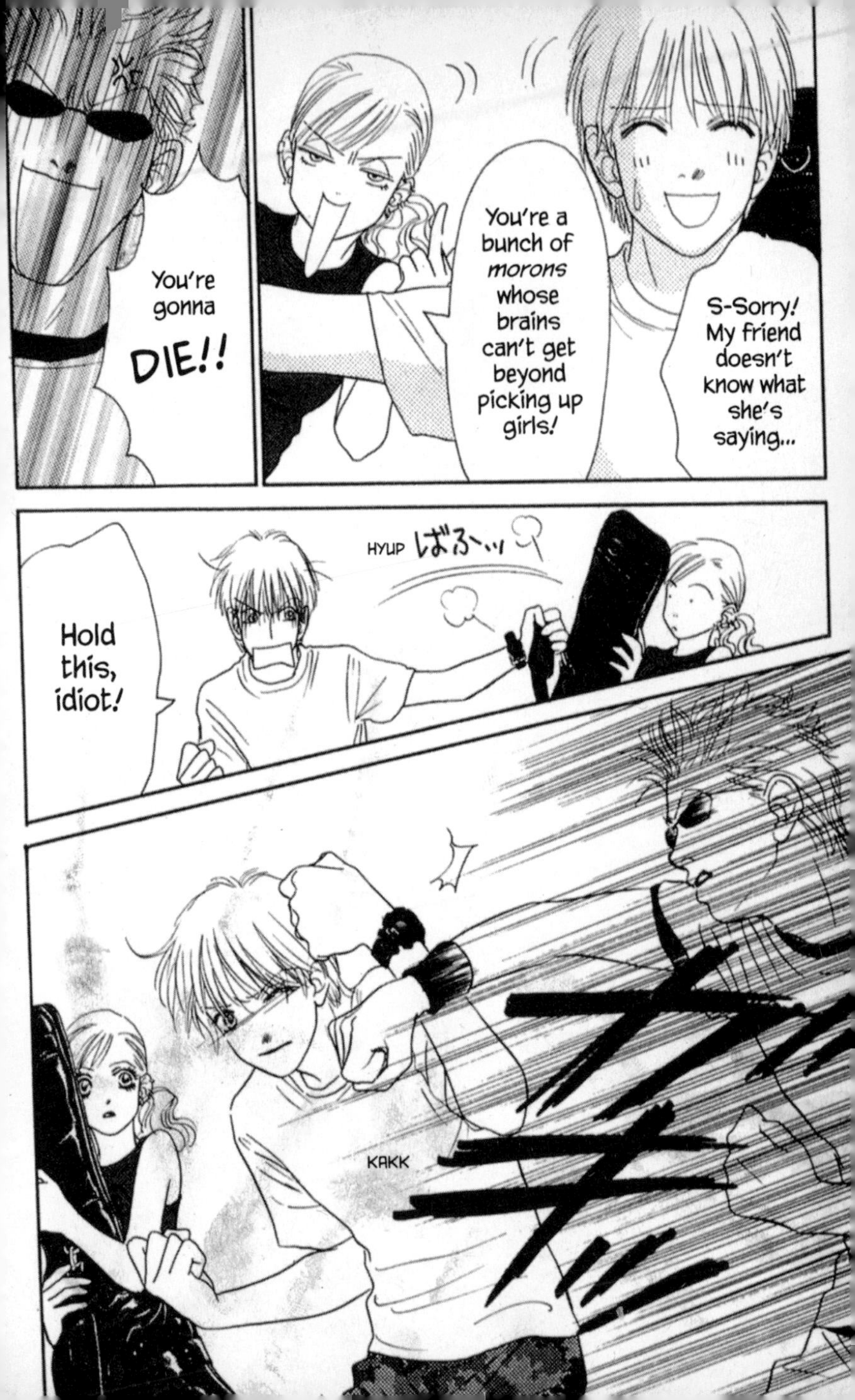
S-Sorry! My friend doesn't know what she's saying...
You're a bunch of *morons* whose brains can't get beyond picking up girls!
You're gonna DIE!!
Hold this, idiot!
HYUP
ばふ〜ッ
KAKK

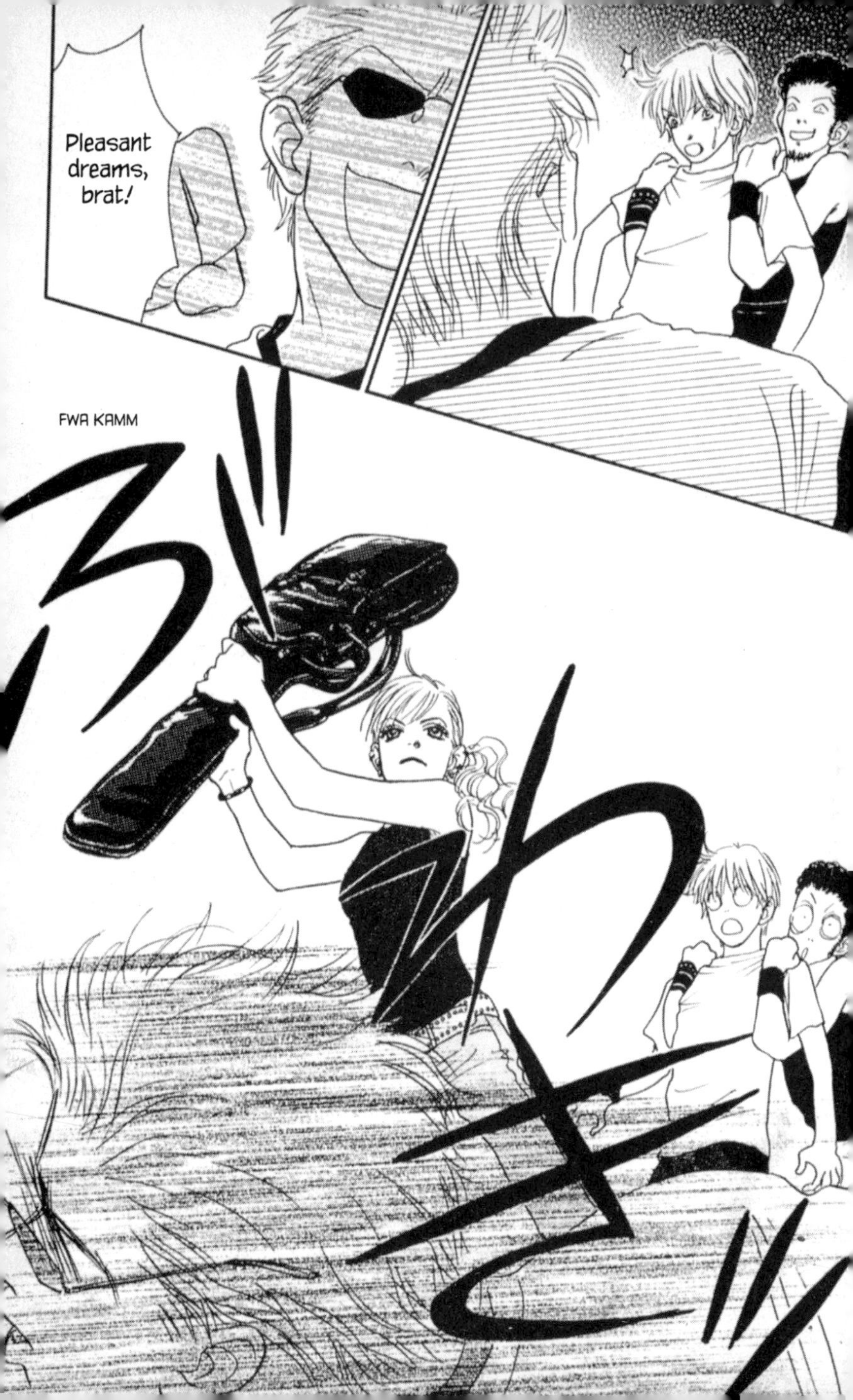
Pleasant dreams, brat!
FWA KAMM

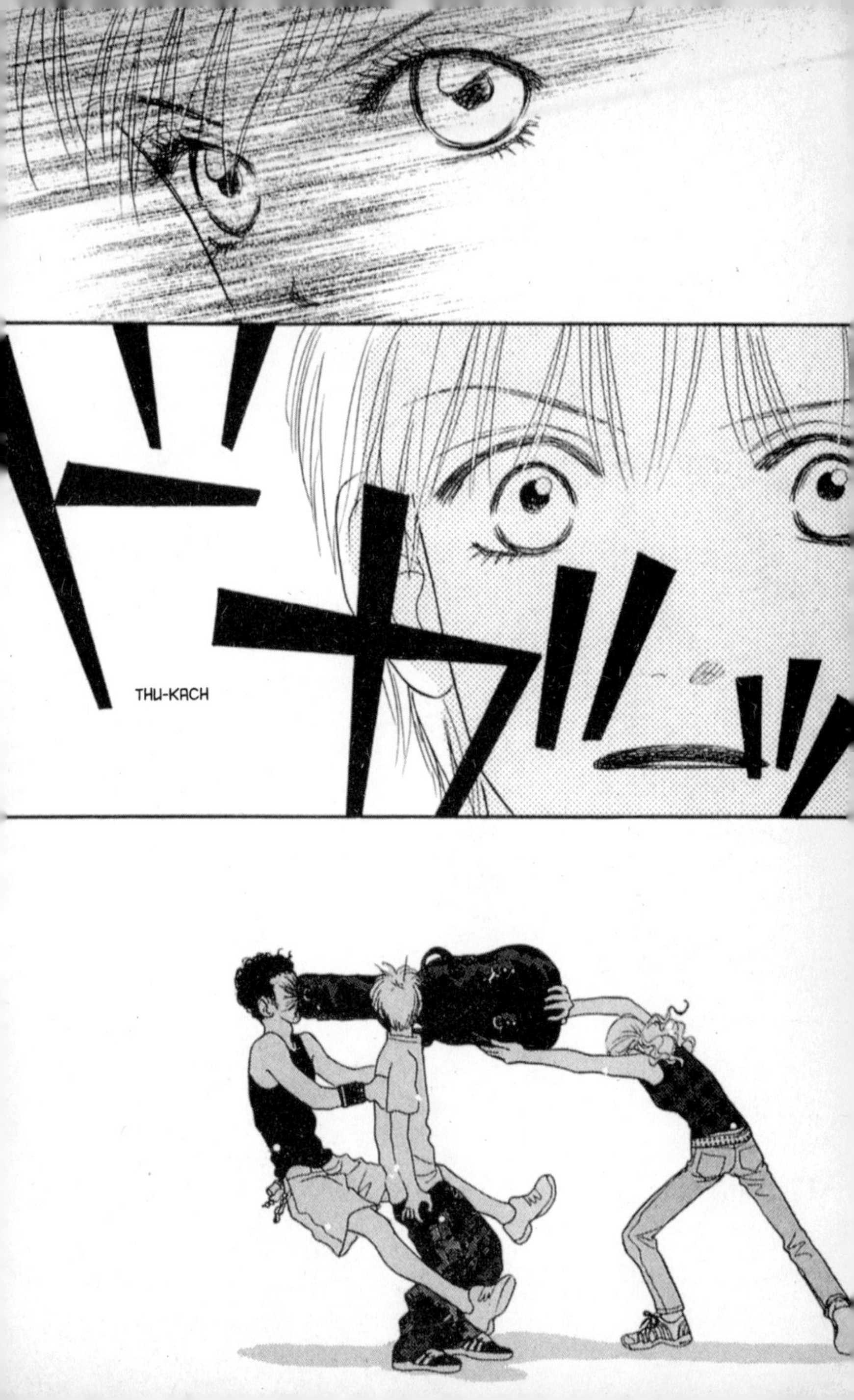
ドキッ
THU-KACH

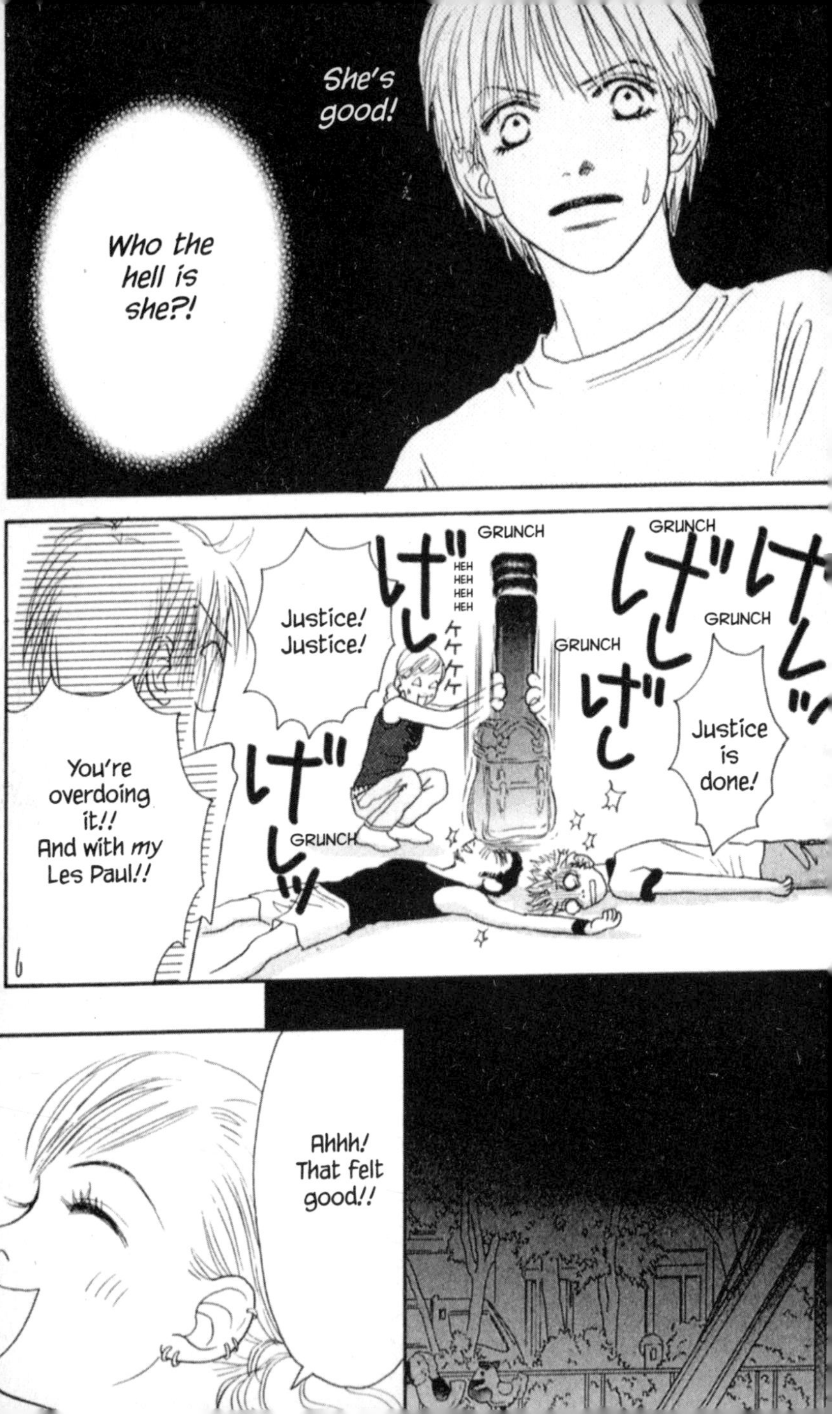
She's good!
Who the hell is she?!
GRUNCH
げしげし
GRUNCH
Justice is done!
GRUNCH
GRUNCH
HEH HEH HEH HEH
ケケケケ
げし
Justice! Justice!
げしッ
GRUNCH
You're overdoing it!! And with *my* Les Paul!!
Ahhh! That felt good!!

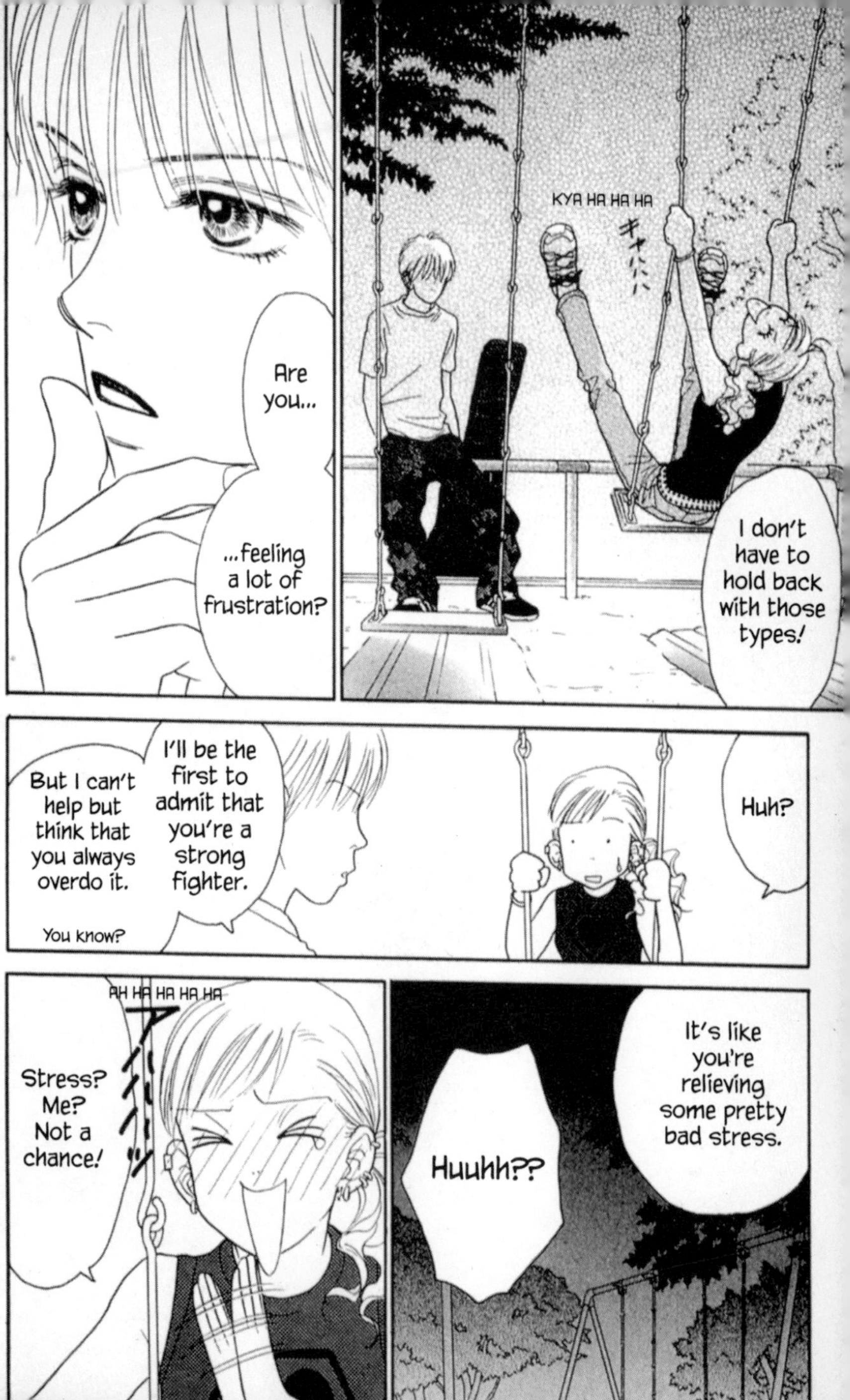
KYA HA HA HA
I don't have to hold back with those types!
Are you...
...feeling a lot of frustration?
Huh?
I'll be the first to admit that you're a strong fighter.
But I can't help but think that you always overdo it.
You know?
It's like you're relieving some pretty bad stress.
Huuhh??
AH HA HA HA HA
Stress? Me? Not a chance!

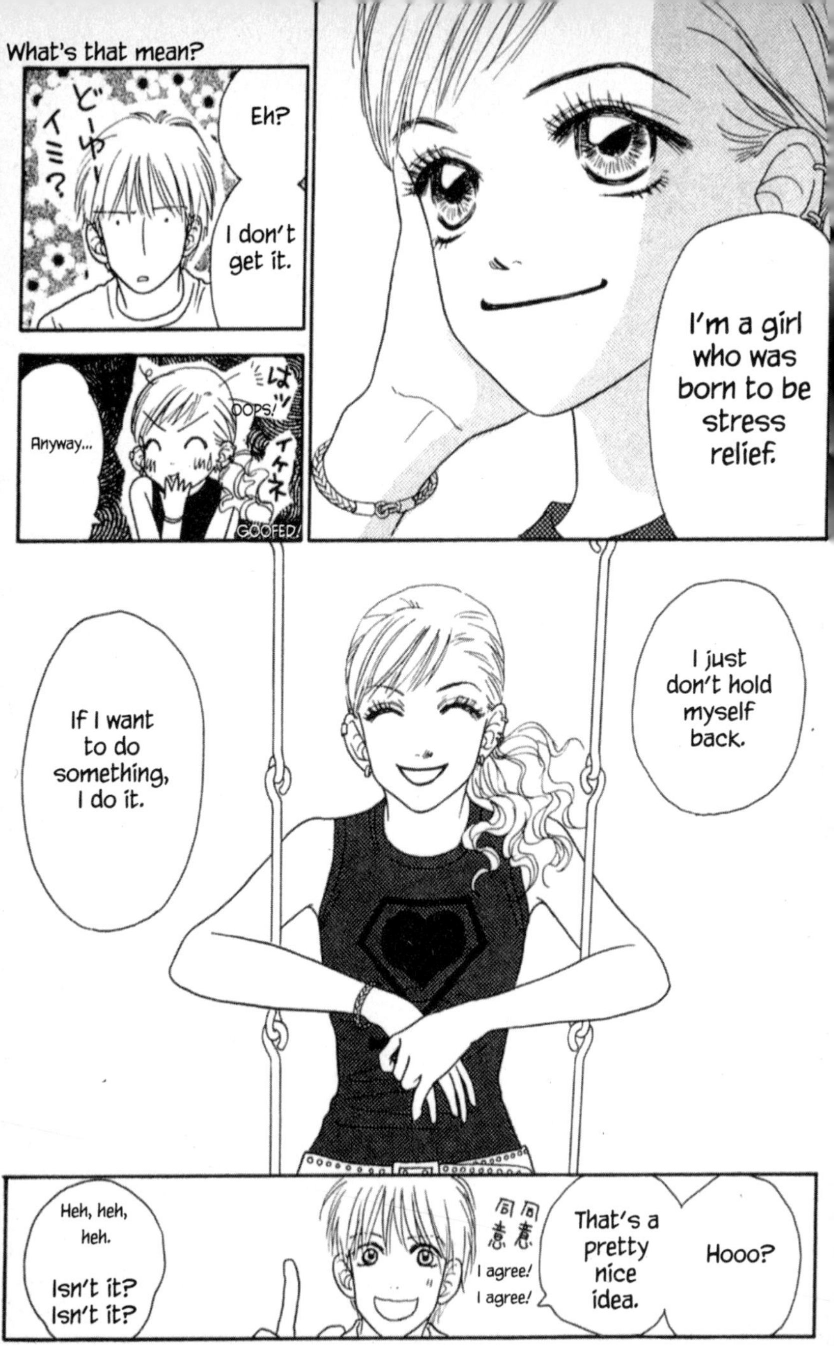

I'm a girl who was born to be stress relief.
What's that mean?
どーゆーイミ?
Eh?
I don't get it.
ぱッ
OOPS!
イケネ
GOOFED!
Anyway...
I just don't hold myself back.
If I want to do something, I do it.
Hooo?
That's a pretty nice idea.
同意同意
I agree! I agree!
Heh, heh, heh.
Isn't it? Isn't it?

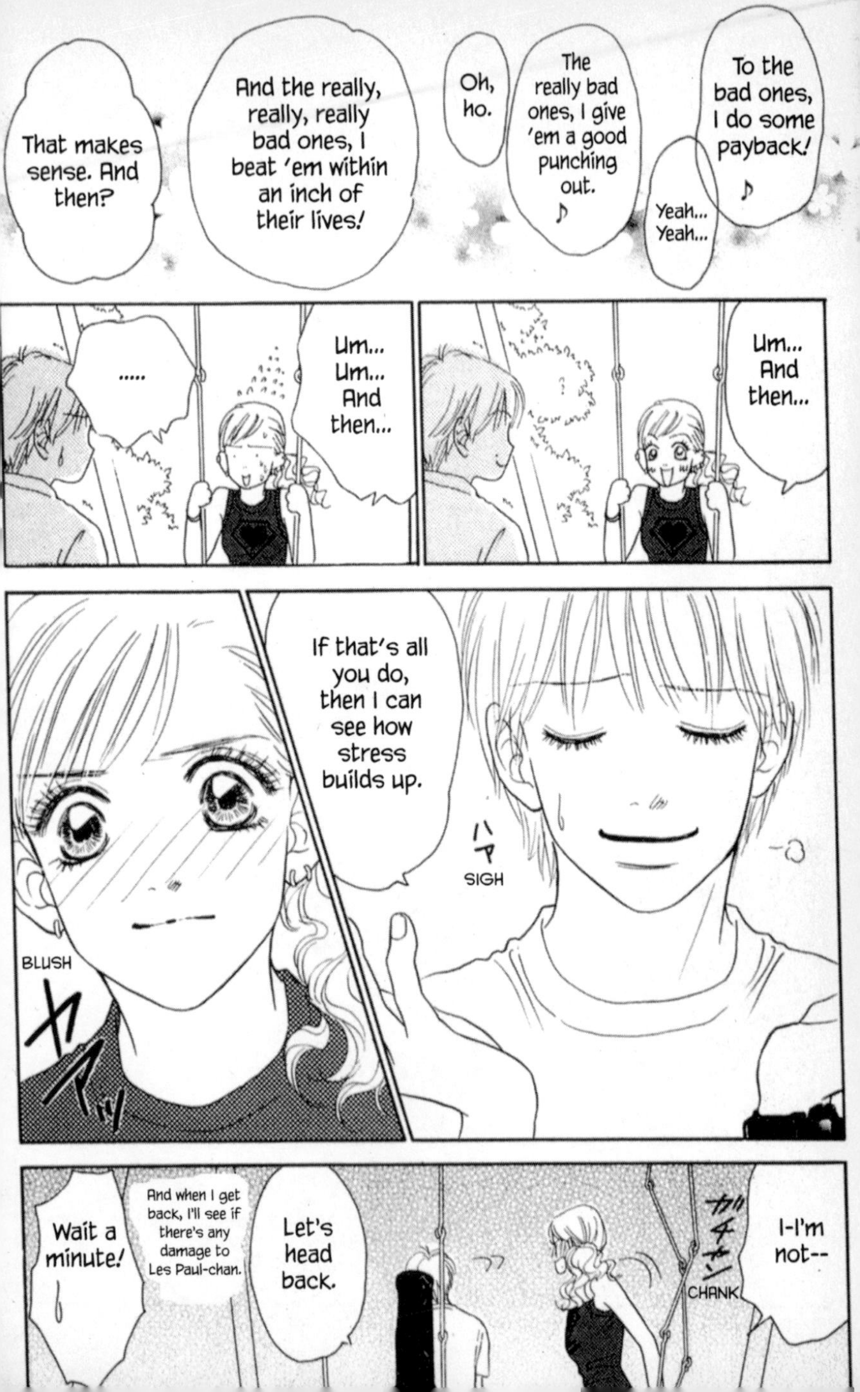
To the bad ones, I do some payback! ♪
Yeah... Yeah...
The really bad ones, I give 'em a good punching out. ♪
Oh, no.
And the really, really, really bad ones, I beat 'em within an inch of their lives!
That makes sense. And then?
Um... And then...
Um... Um... And then...
.....
If that's all you do, then I can see how stress builds up.
SIGH
BLUSH
I-I'm not--
CHANK
Let's head back.
And when I get back, I'll see if there's any damage to Les Paul-chan.
Wait a minute!

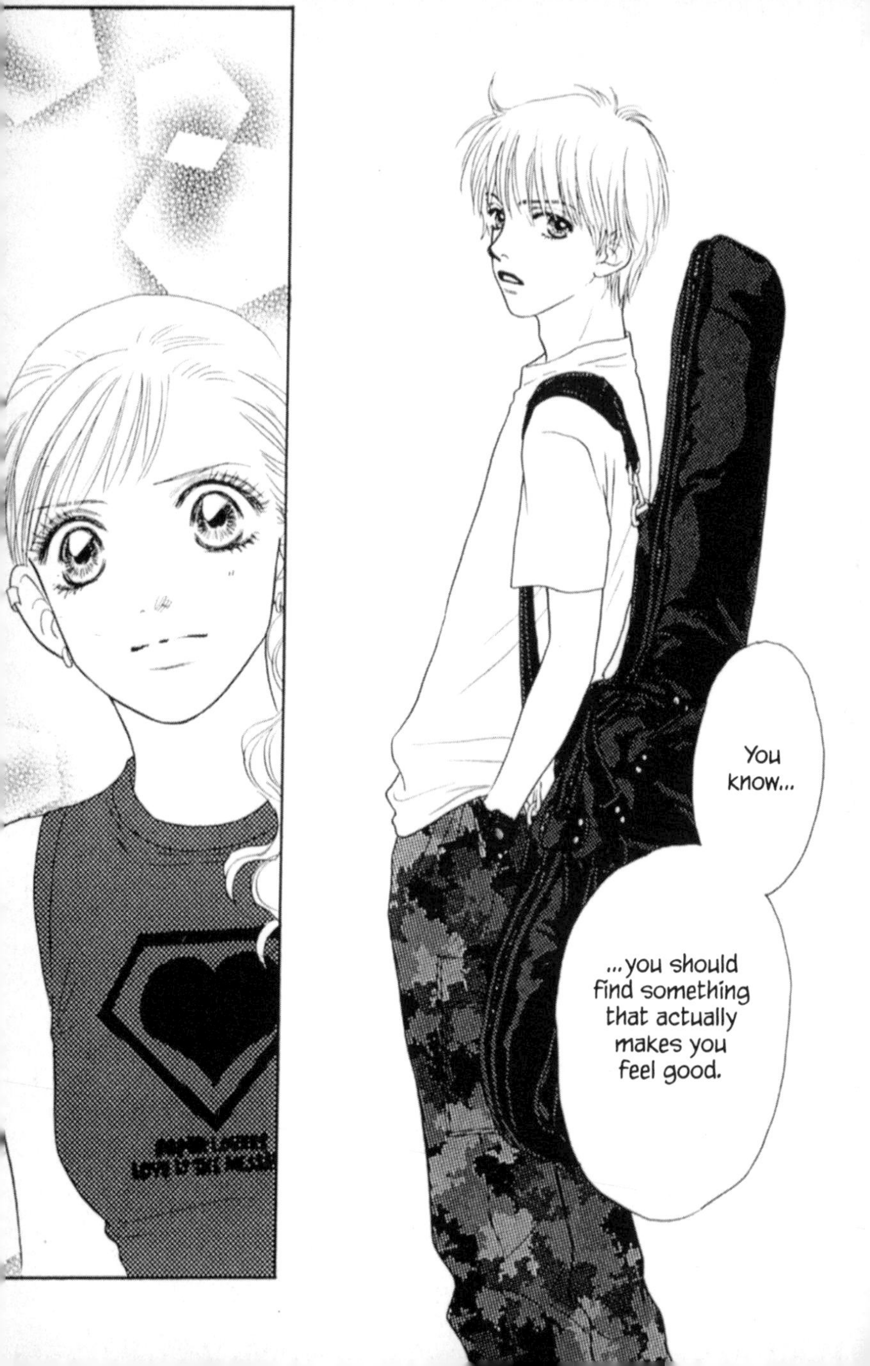
You know...
...you should find something that actually makes you feel good.

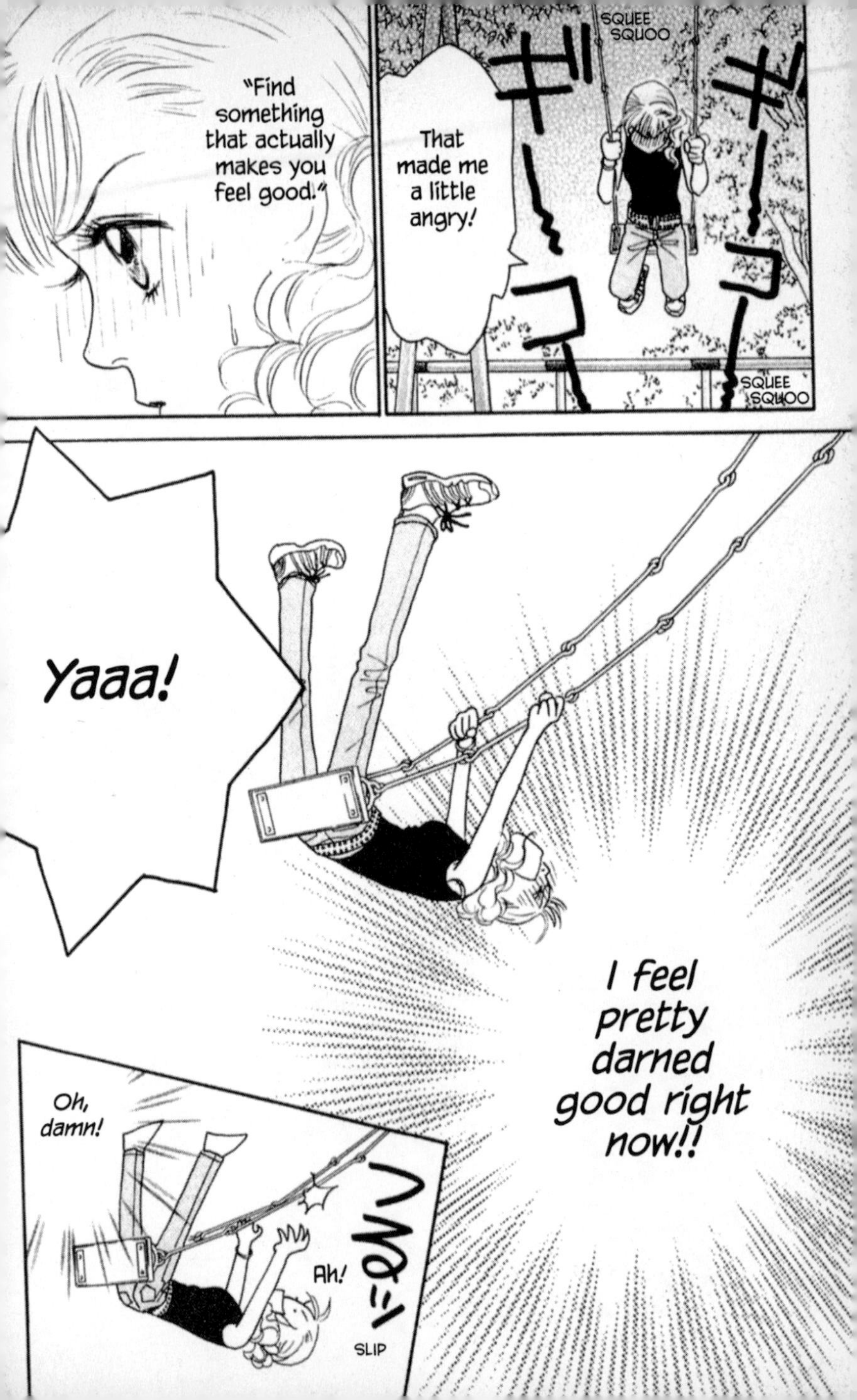
SQUEE SQUOO
That made me a little angry!
"Find something that actually makes you feel good."
SQUEE SQUOO
Yaaa!
I feel pretty darned good right now!!
Ah!
SLIP
Oh, damn!

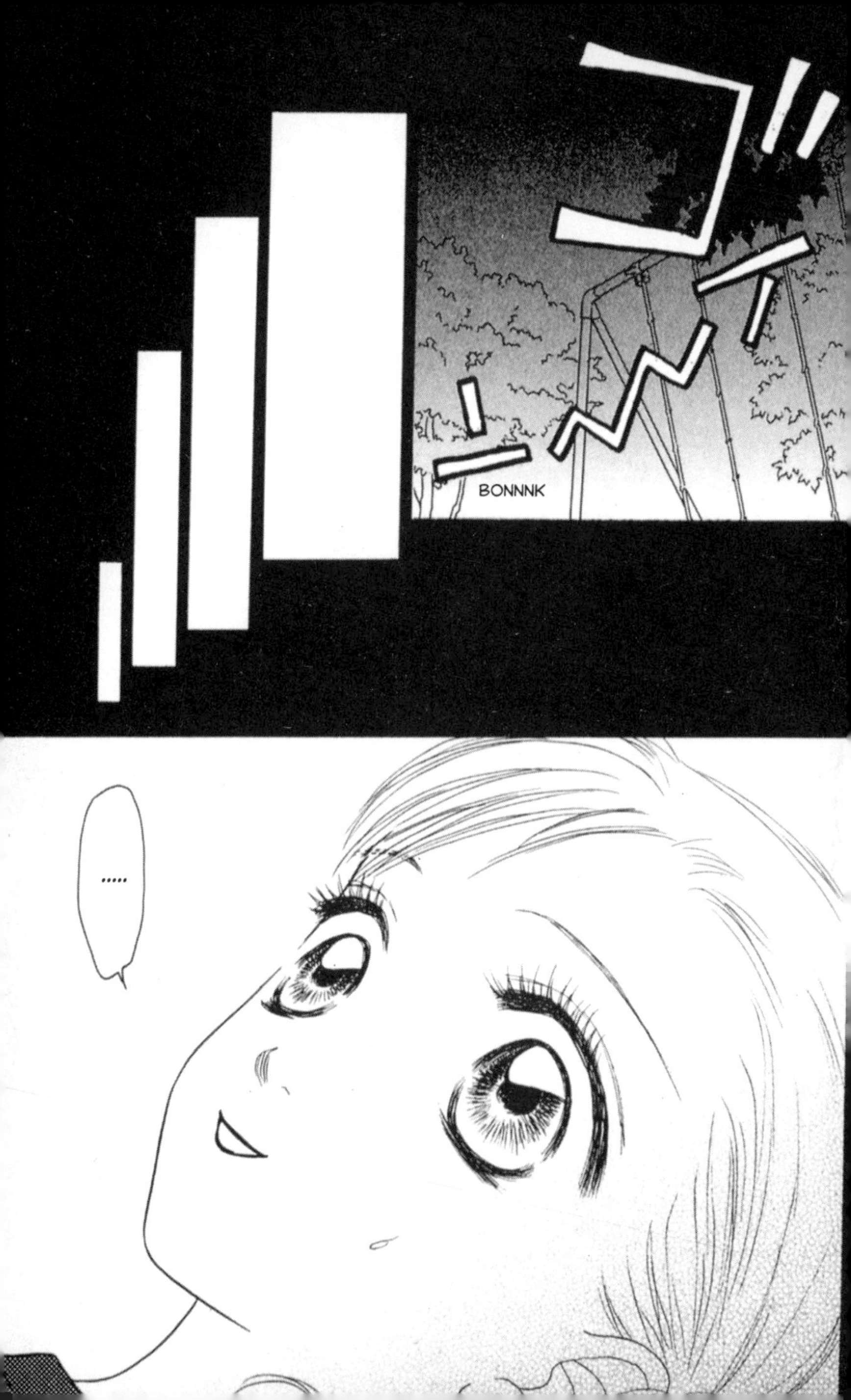
BONNNK
......

Eh?
Um...
Um...
Now let's work this out a minute...
Oww!
Where am I?
When am I?

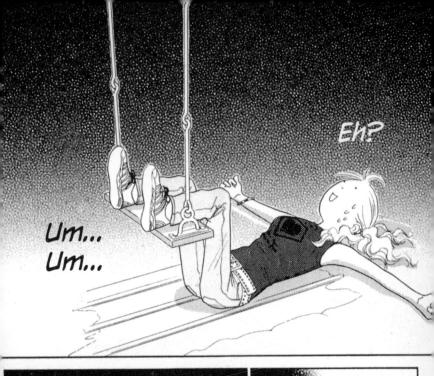

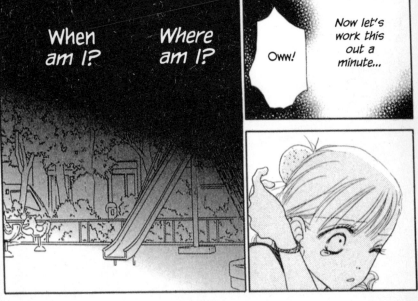

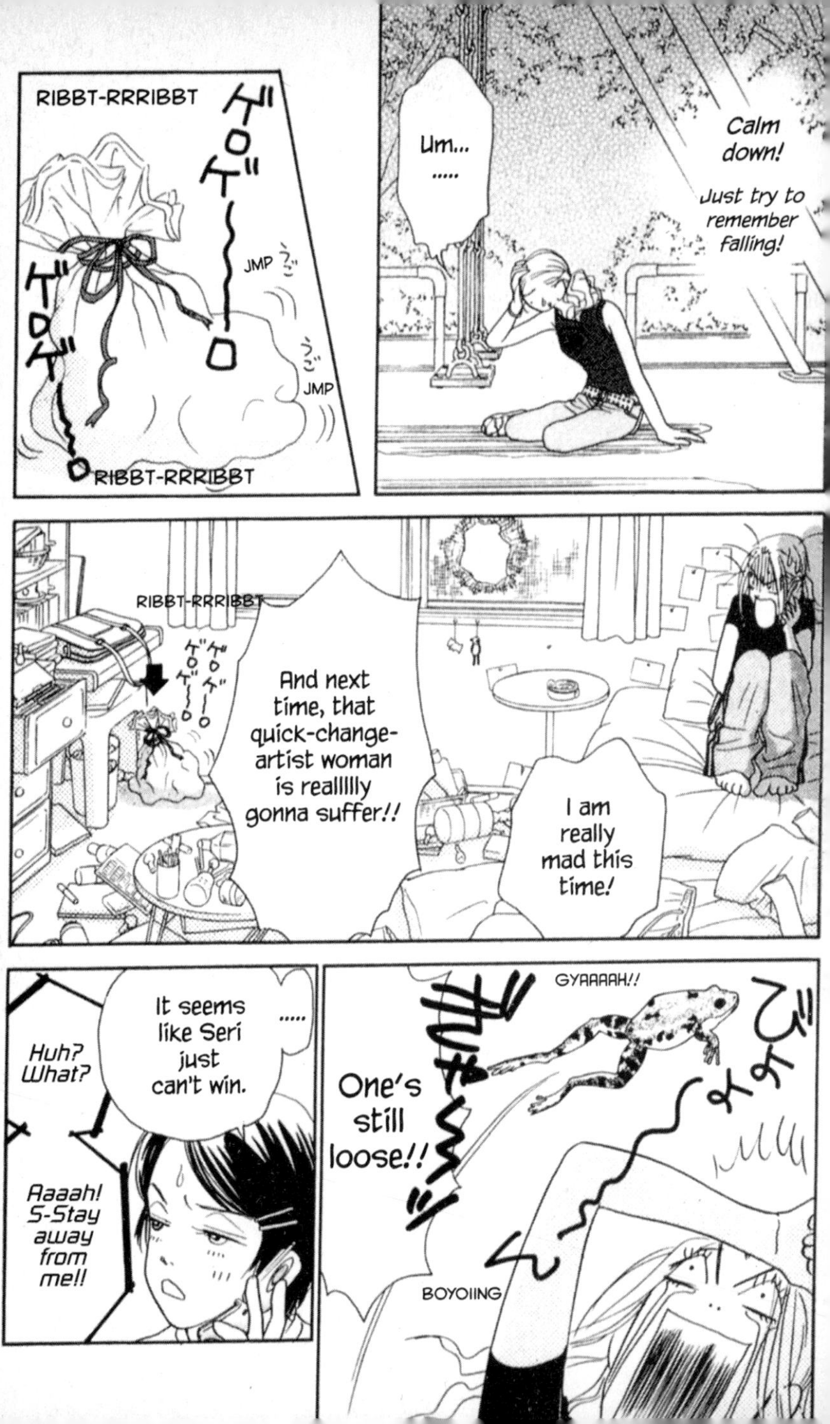
Calm down!
Just try to remember falling!
Um... .....
RIBBT-RRRIBBT
JMP
JMP
RIBBT-RRRIBBT
I am really mad this time!
And next time, that quick-change-artist woman is realllly gonna suffer!!
RIBBT-RRRIBBT
GYAAAAH!!
One's still loose!!
BOYOIING
.....
It seems like Seri just can't win.
Huh? What?
Aaaah! S-Stay away from me!!

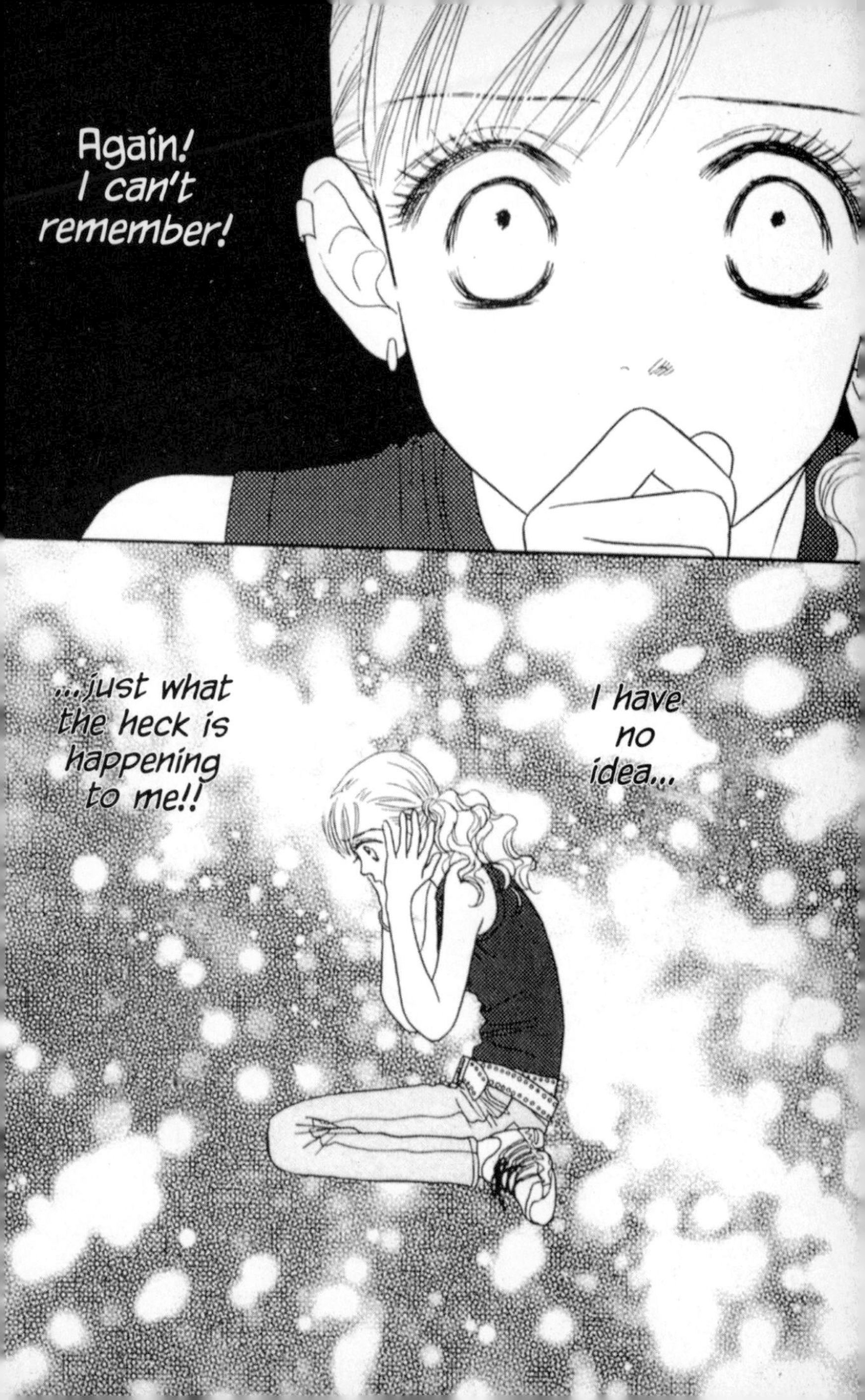
Again! I can't remember!
I have no idea...
...just what the heck is happening to me!!

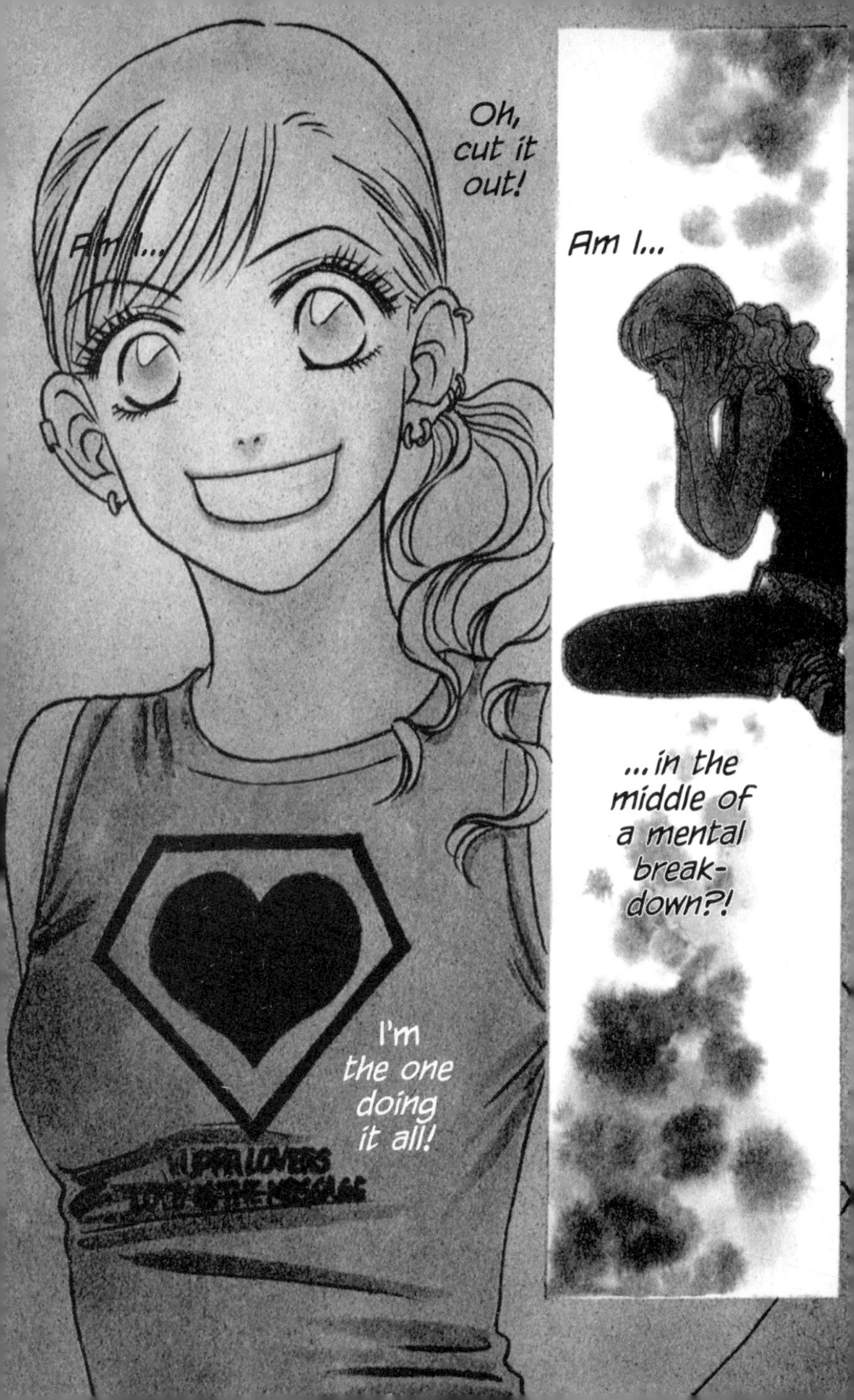
Am I...
...in the middle of a mental breakdown?!
Oh, cut it out!
Am I...
I'm the one doing it all!

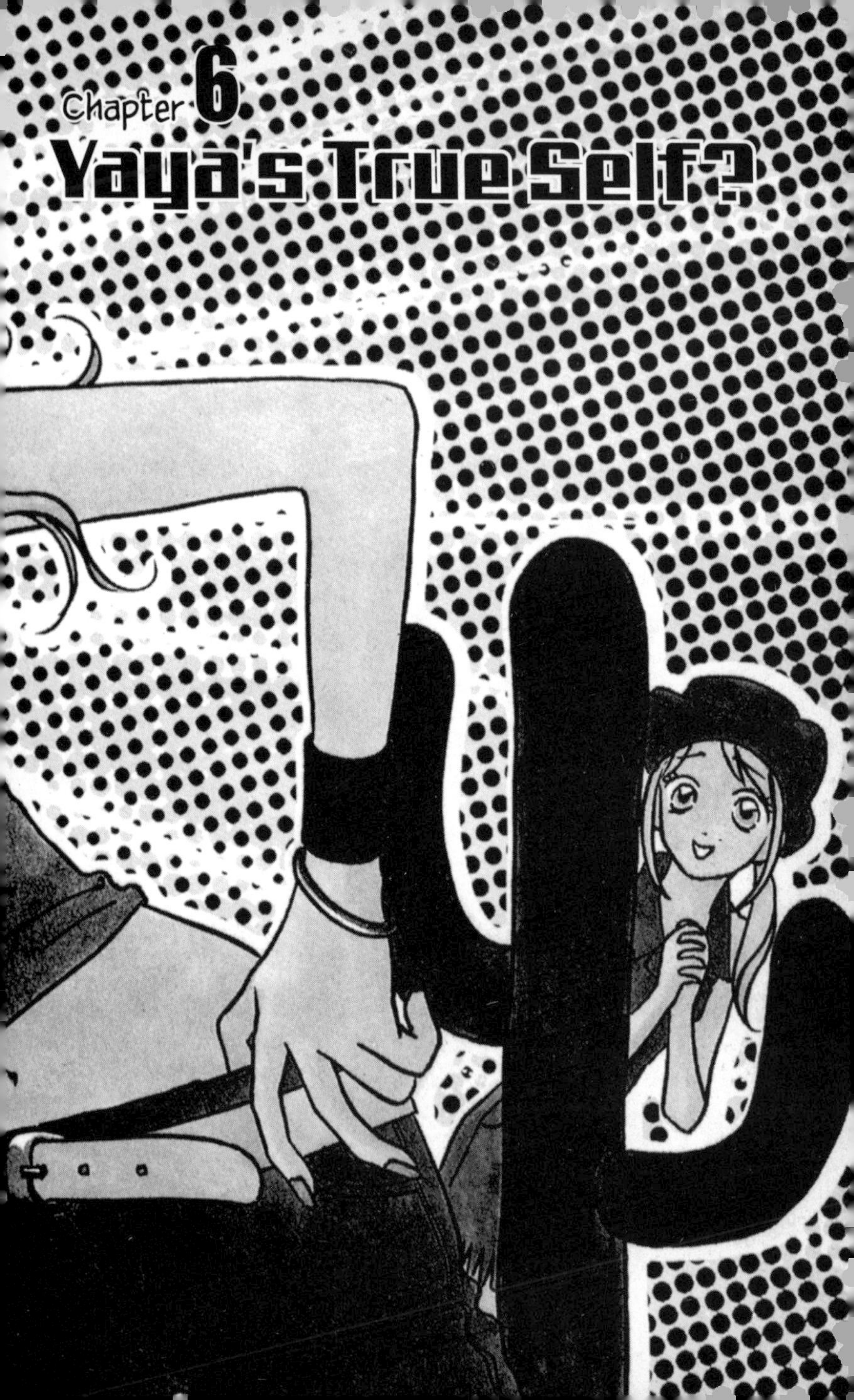
Chapter 6
Yaya's True Self?

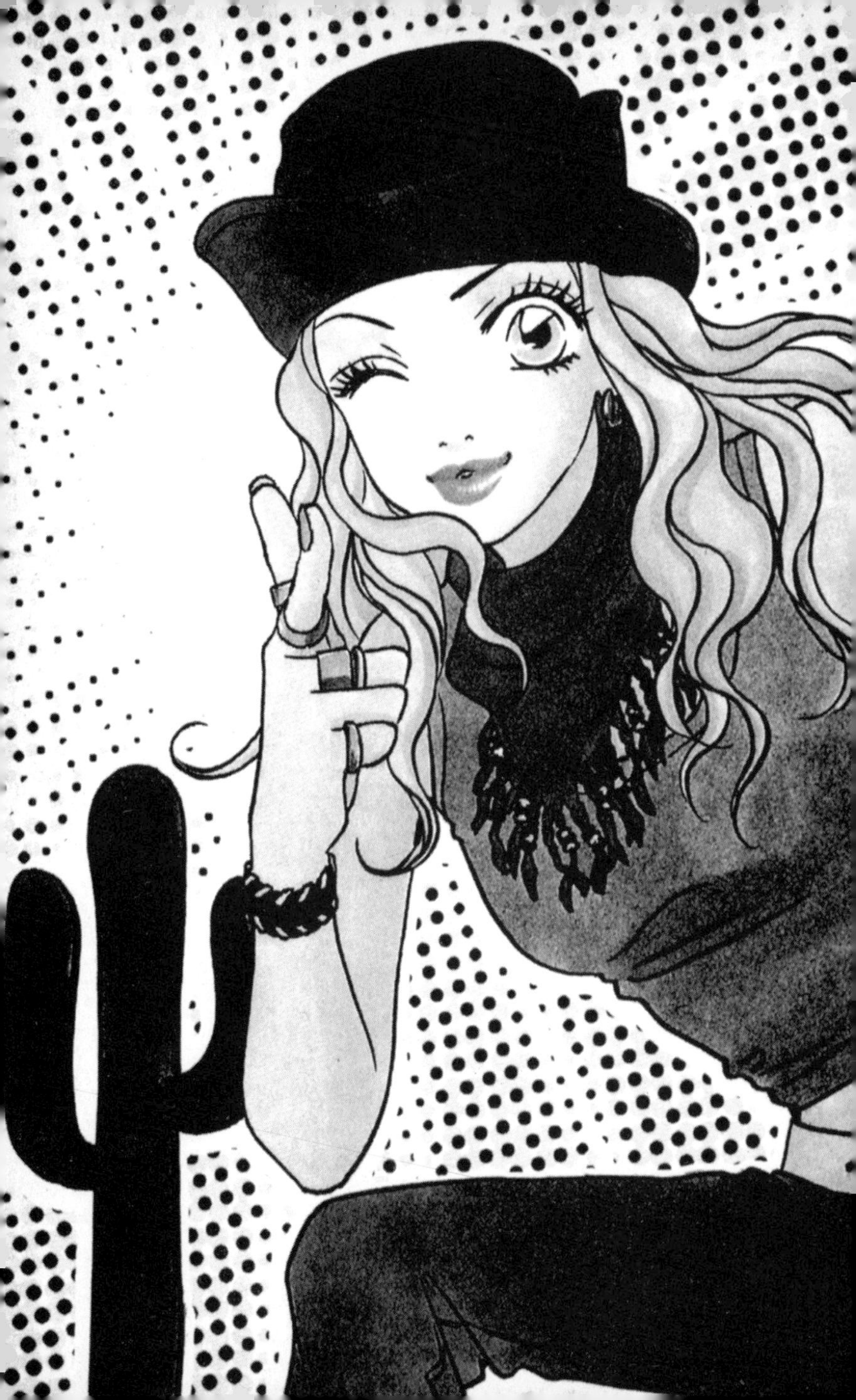

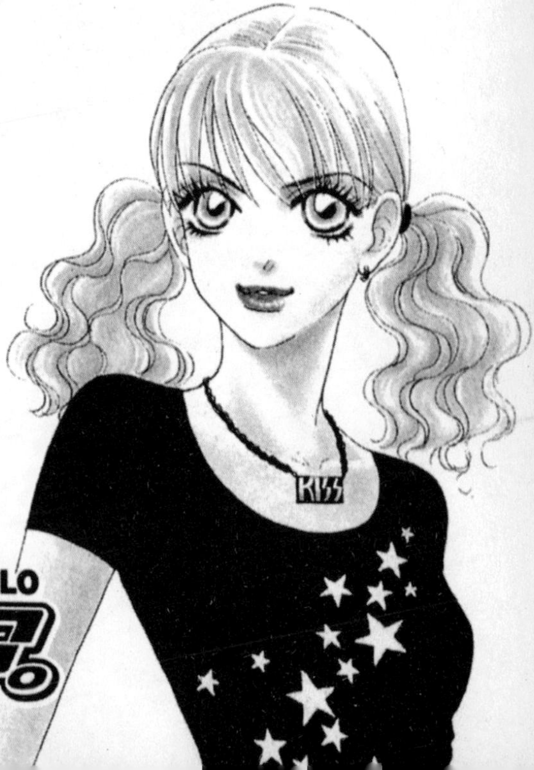
KISS

OTHELLO
オセロ。

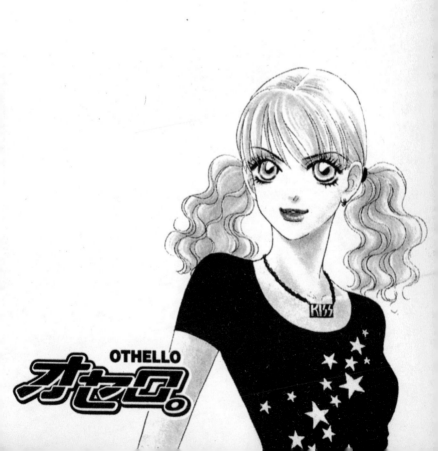

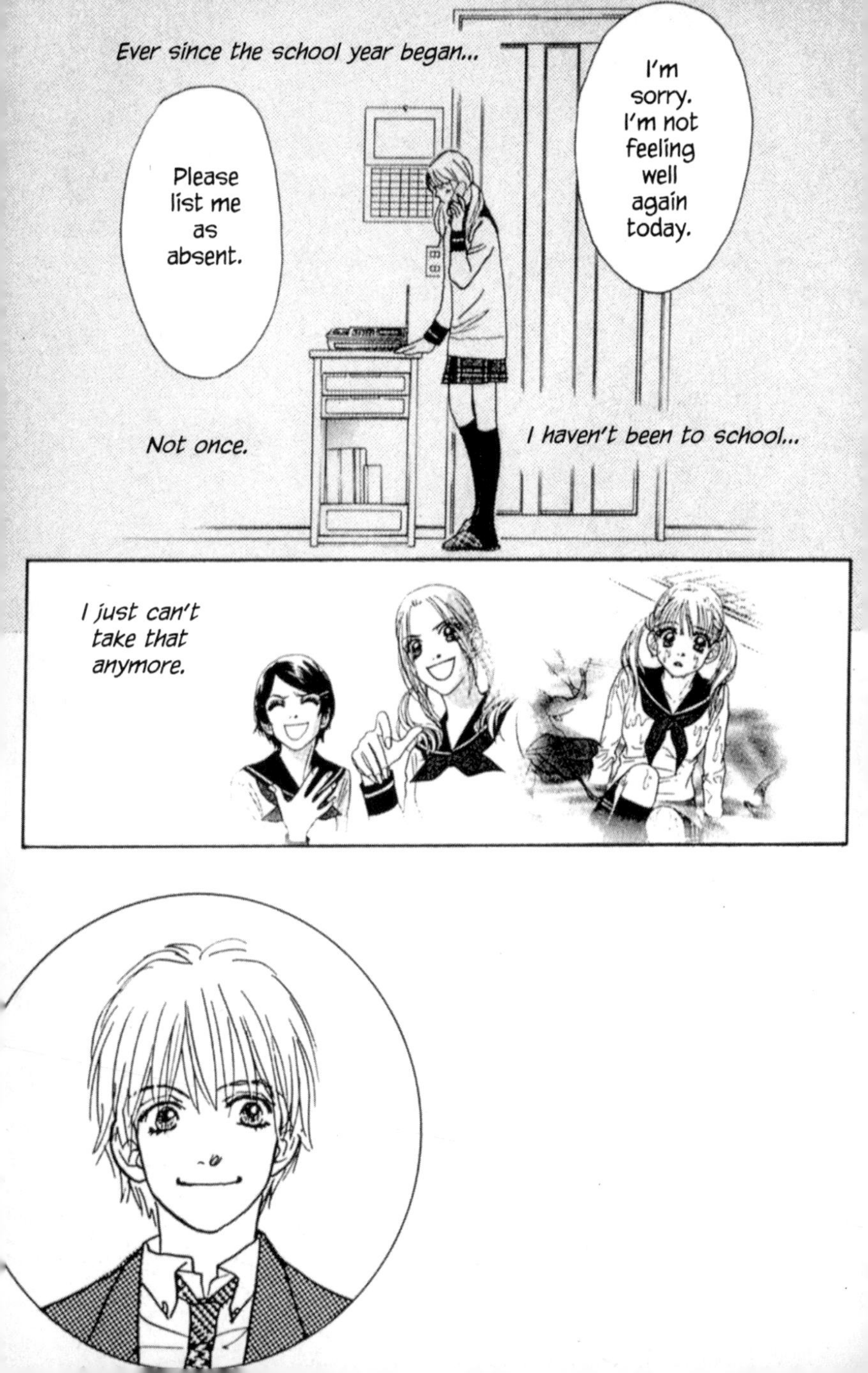
Ever since the school year began...
I'm sorry. I'm not feeling well again today.
Please list me as absent.
I haven't been to school...
Not once.
I just can't take that anymore.

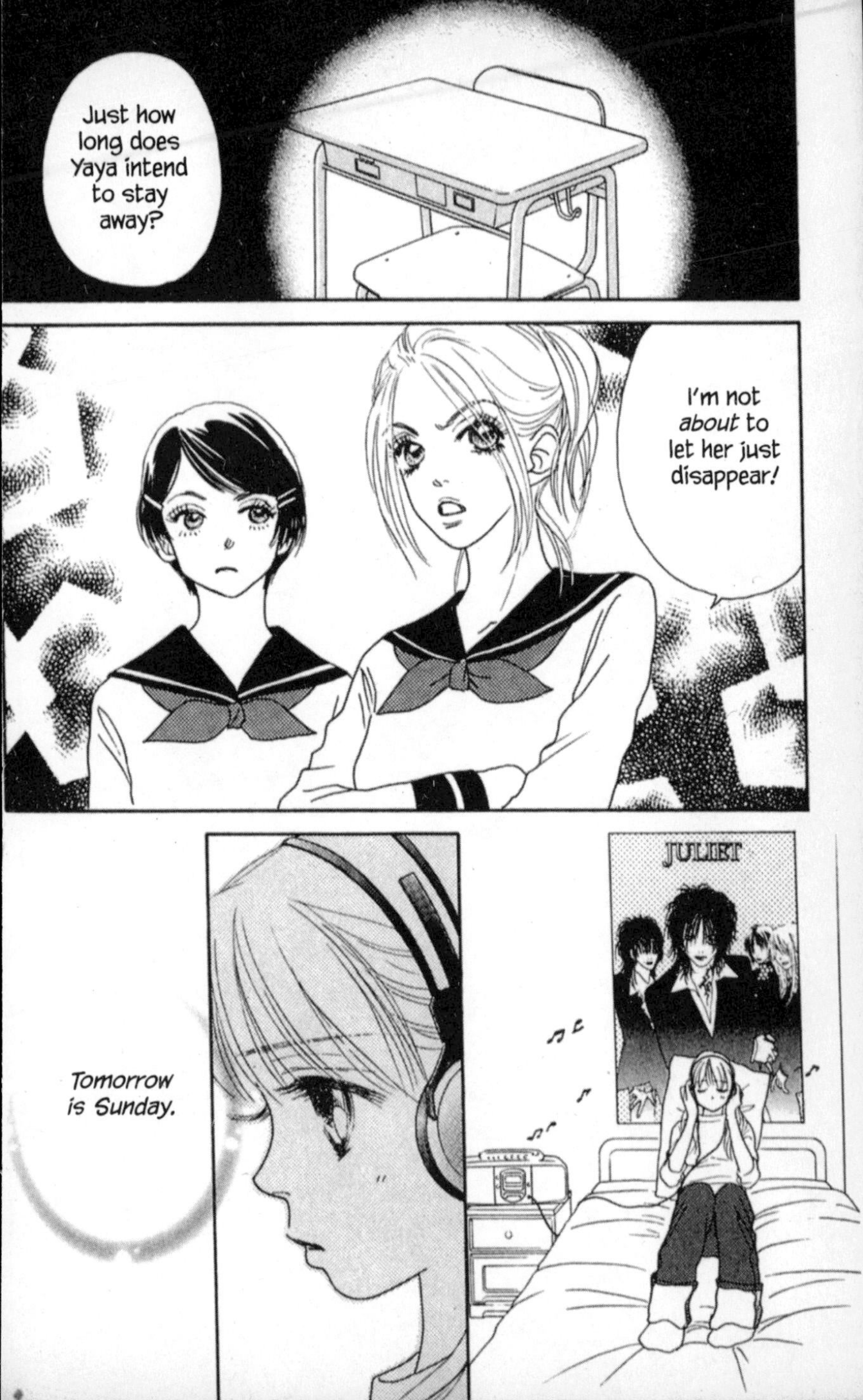
Just how long does Yaya intend to stay away?
I'm not *about* to let her just disappear!
JULIET
Tomorrow is Sunday.

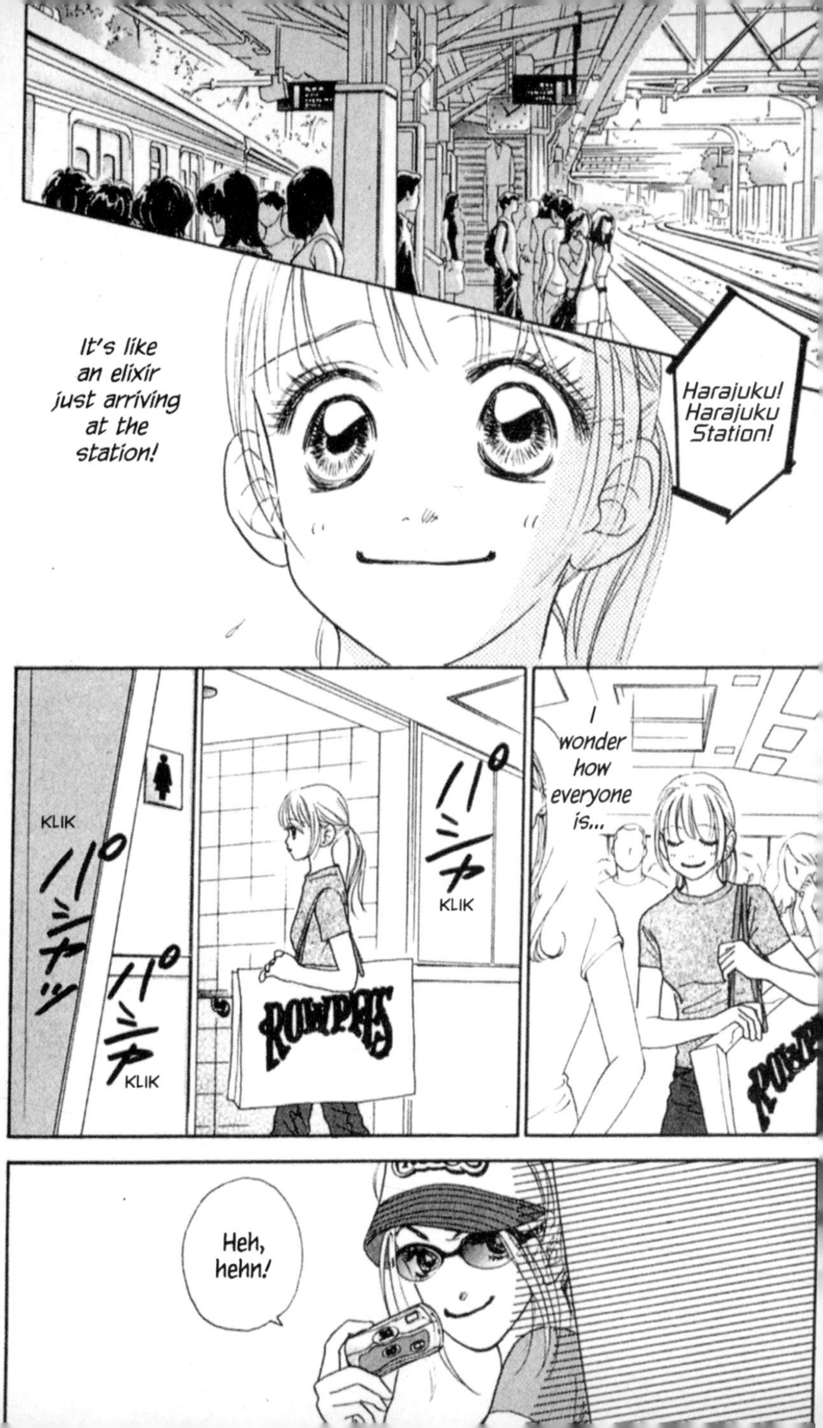

Harajuku! Harajuku Station!
It's like an elixir just arriving at the station!
I wonder how everyone is...
パシャ
KLIK
パシャッ
KLIK
パシャ
KLIK
Heh, hehn!

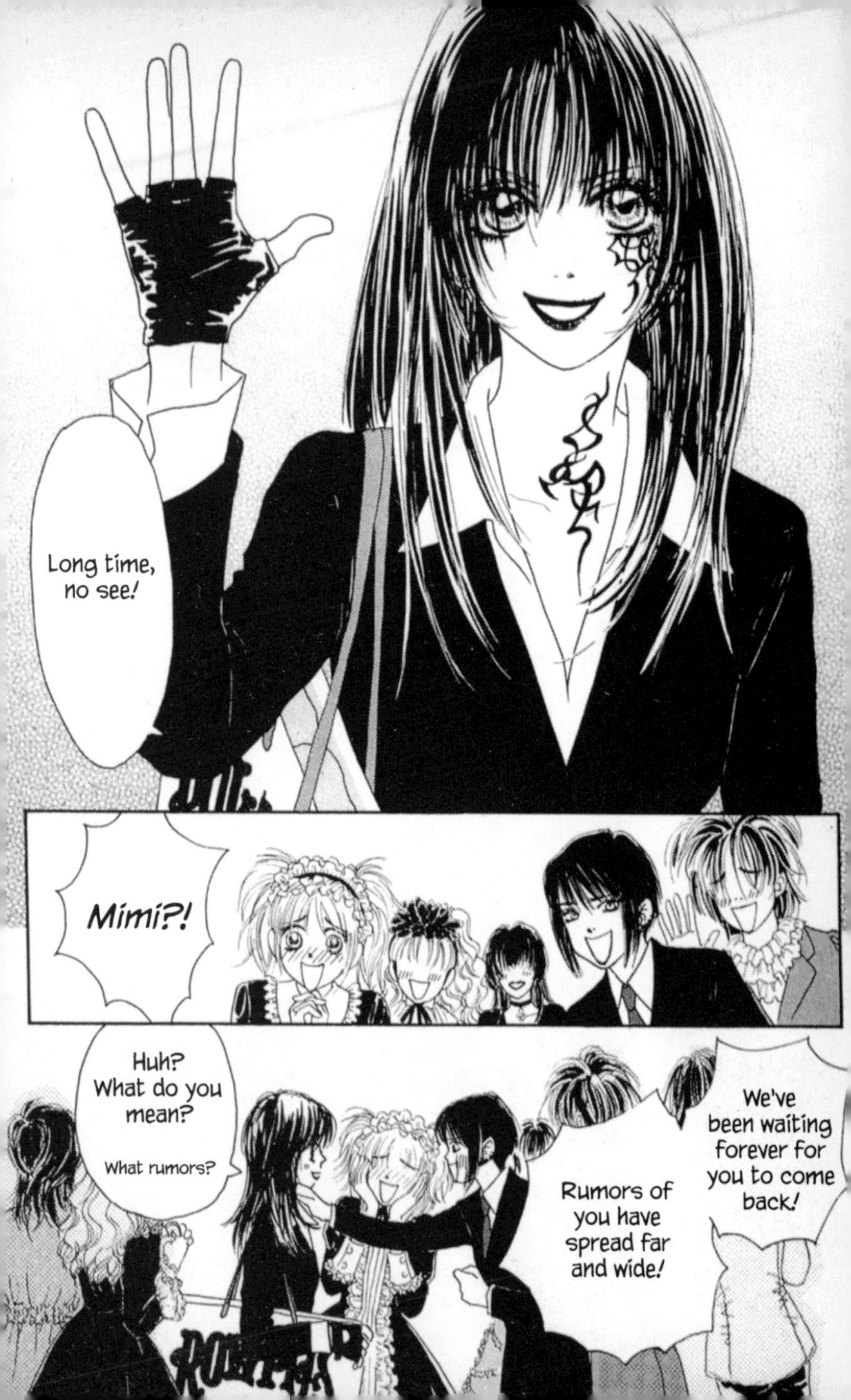
Long time, no see!
Mimi?!
We've been waiting forever for you to come back!
Rumors of you have spread far and wide!
Huh? What do you mean?
What rumors?

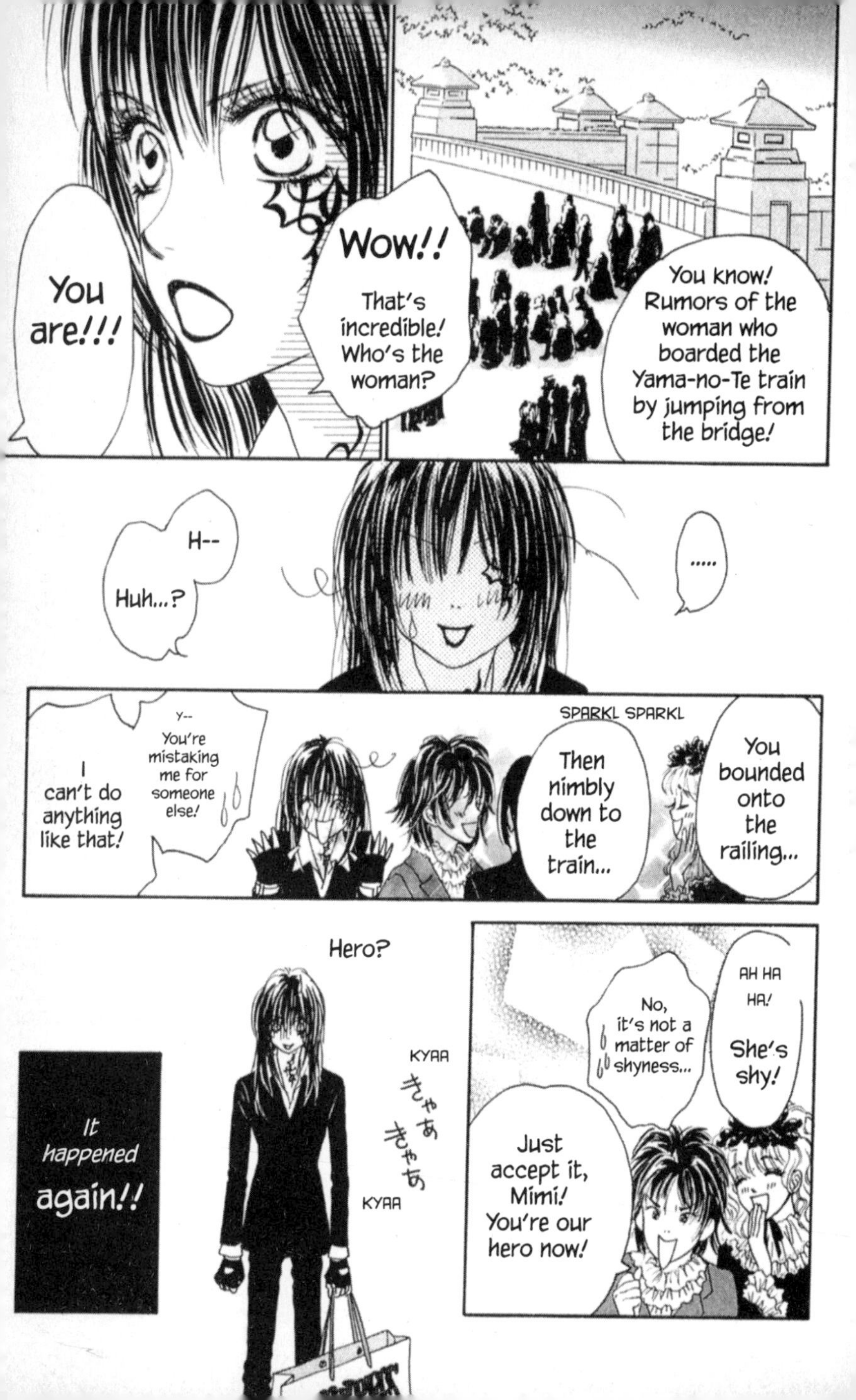

You know! Rumors of the woman who boarded the Yama-no-Te train by jumping from the bridge!
Wow!!
That's incredible! Who's the woman?
You are!!!
.....
H--
Huh...?
You bounded onto the railing...
Then nimbly down to the train...
SPARKL SPARKL
Y--
You're mistaking me for someone else!
I can't do anything like that!
AH HA HA!
She's shy!
No, it's not a matter of shyness...
Just accept it, Mimi! You're our hero now!
Hero?
KYAA
きゃあ きゃあ
KYAA
It happened again!!

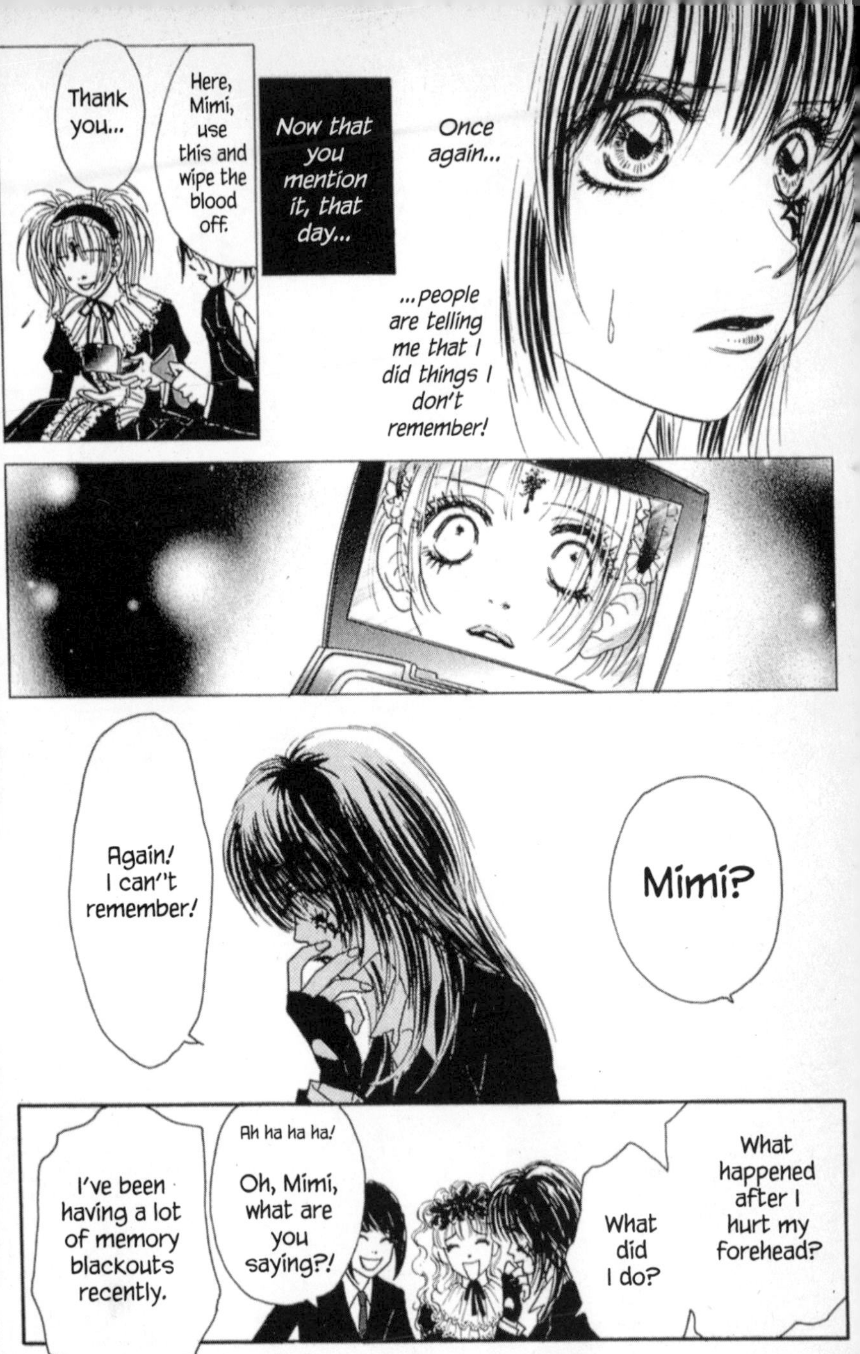
Once again...
...people are telling me that I did things I don't remember!
Now that you mention it, that day...
Here, Mimi, use this and wipe the blood off.
Thank you...
Mimi?
Again! I can''t remember!
What happened after I hurt my forehead?
What did I do?
Ah ha ha ha!
Oh, Mimi, what are you saying?!
I've been having a lot of memory blackouts recently.

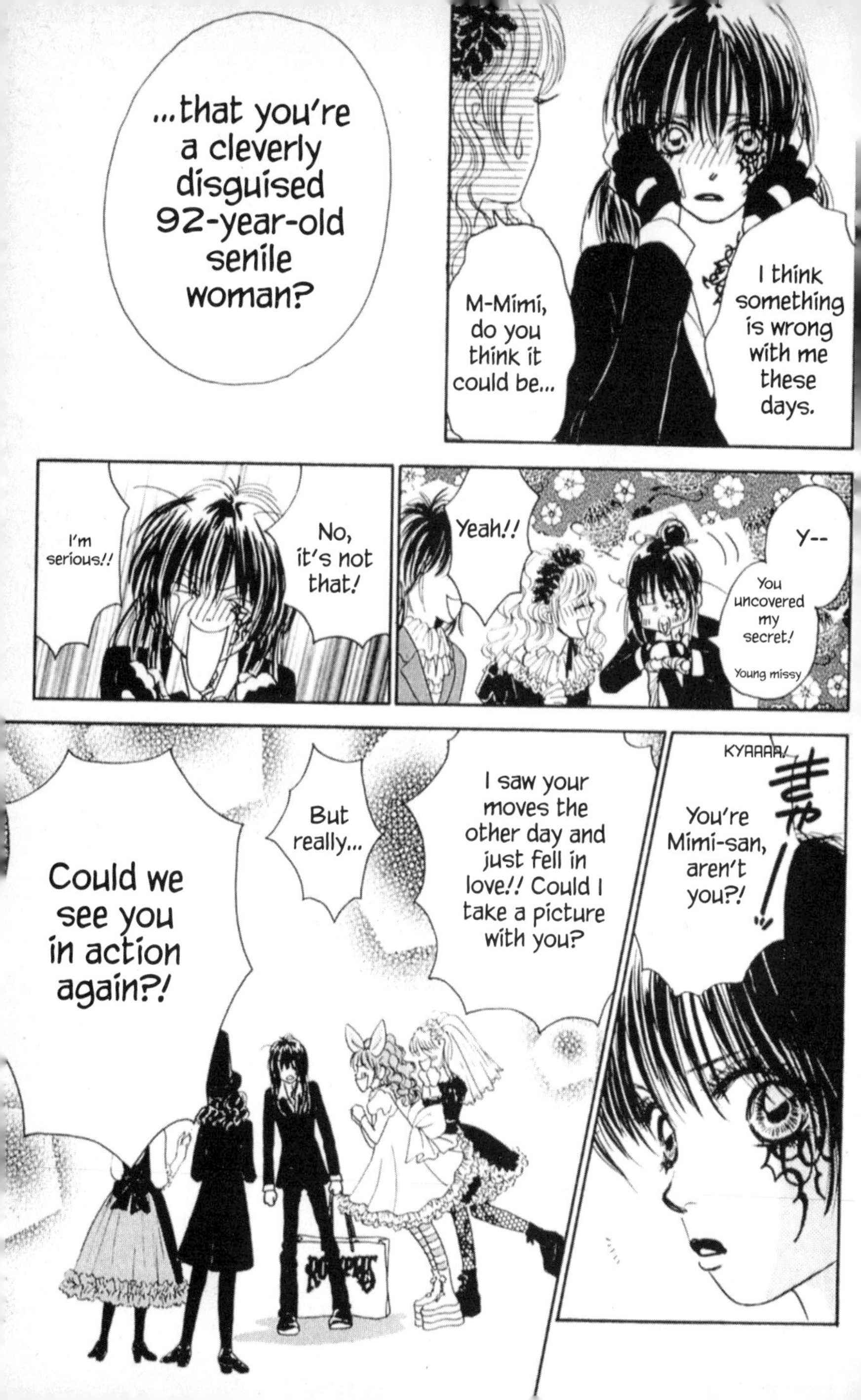

I think something is wrong with me these days.
M-Mimi, do you think it could be...
...that you're a cleverly disguised 92-year-old senile woman?
Y--
You uncovered my secret!
Young missy
Yeah!!
No, it's not that!
I'm serious!!
KYAAAA!
You're Mimi-san, aren't you?!
I saw your moves the other day and just fell in love!! Could I take a picture with you?
But really...
Could we see you in action again?!

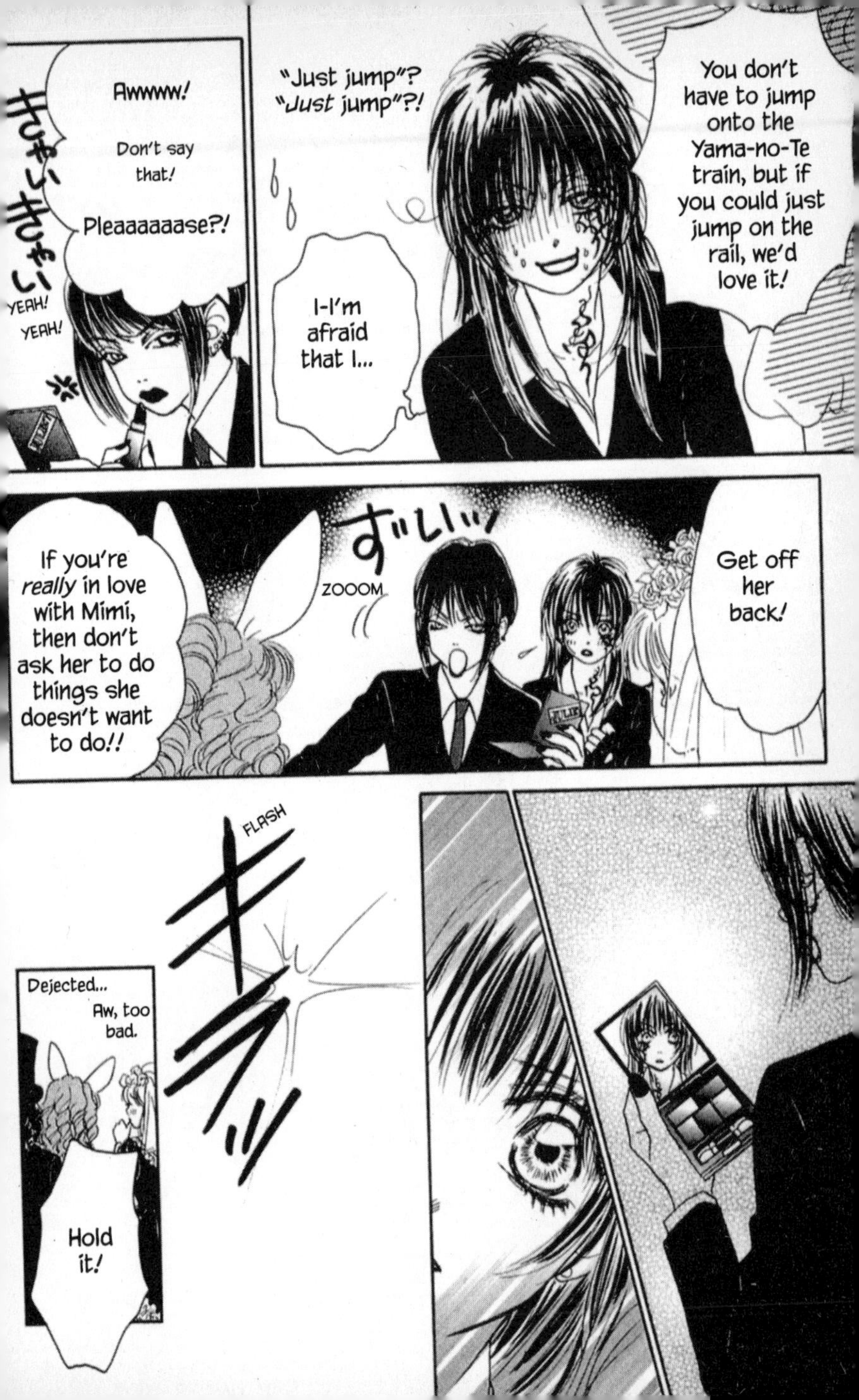

You don't have to jump onto the Yama-no-Te train, but if you could just jump on the rail, we'd love it!
"Just jump"? "*Just* jump"?!
I-I'm afraid that I...
きゃいきゃい
YEAH! YEAH!
Awwww! Don't say that! Pleaaaaaase?!
Get off her back!
ZOOOM
If you're *really* in love with Mimi, then don't ask her to do things she doesn't want to do!!
FLASH
Dejected...
Aw, too bad.
Hold it!

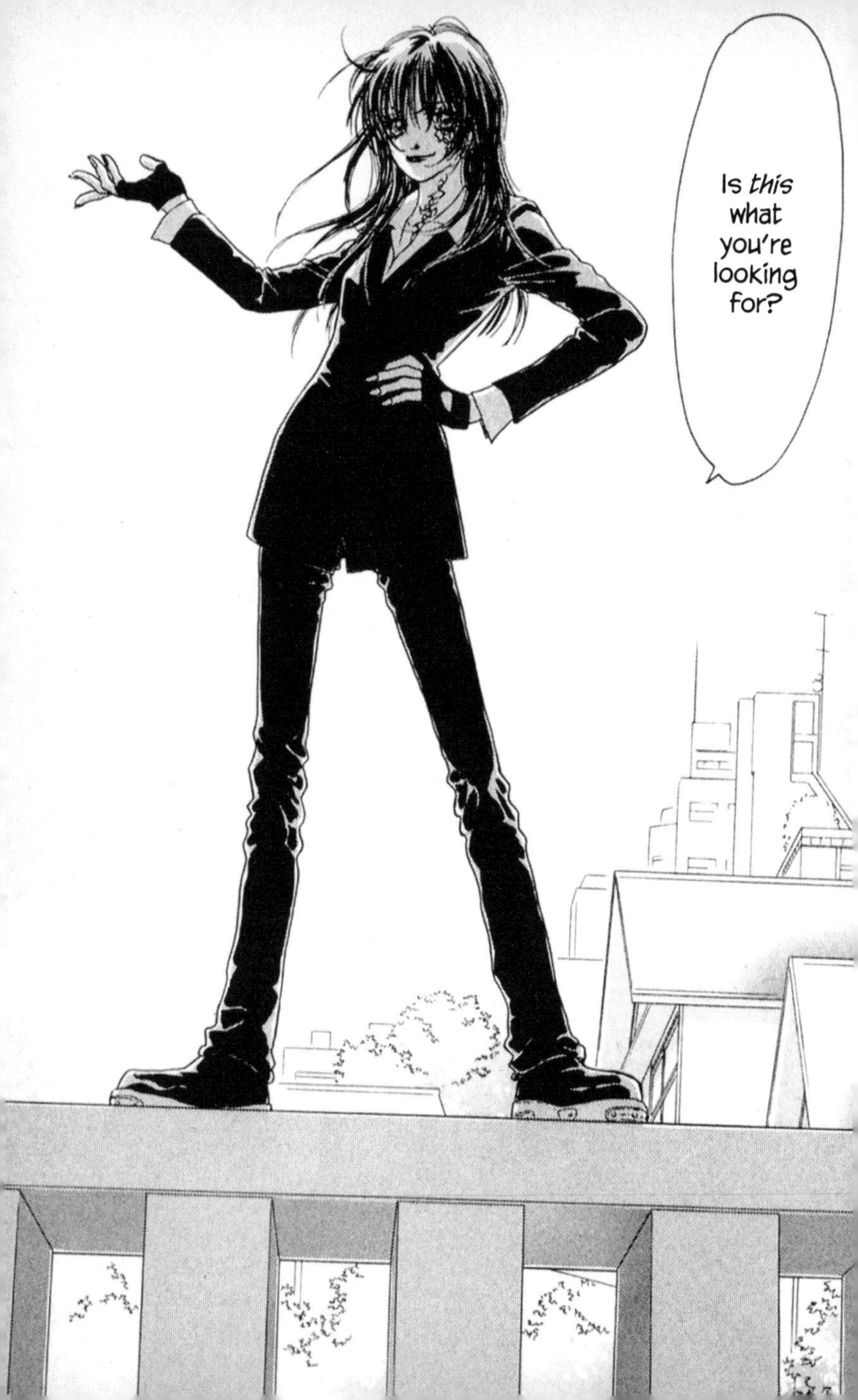
Is *this* what you're looking for?

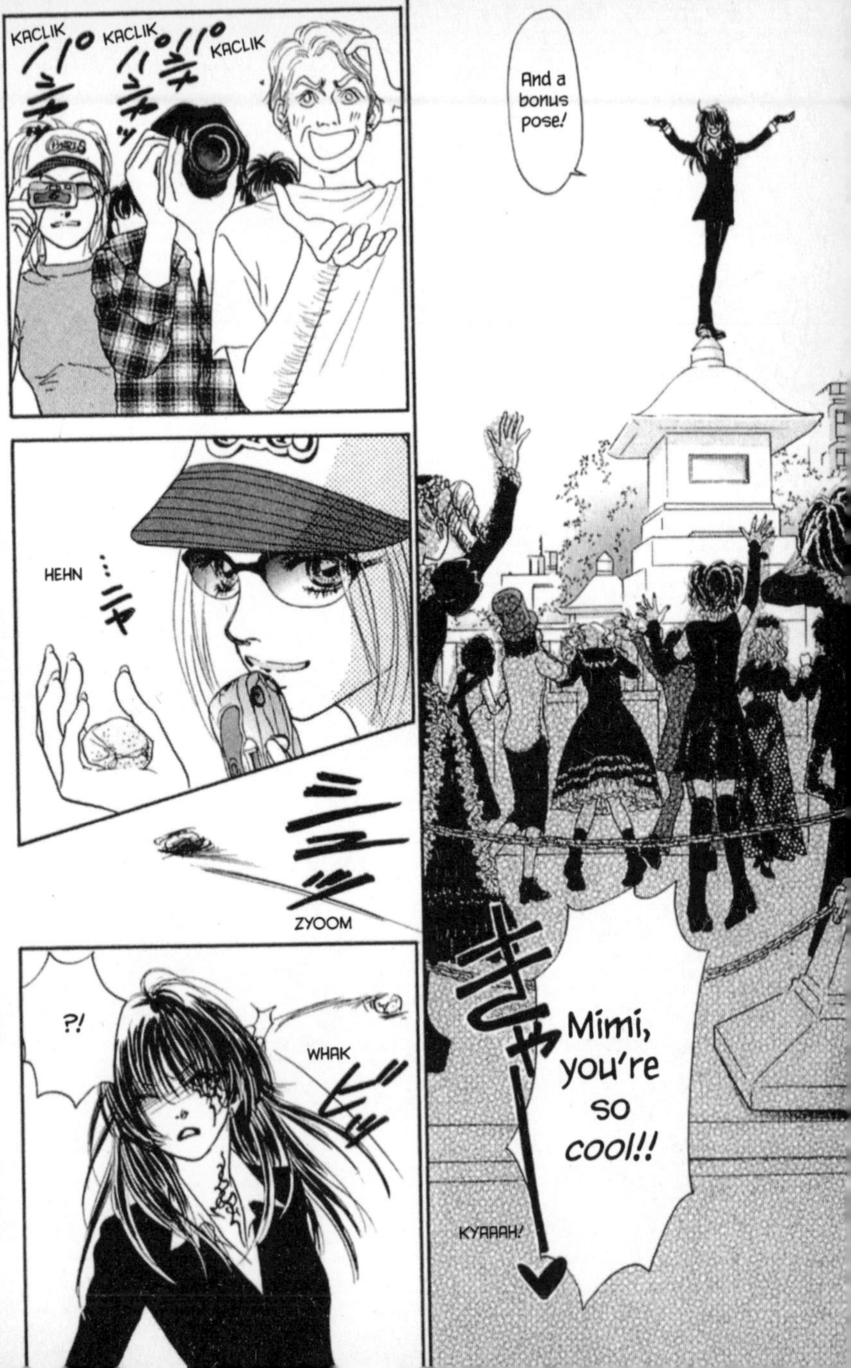

And a bonus pose!
Mimi, you're so cool!!
KYAAAH!
KACLIK
KACLIK
KACLIK
HEHN
ZYOOM
?!
WHAK

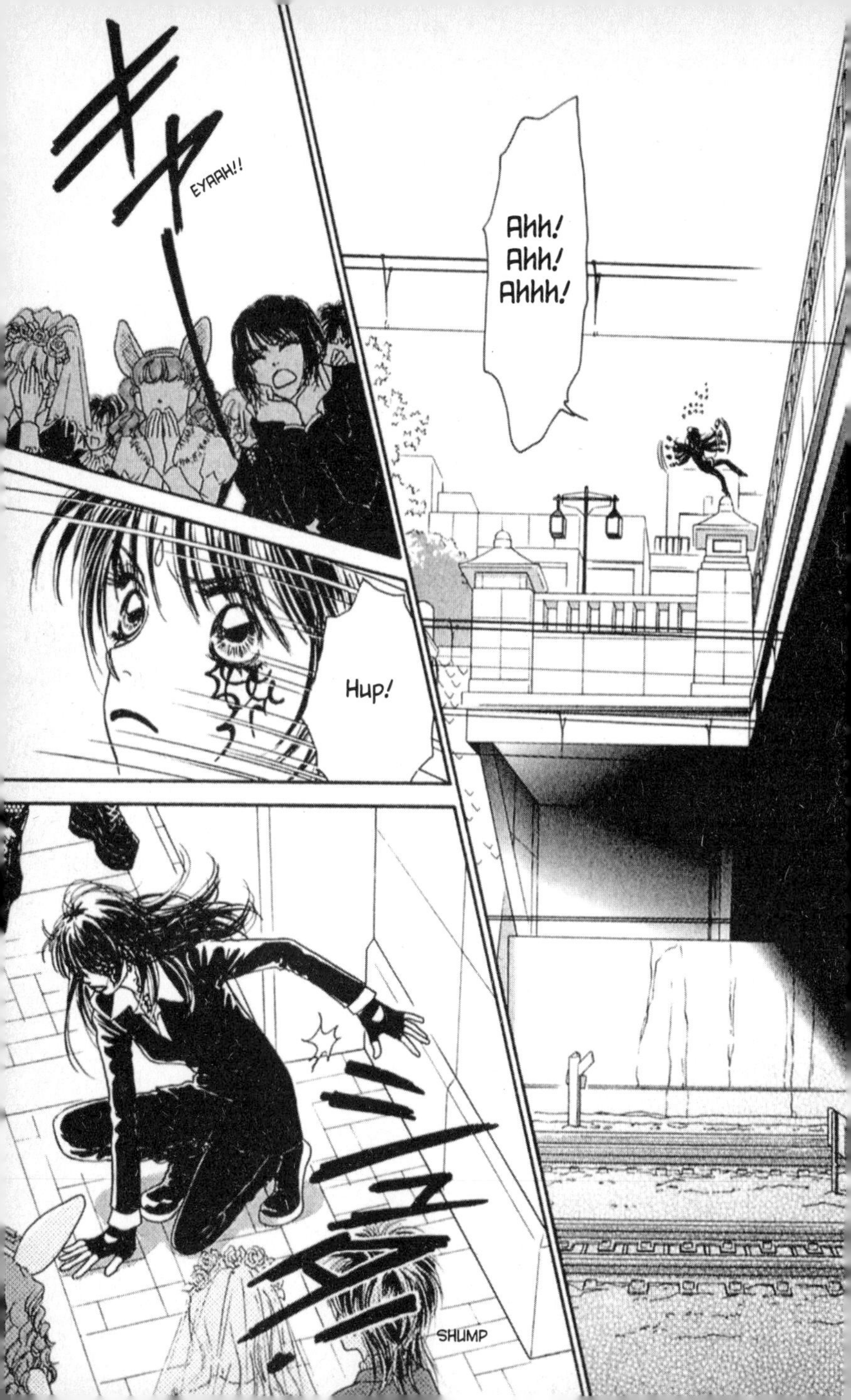
Ahh!
Ahh!
Ahhh!
EYAAH!!
Hup!
SHUMP

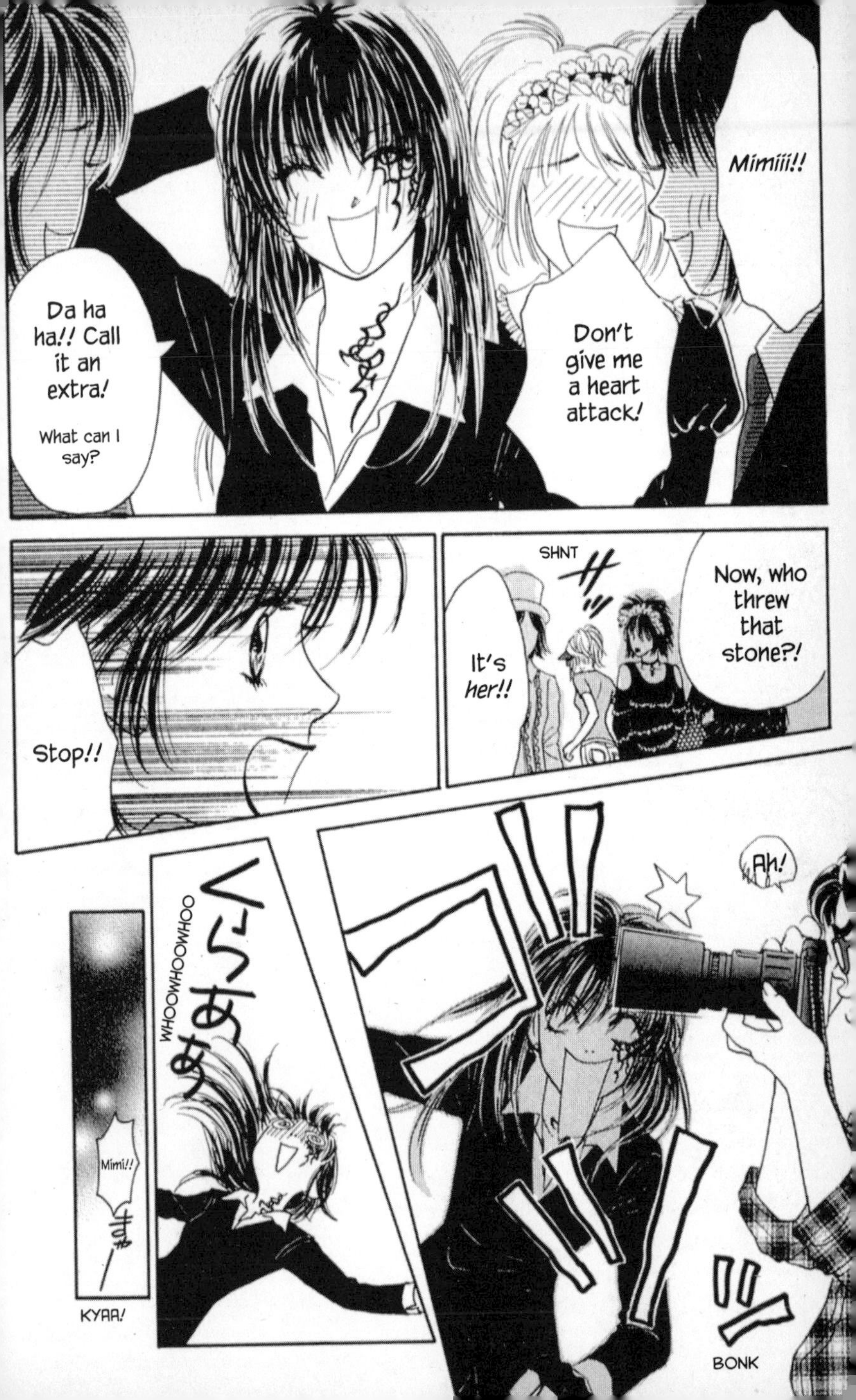
Mimiii!!
Don't give me a heart attack!
Da ha ha!! Call it an extra!
What can I say?
Now, who threw that stone?!
SHNT
It's her!!
Stop!!
Ah!
BONK
WHOOWHOOWHOO
Mimi!!
KYAA!

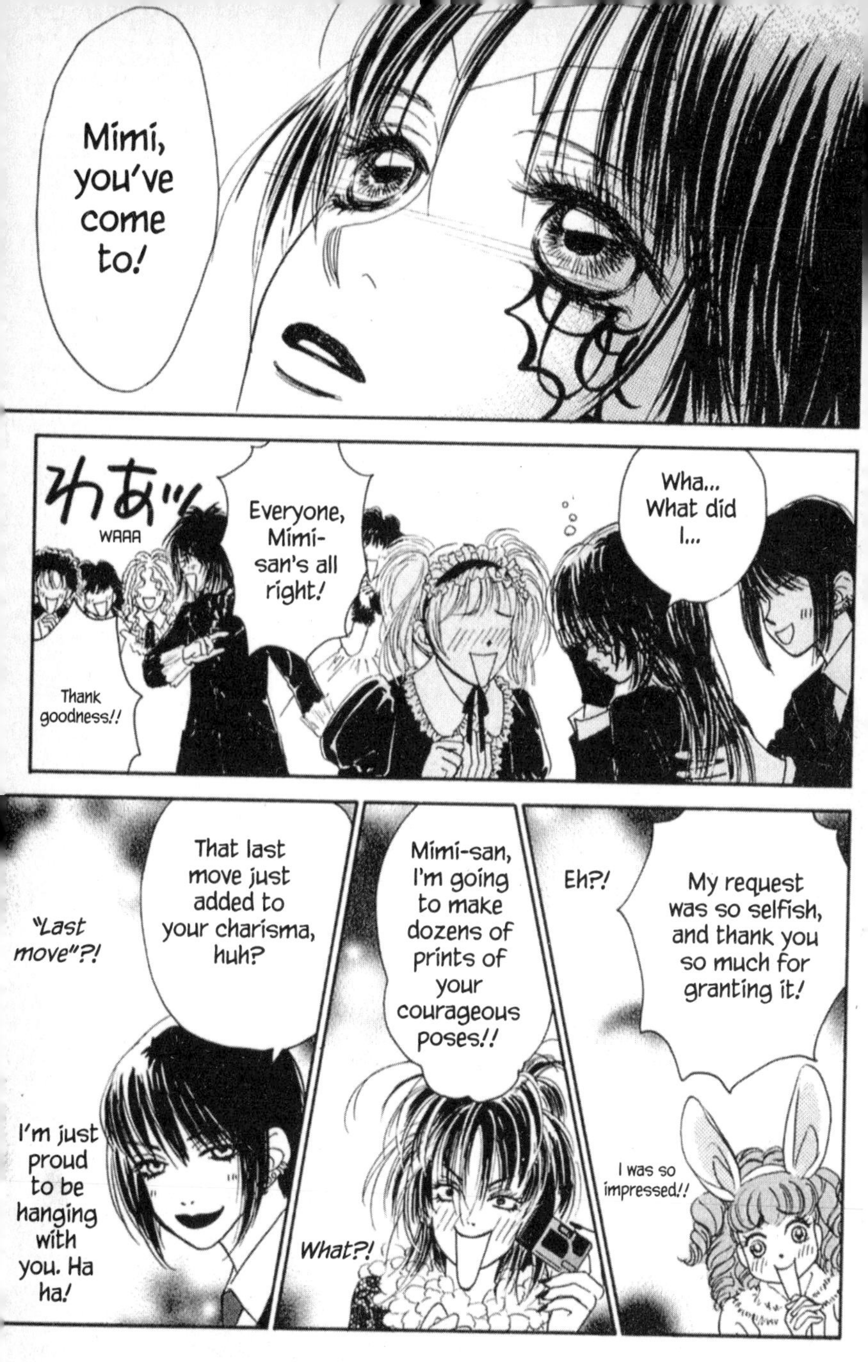
Mimi, you've come to!
Wha... What did I...
Everyone, Mimi-san's all right!
わあッ
WAAA
Thank goodness!!
My request was so selfish, and thank you so much for granting it!
I was so impressed!!
Eh?!
Mimi-san, I'm going to make dozens of prints of your courageous poses!!
What?!
That last move just added to your charisma, huh?
I'm just proud to be hanging with you. Ha ha!
"Last move"?!

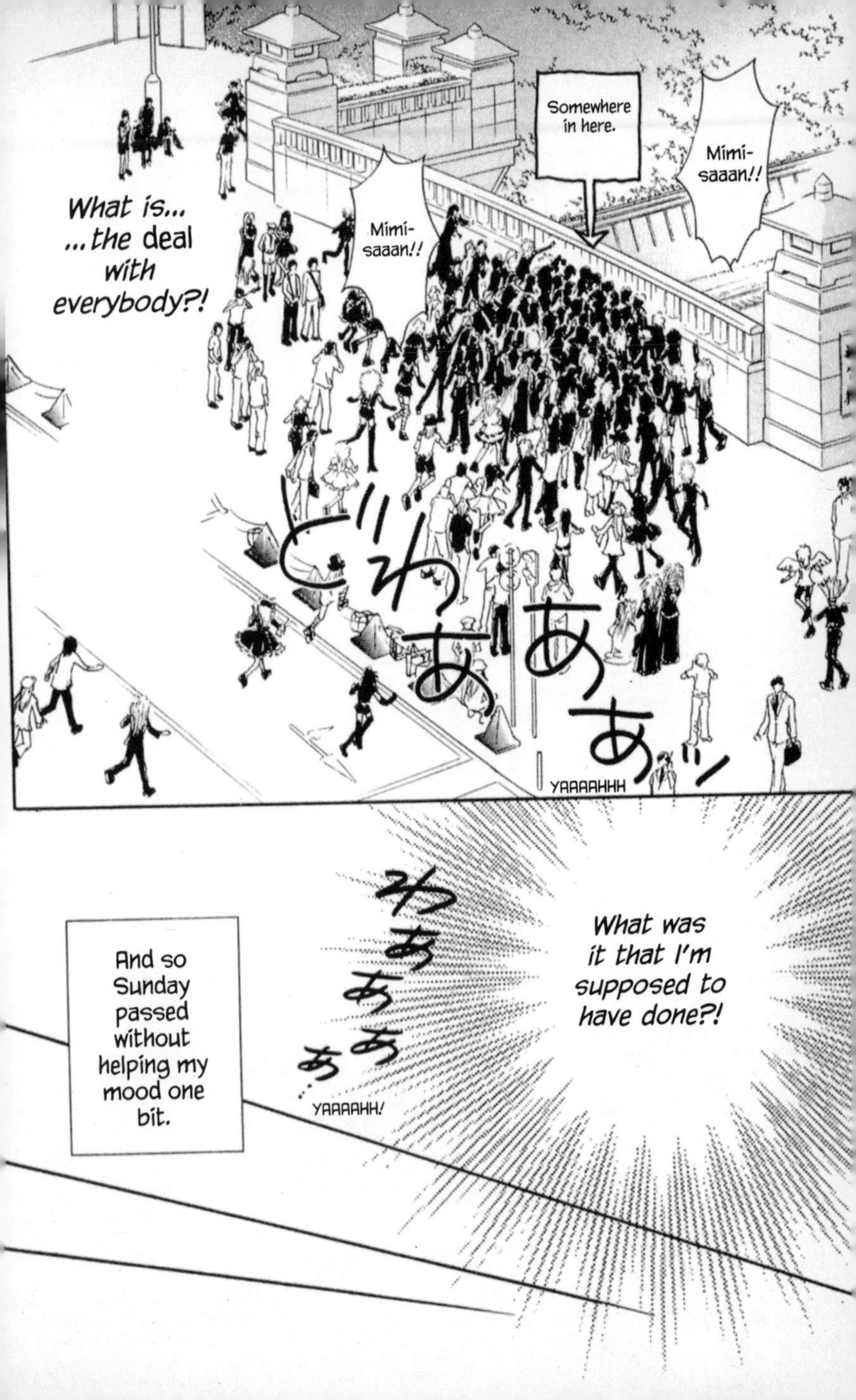
Mimi-saaan!!
Somewhere in here.
Mimi-saaan!!
What is... ...the deal with everybody?!
どわあああッ
YAAAAHHH
What was it that I'm supposed to have done?!
わあああ...
YAAAAHH!
And so Sunday passed without helping my mood one bit.

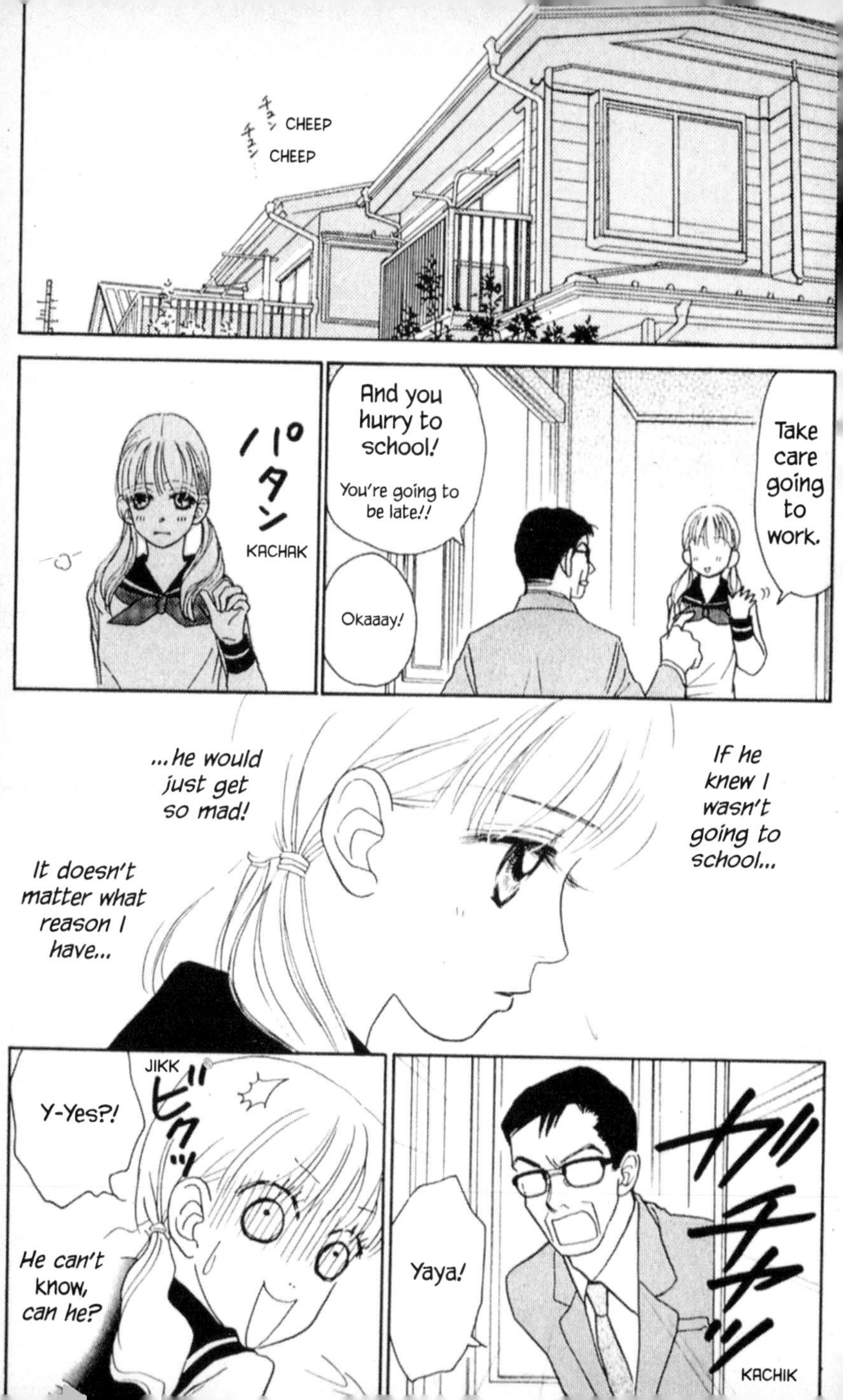
チュン CHEEP
チュン CHEEP
Take care going to work.
And you hurry to school!
You're going to be late!!
Okaaay!
パタン
KACHAK
If he knew I wasn't going to school...
...he would just get so mad!
It doesn't matter what reason I have...
ガチャッ
KACHIK
Yaya!
ビクッ
JIKK
Y-Yes?!
He can't know, can he?

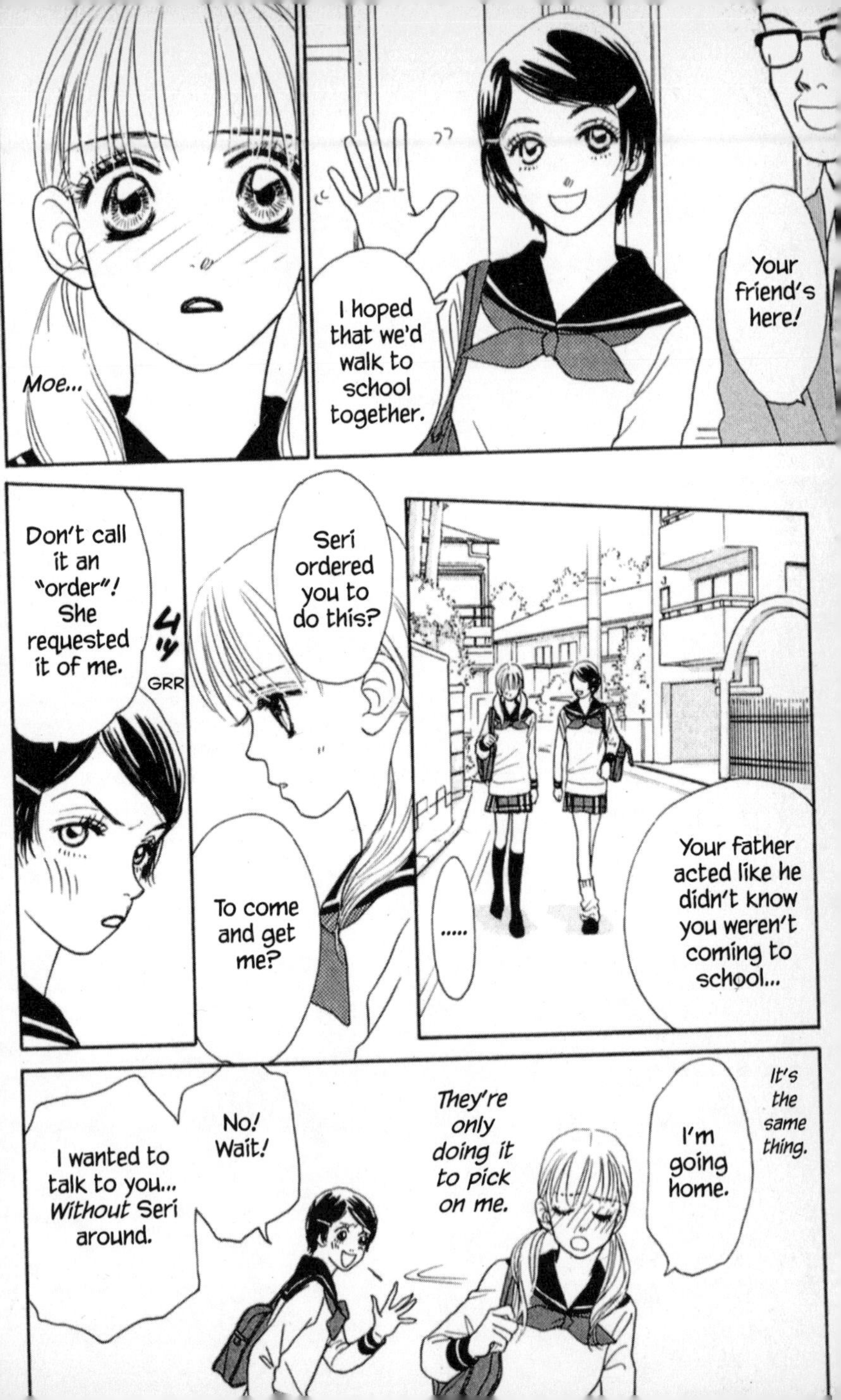
Your friend's here!
I hoped that we'd walk to school together.
Moe...
Your father acted like he didn't know you weren't coming to school...
.....
Seri ordered you to do this?
To come and get me?
Don't call it an "order"! She requested it of me.
GRR
It's the same thing.
I'm going home.
They're only doing it to pick on me.
No! Wait!
I wanted to talk to you... Without Seri around.

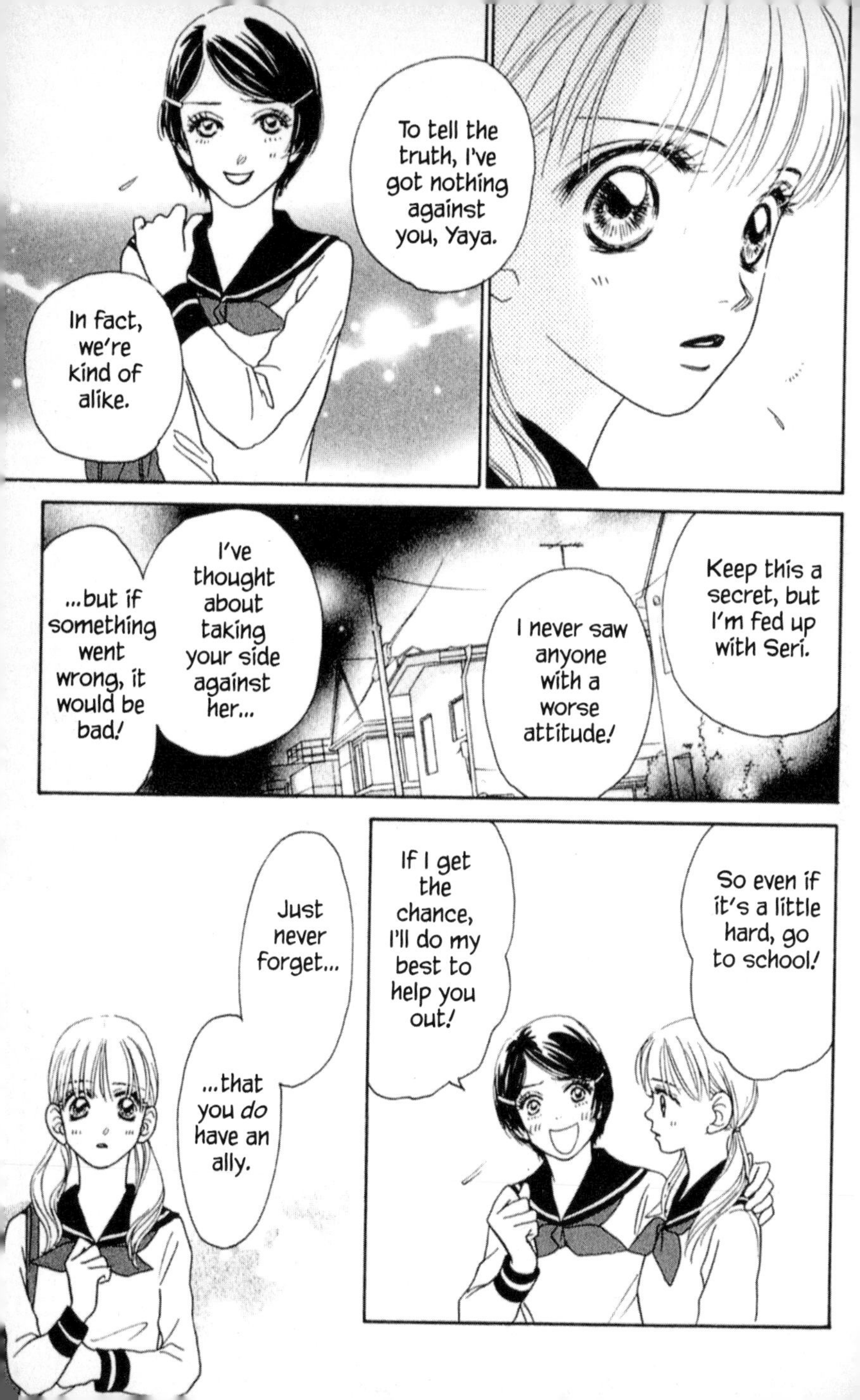
To tell the truth, I've got nothing against you, Yaya.
In fact, we're kind of alike.
Keep this a secret, but I'm fed up with Seri.
I never saw anyone with a worse attitude!
I've thought about taking your side against her...
...but if something went wrong, it would be bad!
So even if it's a little hard, go to school!
If I get the chance, I'll do my best to help you out!
Just never forget...
...that you *do* have an ally.

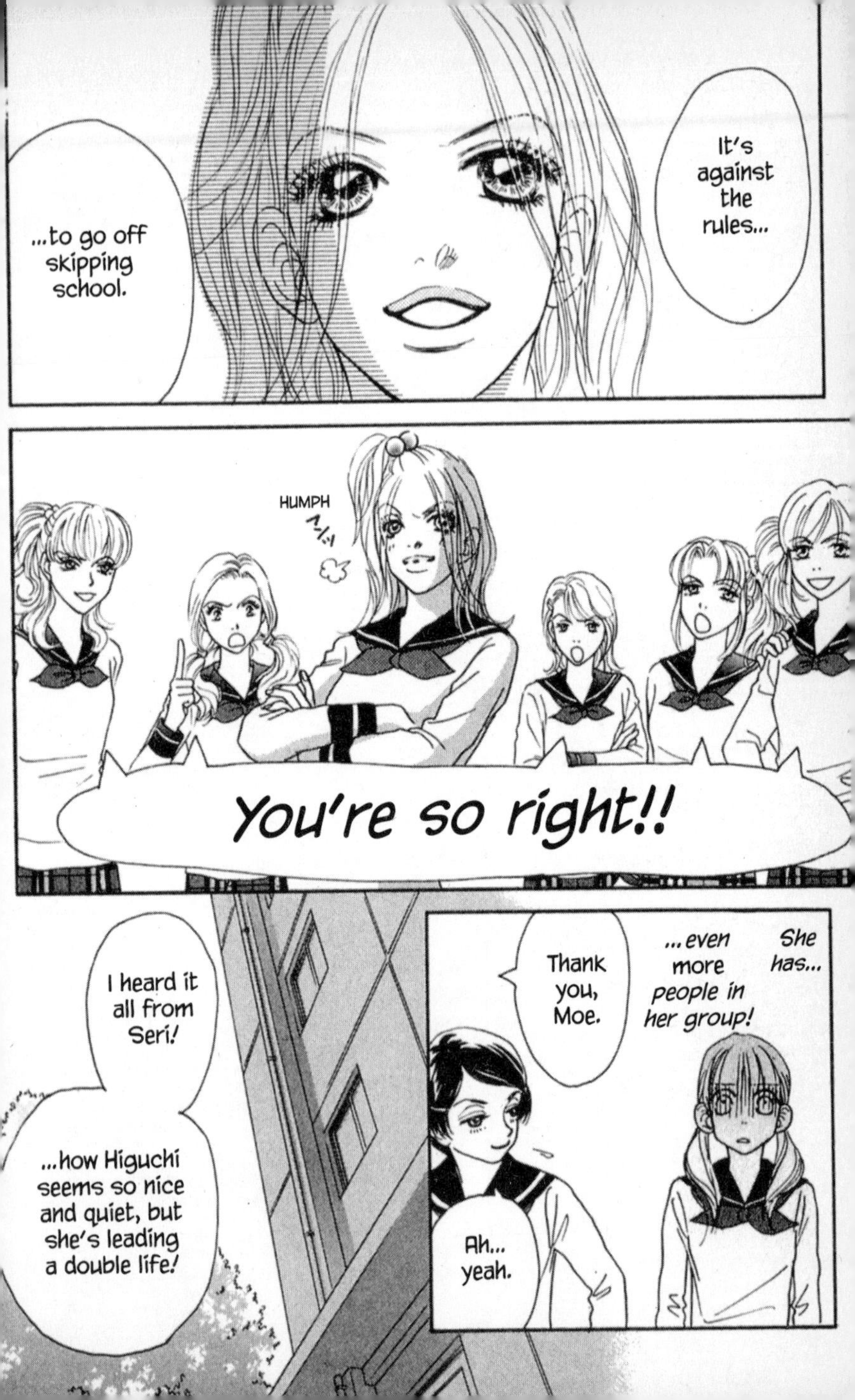
It's against the rules...
...to go off skipping school.
HUMPH
You're so right!!
She has...
...even more people in her group!
Thank you, Moe.
Ah... yeah.
I heard it all from Seri!
...how Higuchi seems so nice and quiet, but she's leading a double life!

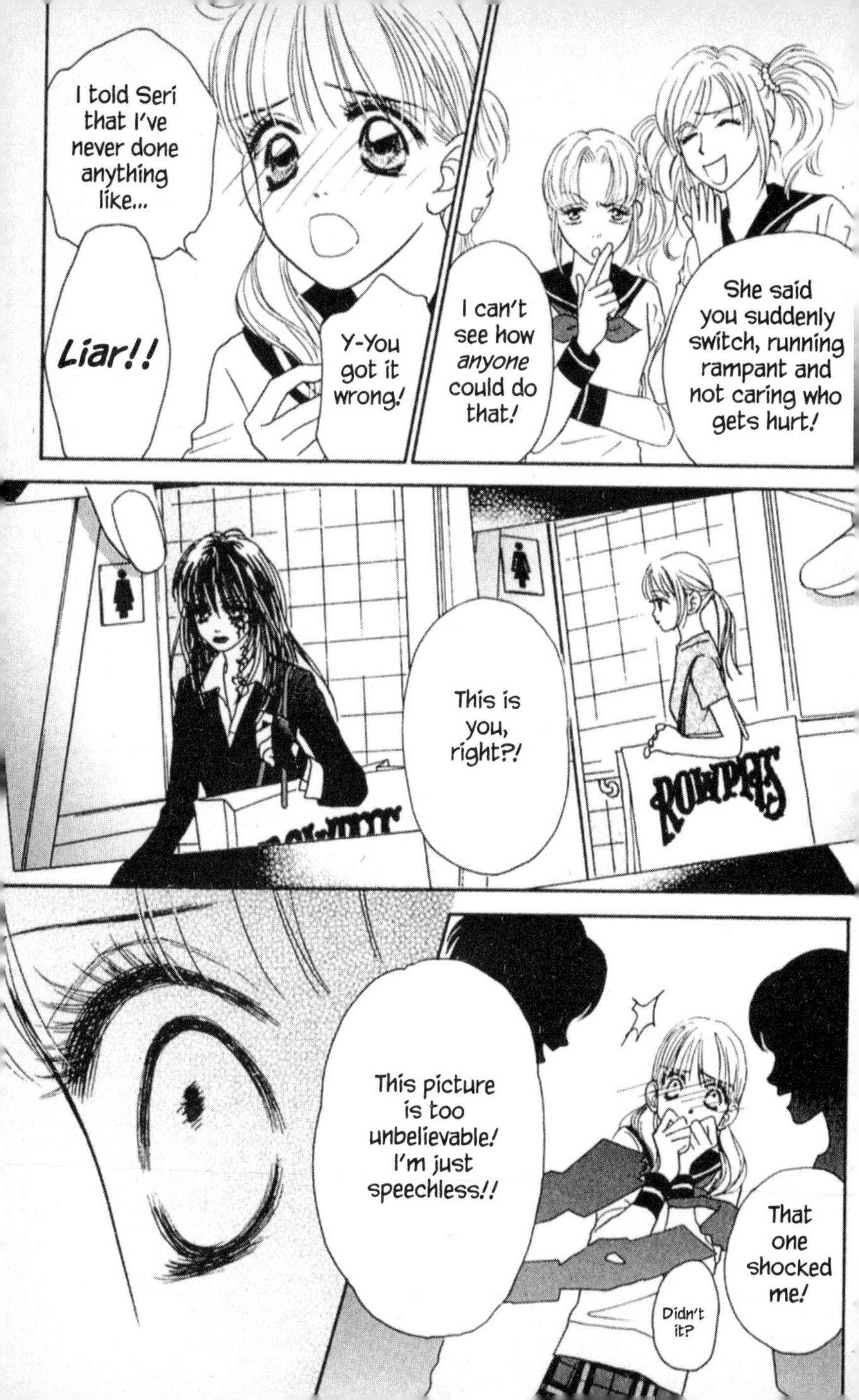
She said you suddenly switch, running rampant and not caring who gets hurt!
I can't see how *anyone* could do that!
Y-You got it wrong!
I told Seri that I've never done anything like...
Liar!!
This is you, right?!
ROWPAS
That one shocked me!
Didn't it?
This picture is too unbelievable! I'm just speechless!!

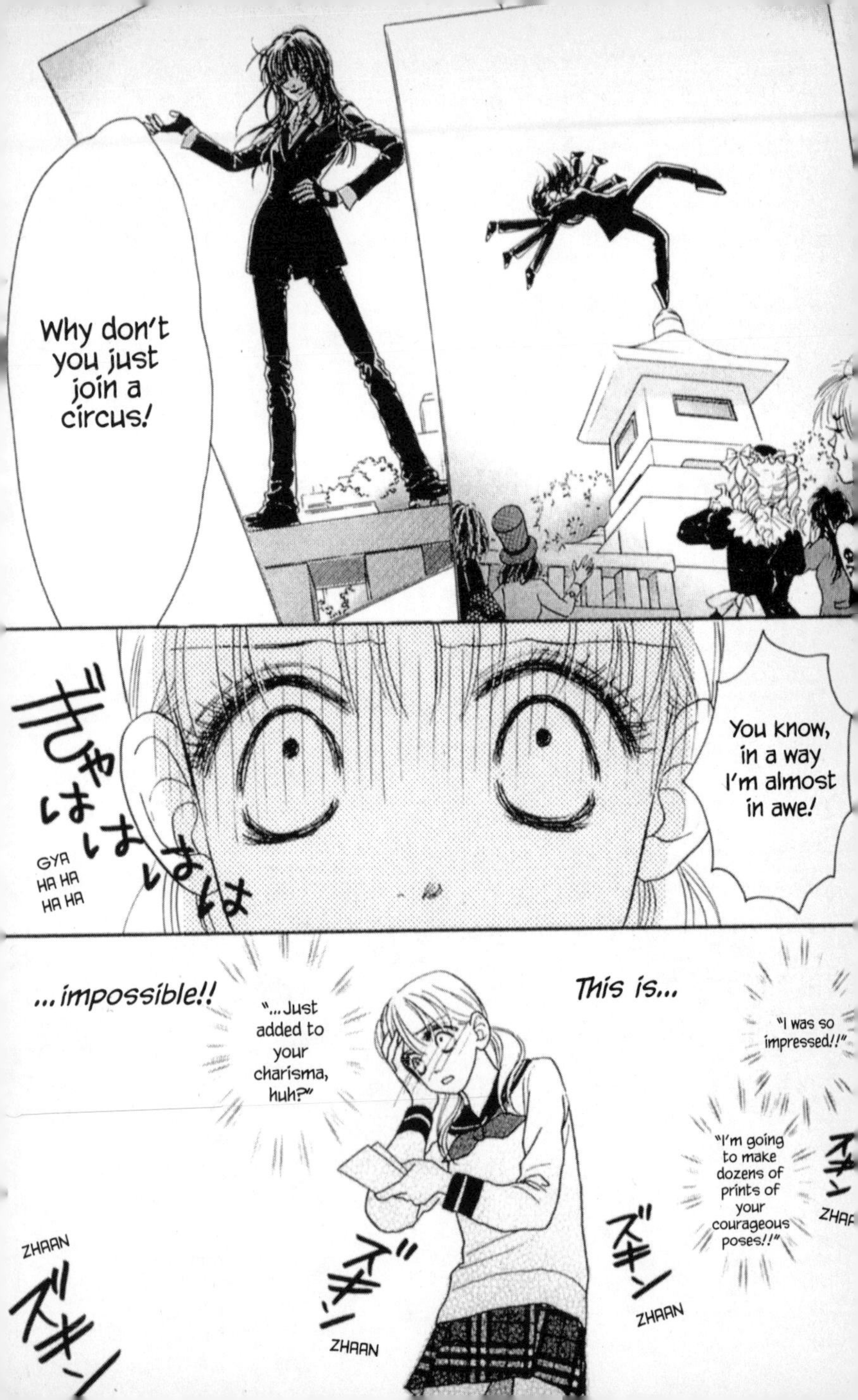
Why don't you just join a circus!
You know, in a way I'm almost in awe!
GYA HA HA HA HA
"I was so impressed!!"
"I'm going to make dozens of prints of your courageous poses!!"
ZHAAN
This is...
"...Just added to your charisma, huh?"
...impossible!!
ZHAAN
ZHAAN
ZHAAN

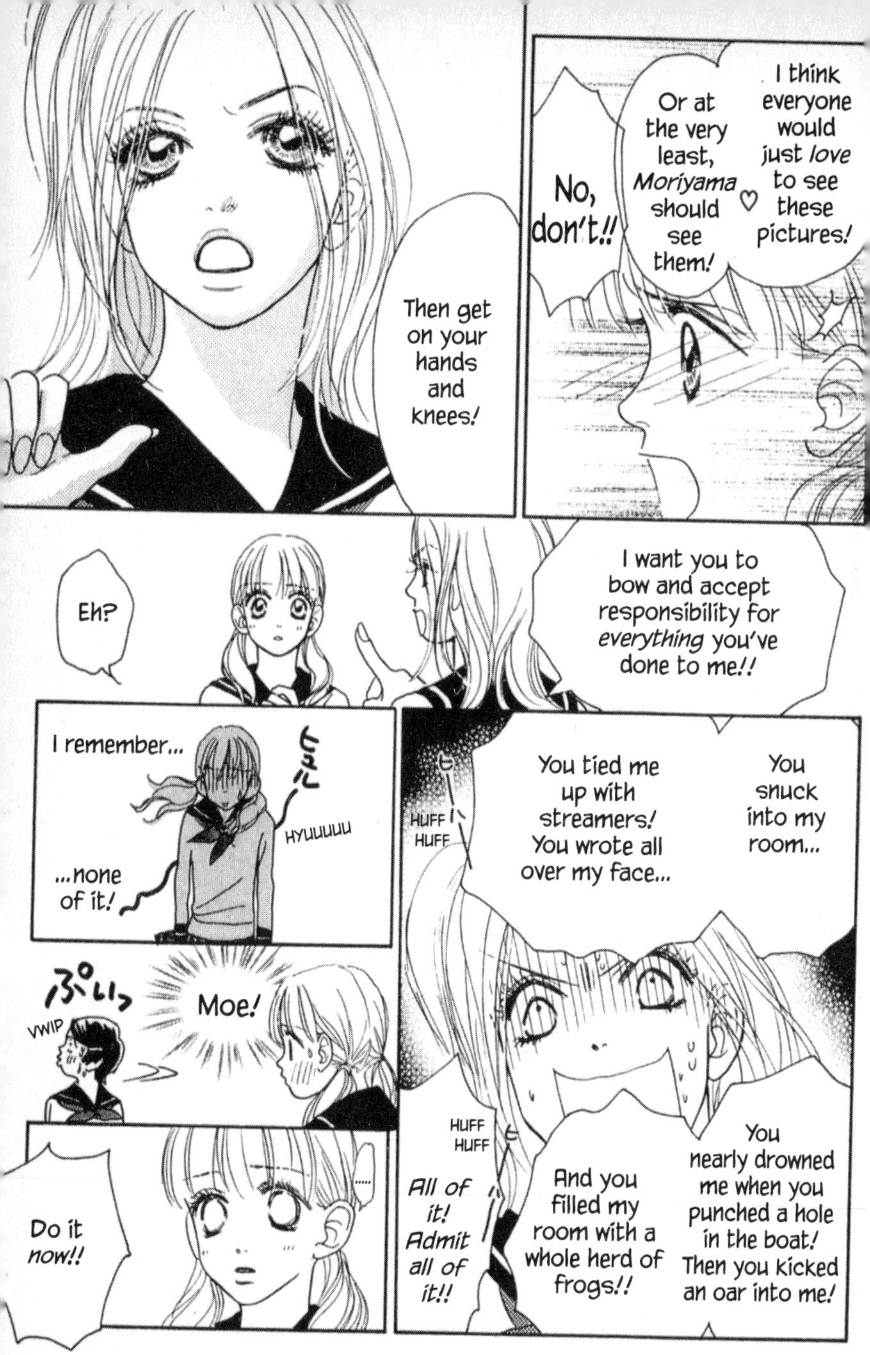

I think everyone would just *love* to see these pictures!
Or at the very least, *Moriyama* should see them! ♡
No, don't!!
Then get on your hands and knees!
I want you to bow and accept responsibility for *everything* you've done to me!!
Eh?
You snuck into my room...
You tied me up with streamers! You wrote all over my face...
HUFF HUFF
I remember...
HYUUUUU
...none of it!
Moe!
ぷいっ
VWIP
You nearly drowned me when you punched a hole in the boat! Then you kicked an oar into me!
And you filled my room with a whole herd of frogs!!
HUFF HUFF
All of it! Admit all of it!!
Do it *now!!*

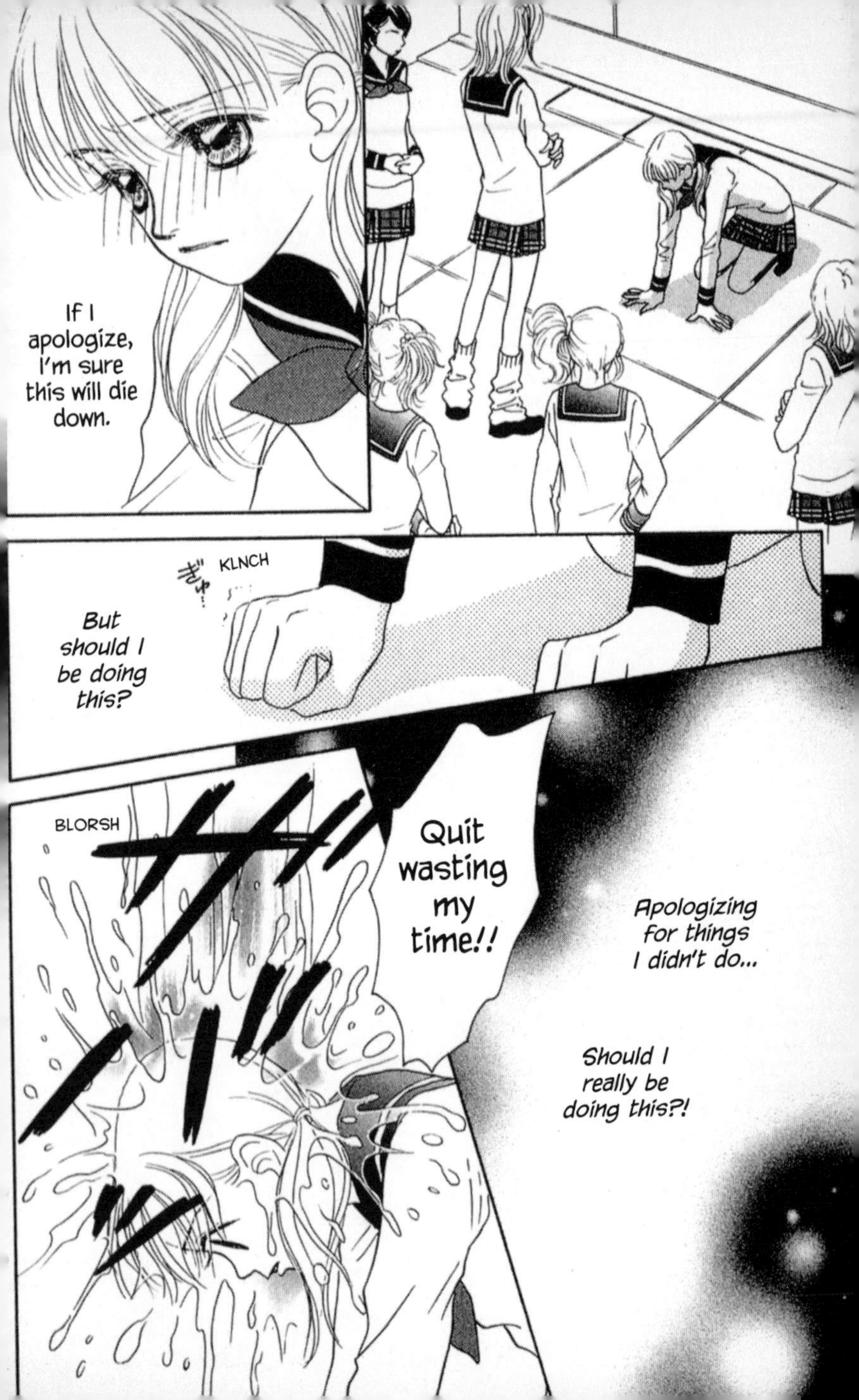
If I apologize, I'm sure this will die down.
ぎゅ…
KLNCH
But should I be doing this?
BLORSH
Quit wasting my time!!
Apologizing for things I didn't do...
Should I really be doing this?!

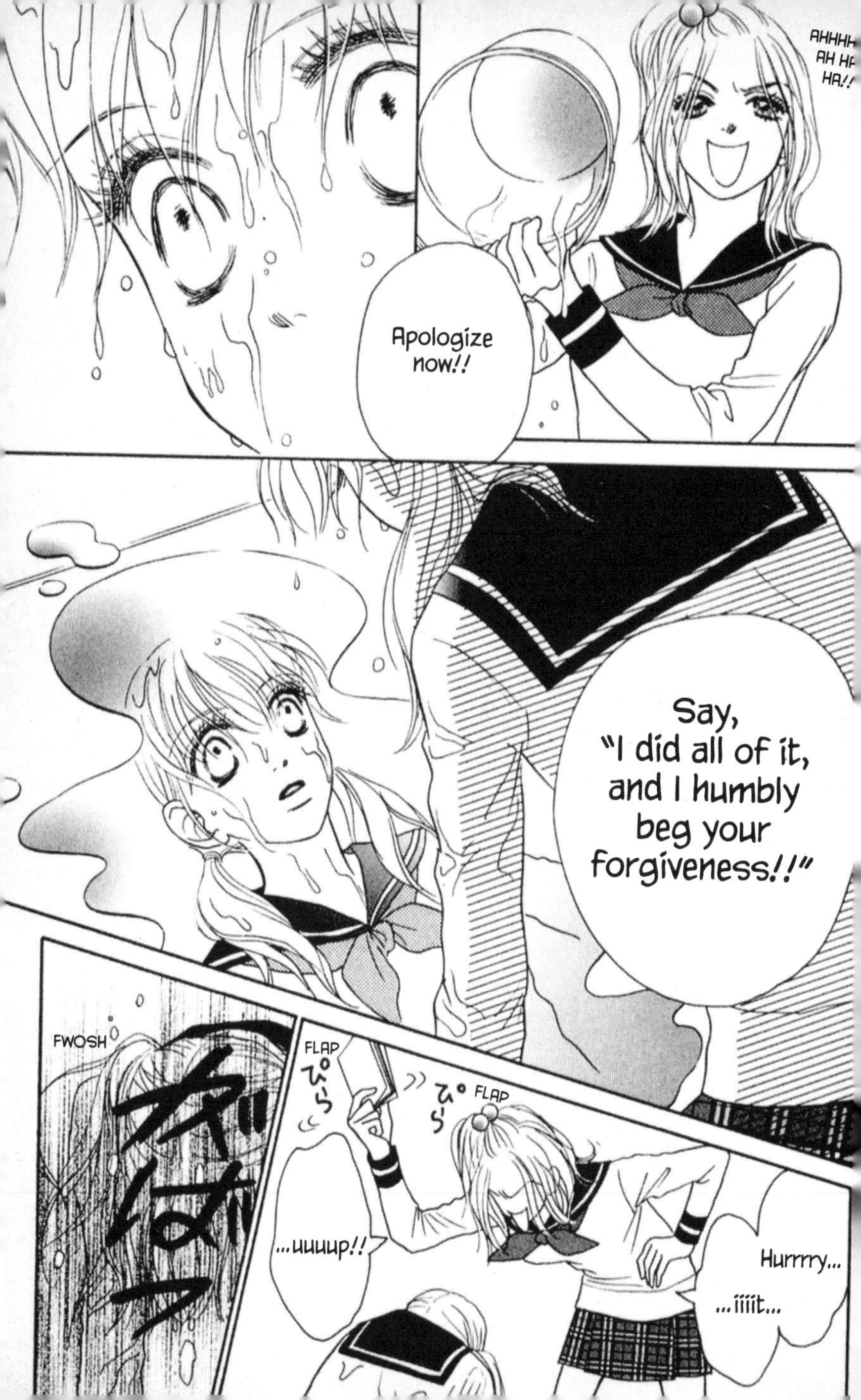
AHHHH AH HA HA!!
Apologize now!!
Say, "I did all of it, and I humbly beg your forgiveness!!"
Hurrrry...
...iiiit...
FLAP
FLAP
...uuuup!!
FWOSH

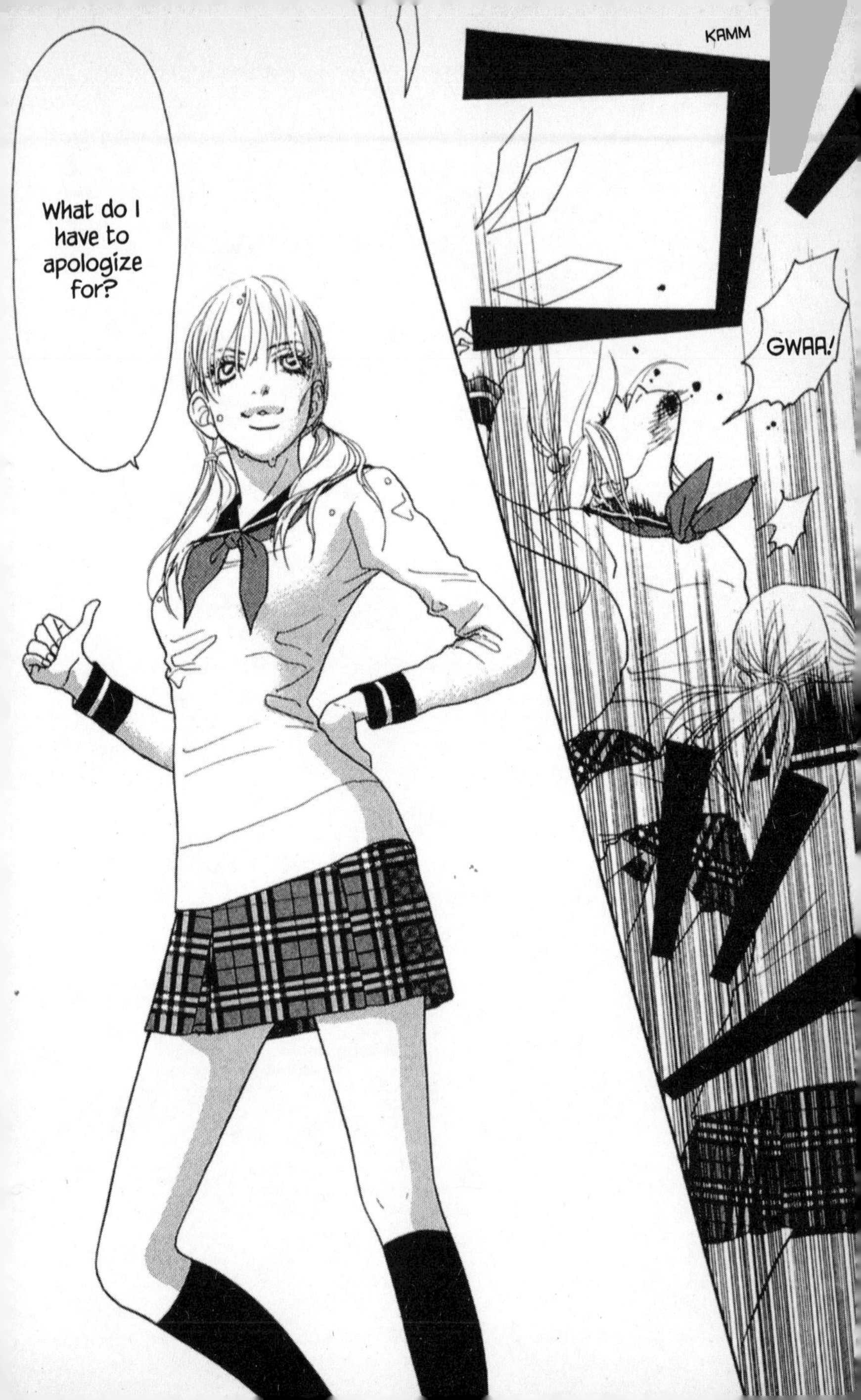
KAMM
GWAA!
What do I have to apologize for?

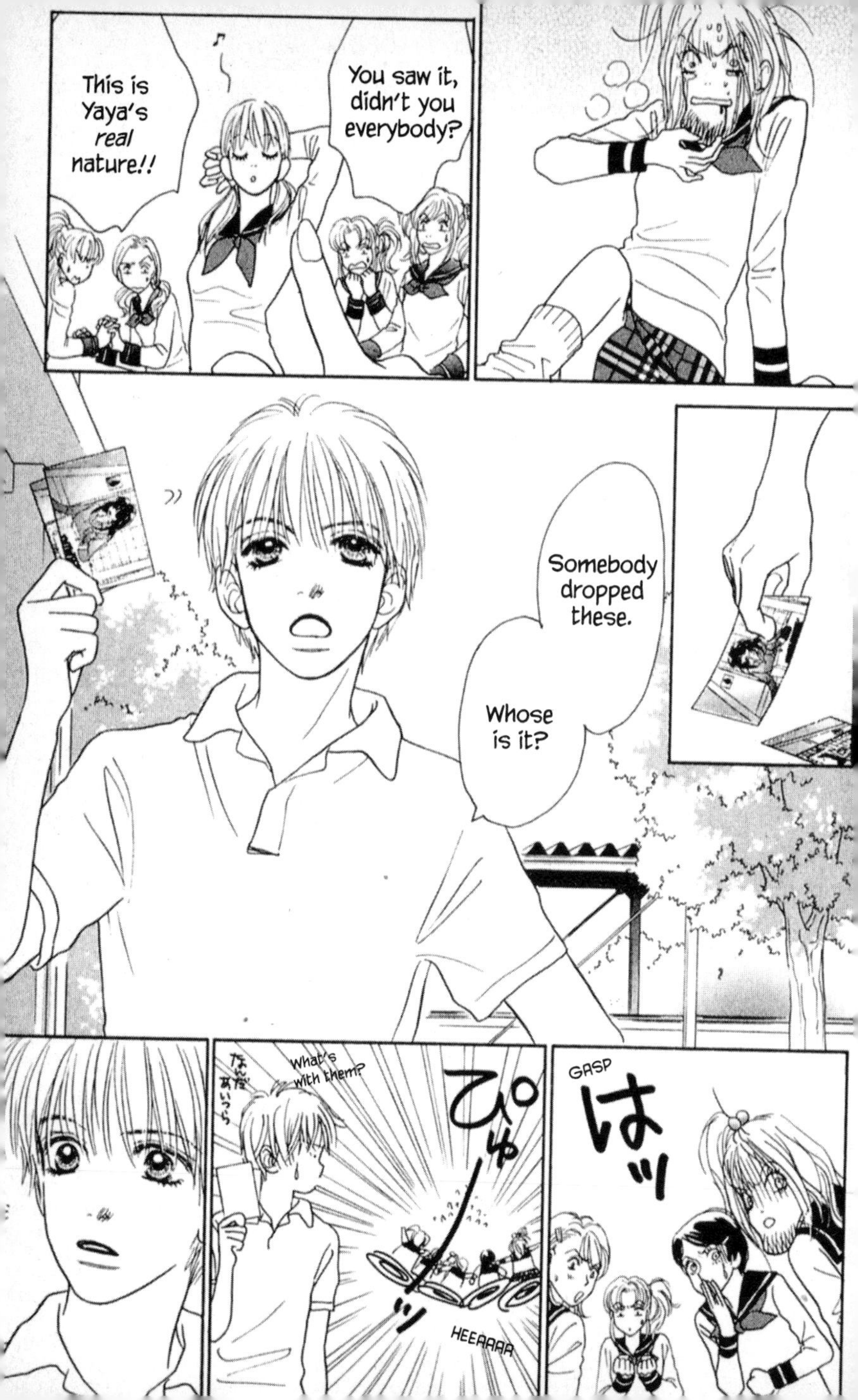
You saw it, didn't you everybody?
This is Yaya's *real* nature!!
Somebody dropped these.
Whose is it?
GASP
はッ
ぴゅ
ッ
HEEAAAA
What's with them?
なんだ あいつら

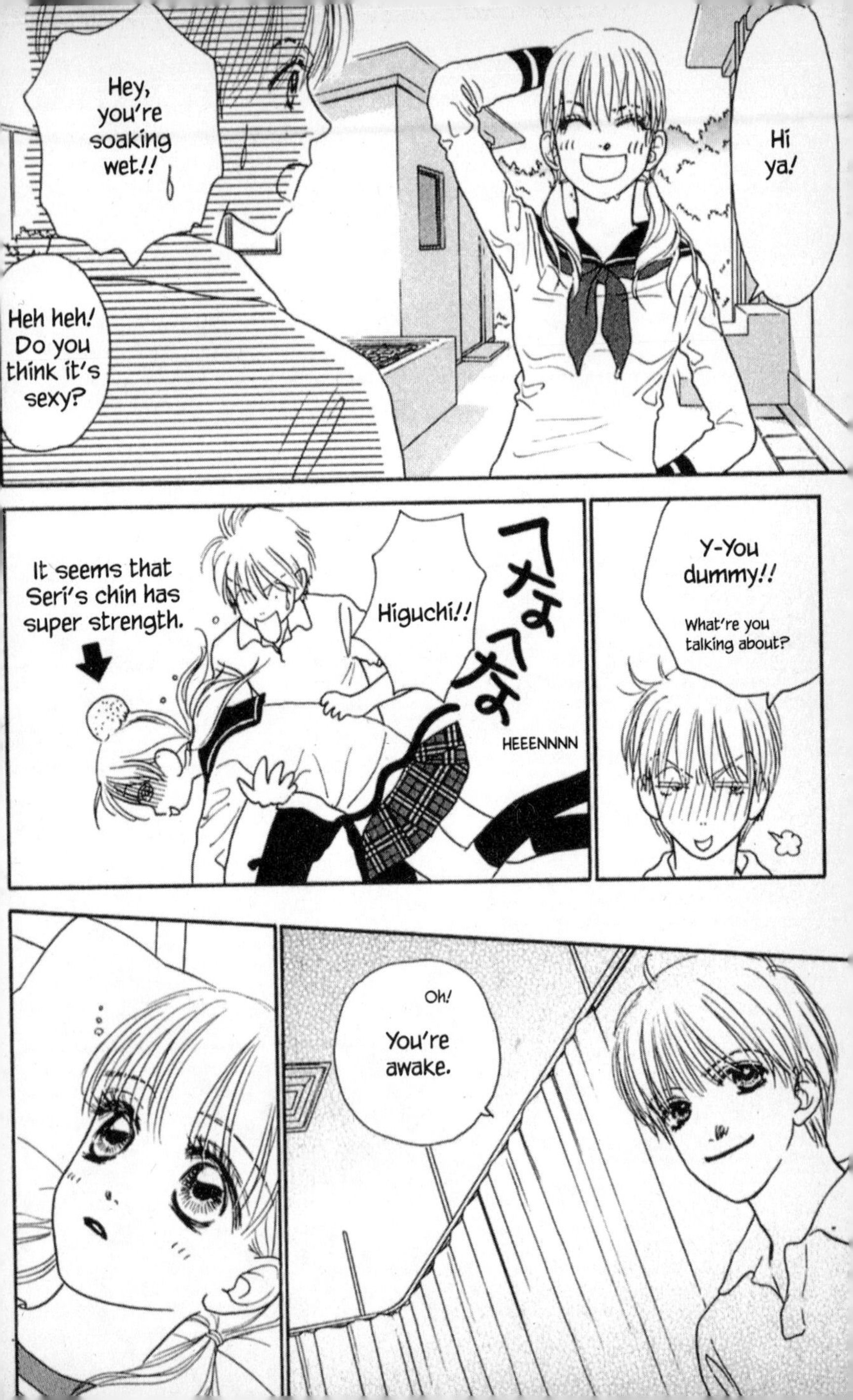
Hi ya!
Hey, you're soaking wet!!
Heh heh! Do you think it's sexy?
Y-You dummy!!
What're you talking about?
Higuchi!!
へなへな
HEEENNNN
It seems that Seri's chin has super strength.
Oh!
You're awake.

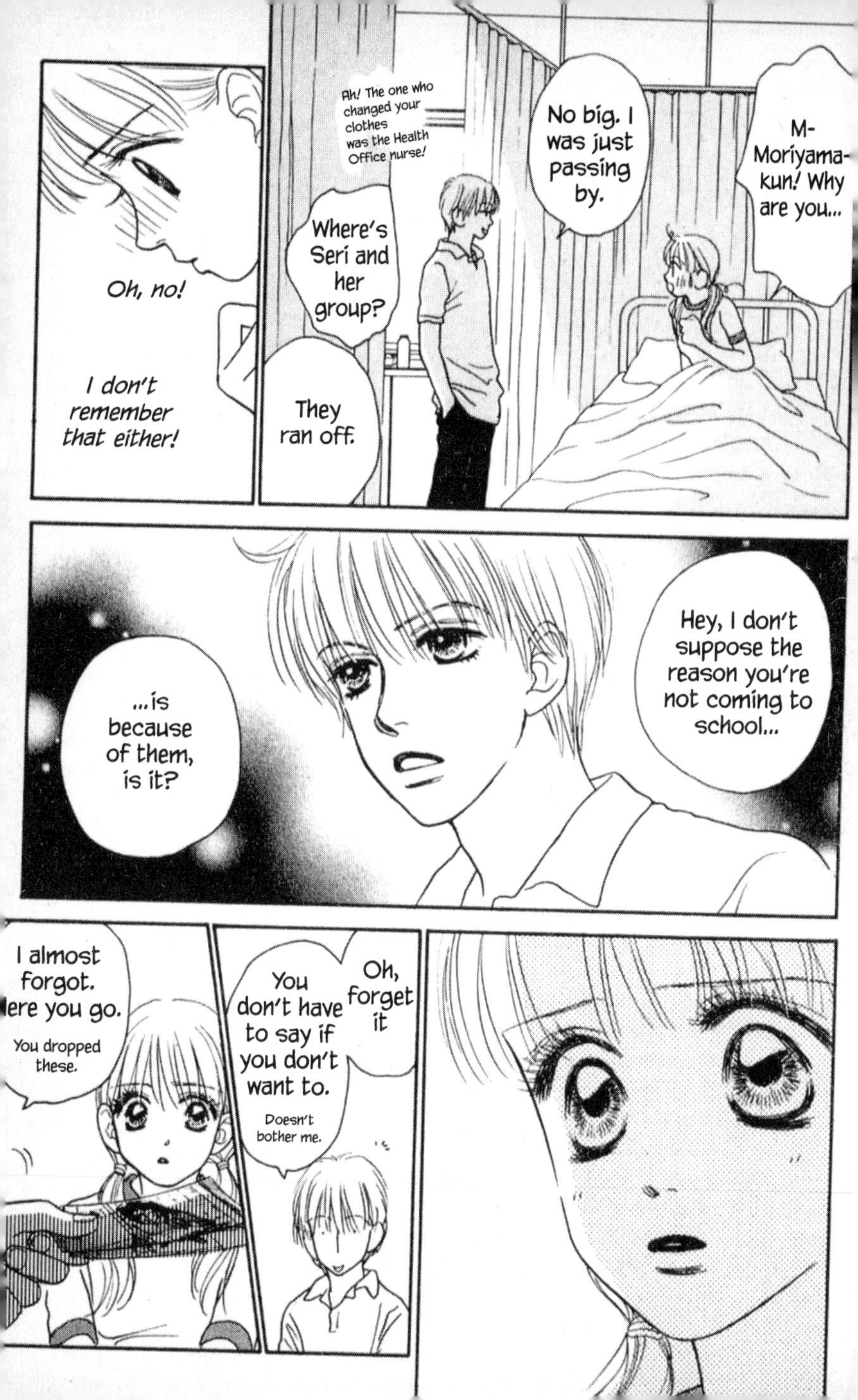
M-Moriyama-kun! Why are you...
No big. I was just passing by.
Where's Seri and her group?
They ran off.
Ah! The one who changed your clothes was the Health Office nurse!
Oh, no!
I don't remember that either!
Hey, I don't suppose the reason you're not coming to school...
...is because of them, is it?
Oh, forget it
You don't have to say if you don't want to.
Doesn't bother me.
I almost forgot. ere you go.
You dropped these.

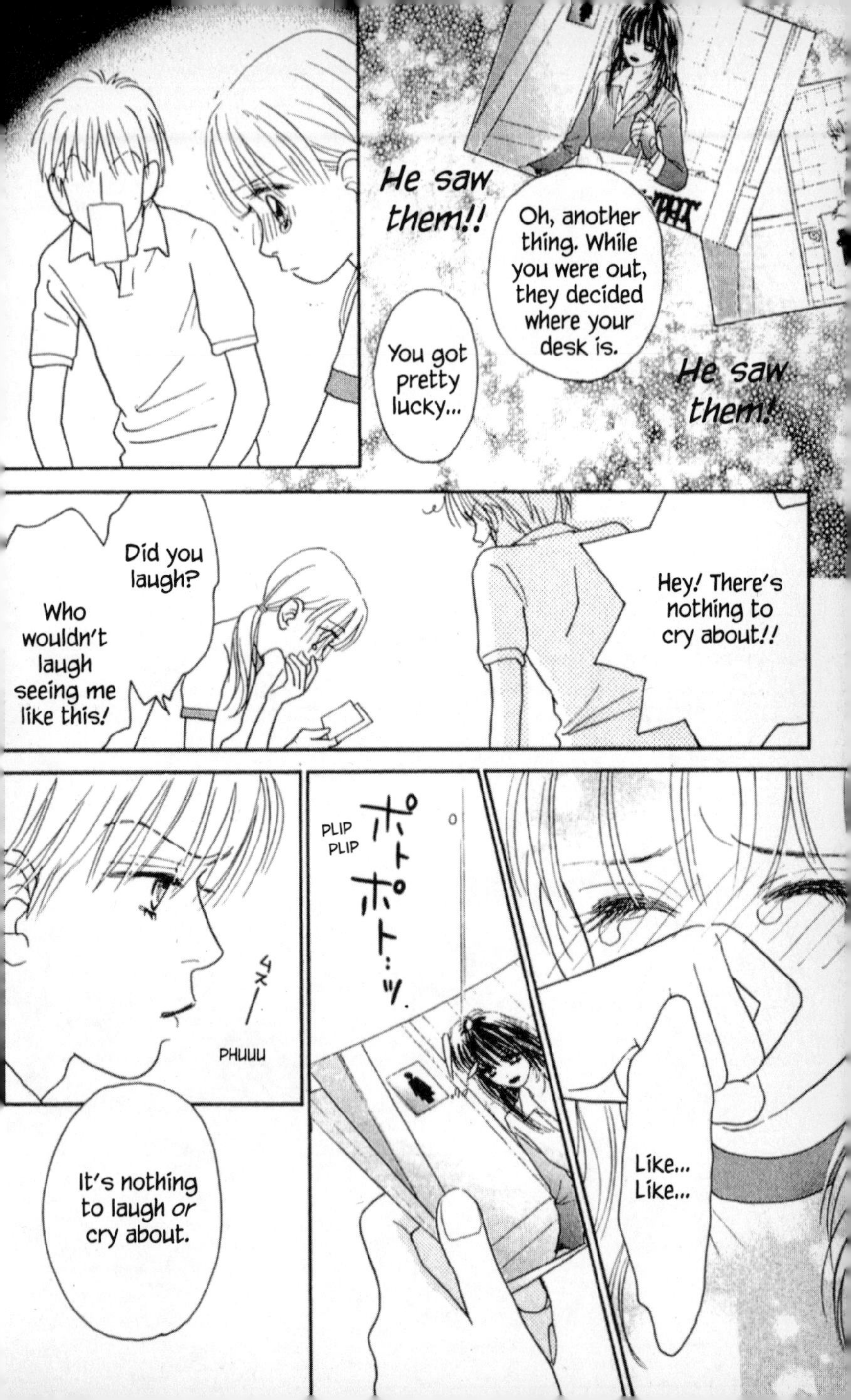
Oh, another thing. While you were out, they decided where your desk is.
You got pretty lucky...
He saw them!!
He saw them!
Hey! There's nothing to cry about!!
Did you laugh?
Who wouldn't laugh seeing me like this!
Like... Like...
ポトポト…ッ
PLIP PLIP
ムスー
PHUUU
It's nothing to laugh *or* cry about.

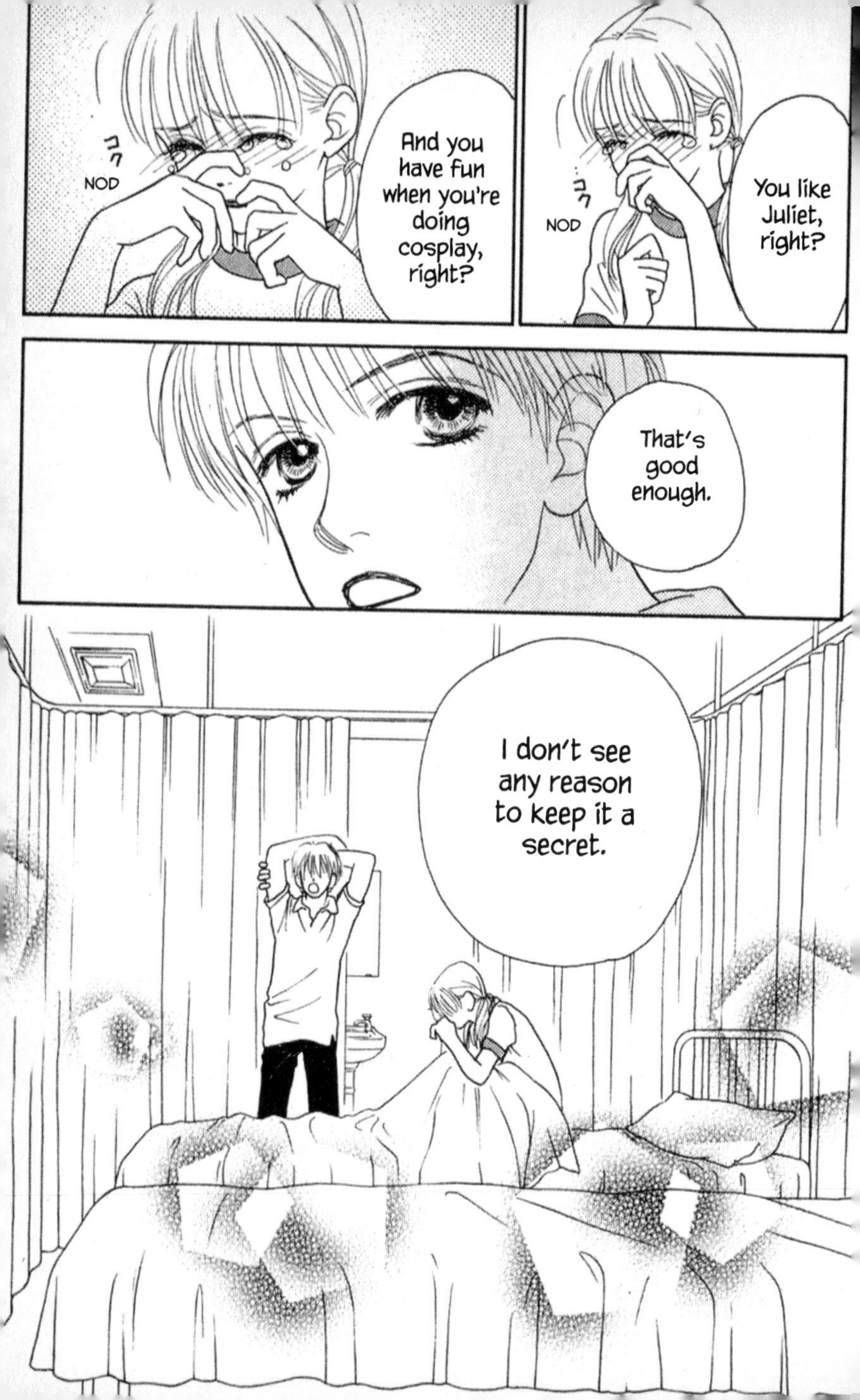
You like Juliet, right?
コク
NOD
And you have fun when you're doing cosplay, right?
コク
NOD
That's good enough.
I don't see any reason to keep it a secret.

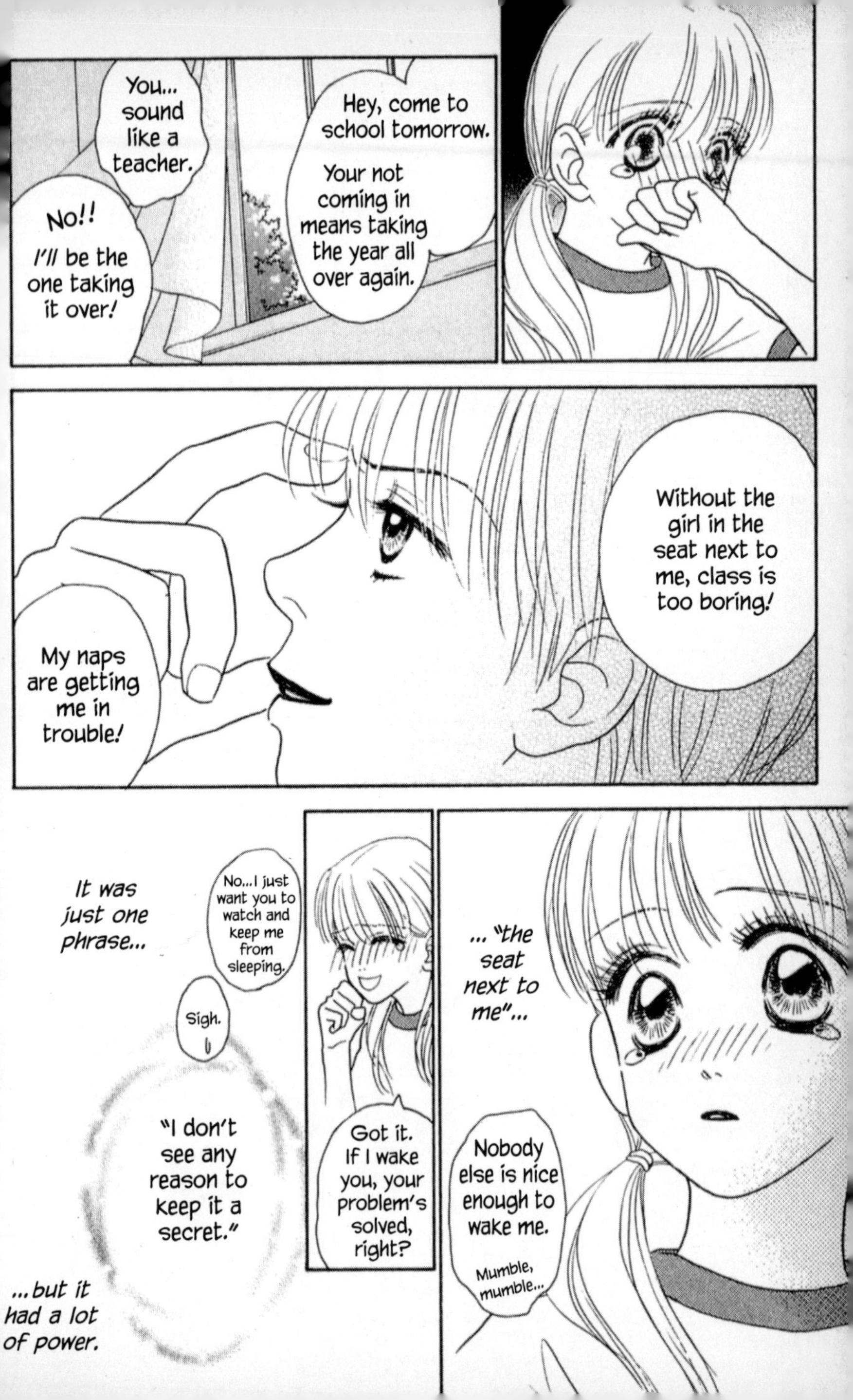

Hey, come to school tomorrow.
Your not coming in means taking the year all over again.
You... sound like a teacher.
No!!
I'll be the one taking it over!
Without the girl in the seat next to me, class is too boring!
My naps are getting me in trouble!
... "the seat next to me"...
Nobody else is nice enough to wake me.
Mumble, mumble...
Got it. If I wake you, your problem's solved, right?
No...I just want you to watch and keep me from sleeping.
Sigh.
It was just one phrase...
"I don't see any reason to keep it a secret."
...but it had a lot of power.

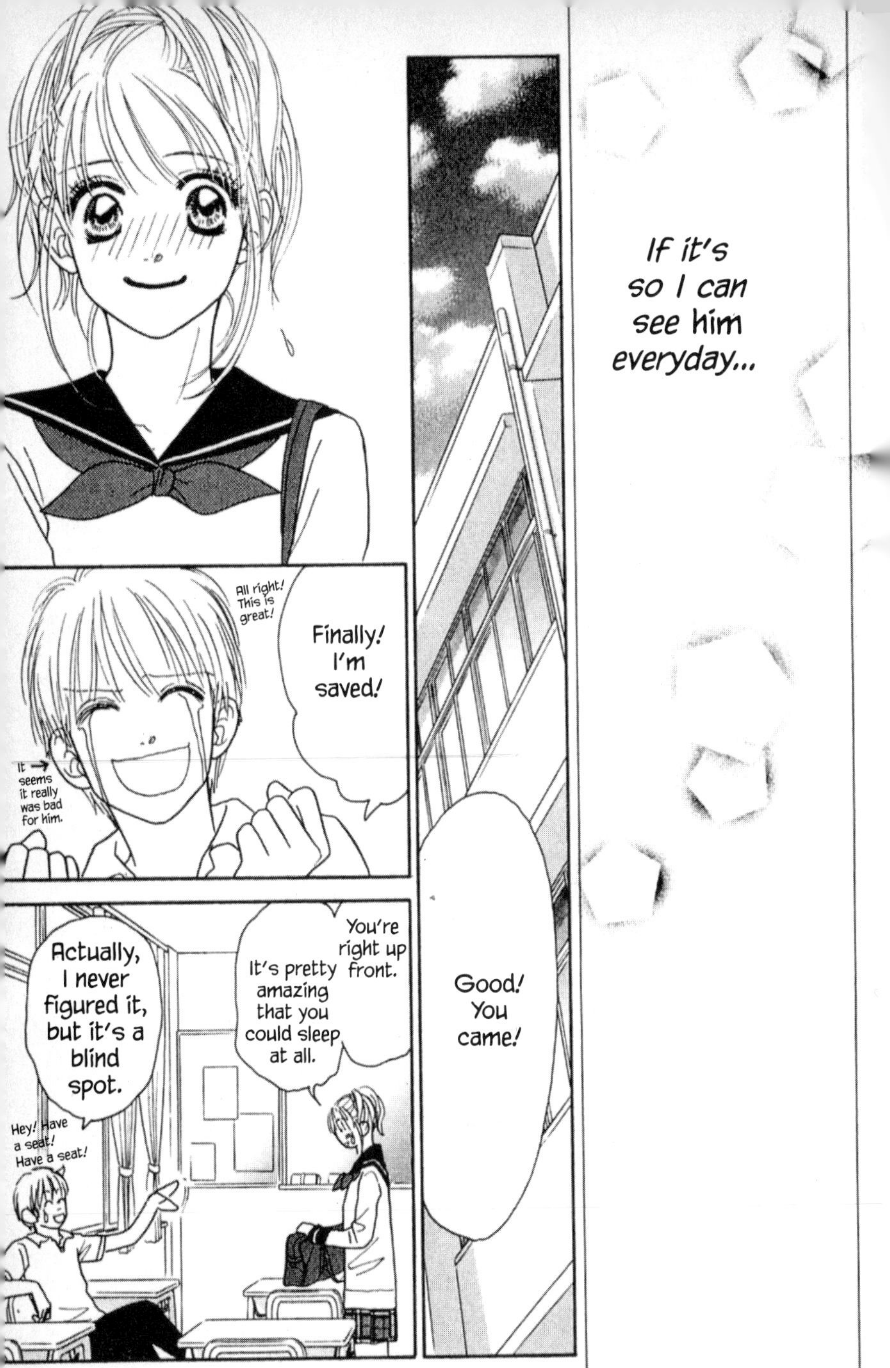

If it's so I can see him everyday...
Good! You came!
Finally! I'm saved!
All right! This is great!
It → seems it really was bad for him.
You're right up front.
It's pretty amazing that you could sleep at all.
Actually, I never figured it, but it's a blind spot.
Hey! Have a seat! Have a seat!

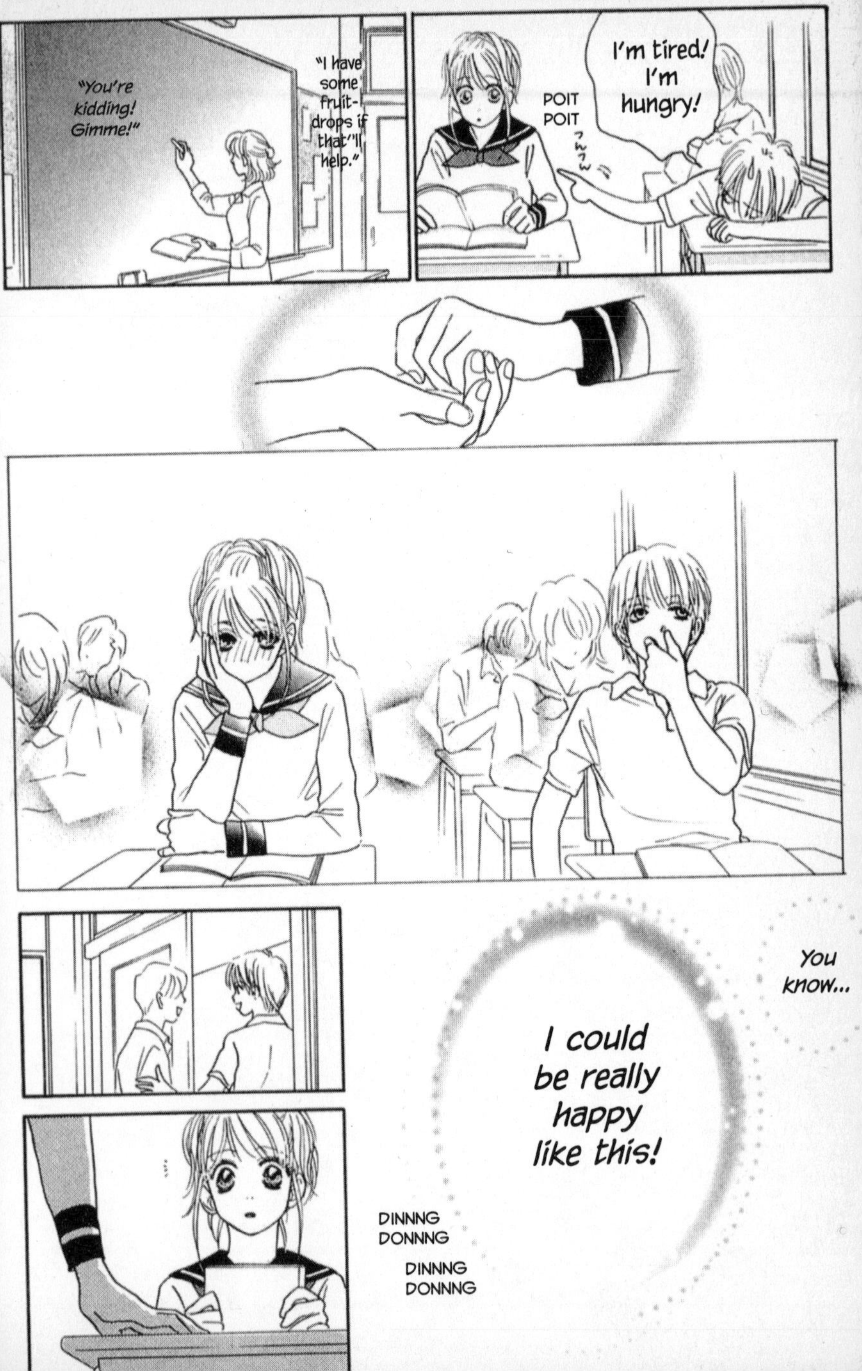
I'm tired! I'm hungry!
POIT POIT
"I have some fruit-drops if that'll help."
"You're kidding! Gimme!"
You know...
I could be really happy like this!
DINNNG DONNNG
DINNNG DONNNG

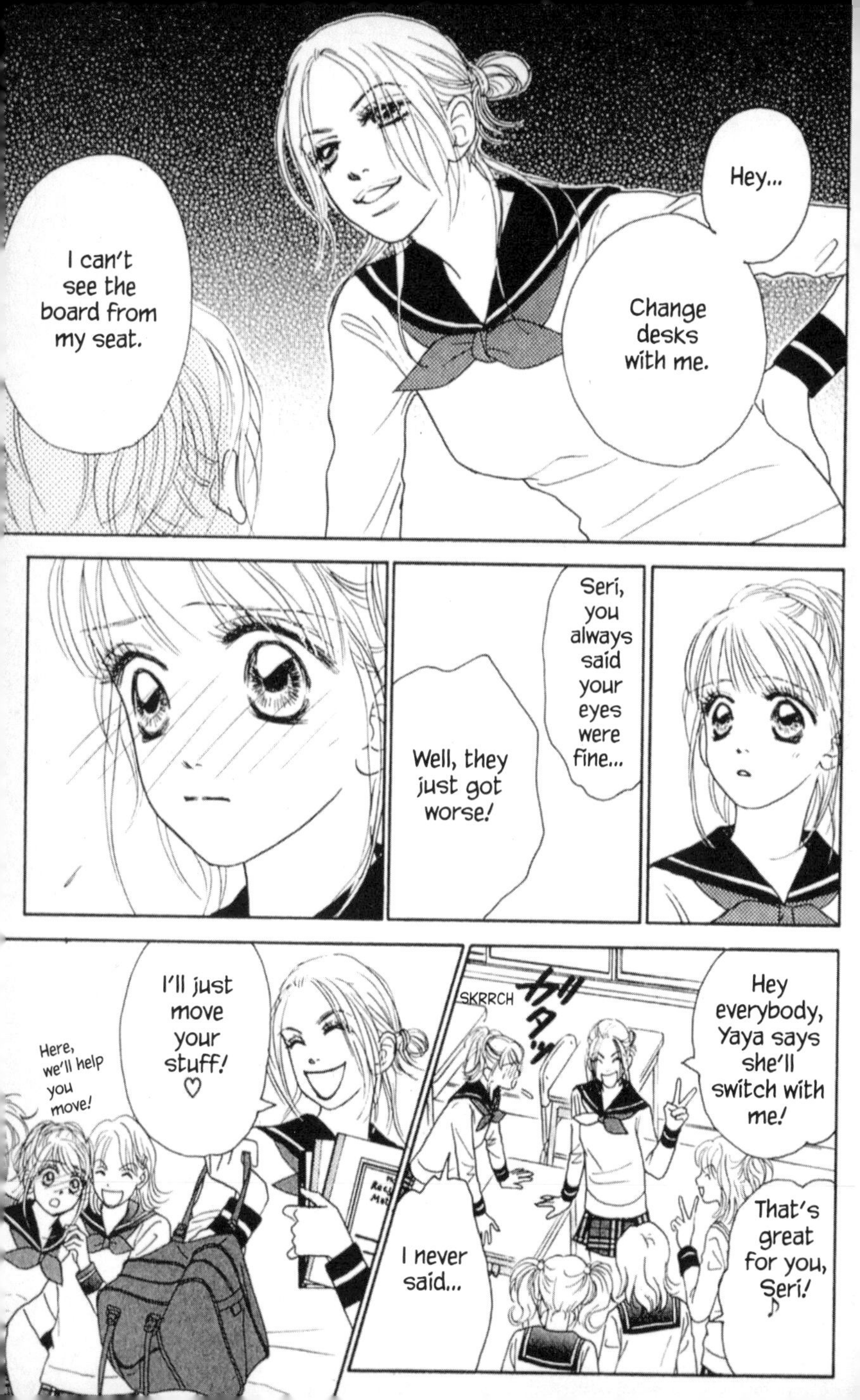
Hey...
Change desks with me.
I can't see the board from my seat.
Seri, you always said your eyes were fine...
Well, they just got worse!
SKRRCH
Hey everybody, Yaya says she'll switch with me!
That's great for you, Seri! ♪
I never said...
I'll just move your stuff! ♡
Here, we'll help you move!

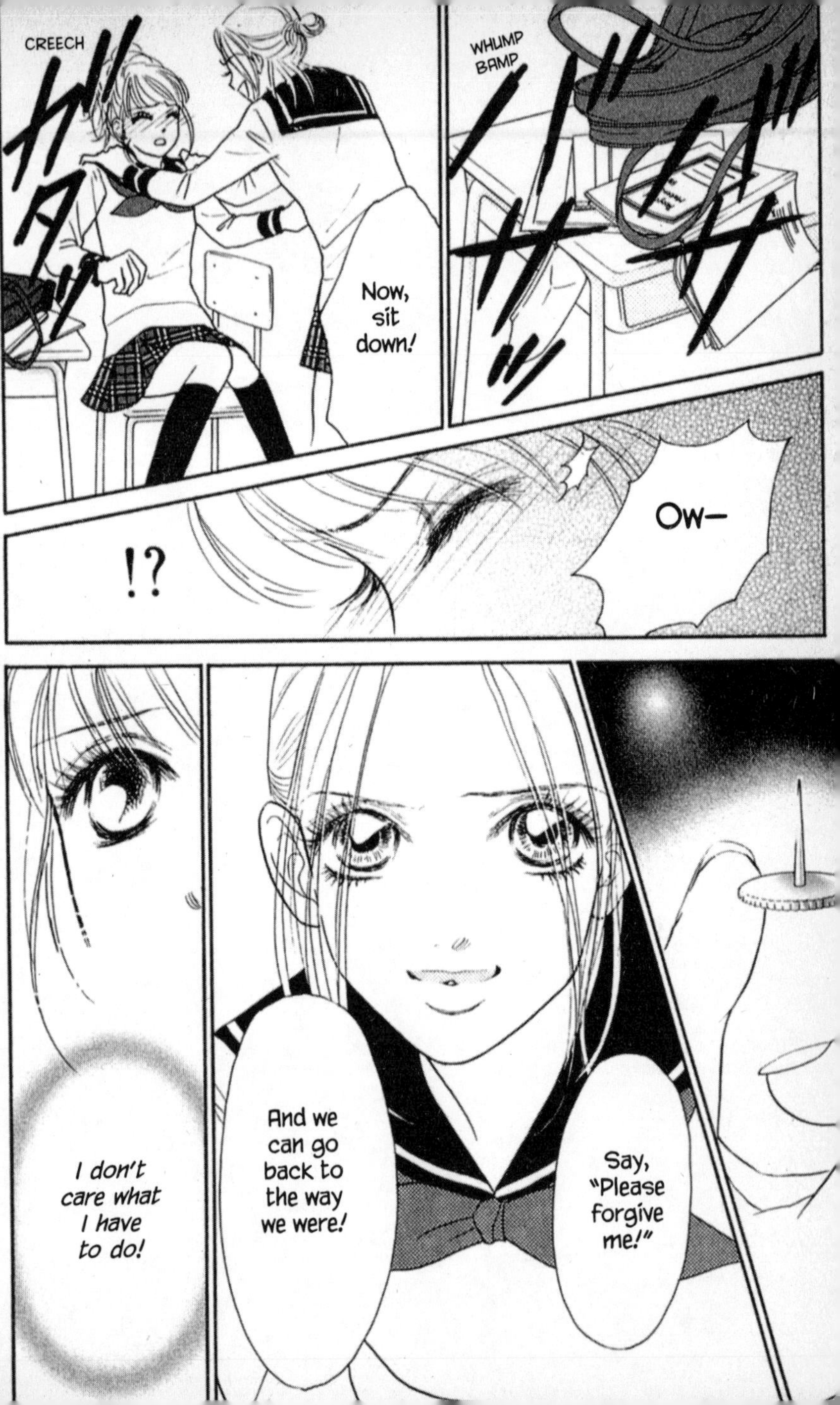
WHUMP
BAMP
CREECH
Now, sit down!
Ow–
!?
Say, "Please forgive me!"
And we can go back to the way we were!
I don't care what I have to do!

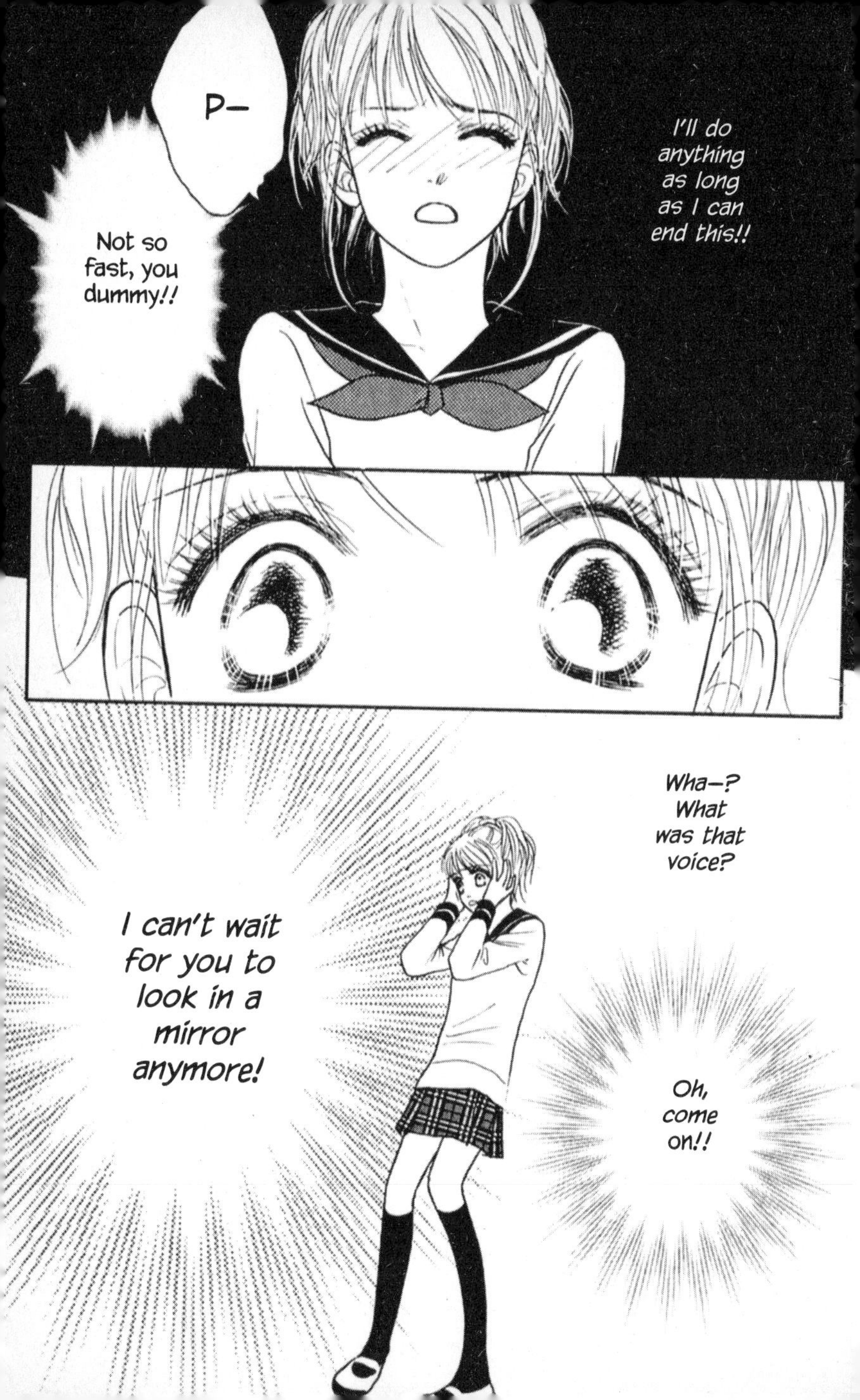
I'll do anything as long as I can end this!!
P–
Not so fast, you dummy!!
Wha–? What was that voice?
Oh, come on!!
I can't wait for you to look in a mirror anymore!

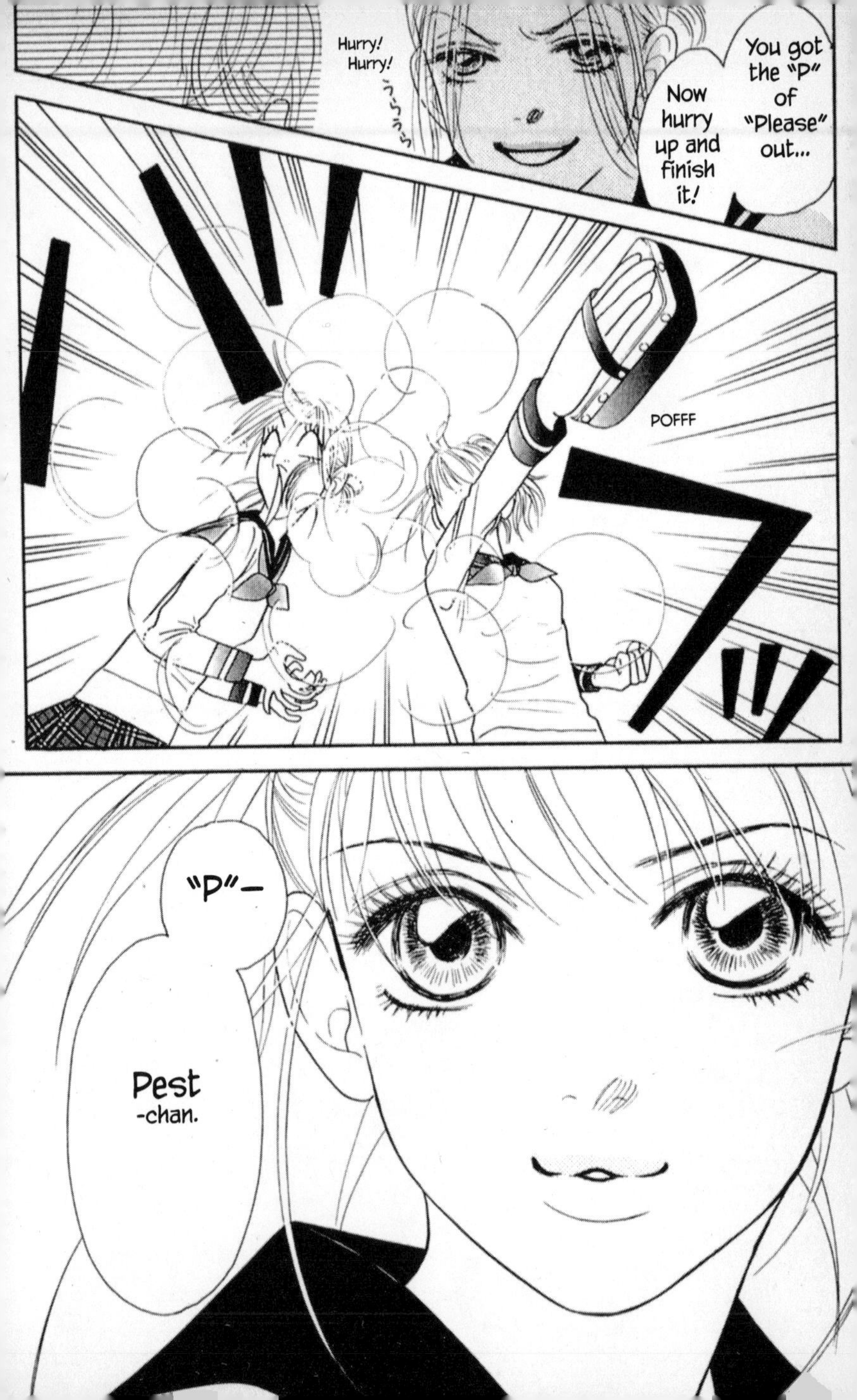

You got the "P" of "Please" out...
Now hurry up and finish it!
Hurry! Hurry!
POFFF
"P"–
Pest -chan.

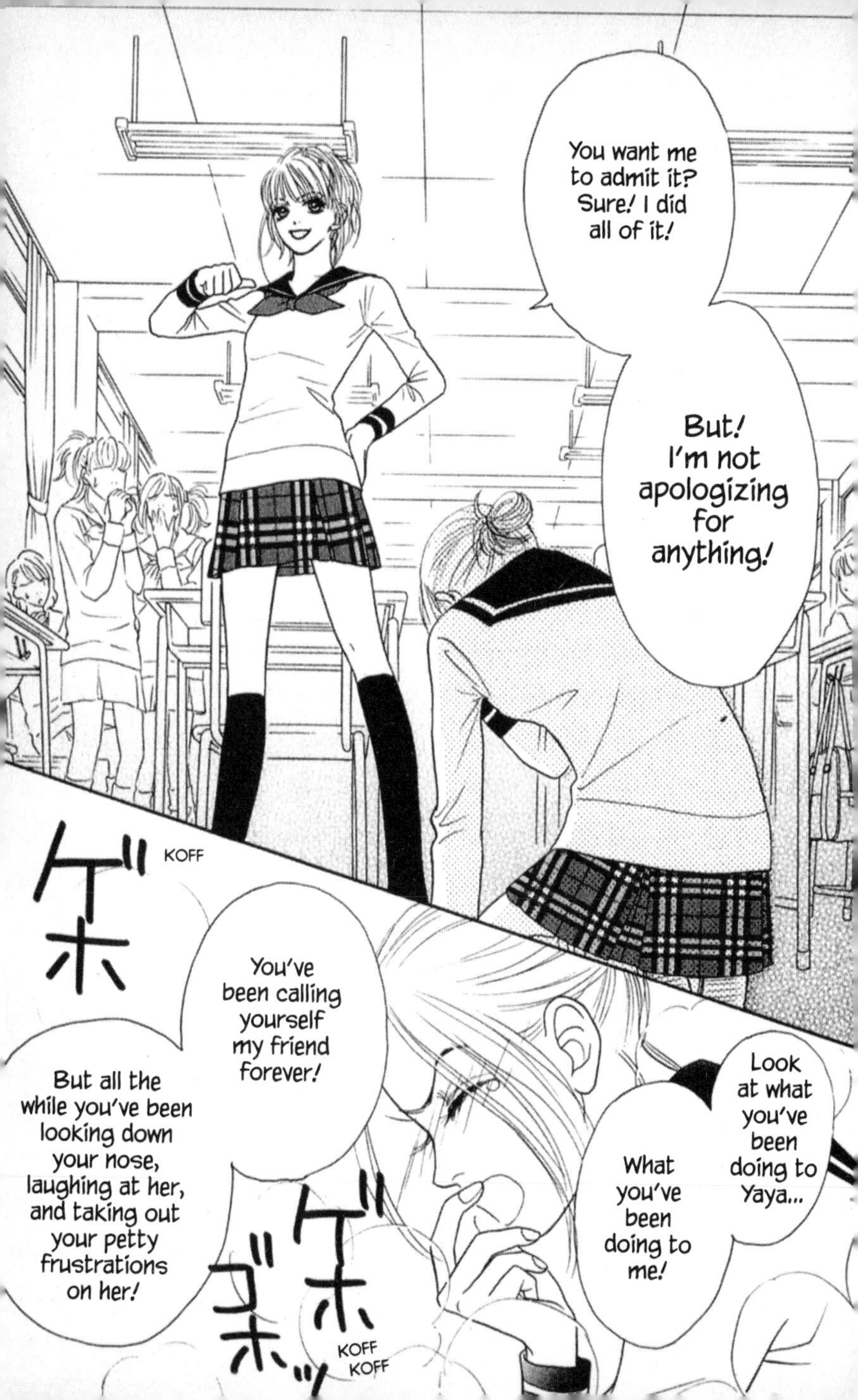
You want me to admit it? Sure! I did all of it!
But! I'm not apologizing for anything!
Look at what you've been doing to Yaya...
What you've been doing to me!
ゲホ
KOFF
You've been calling yourself my friend forever!
But all the while you've been looking down your nose, laughing at her, and taking out your petty frustrations on her!
ゲホ ゴホッ
KOFF KOFF

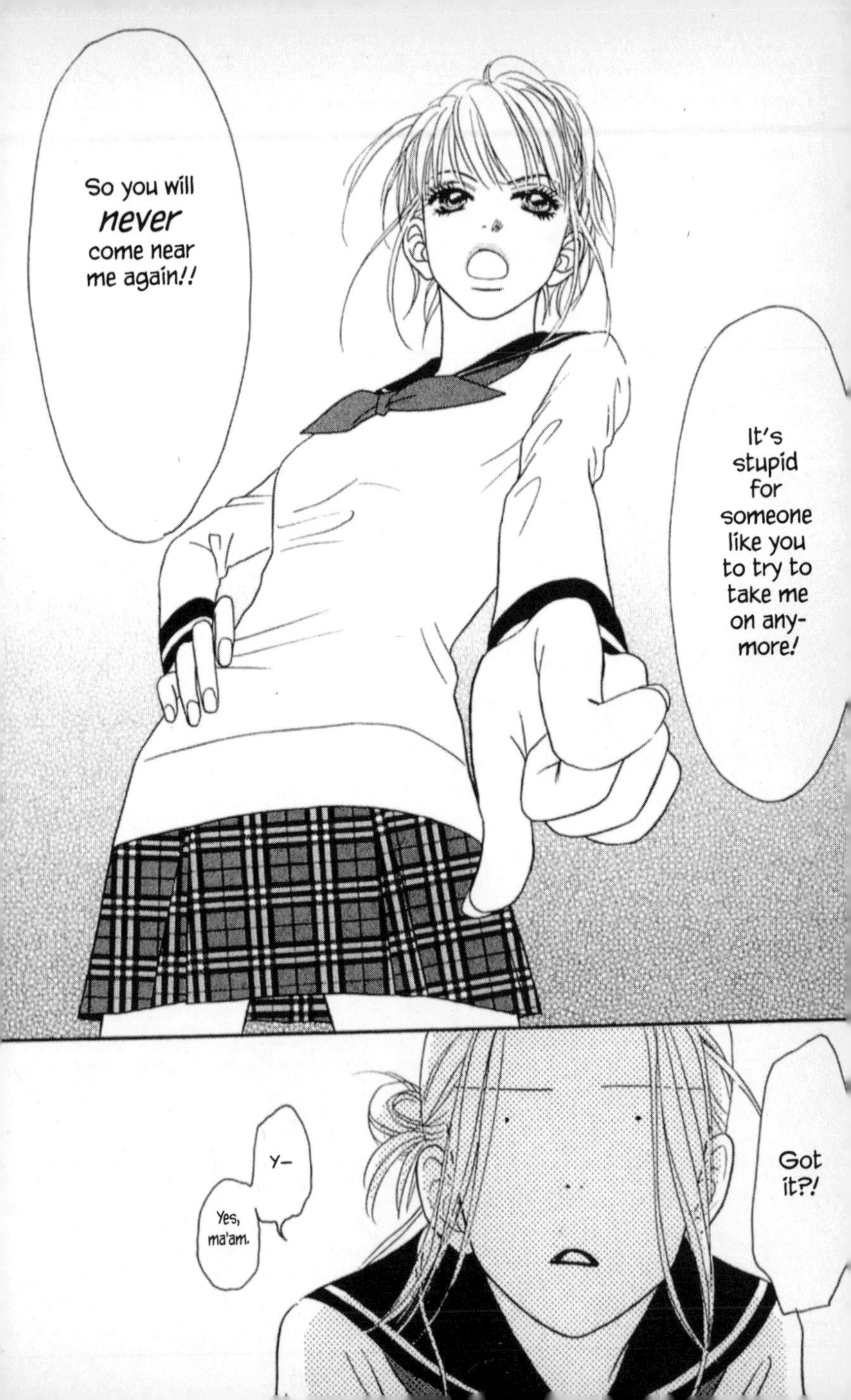
It's stupid for someone like you to try to take me on any-more!
So you will *never* come near me again!!
Got it?!
Y—
Yes, ma'am.

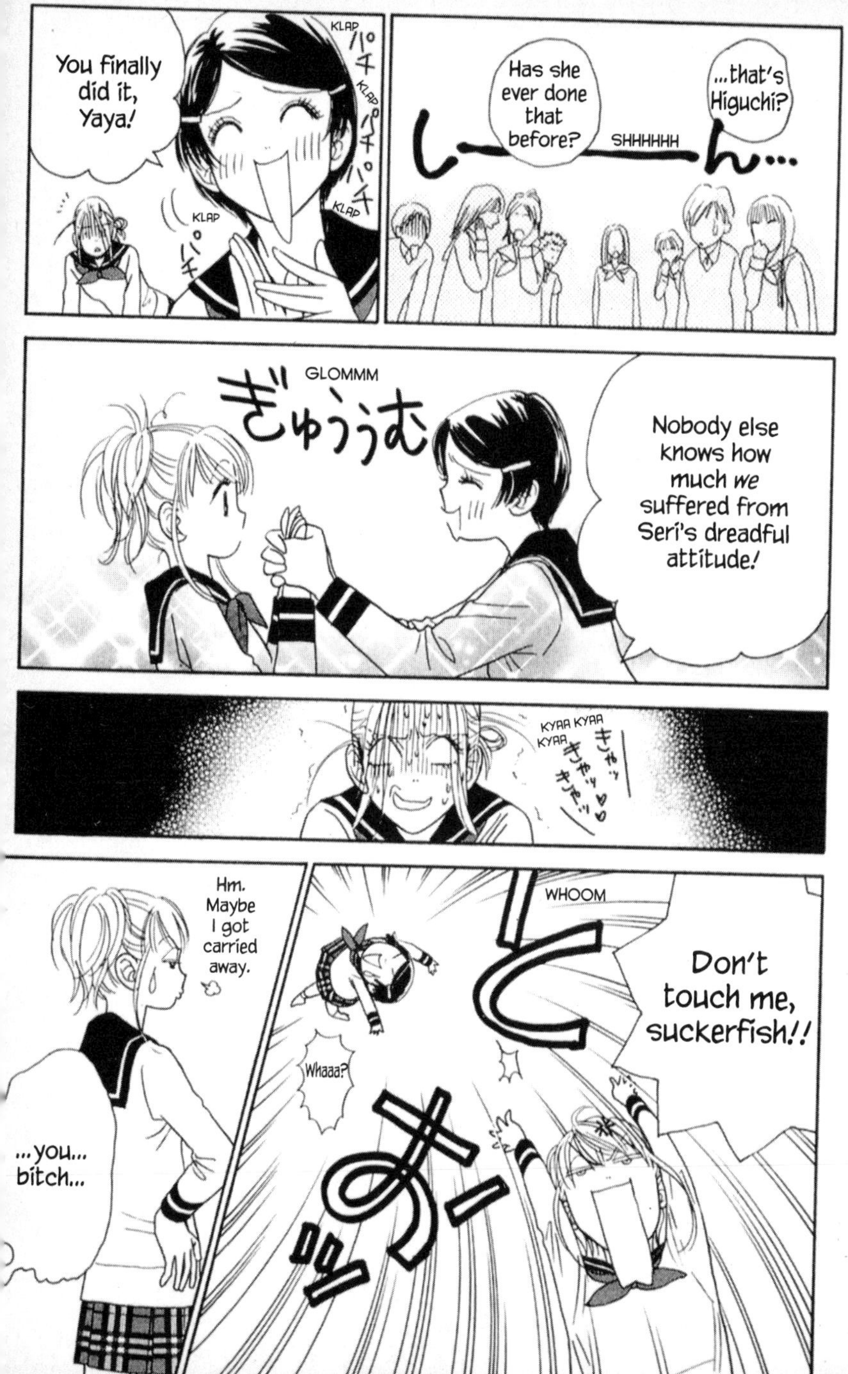

...that's Higuchi?
Has she ever done that before?
SHHHHHH
しーーん...
KLAP
パチ
KLAP
パチ
KLAP
パチ
You finally did it, Yaya!
KLAP
パチ
GLOMMM
ぎゅううむ
Nobody else knows how much *we* suffered from Seri's dreadful attitude!
KYAA KYAA KYAA
WHOOM
Don't touch me, suckerfish!!
Whaaa?
Hm. Maybe I got carried away.
...you... bitch...

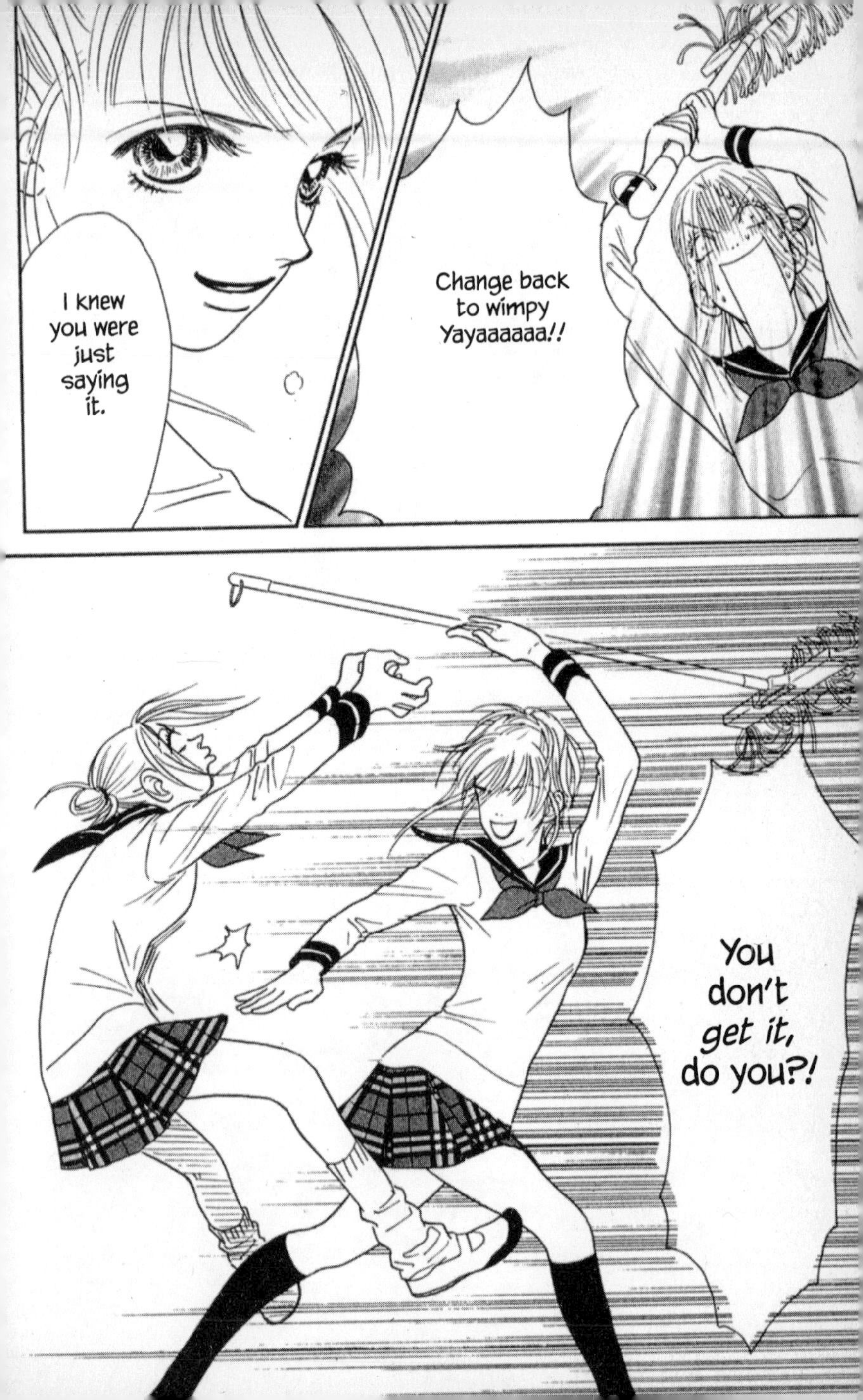
Change back to wimpy Yayaaaaaa!!
I knew you were just saying it.
You don't *get it*, do you?!

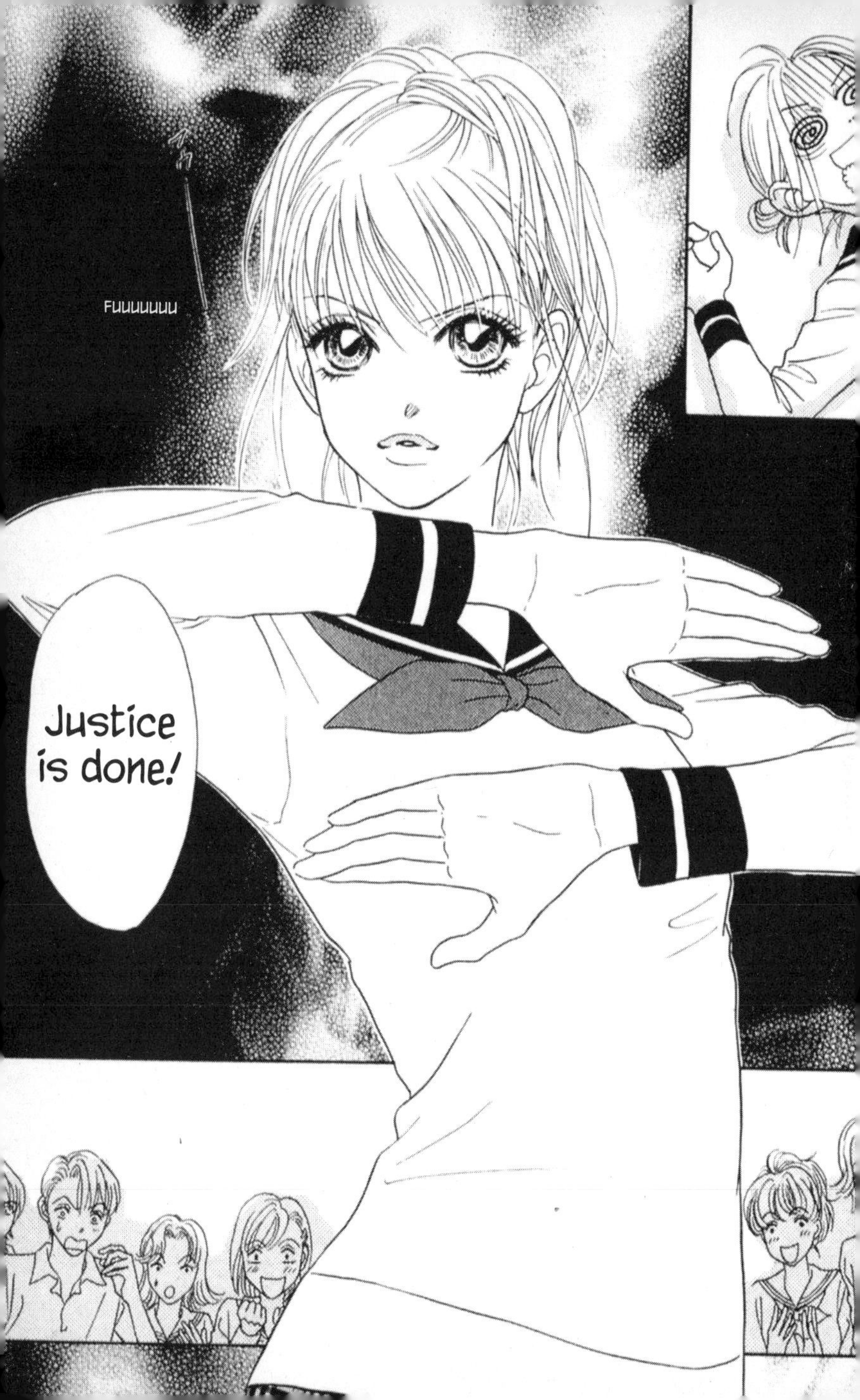
Fuuuuuuu
Justice is done!

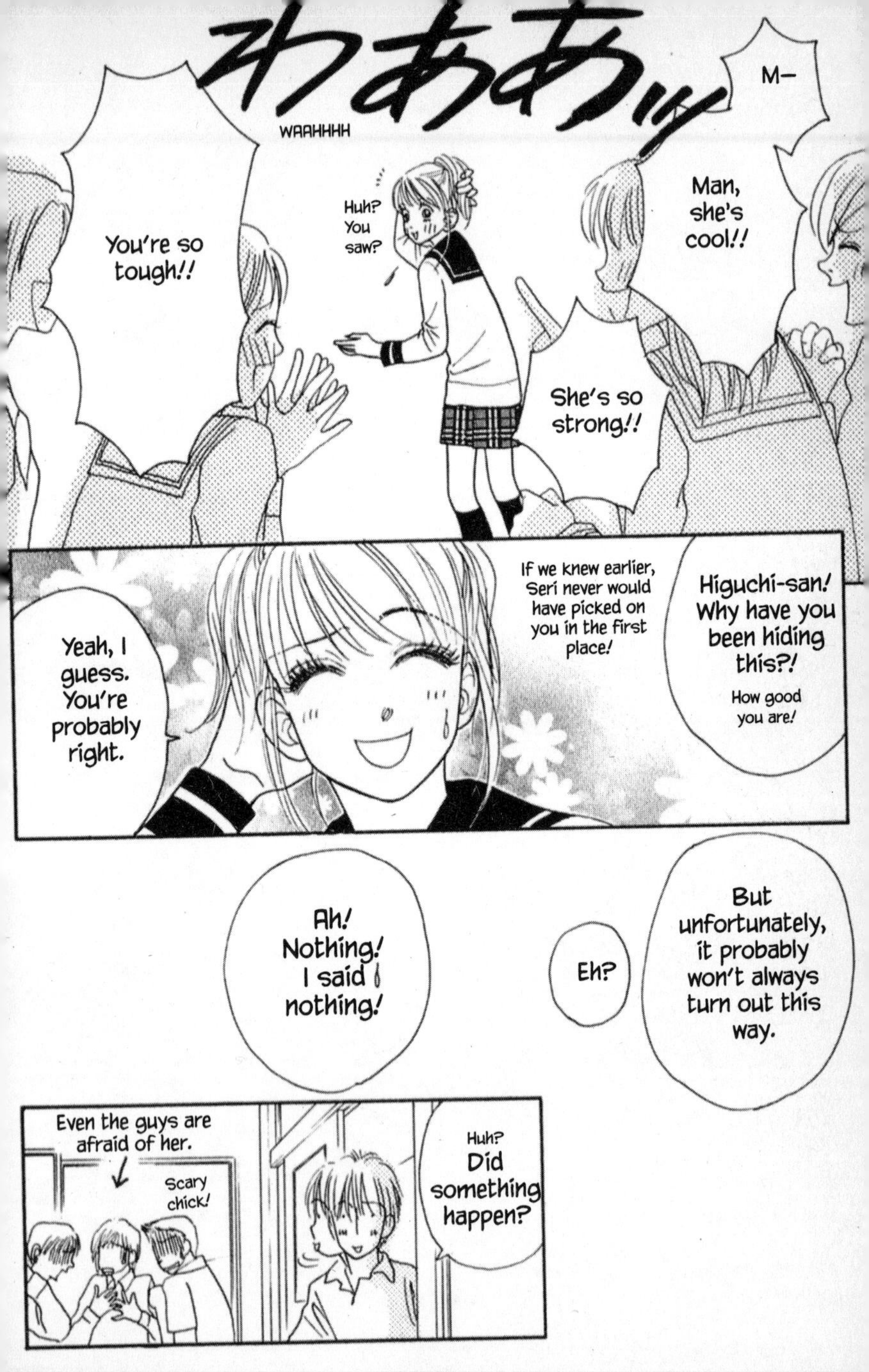

わああッ
WAAHHHH
M–
Man, she's cool!!
She's so strong!!
You're so tough!!
Huh? You saw?
Higuchi-san! Why have you been hiding this?!
How good you are!
If we knew earlier, Seri never would have picked on you in the first place!
Yeah, I guess. You're probably right.
But unfortunately, it probably won't always turn out this way.
Eh?
Ah! Nothing! I said nothing!
Huh? Did something happen?
Even the guys are afraid of her.
Scary chick!

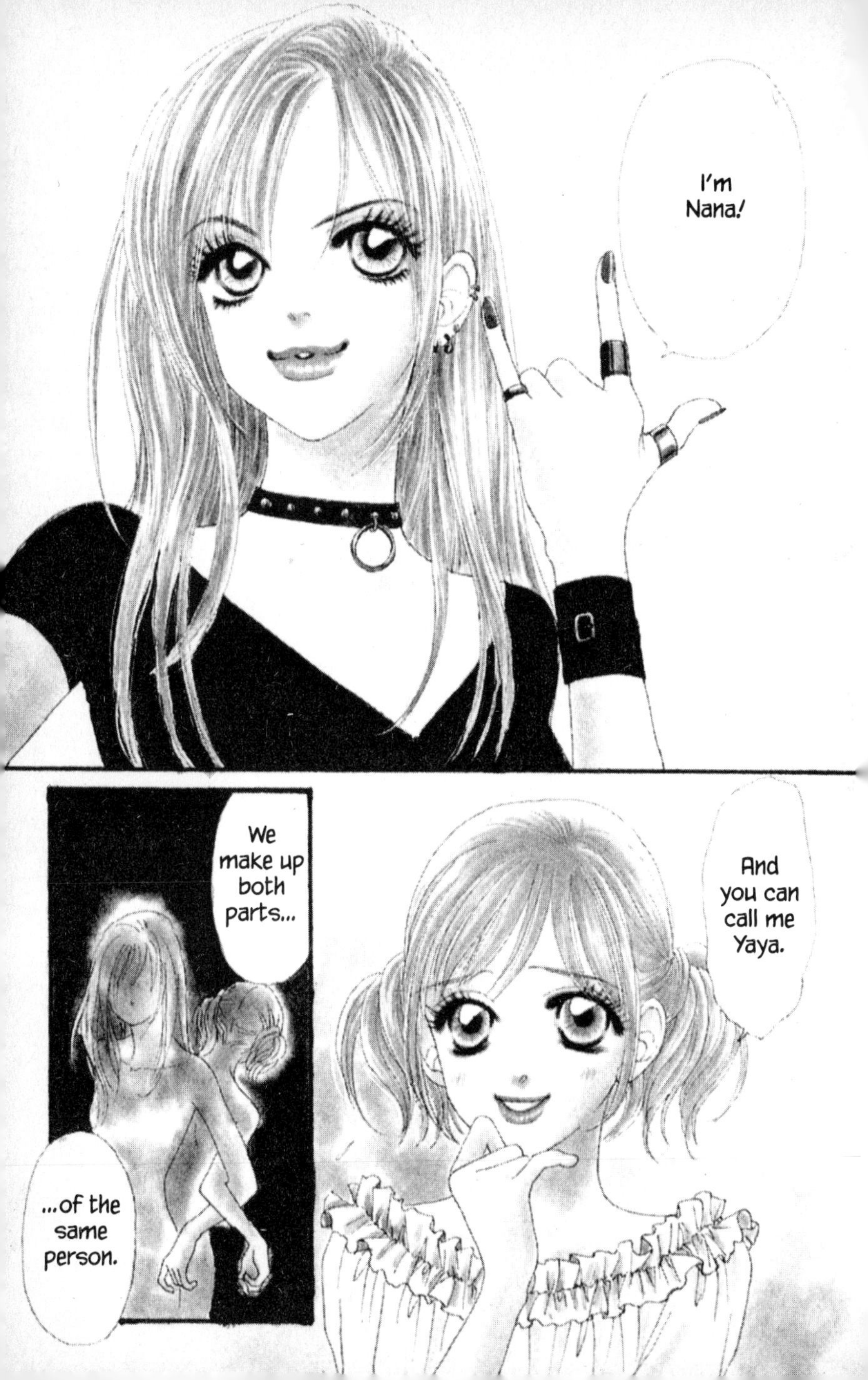
I'm Nana!
And you can call me Yaya.
We make up both parts...
...of the same person.

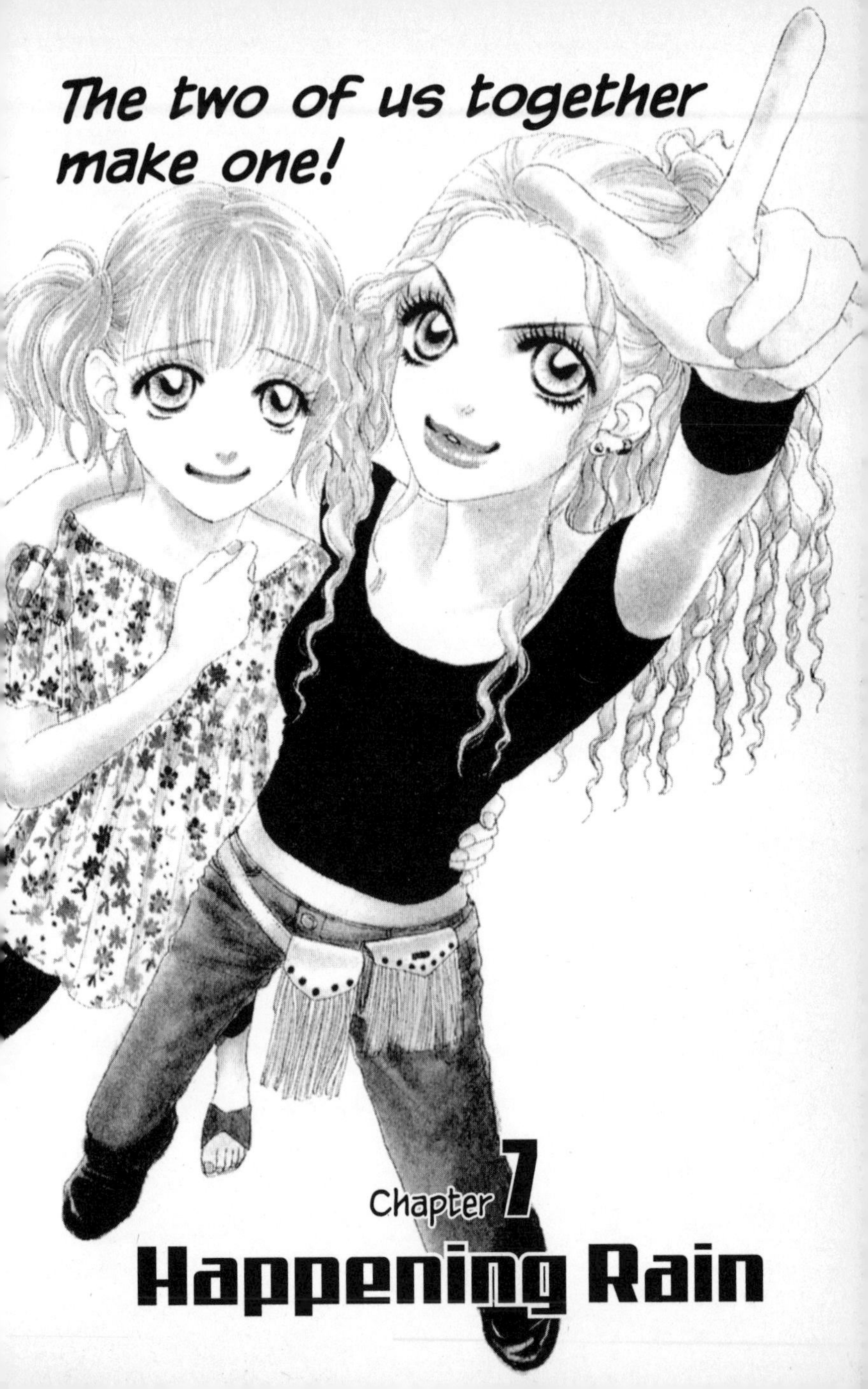
The two of us together make one!
Chapter 7
Happening Rain

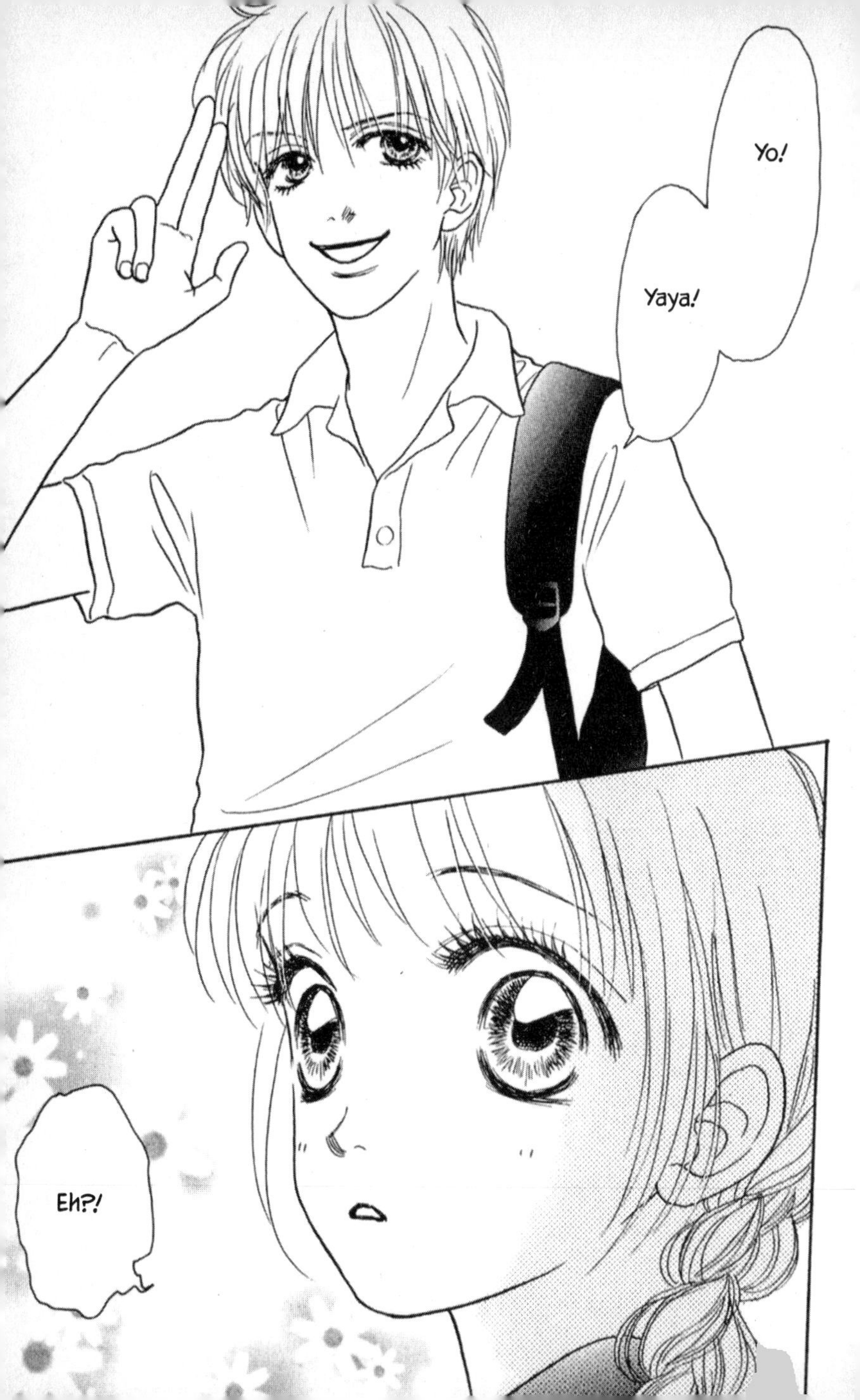
Yo!
Yaya!
Eh?!

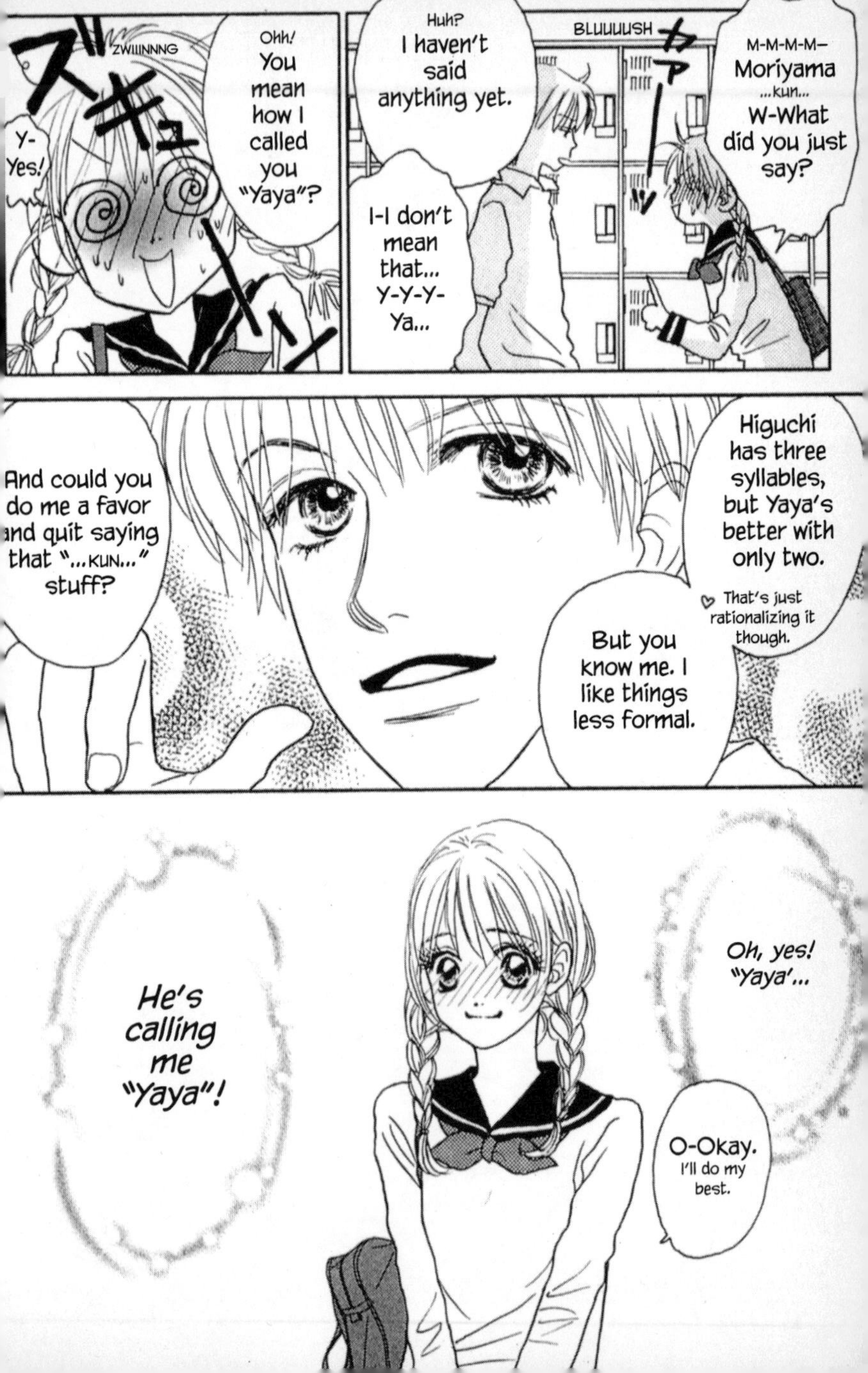
BLUUUUSH
M-M-M-M— Moriyama ...kun... W-What did you just say?
Huh? I haven't said anything yet.
I-I don't mean that... Y-Y-Y-Ya...
Ohh! You mean how I called you "Yaya"?
ZWIIINNNG
Y- Yes!
Higuchi has three syllables, but Yaya's better with only two.
That's just rationalizing it though.
But you know me. I like things less formal.
And could you do me a favor and quit saying that "...KUN..." stuff?
Oh, yes! "Yaya'...
O-Okay. I'll do my best.
He's calling me "Yaya"!

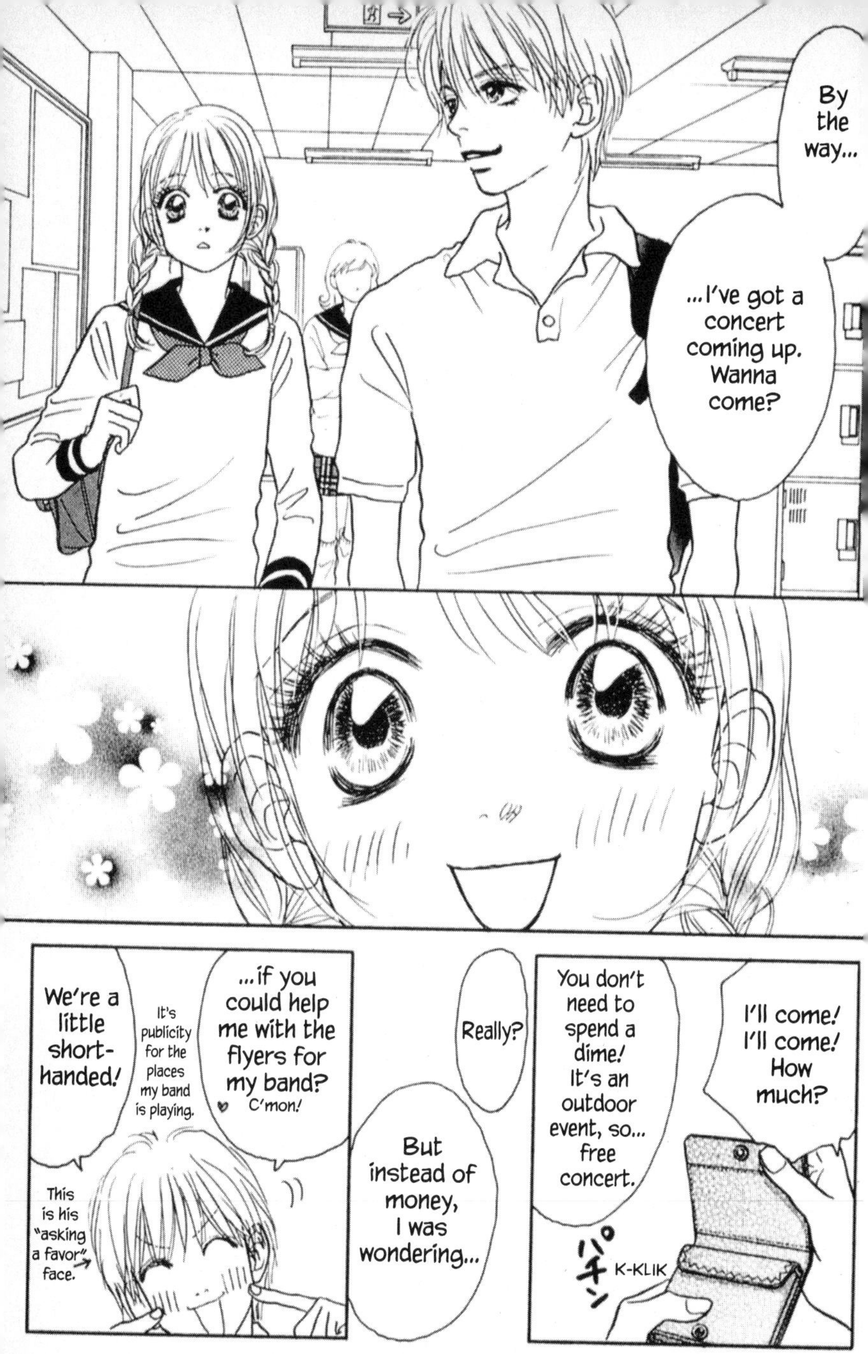
By the way...
...I've got a concert coming up. Wanna come?
I'll come! I'll come! How much?
パチン
K-KLIK
You don't need to spend a dime! It's an outdoor event, so... free concert.
Really?
But instead of money, I was wondering...
...if you could help me with the flyers for my band? C'mon!
It's publicity for the places my band is playing.
We're a little short-handed!
This is his "asking a favor" face.

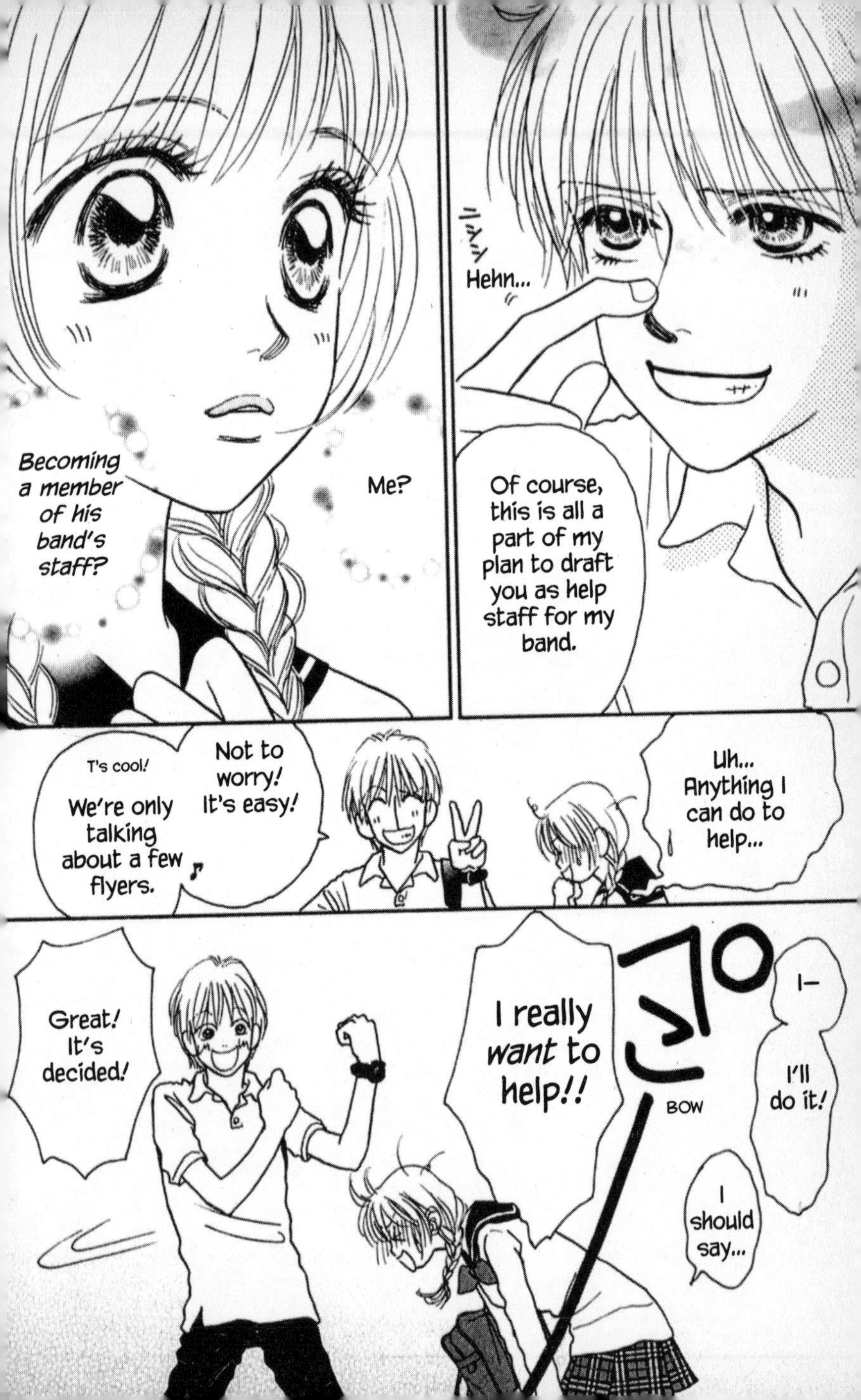
Hehn...
Of course, this is all a part of my plan to draft you as help staff for my band.
Me?
Becoming a member of his band's staff?
Uh... Anything I can do to help...
Not to worry! It's easy!
T's cool!
We're only talking about a few flyers.
I—
I'll do it!
I should say...
I really *want* to help!!
BOW
Great! It's decided!

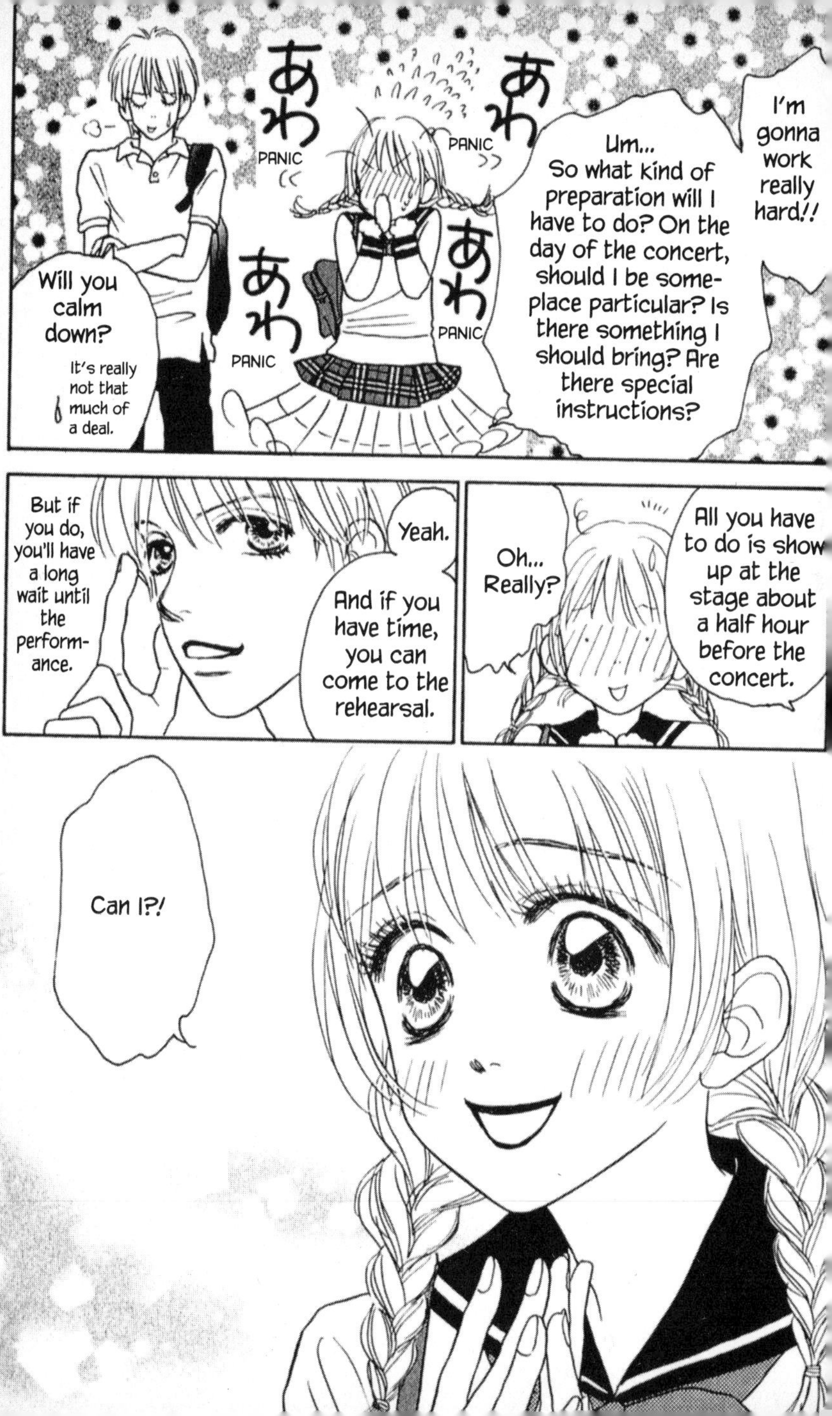

I'm gonna work really hard!!
Um... So what kind of preparation will I have to do? On the day of the concert, should I be someplace particular? Is there something I should bring? Are there special instructions?
あわ
PANIC
あわ
PANIC
あわ
PANIC
あわ
PANIC
Will you calm down?
It's really not that much of a deal.
All you have to do is show up at the stage about a half hour before the concert.
Oh... Really?
Yeah.
And if you have time, you can come to the rehearsal.
But if you do, you'll have a long wait until the performance.
Can I?!

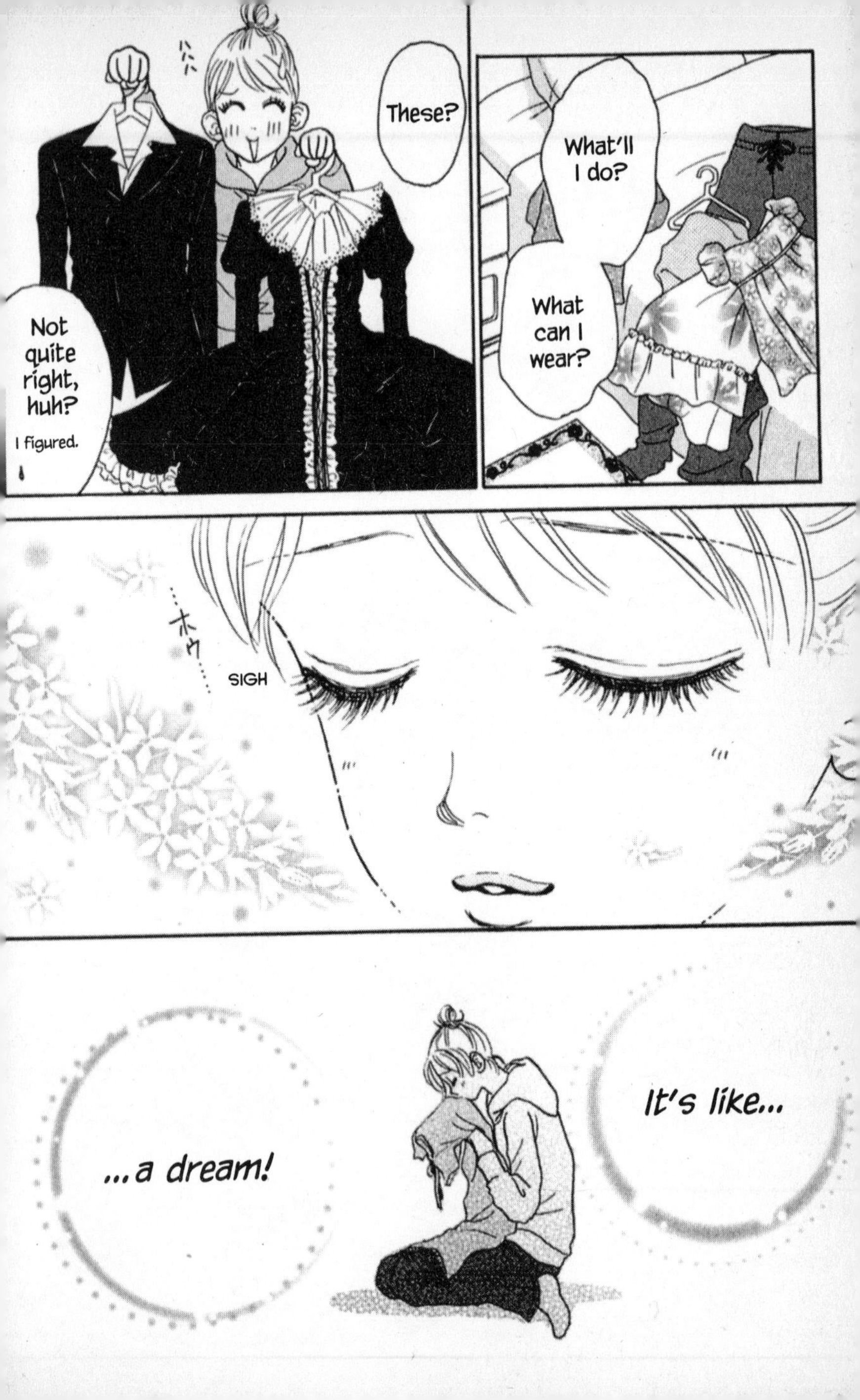
What'll I do?
What can I wear?
These?
Not quite right, huh?
I figured.
SIGH
It's like...
...a dream!

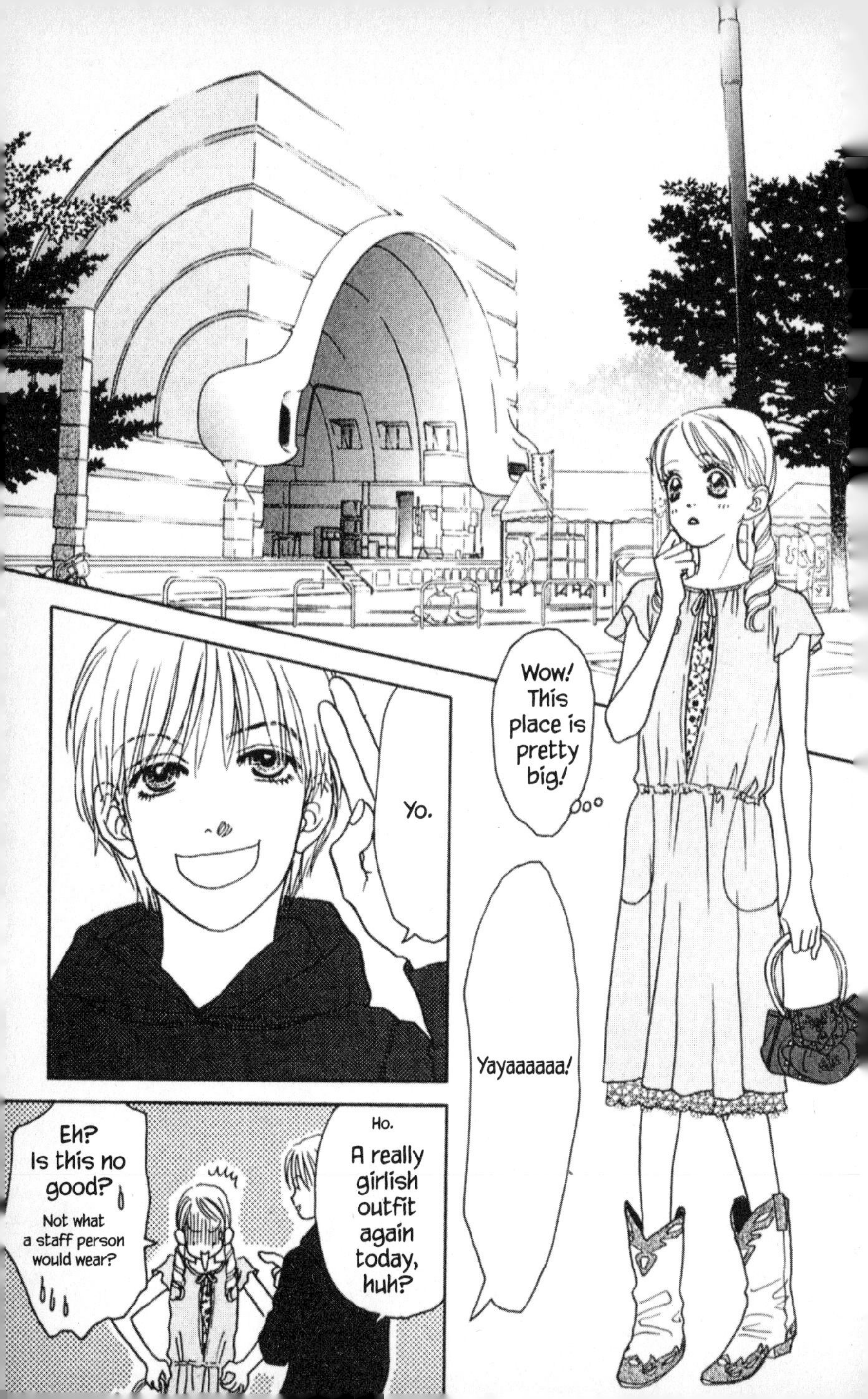
Wow! This place is pretty big!
Yayaaaaaa!
Yo.
Ho.
A really girlish outfit again today, huh?
Eh? Is this no good?
Not what a staff person would wear?

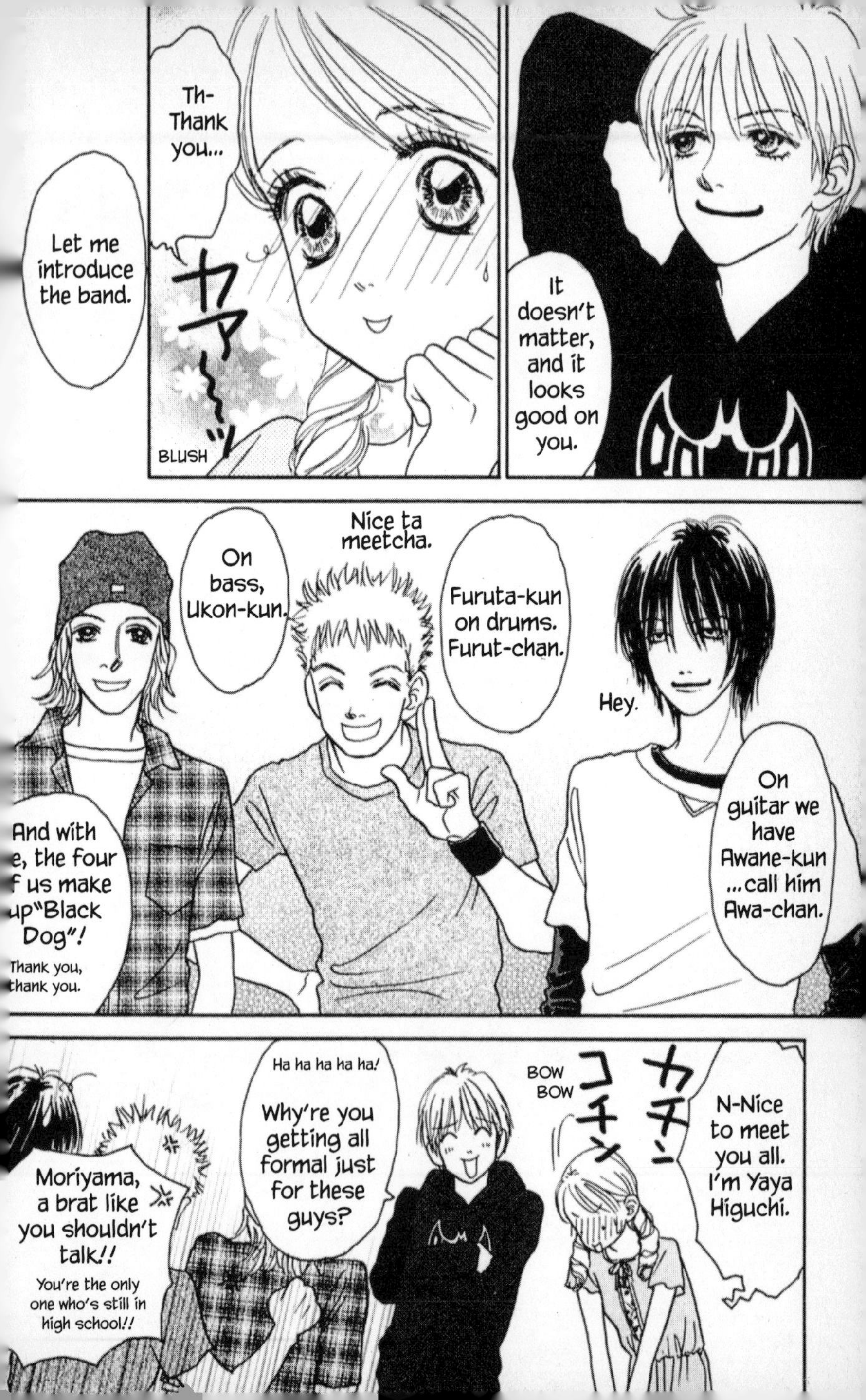
It doesn't matter, and it looks good on you.
Th- Thank you...
BLUSH
Let me introduce the band.
On guitar we have Awane-kun ...call him Awa-chan.
Hey.
Furuta-kun on drums. Furut-chan.
Nice ta meetcha.
On bass, Ukon-kun.
And with e, the four f us make up"Black Dog"!
Thank you, thank you.
N-Nice to meet you all. I'm Yaya Higuchi.
BOW BOW
Ha ha ha ha ha!
Why're you getting all formal just for these guys?
Moriyama, a brat like you shouldn't talk!!
You're the only one who's still in high school!!

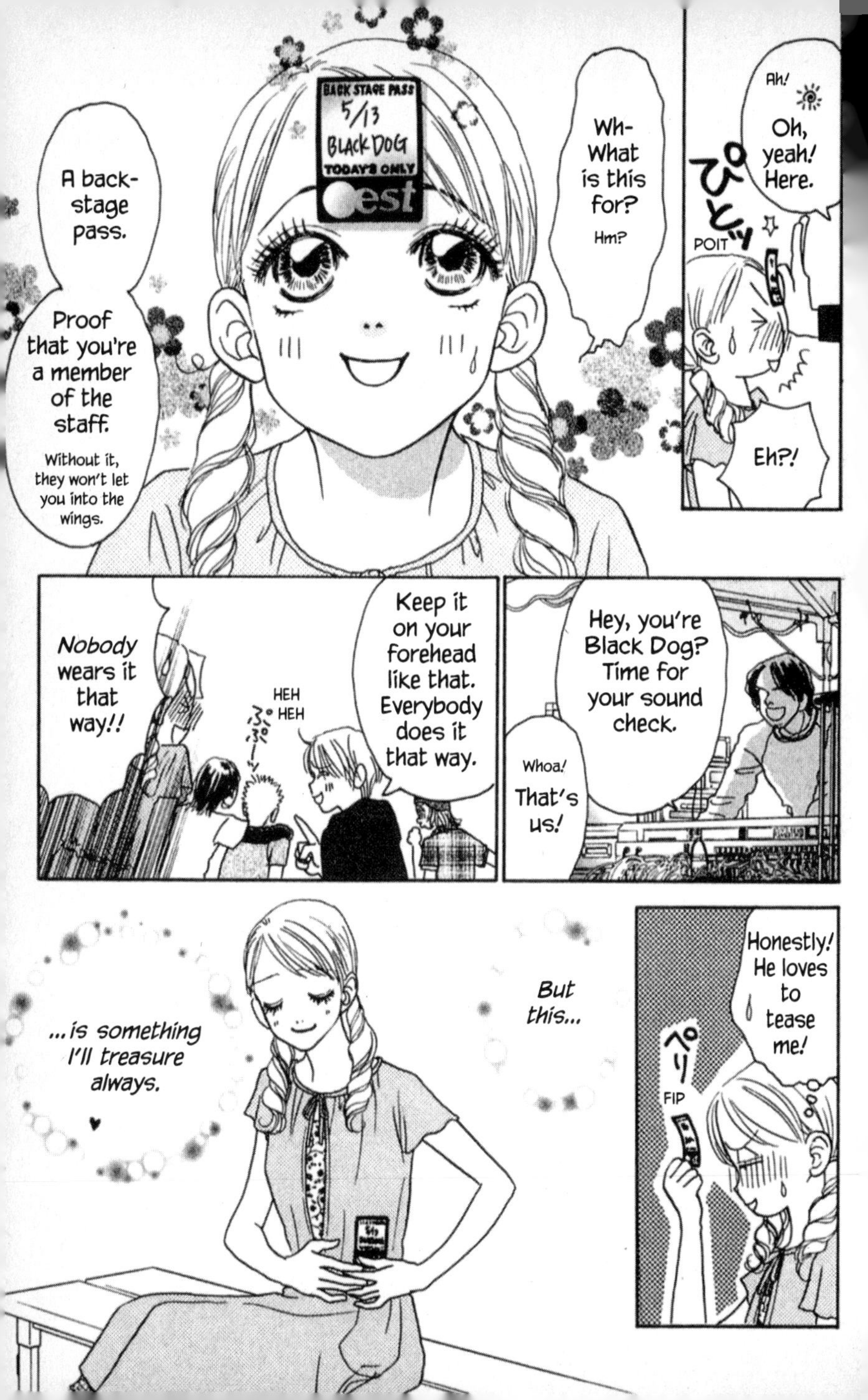
Ah!
Oh, yeah! Here.
ぴとッ
POIT
Eh?!
Wh- What is this for?
Hm?
BACK STAGE PASS 5/13 BLACK DOG TODAY'S ONLY est
A back-stage pass.
Proof that you're a member of the staff.
Without it, they won't let you into the wings.
Hey, you're Black Dog? Time for your sound check.
Whoa! That's us!
Keep it on your forehead like that. Everybody does it that way.
ふっふっ
HEH HEH
Nobody wears it that way!!
Honestly! He loves to tease me!
ぺり
FIP
But this...
...is something I'll treasure always.

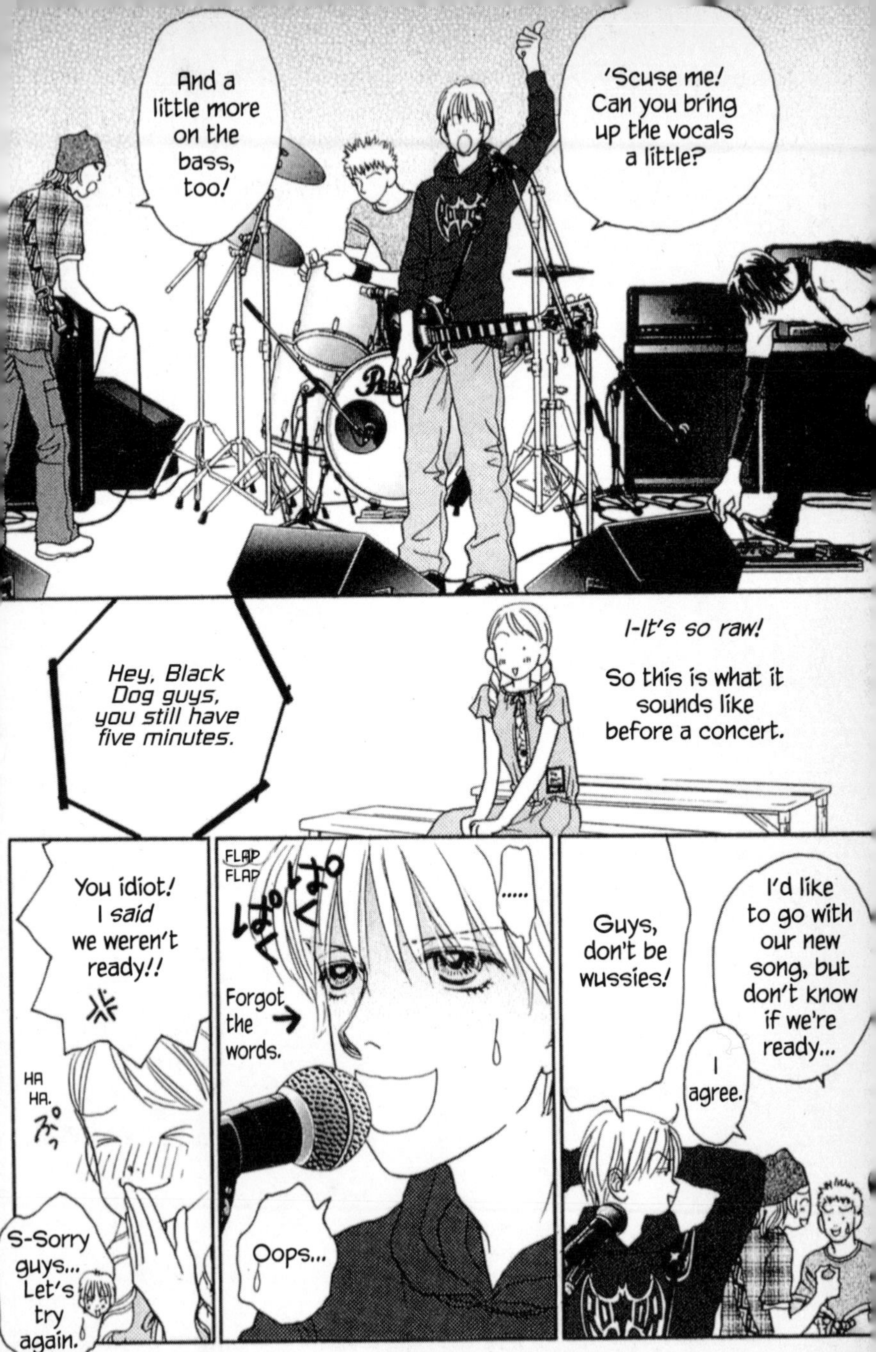
'Scuse me! Can you bring up the vocals a little?
And a little more on the bass, too!
I-It's so raw!
So this is what it sounds like before a concert.
Hey, Black Dog guys, you still have five minutes.
I'd like to go with our new song, but don't know if we're ready...
I agree.
Guys, don't be wussies!
.....
FLAP FLAP
Forgot the words.
Oops...
You idiot! I *said* we weren't ready!!
HA HA.
S-Sorry guys... Let's try again.

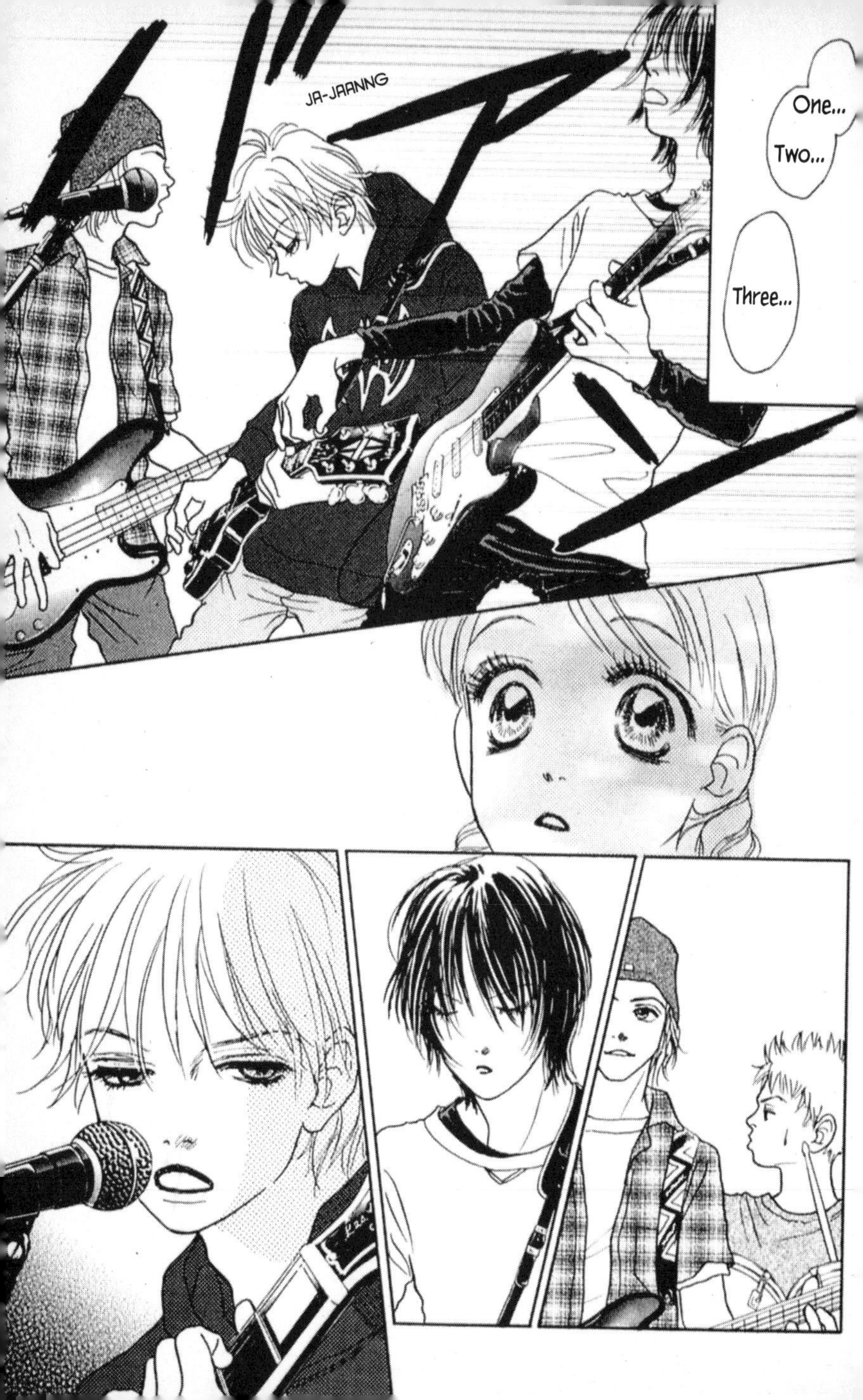
One...
Two...
Three...
JA-JAANNG

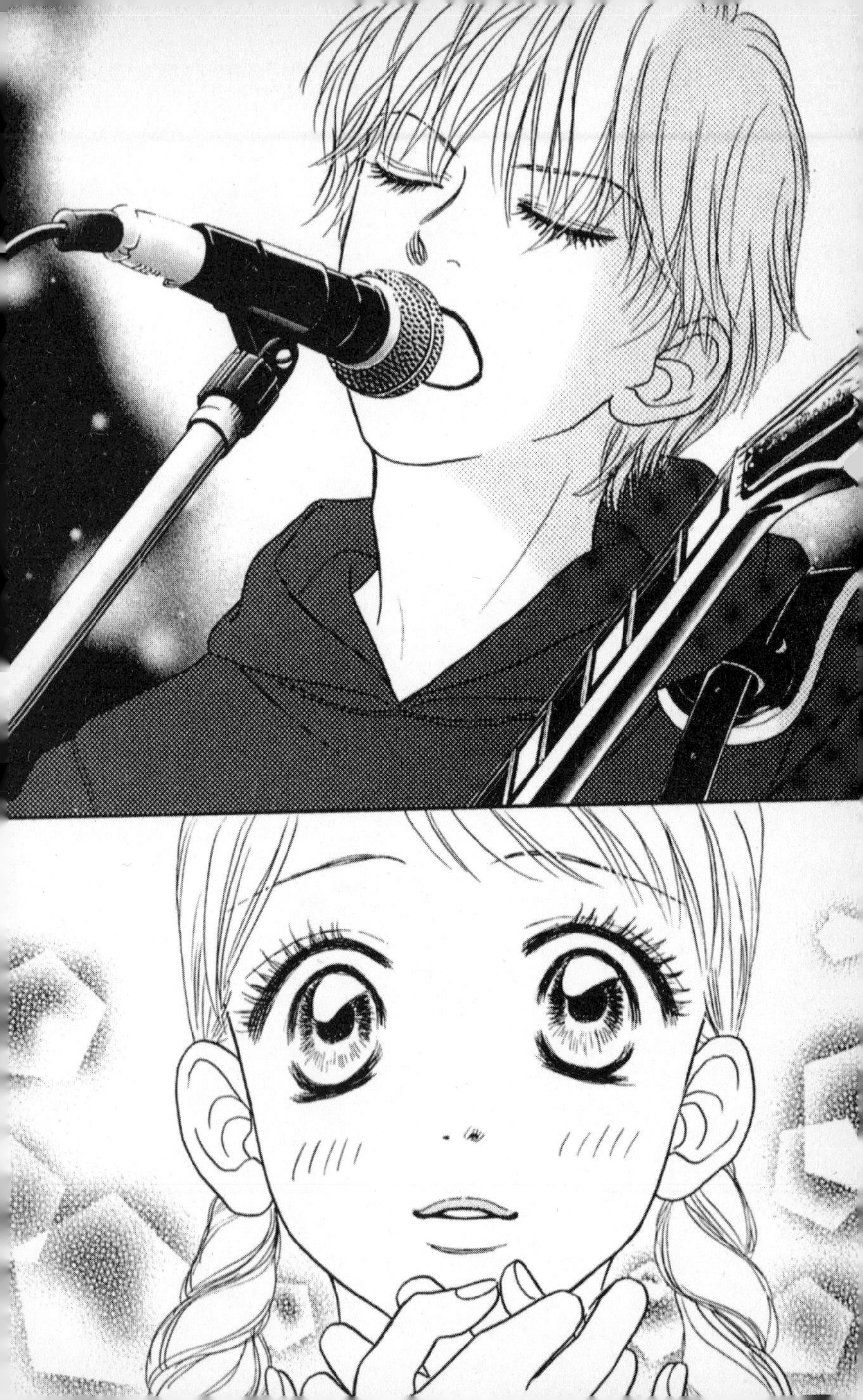

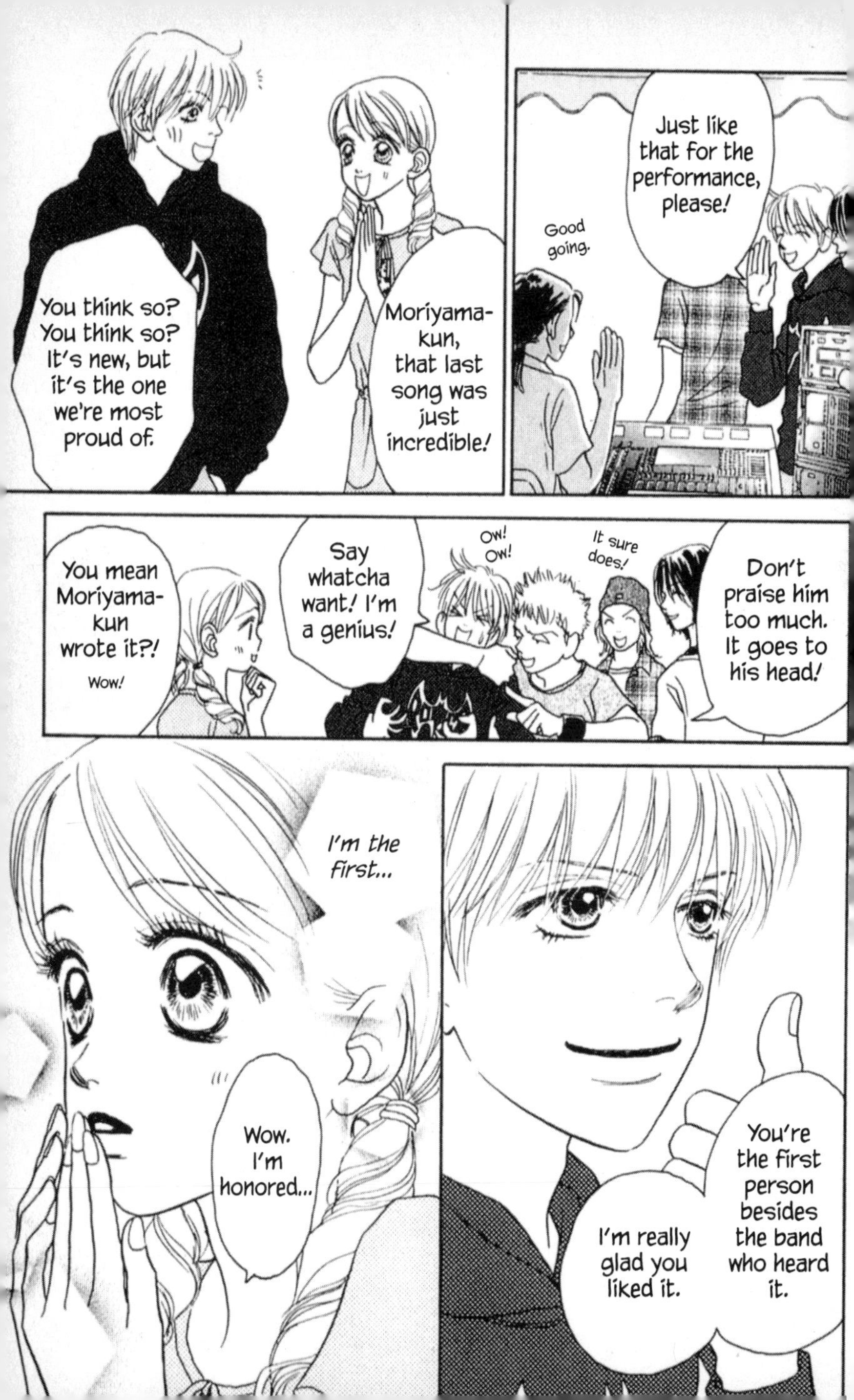
Good going.
Just like that for the performance, please!
Moriyama-kun, that last song was just incredible!
You think so? You think so? It's new, but it's the one we're most proud of.
Don't praise him too much. It goes to his head!
It sure does!
Ow! Ow!
Say whatcha want! I'm a genius!
You mean Moriyama-kun wrote it?!
Wow!
You're the first person besides the band who heard it.
I'm really glad you liked it.
Wow. I'm honored...
I'm the first...

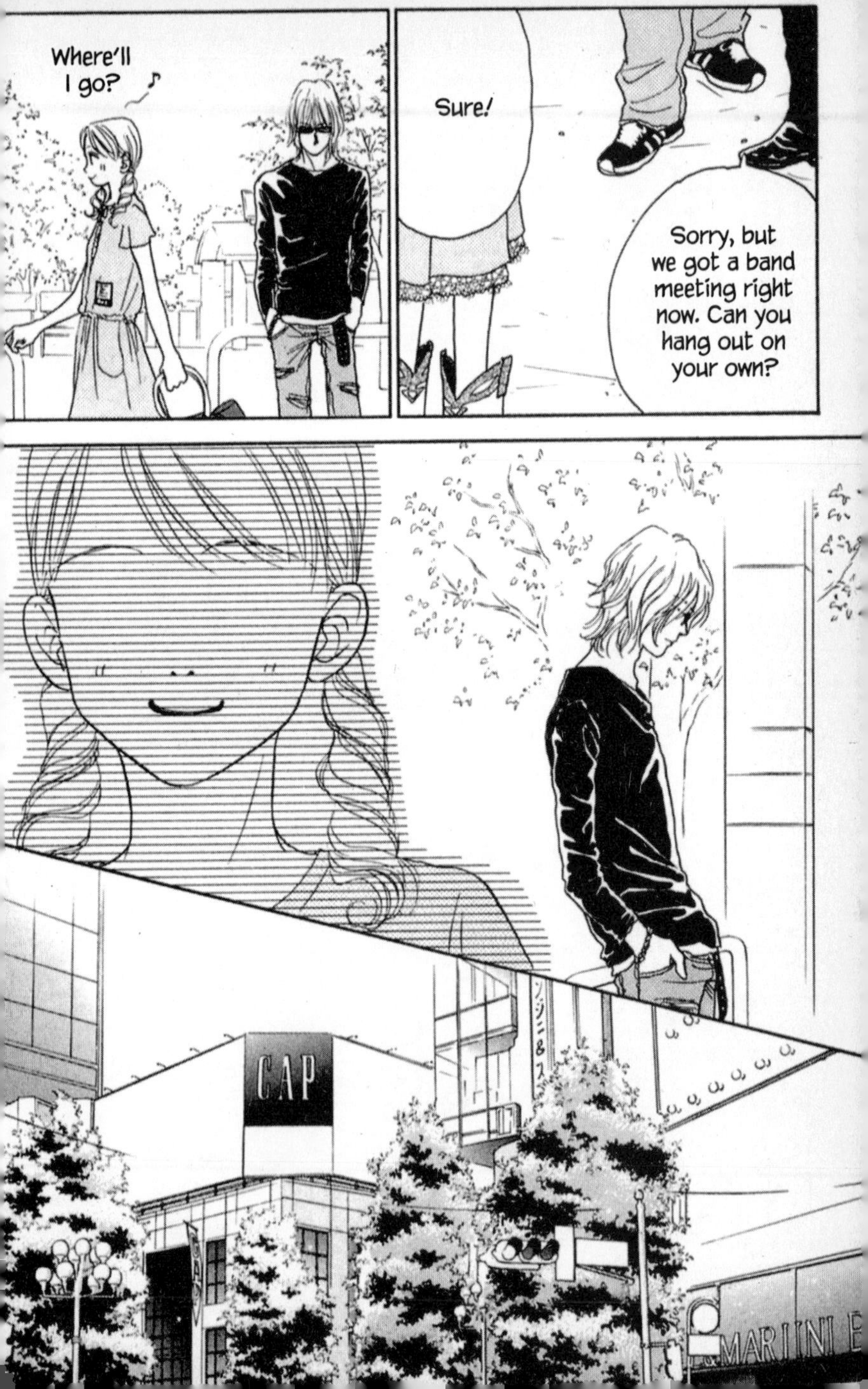
Sorry, but we got a band meeting right now. Can you hang out on your own?
Sure!
Where'll I go? ♪
CAP

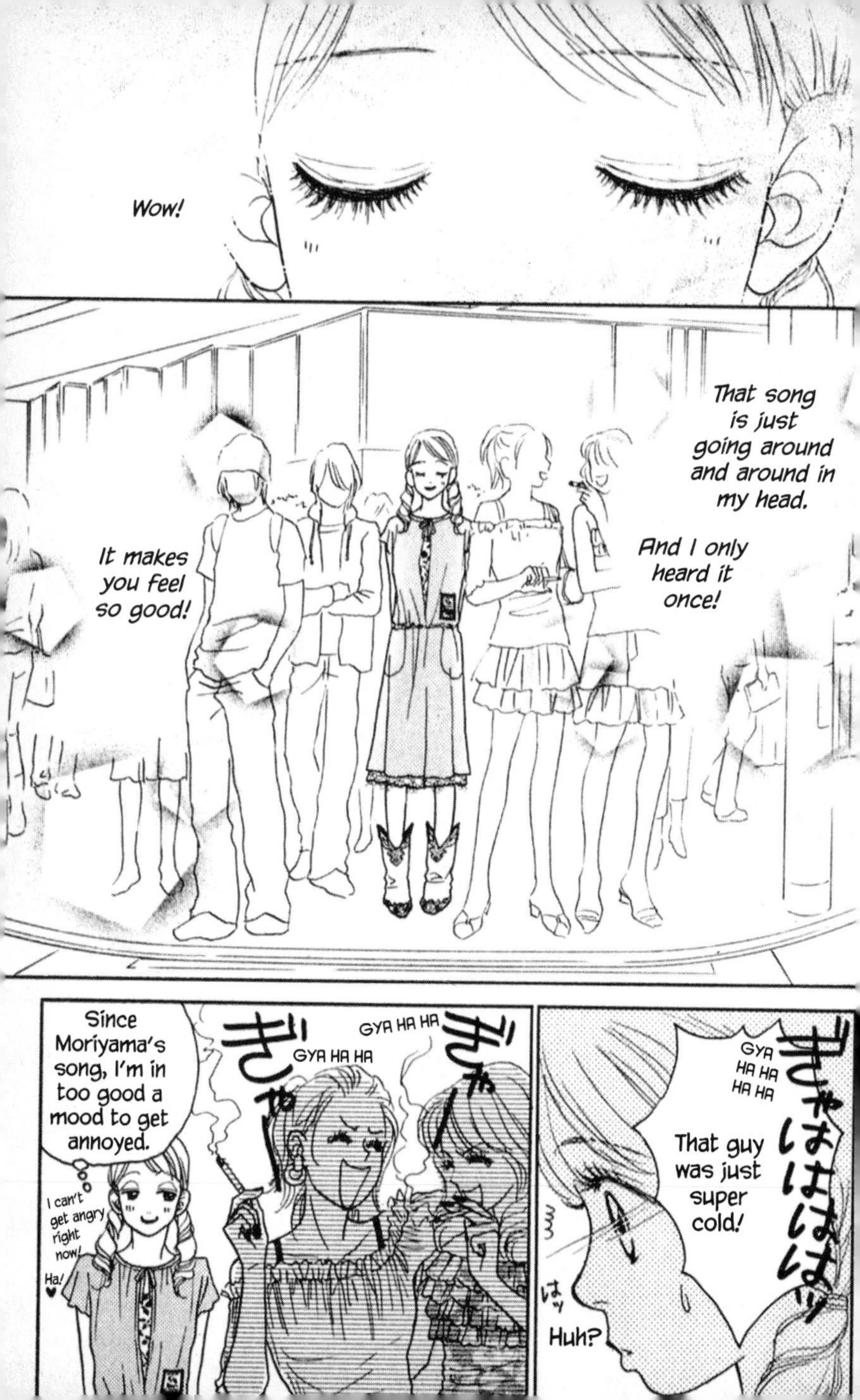
Wow!
That song is just going around and around in my head.
And I only heard it once!
It makes you feel so good!
GYA HA HA HA HA
That guy was just super cold!
Huh?
GYA HA HA
GYA HA HA
Since Moriyama's song, I'm in too good a mood to get annoyed.
I can't get angry right now!
Ha!

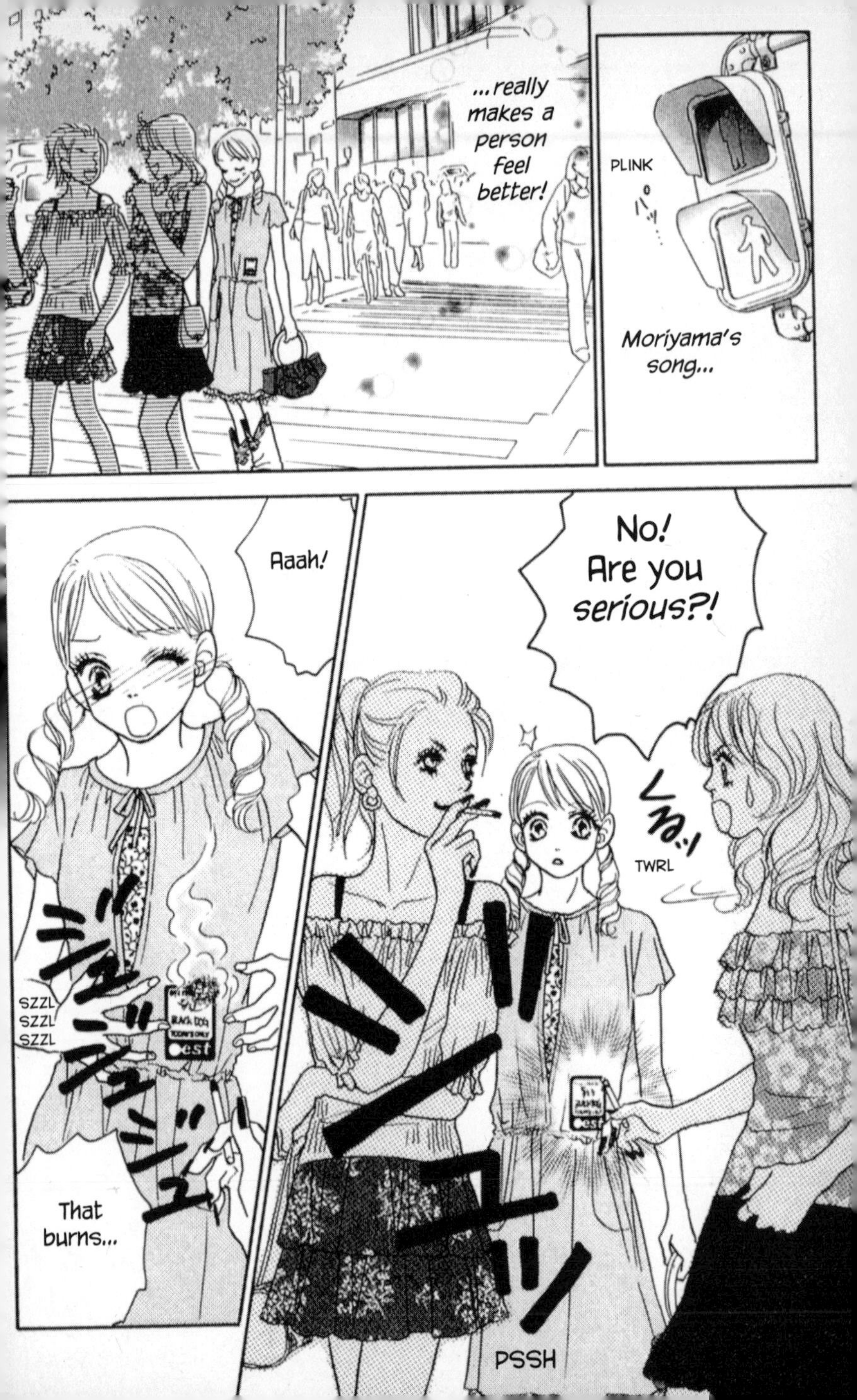
PLINK
Moriyama's song...
...really makes a person feel better!
No! Are you serious?!
TWRL
PSSH
Aaah!
SZZL SZZL SZZL
That burns...

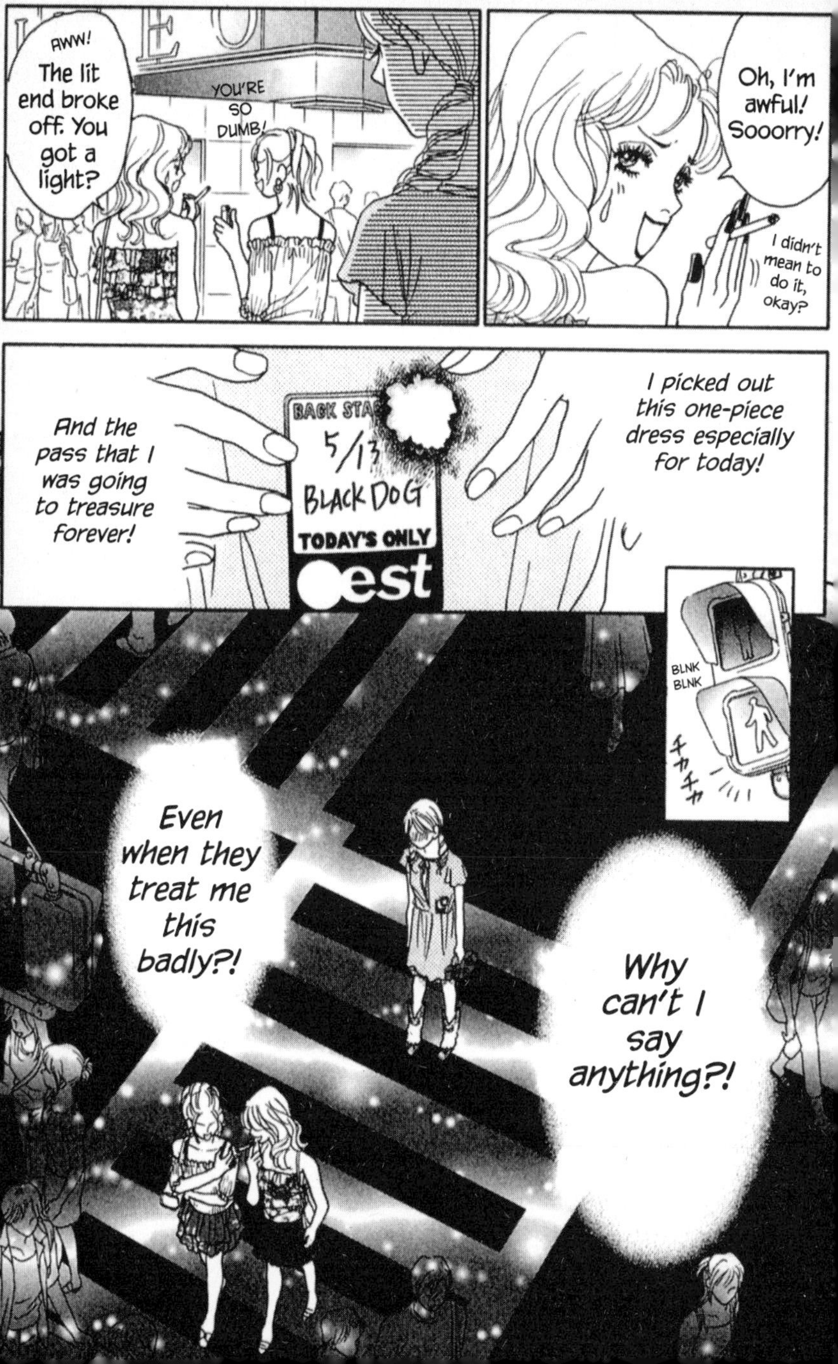
AWW!
The lit end broke off. You got a light?
YOU'RE SO DUMB!
Oh, I'm awful! Sooorry!
I didn't mean to do it, okay?
And the pass that I was going to treasure forever!
BACK STA
5/13
BLACK DOG
TODAY'S ONLY
est
I picked out this one-piece dress especially for today!
BLNK BLNK
チカチカ
Even when they treat me this badly?!
Why can't I say anything?!

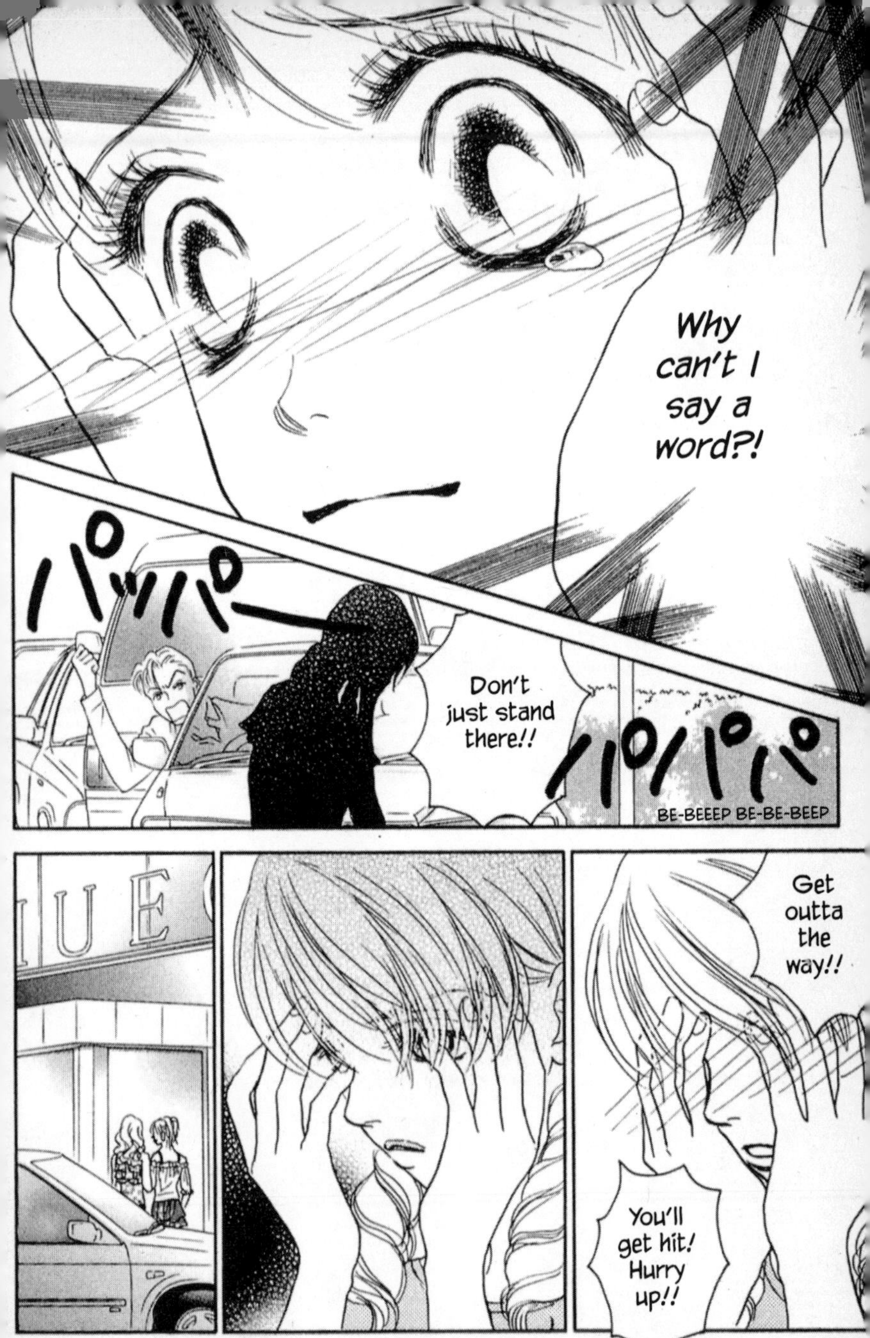
Why can't I say a word?!
パパパ
BE-BEEEP BE-BE-BEEP
Don't just stand there!!
パッパ
Get outta the way!!
You'll get hit! Hurry up!!

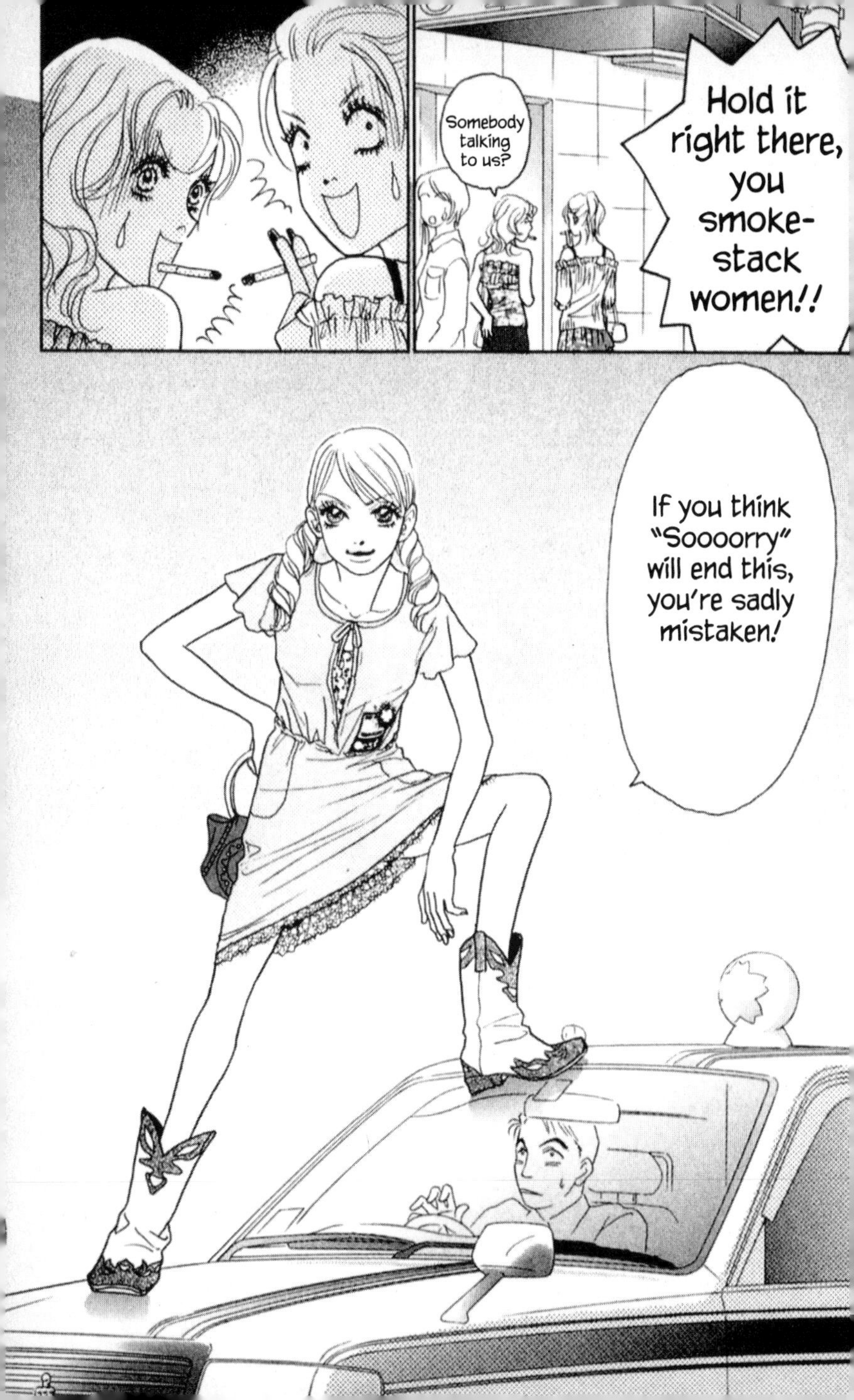
Somebody talking to us?
Hold it right there, you smoke-stack women!!
If you think "Soooorry" will end this, you're sadly mistaken!

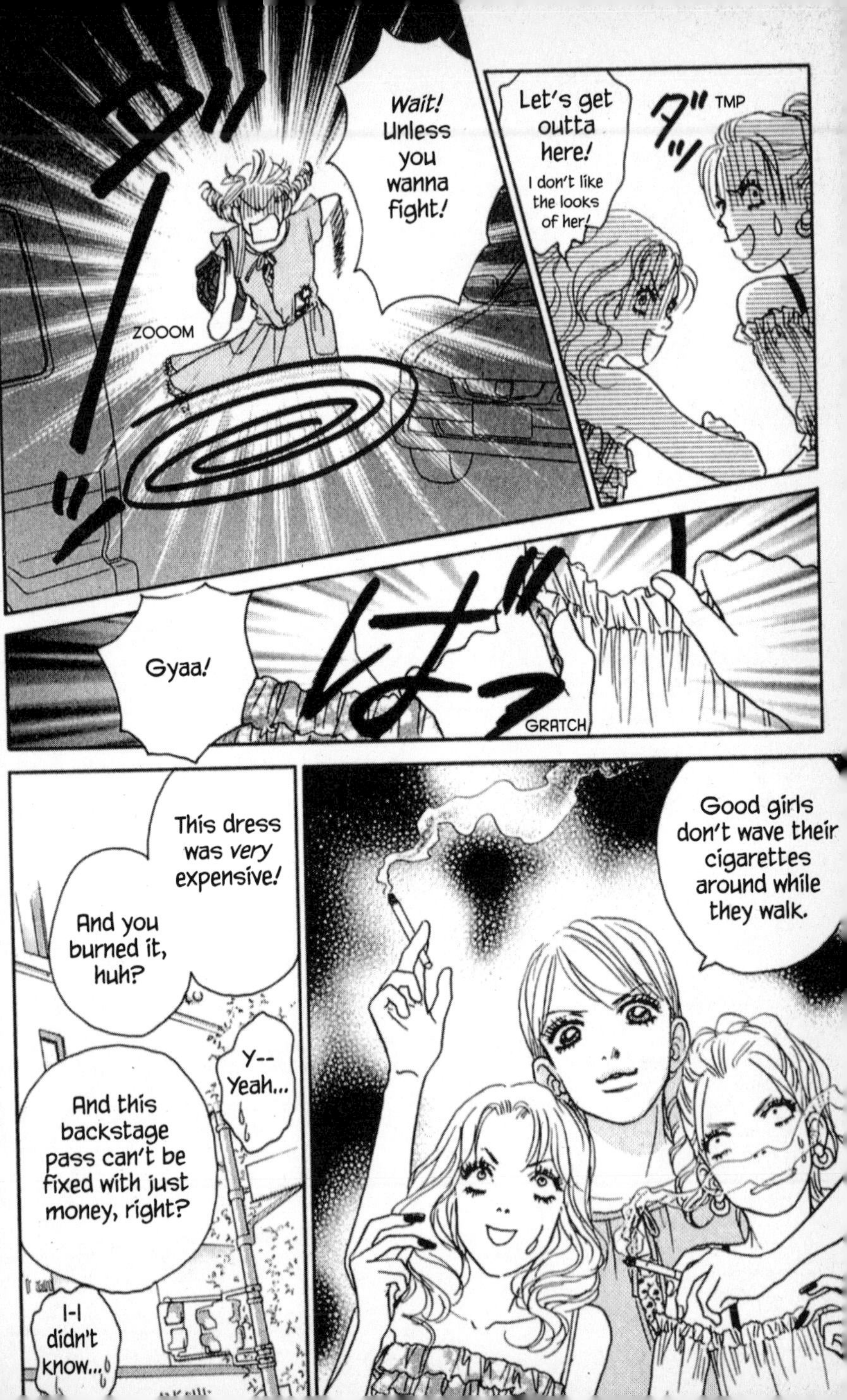

Let's get outta here!
I don't like the looks of her!
タッ
TMP
Wait! Unless you wanna fight!
ZOOOM
はっ
GRATCH
Gyaa!
Good girls don't wave their cigarettes around while they walk.
This dress was *very* expensive!
And you burned it, huh?
Y-- Yeah...
And this backstage pass can't be fixed with just money, right?
I-I didn't know...

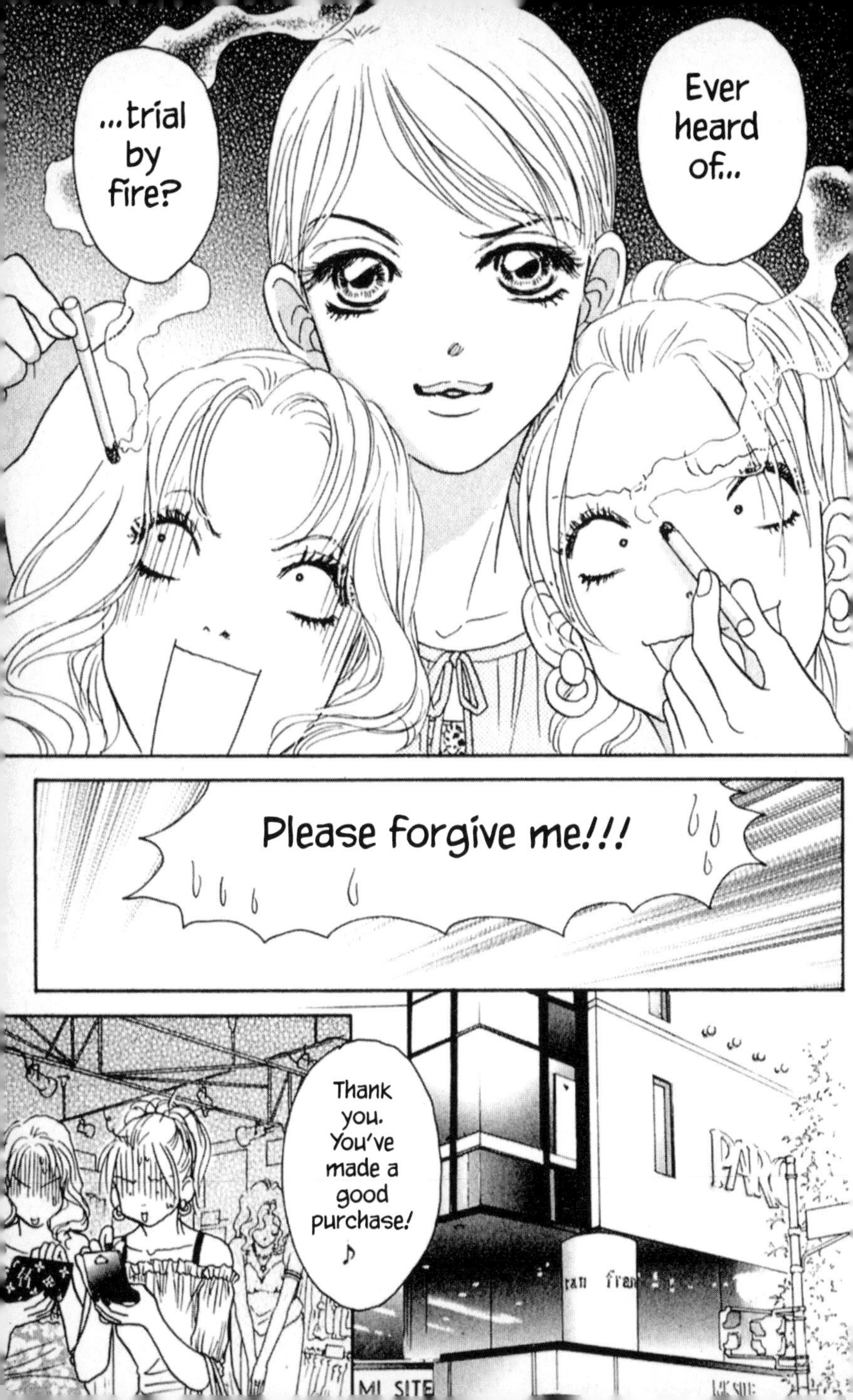
Ever heard of...
...trial by fire?
Please forgive me!!!
Thank you. You've made a good purchase! ♪

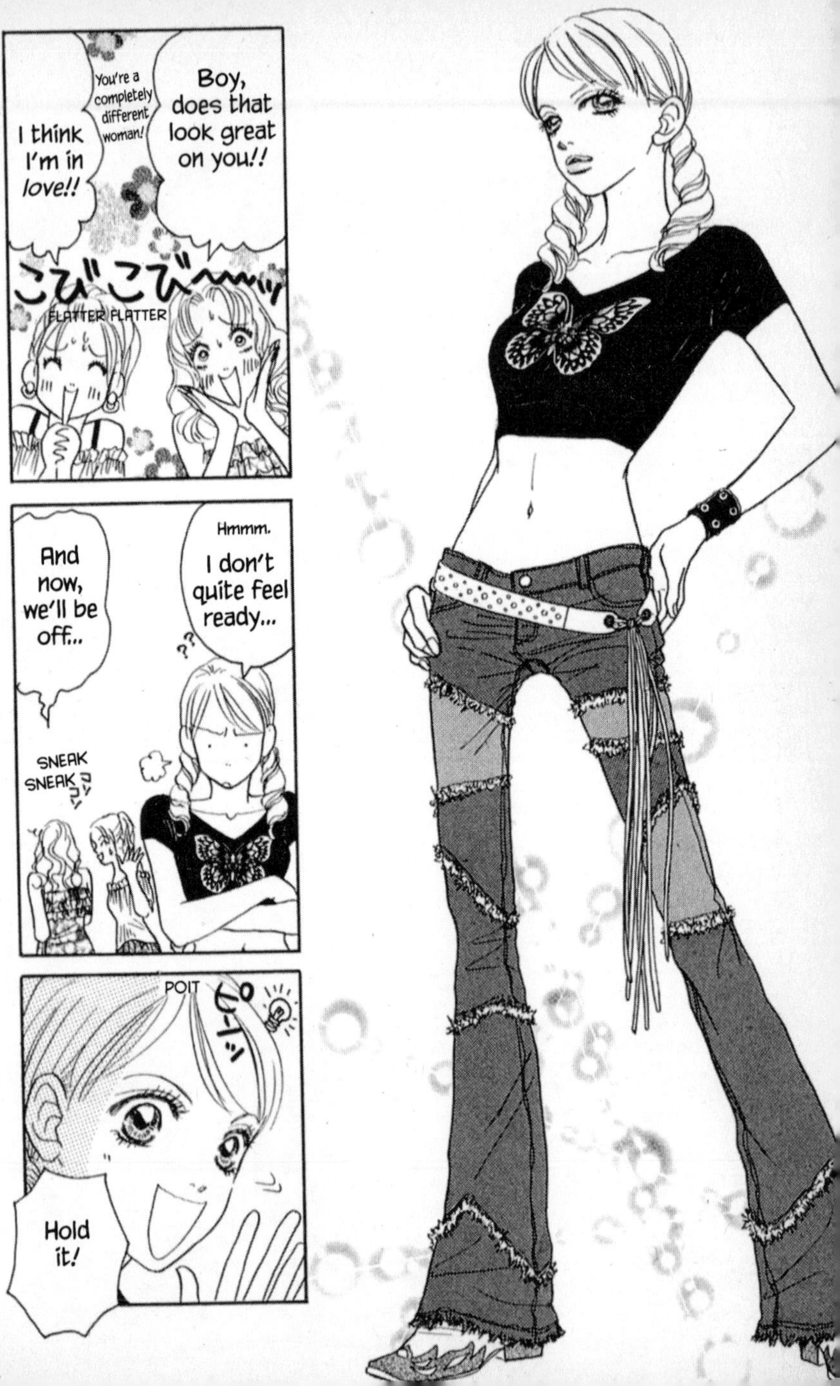
Boy, does that look great on you!!
You're a completely different woman!
I think I'm in love!!
こびこび〜〜ッ
FLATTER FLATTER
Hmmm.
I don't quite feel ready...
And now, we'll be off...
SNEAK SNEAK
POIT
Hold it!

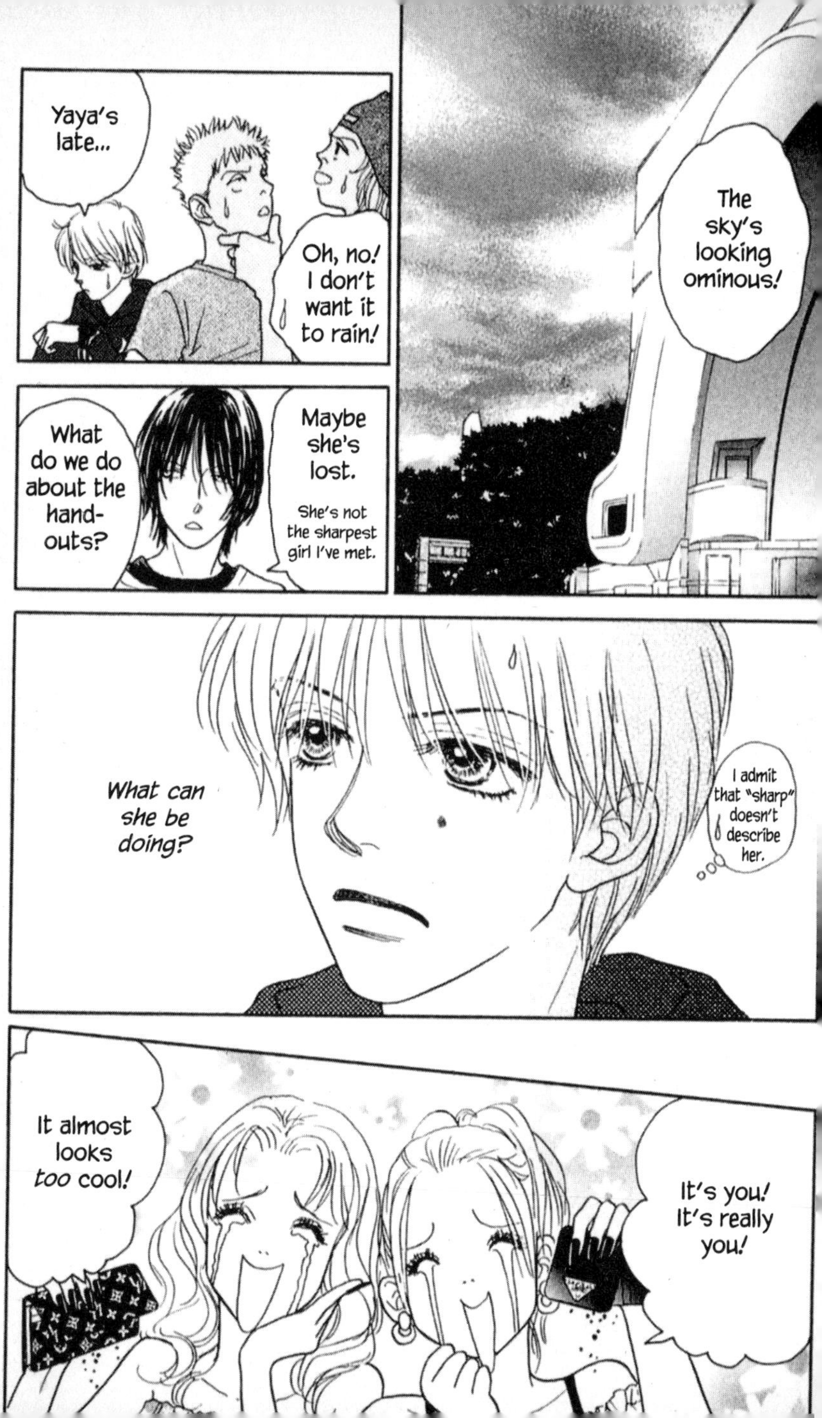

The sky's looking ominous!
Oh, no! I don't want it to rain!
Yaya's late...
Maybe she's lost.
She's not the sharpest girl I've met.
What do we do about the hand-outs?
I admit that "sharp" doesn't describe her.
What can she be doing?
It's you! It's really you!
It almost looks *too* cool!

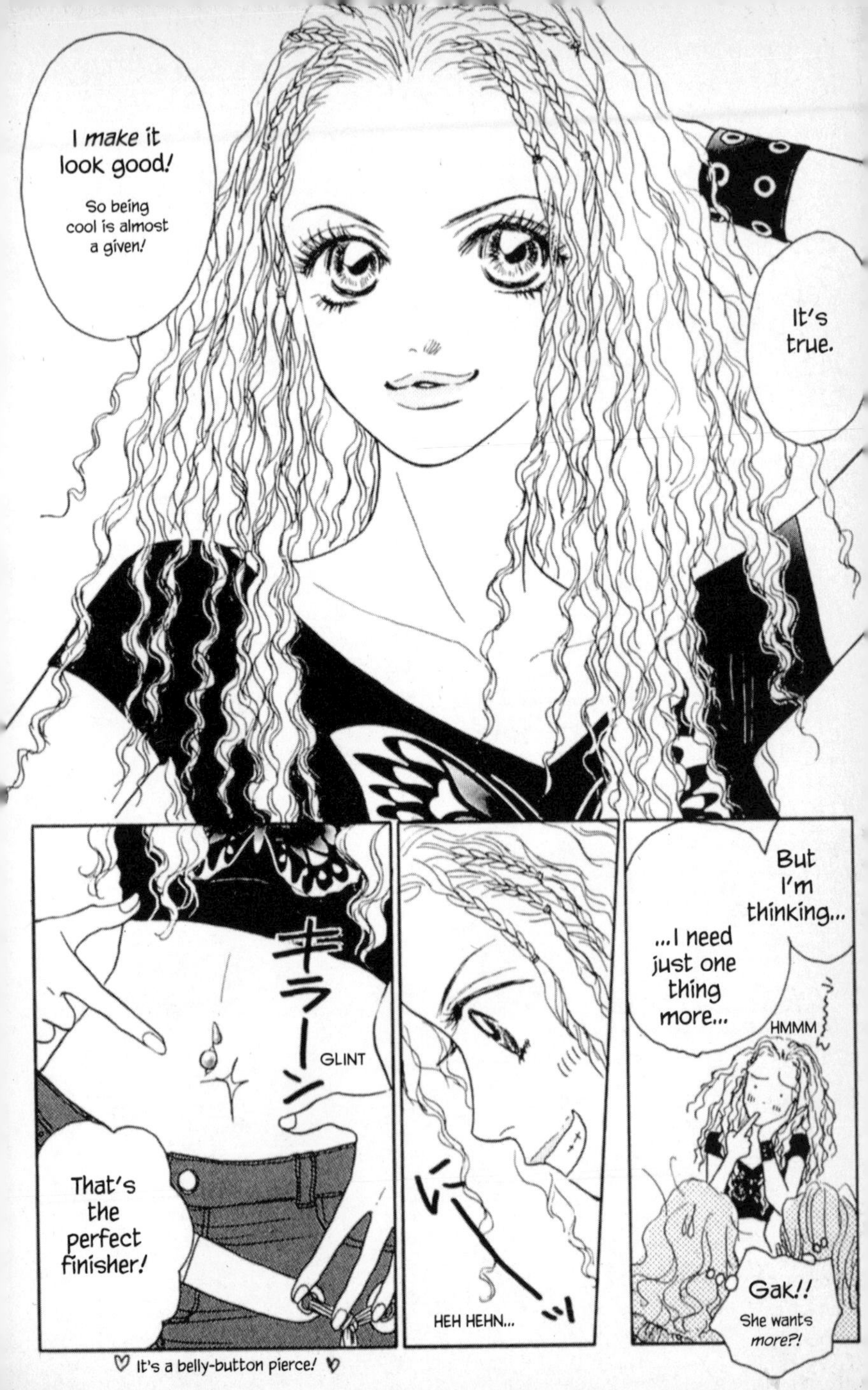
I *make* it look good!
So being cool is almost a given!
It's true.
But I'm thinking...
...I need just one thing more...
HMMM
Gak!!
She wants *more?!*
HEH HEHN...
GLINT
キラーン
That's the perfect finisher!

♡ It's a belly-button pierce! ♡

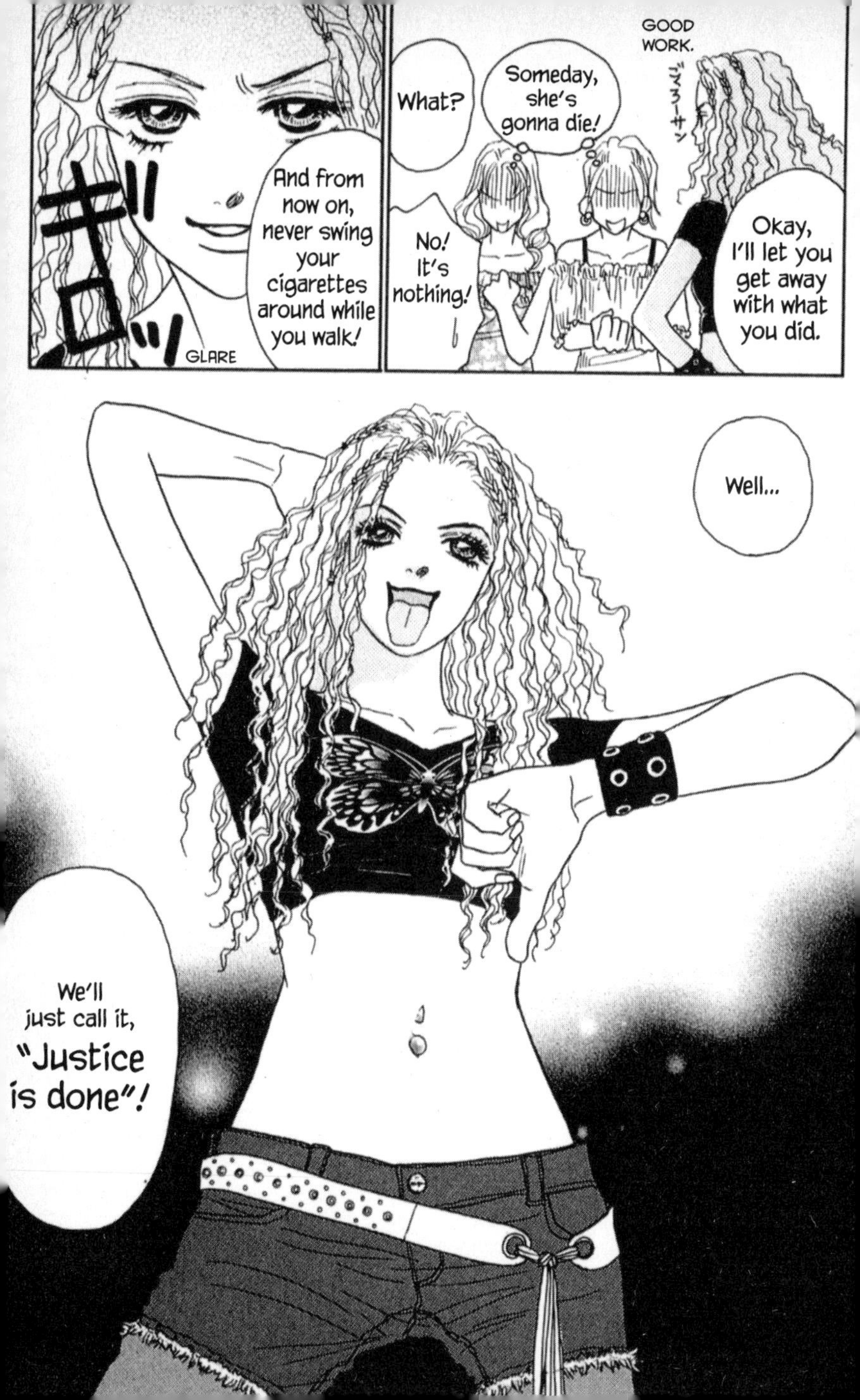
GOOD WORK.
Okay, I'll let you get away with what you did.
What?
Someday, she's gonna die!
No! It's nothing!
And from now on, never swing your cigarettes around while you walk!
GLARE
Well...
We'll just call it, "Justice is done"!

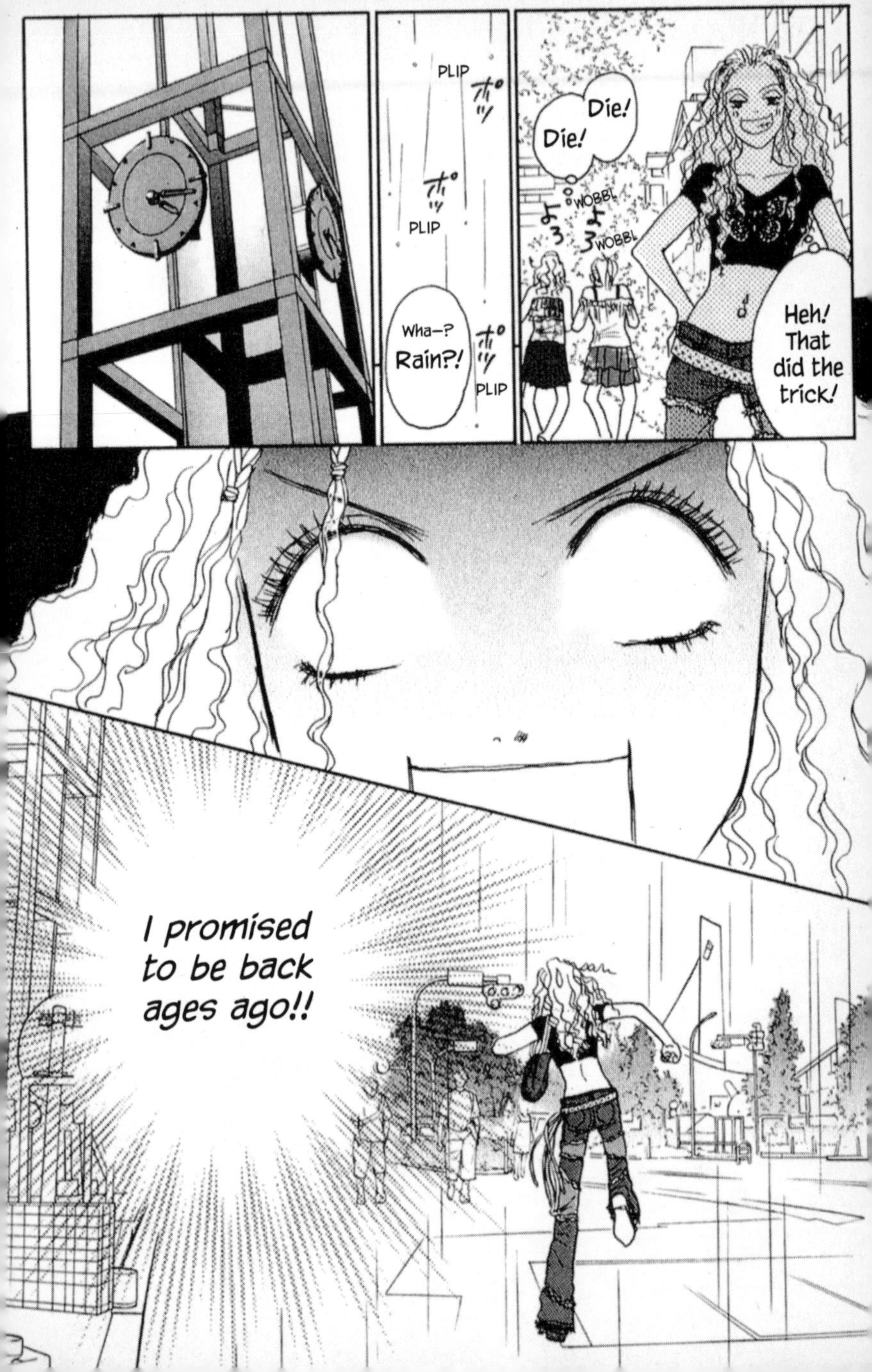
Die!
Die!
WOBBL
WOBBL
Heh! That did the trick!
PLIP
PLIP
Wha–? Rain?!
PLIP
I promised to be back ages ago!!

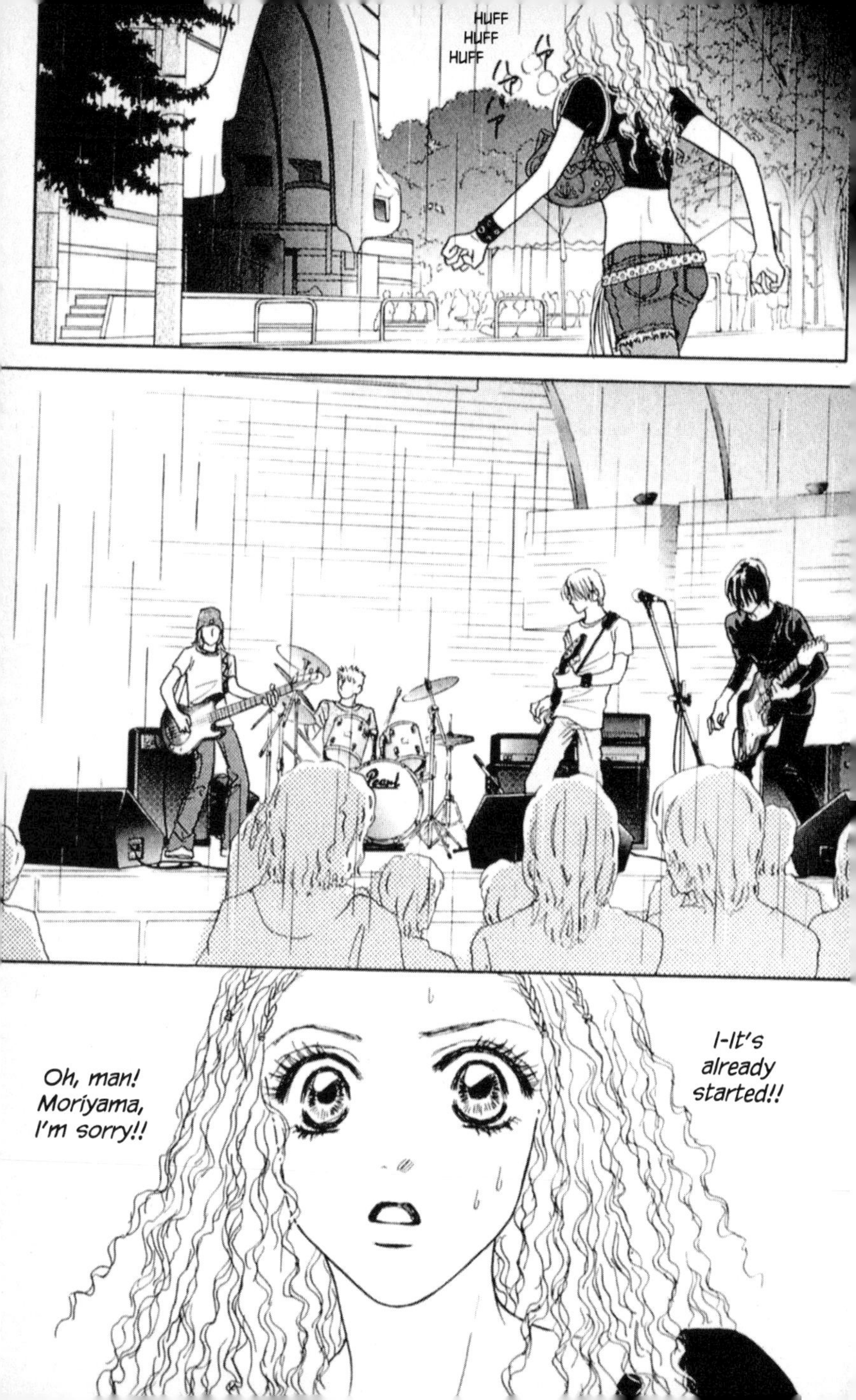
HUFF
HUFF
HUFF
I-It's already started!!
Oh, man! Moriyama, I'm sorry!!

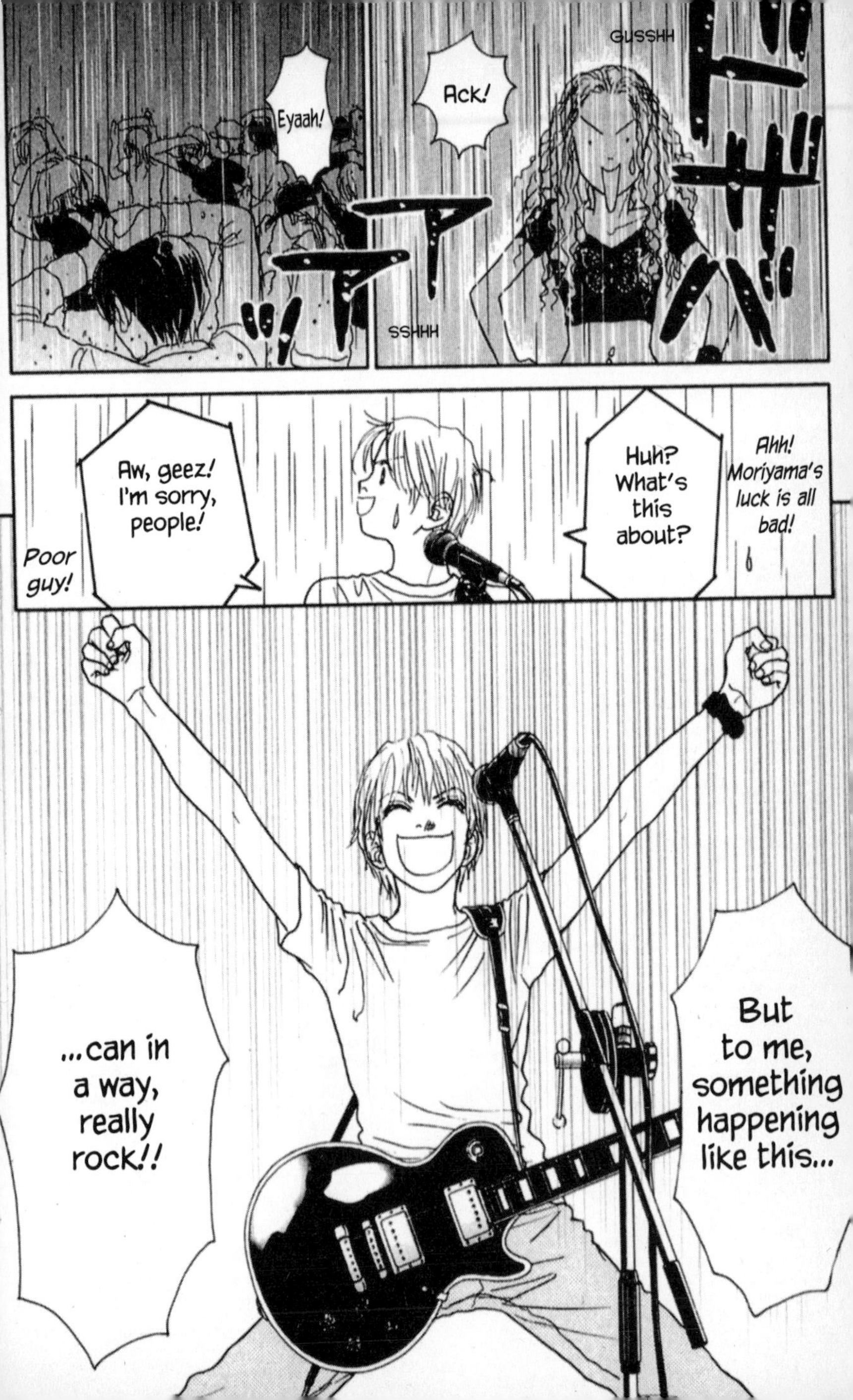
GUSSHH
Ack!
SSHHH
Eyaah!
Ahh! Moriyama's luck is all bad!
Huh? What's this about?
Aw, geez! I'm sorry, people!
Poor guy!
But to me, something happening like this...
...can in a way, really rock!!

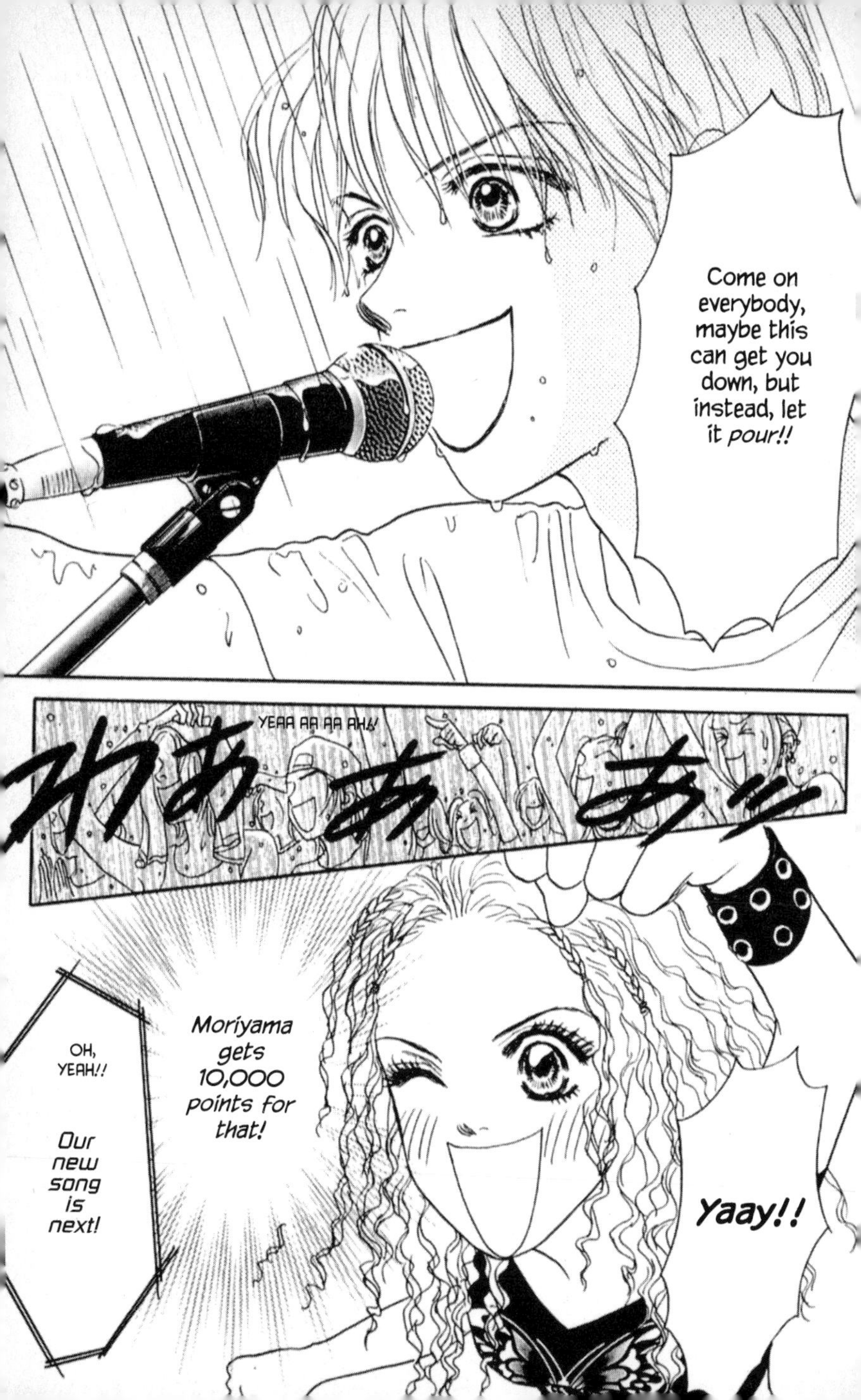
Come on everybody, maybe this can get you down, but instead, let it *pour!!*
YEAA AA AA AH!
わあああッ
Yaay!!
Moriyama gets 10,000 points for that!
OH, YEAH!!
Our new song is next!

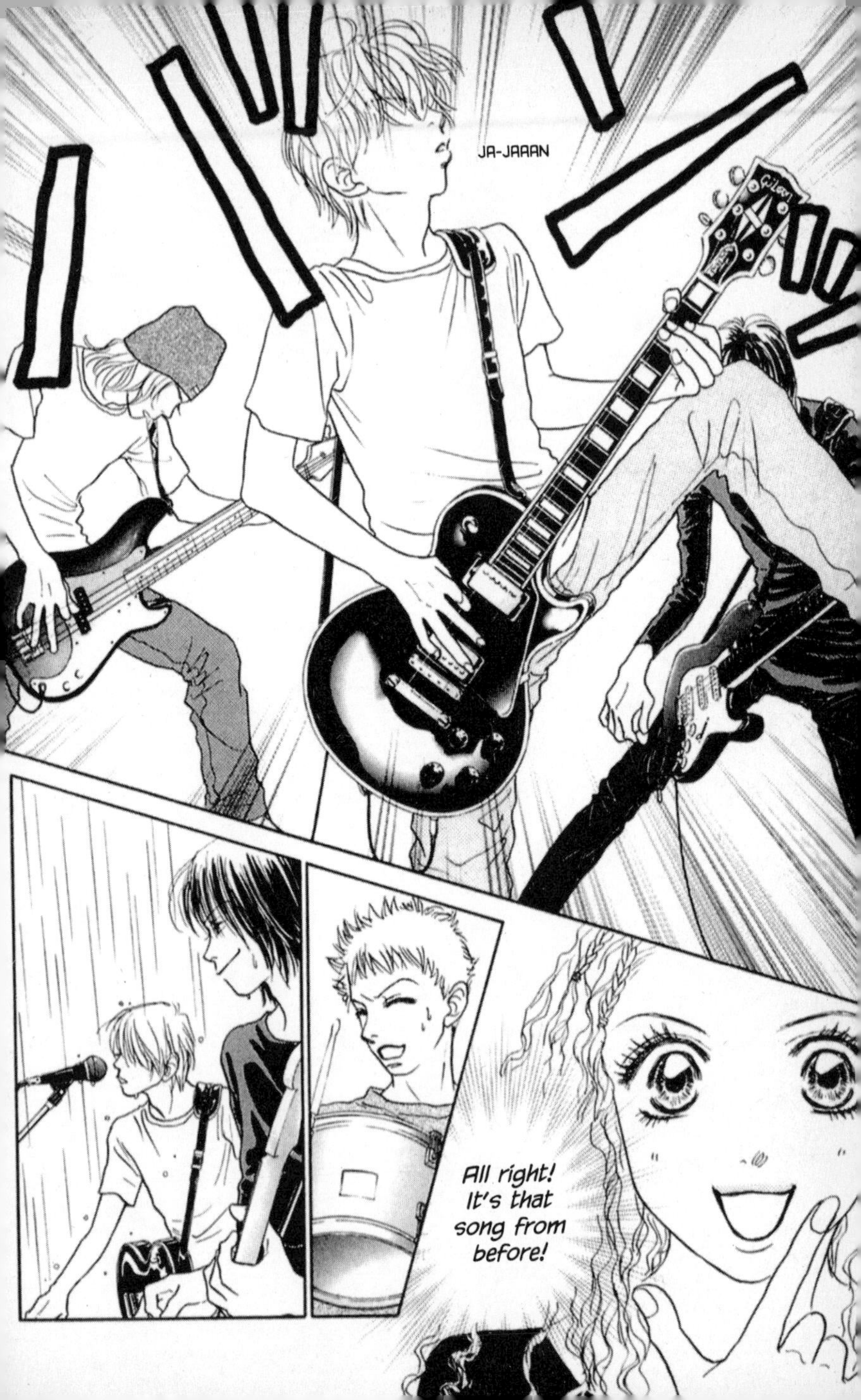
JA-JAAAN
All right! It's that song from before!

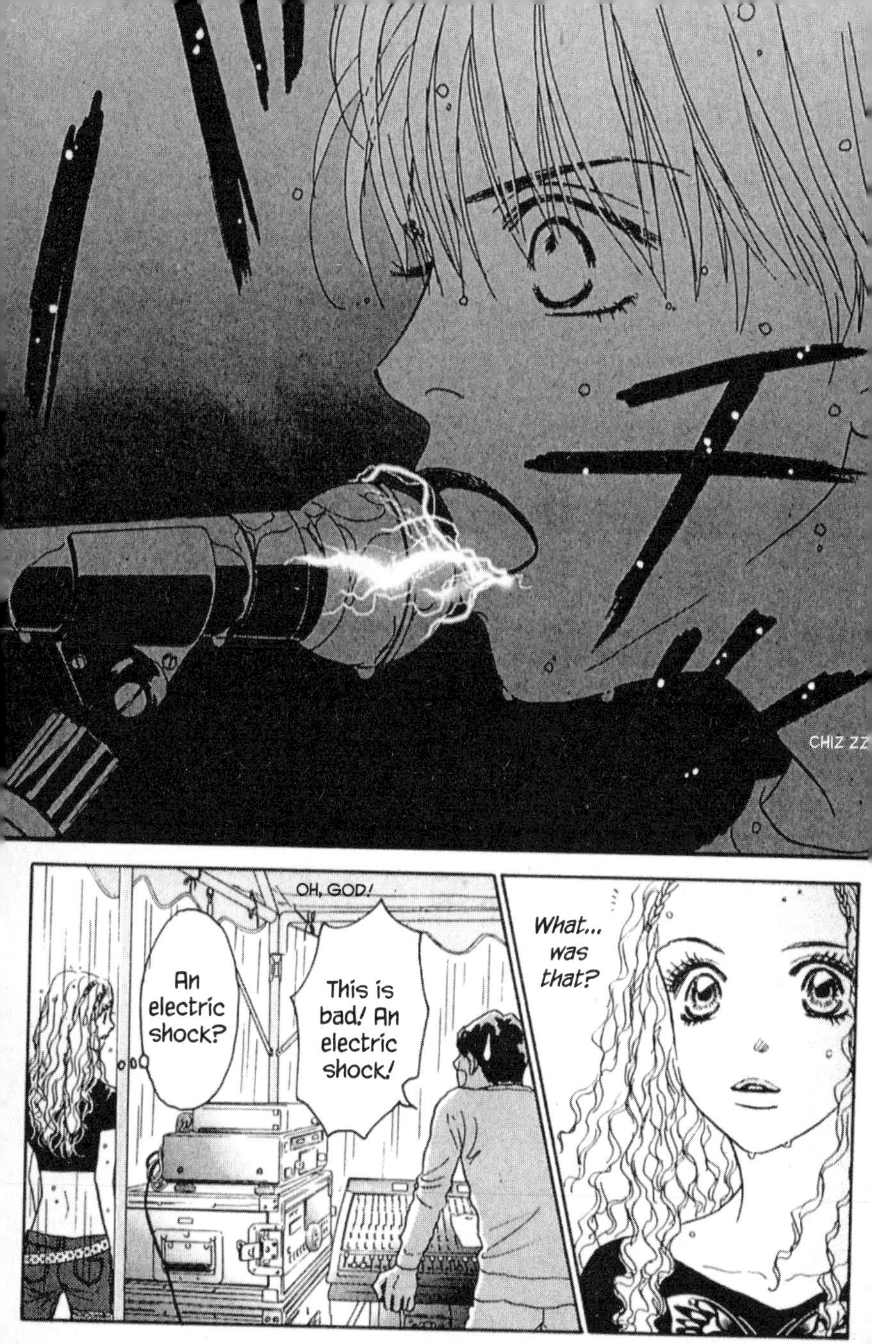
CHIZ ZZ
What... was that?
OH, GOD!
This is bad! An electric shock!
An electric shock?

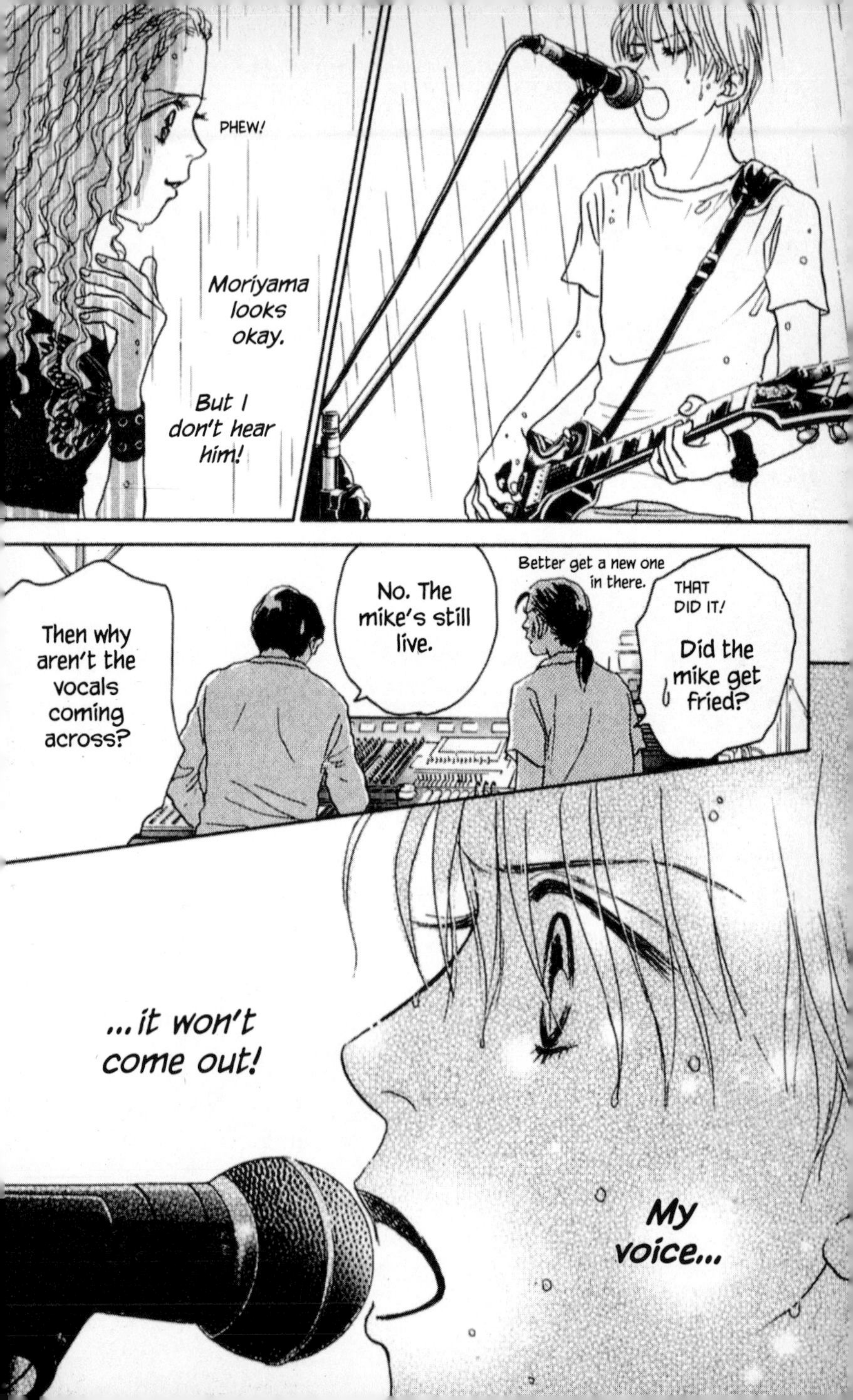
PHEW!
Moriyama looks okay.
But I don't hear him!
THAT DID IT!
Did the mike get fried?
Better get a new one in there.
No. The mike's still live.
Then why aren't the vocals coming across?
My voice...
...it won't come out!

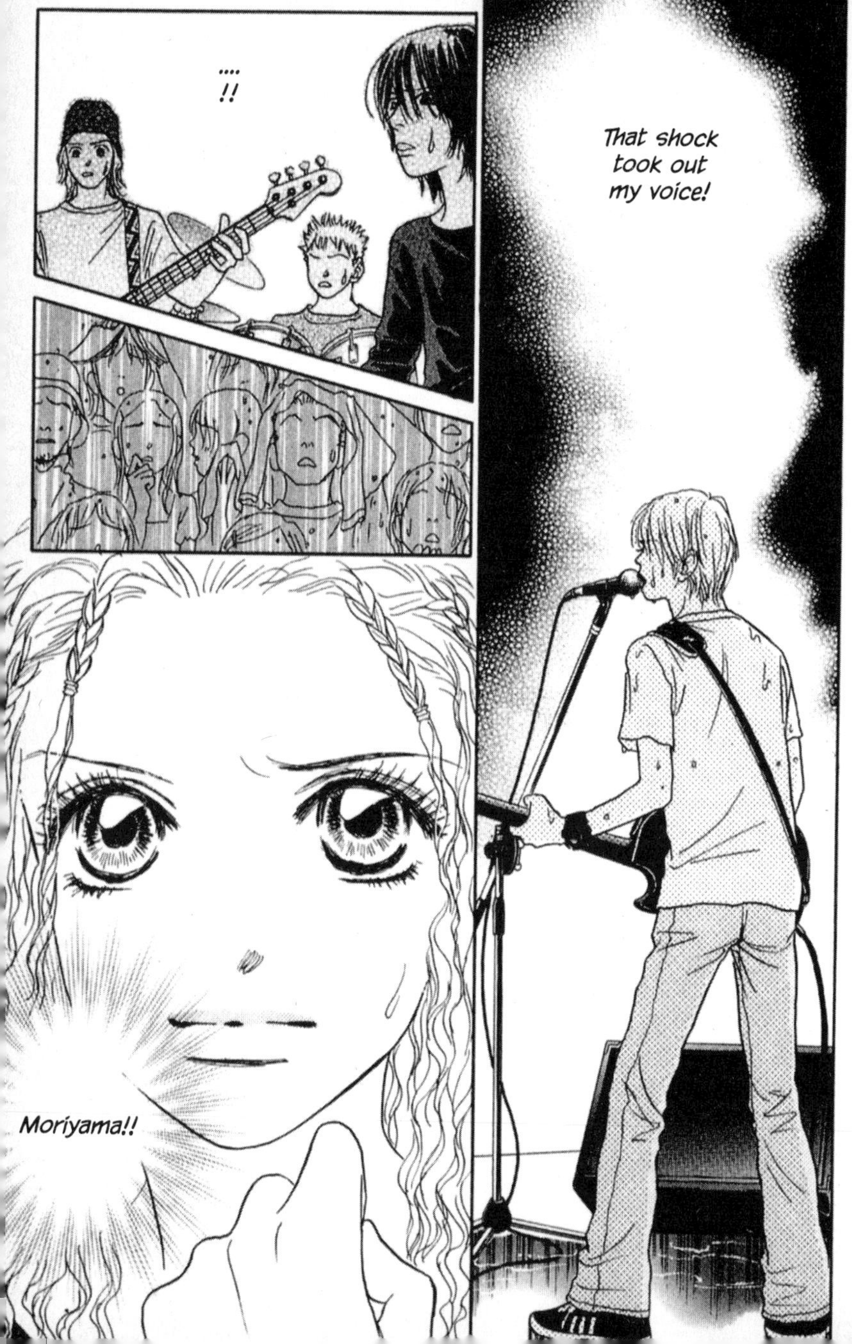
That shock took out my voice!
....!!
Moriyama!!

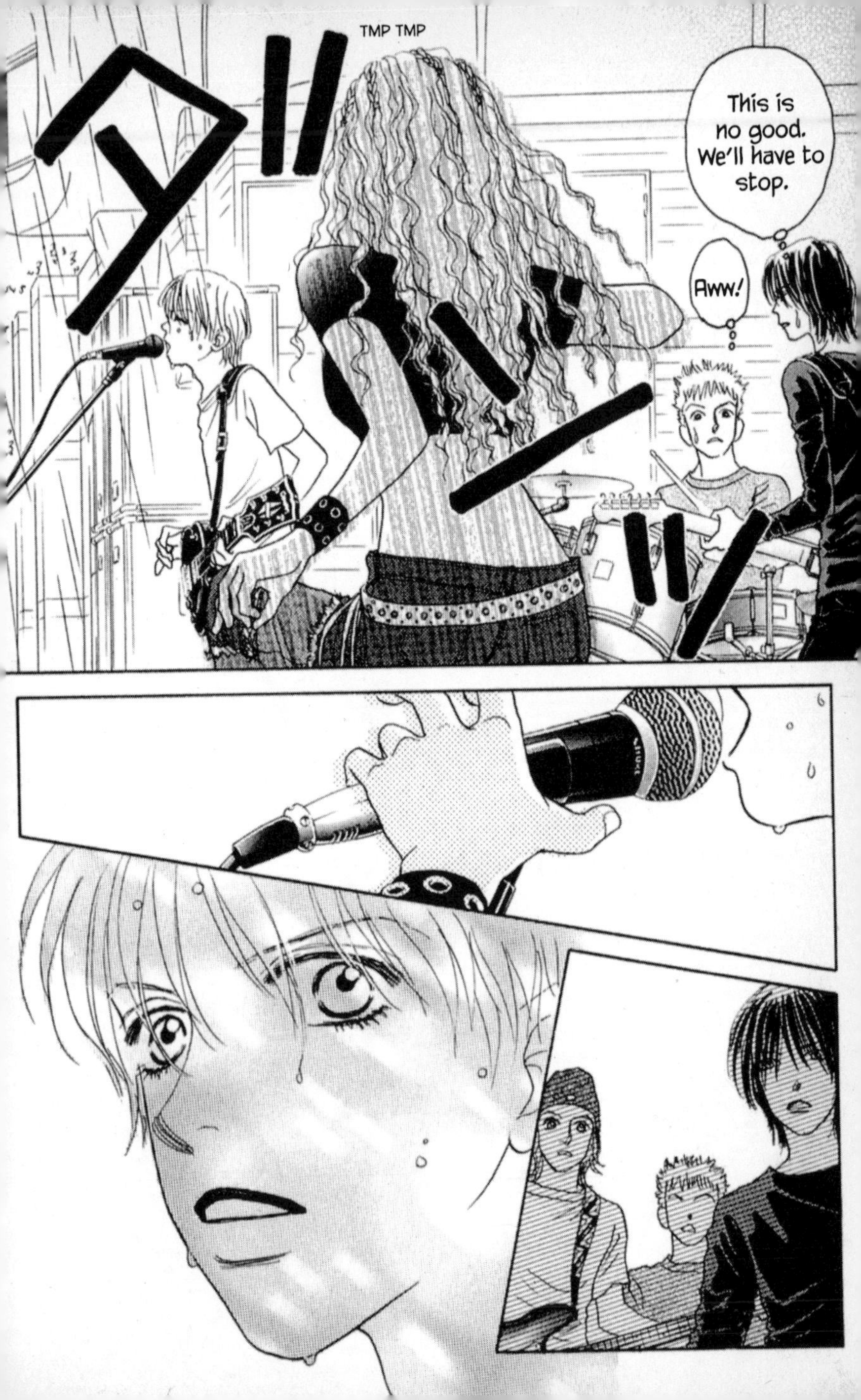
TMP TMP
This is no good. We'll have to stop.
Aww!

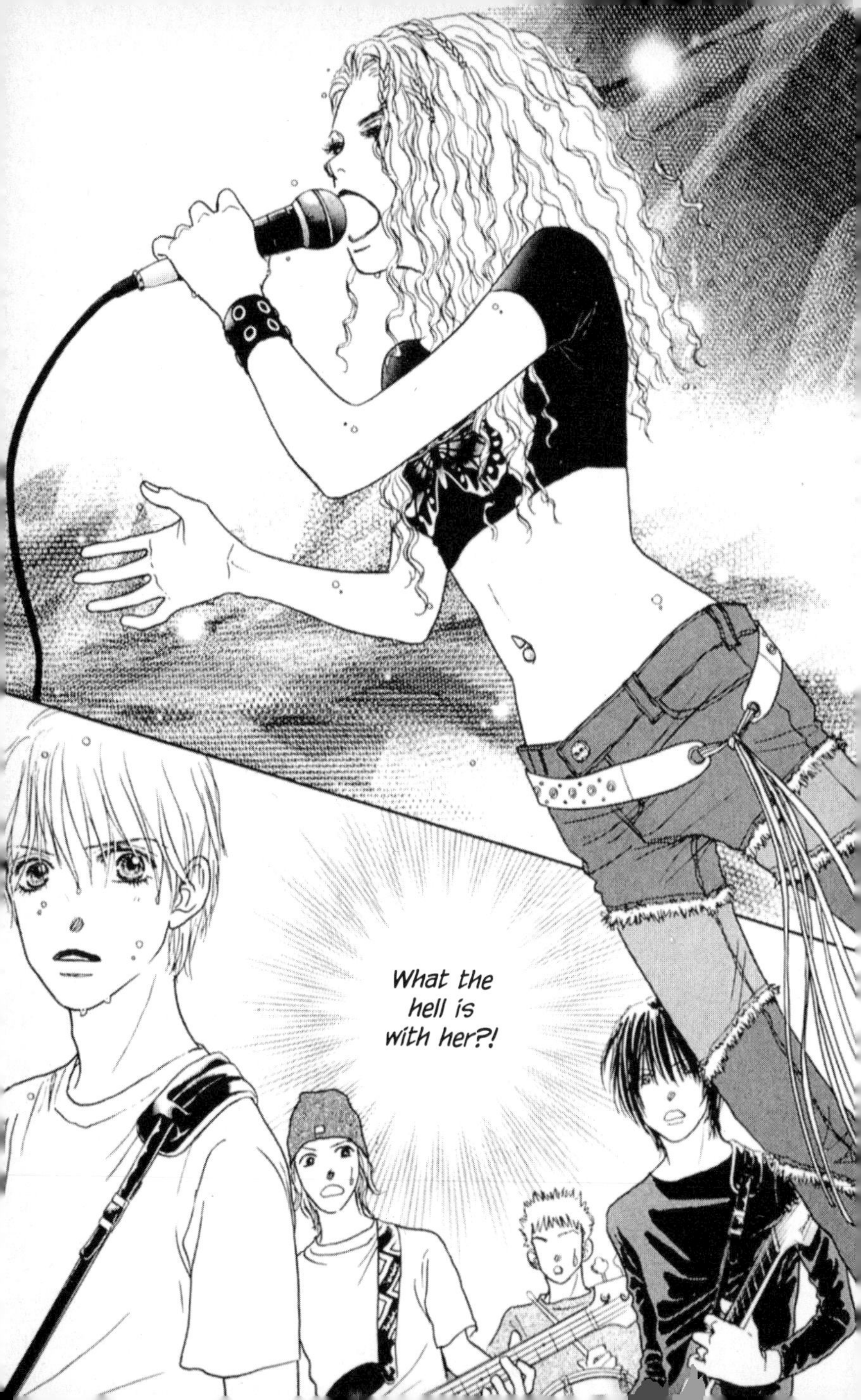
What the hell is with her?!

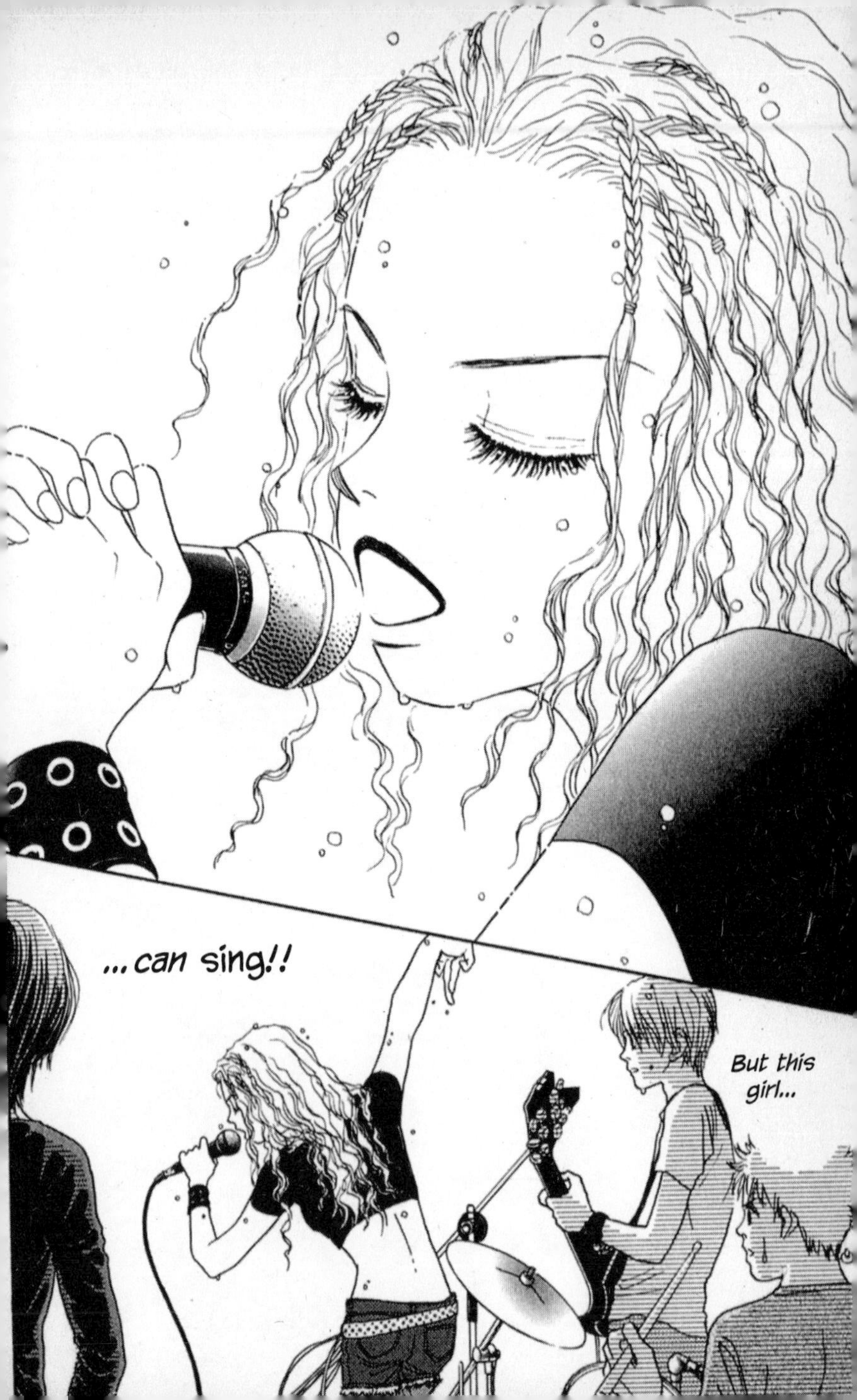
But this girl...
...can sing!!

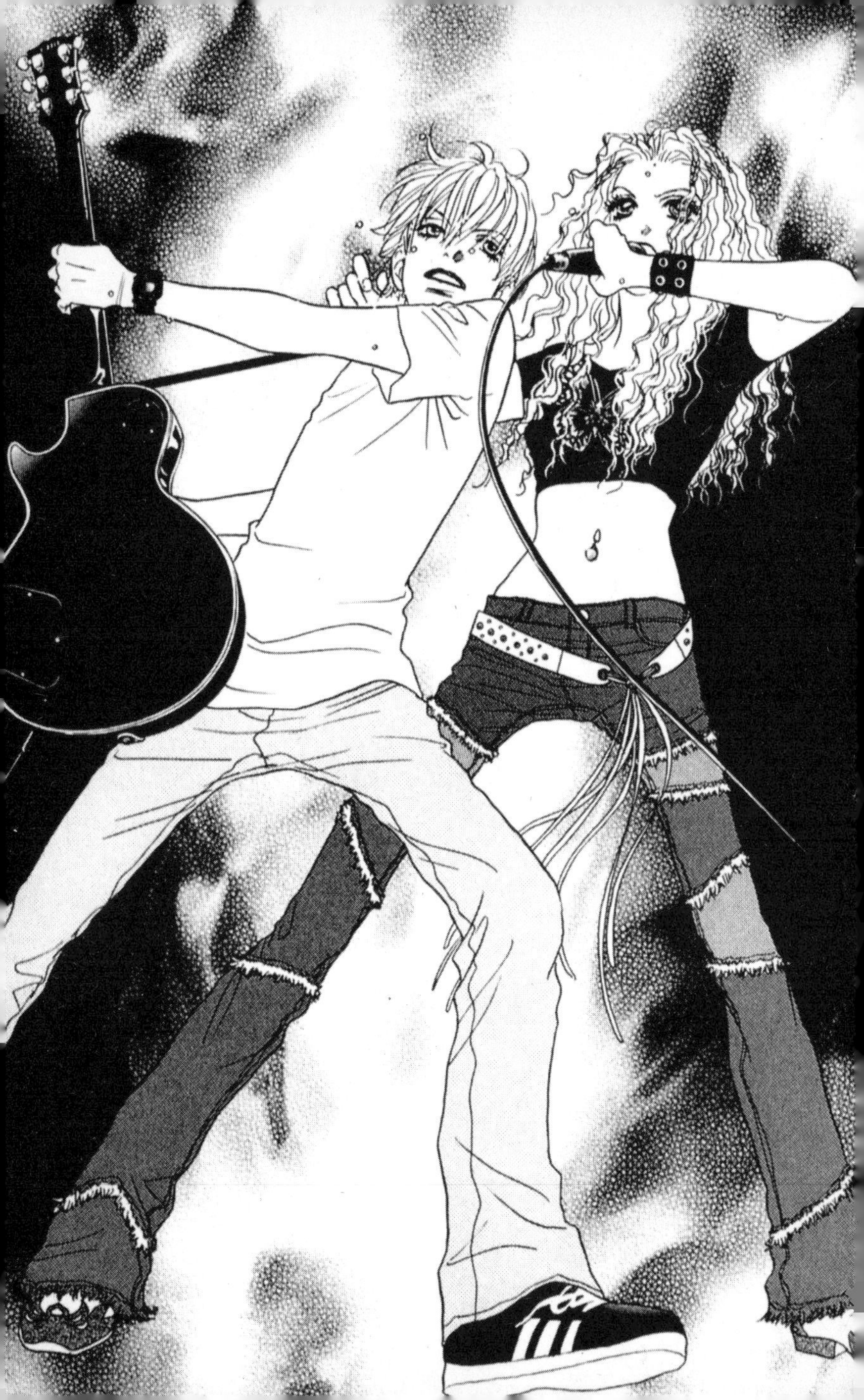

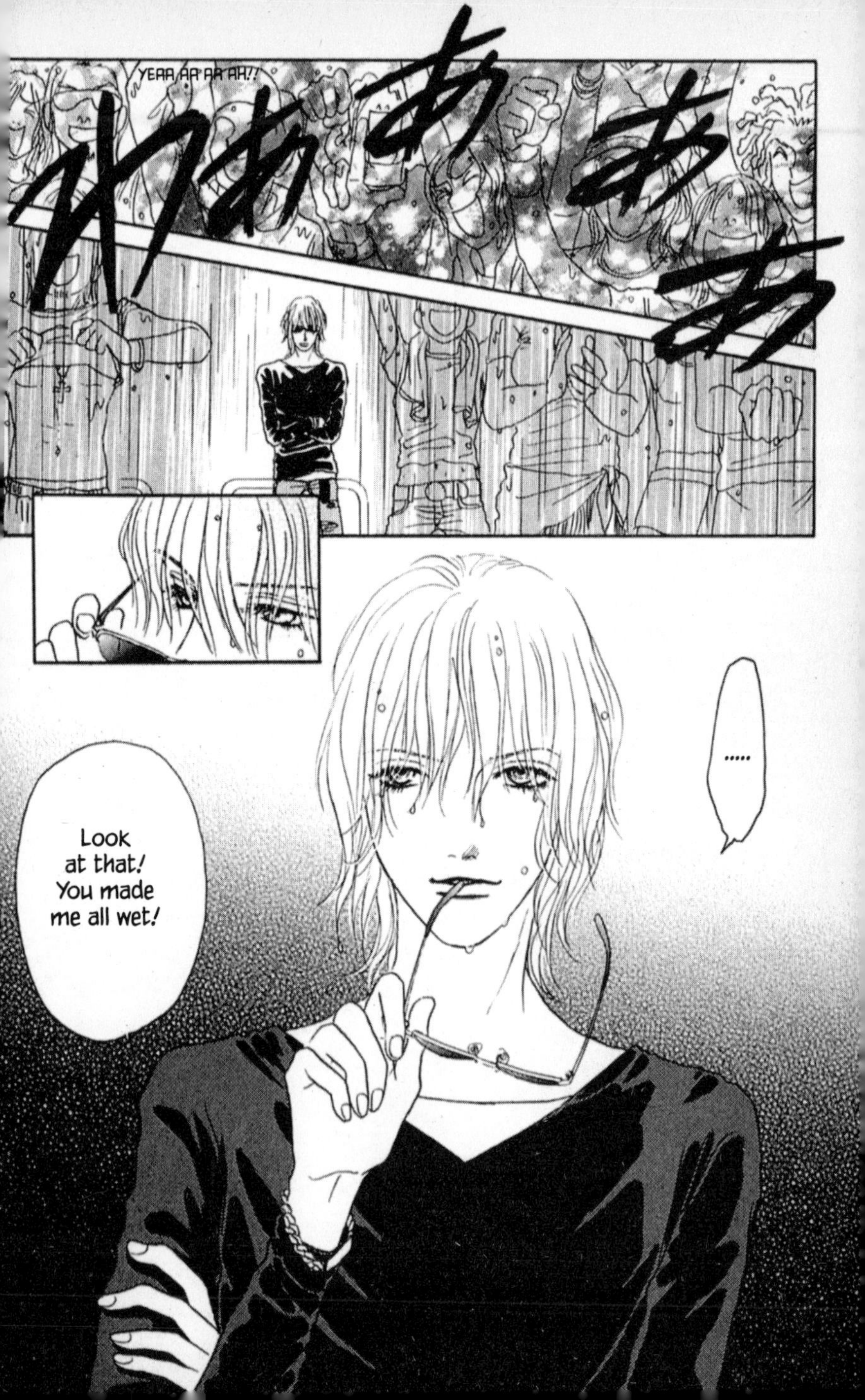
YEAA AA AA AH!!
.....
Look at that! You made me all wet!

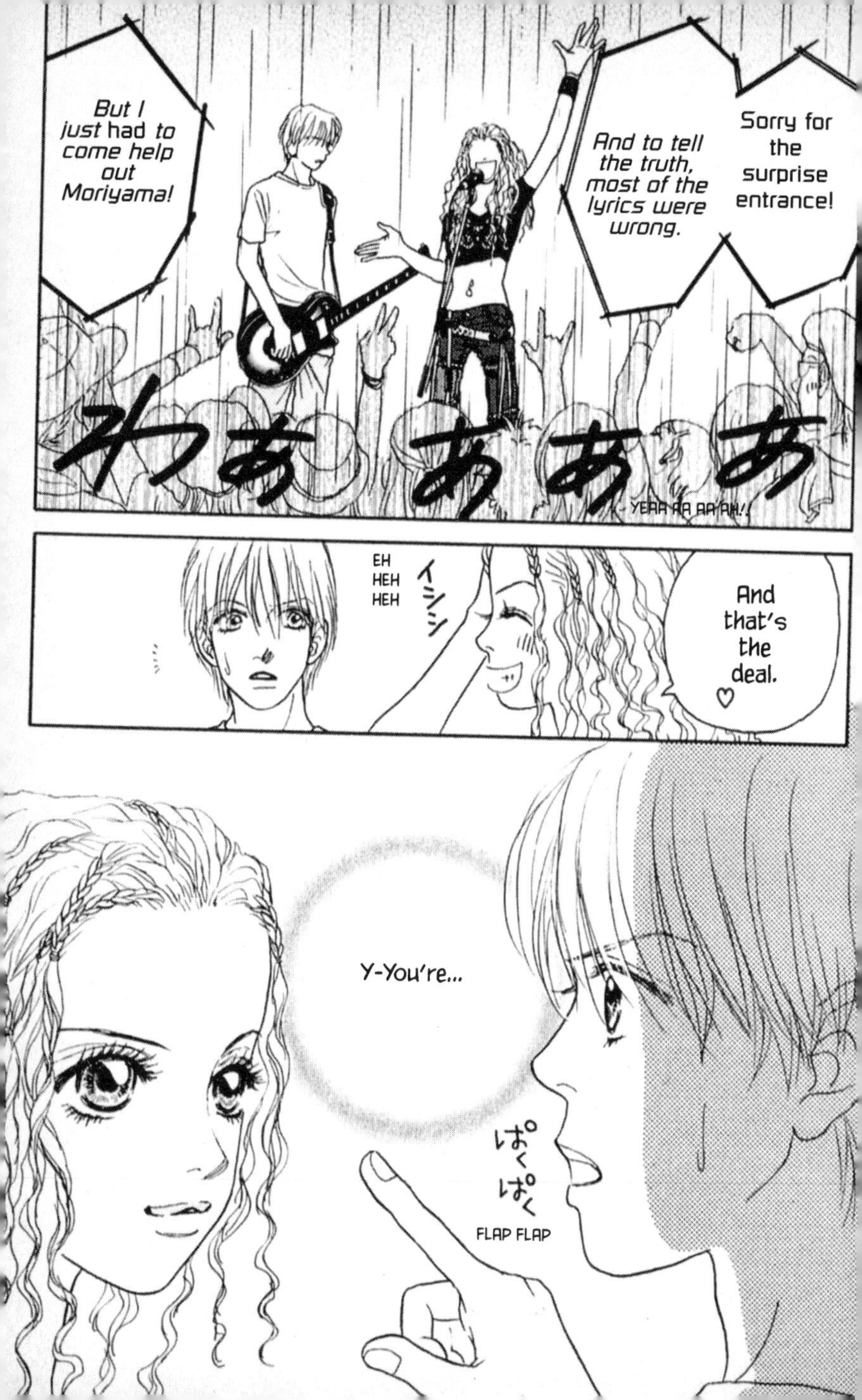
Sorry for the surprise entrance!
And to tell the truth, most of the lyrics were wrong.
But I just had to come help out Moriyama!
わあああ
YEAA AA AA AH!!
And that's the deal. ♡
イシシ
EH HEH HEH
Y-You're...
ぱくぱく
FLAP FLAP

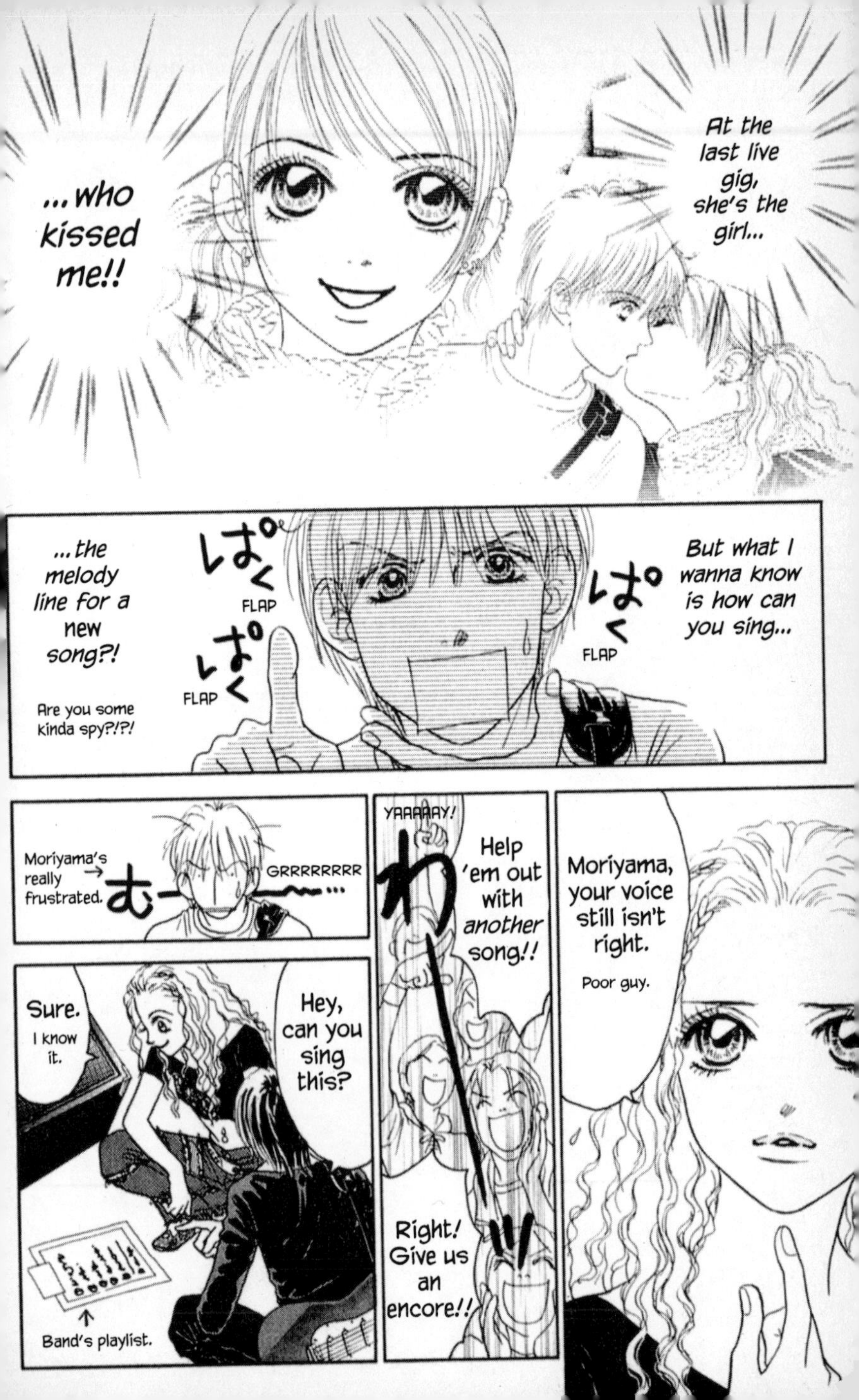
At the last live gig, she's the girl...
...who kissed me!!
But what I wanna know is how can you sing...
ぱく
FLAP
ぱく
FLAP
ぱく
FLAP
...the melody line for a new song?!
Are you some kinda spy?!?!
Moriyama, your voice still isn't right.
Poor guy.
YAAAAAY!
わ
Help 'em out with another song!!
Right! Give us an encore!!
GRRRRRRRR
む
Moriyama's really frustrated.
Hey, can you sing this?
Sure.
I know it.
Band's playlist.

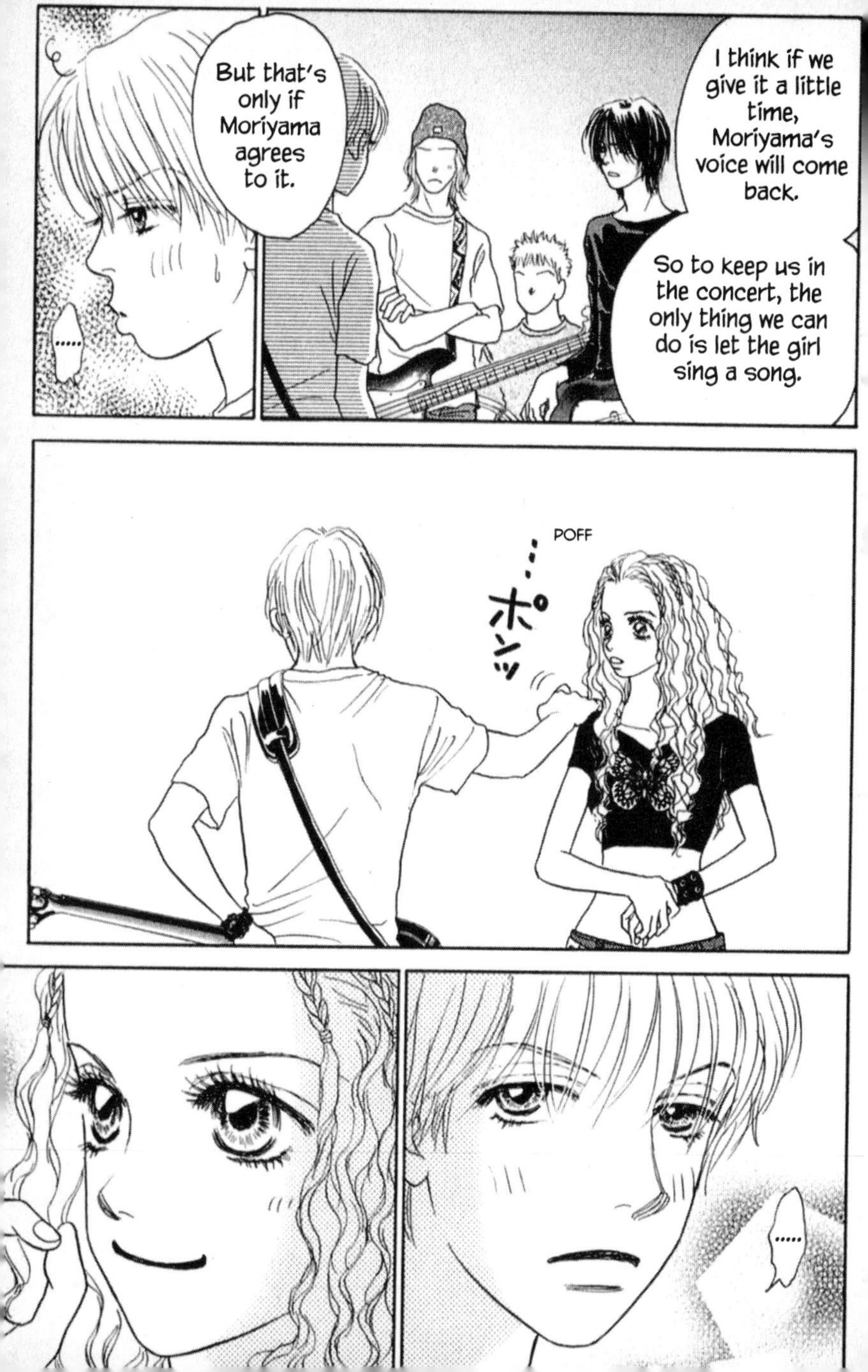
I think if we give it a little time, Moriyama's voice will come back.
So to keep us in the concert, the only thing we can do is let the girl sing a song.
But that's only if Moriyama agrees to it.
.....
ポンッ
POFF
.....

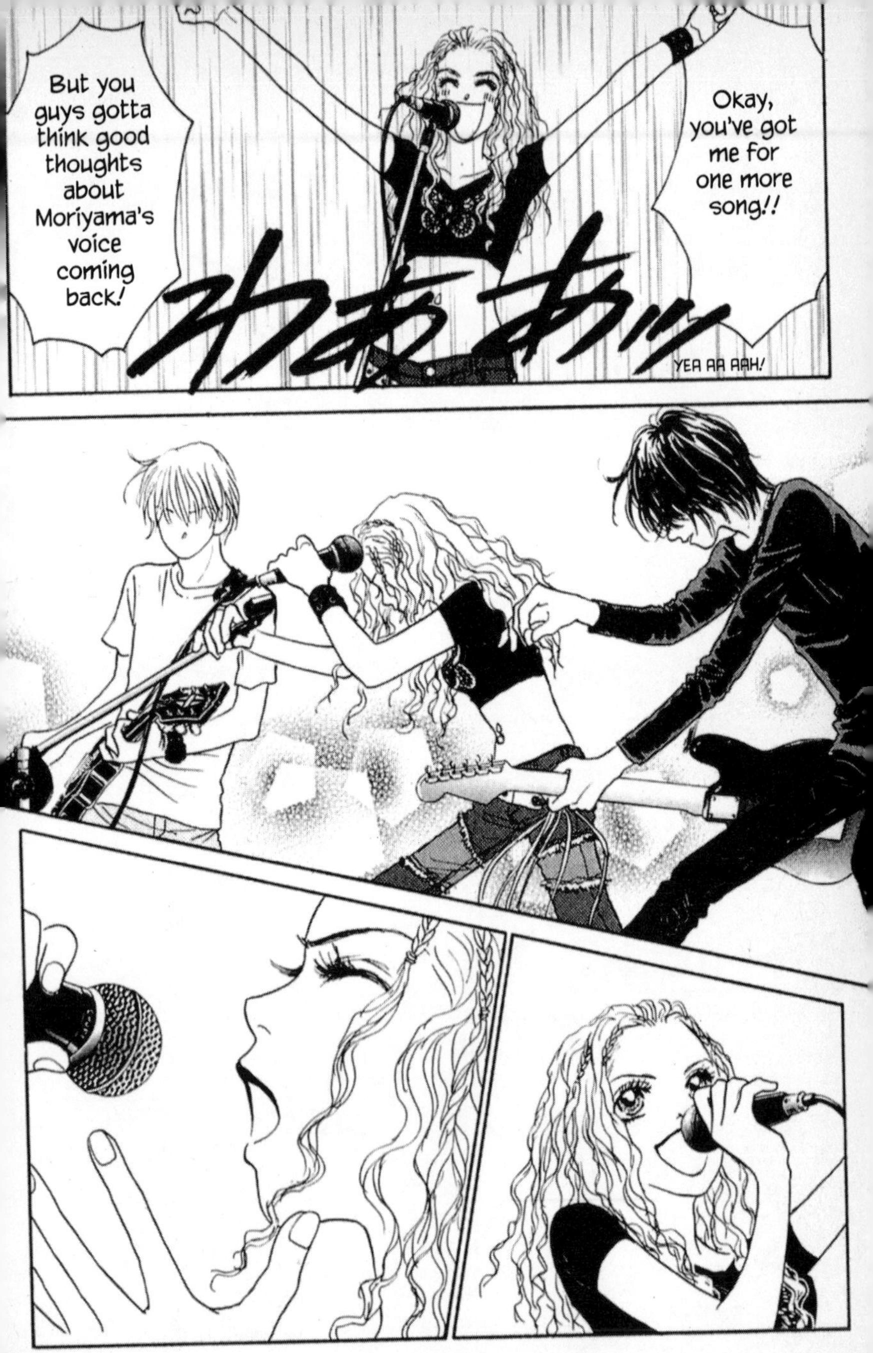
Okay, you've got me for one more song!!
But you guys gotta think good thoughts about Moriyama's voice coming back!
YEA AA AAH!

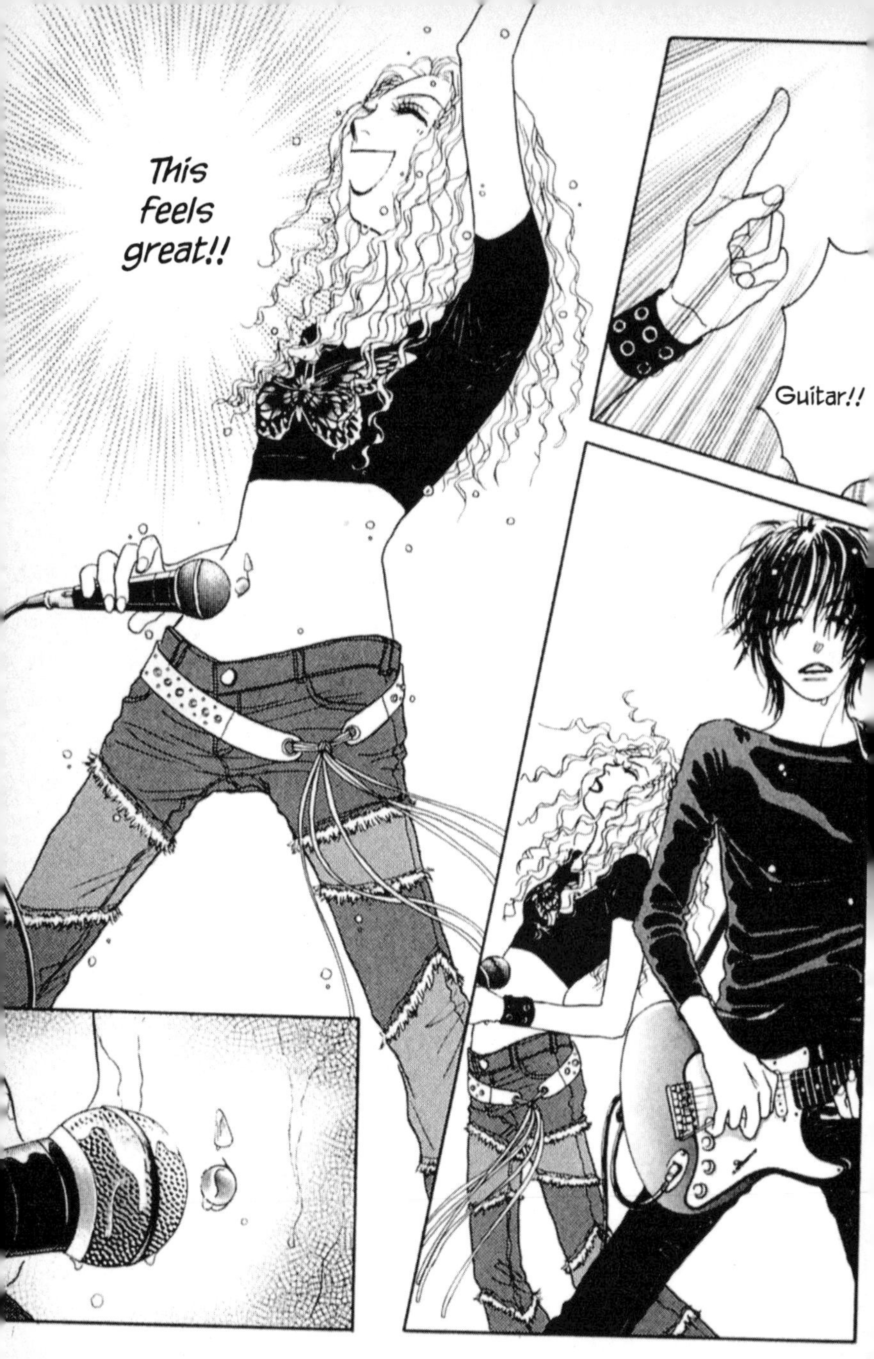
This feels great!!
Guitar!!

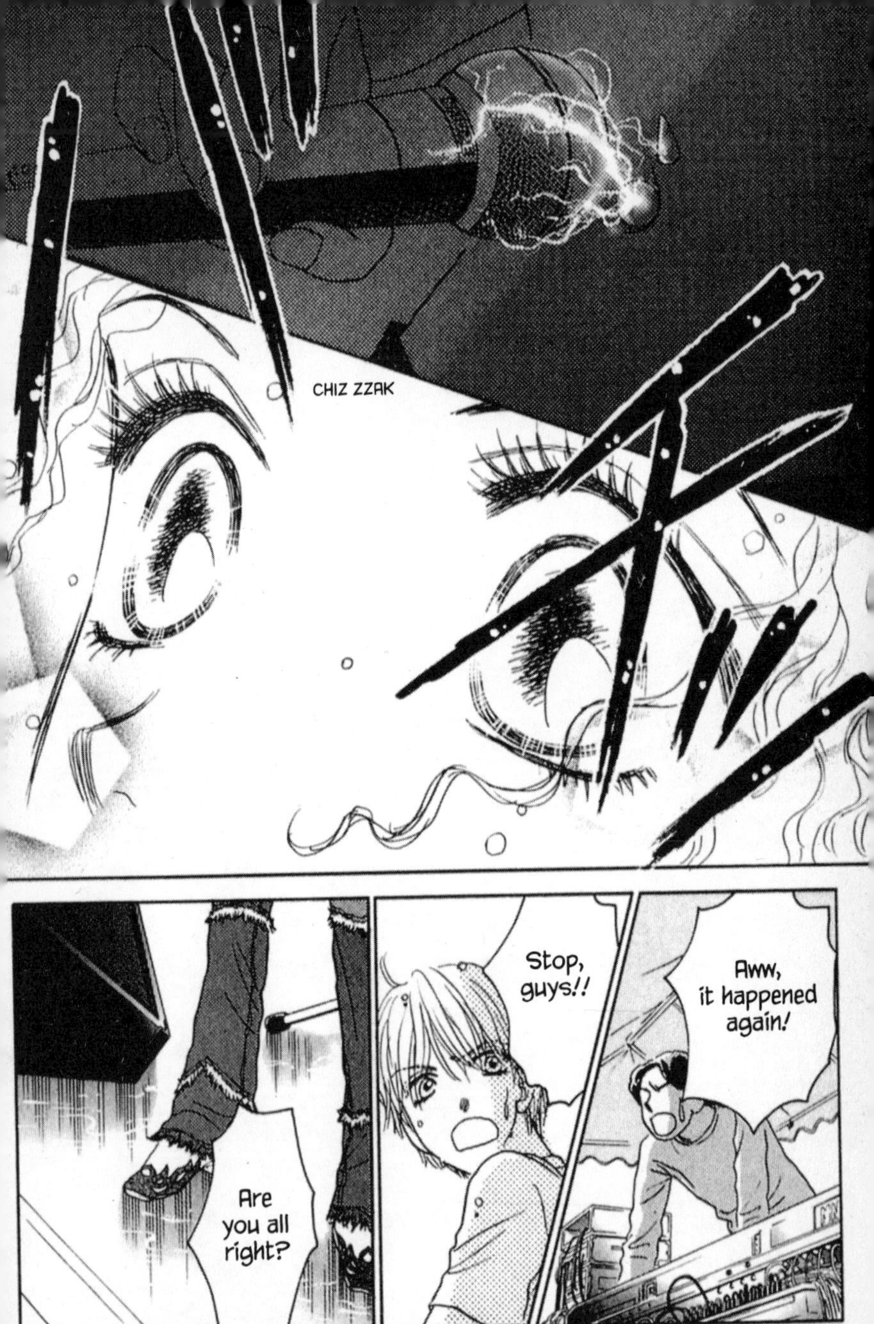
CHIZ ZZAK
Aww, it happened again!
Stop, guys!!
Are you all right?

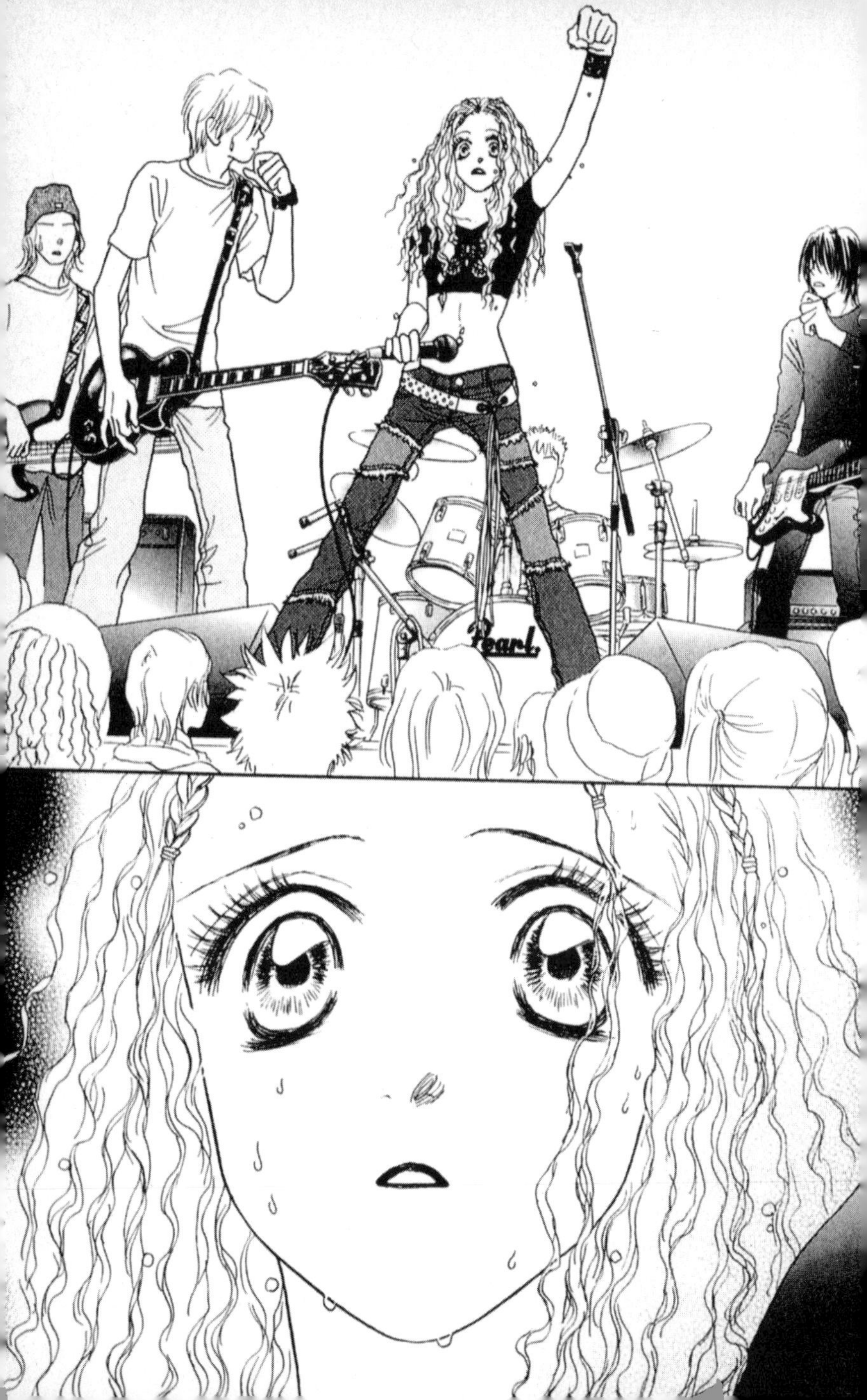
Pearl

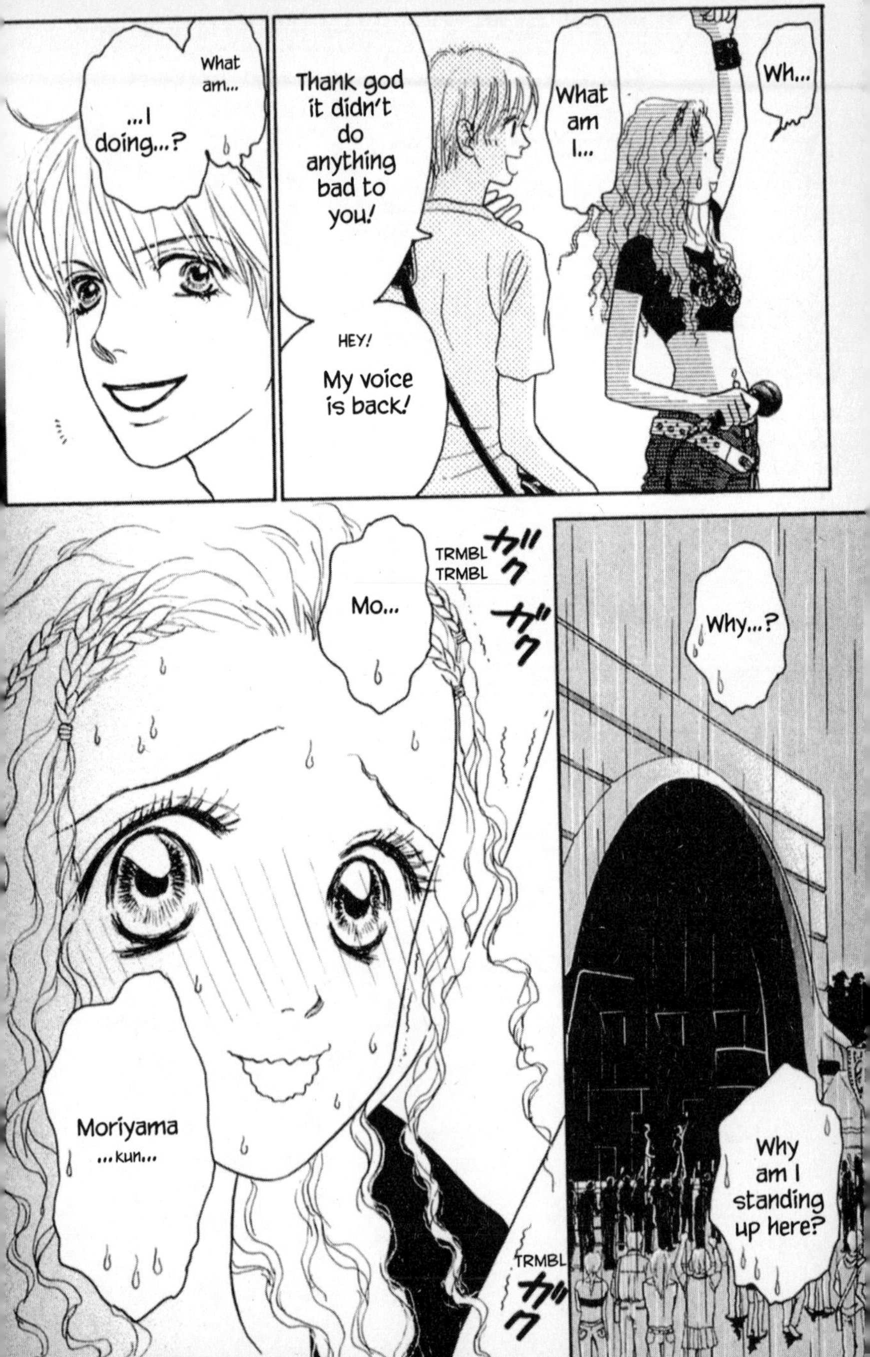
Wh...
What am I...
Thank god it didn't do anything bad to you!
HEY!
My voice is back!
What am...
...I doing...?
Why...?
Why am I standing up here?
TRMBL
ガク ガク
TRMBL TRMBL
ガク ガク
Mo...
Moriyama ...kun...

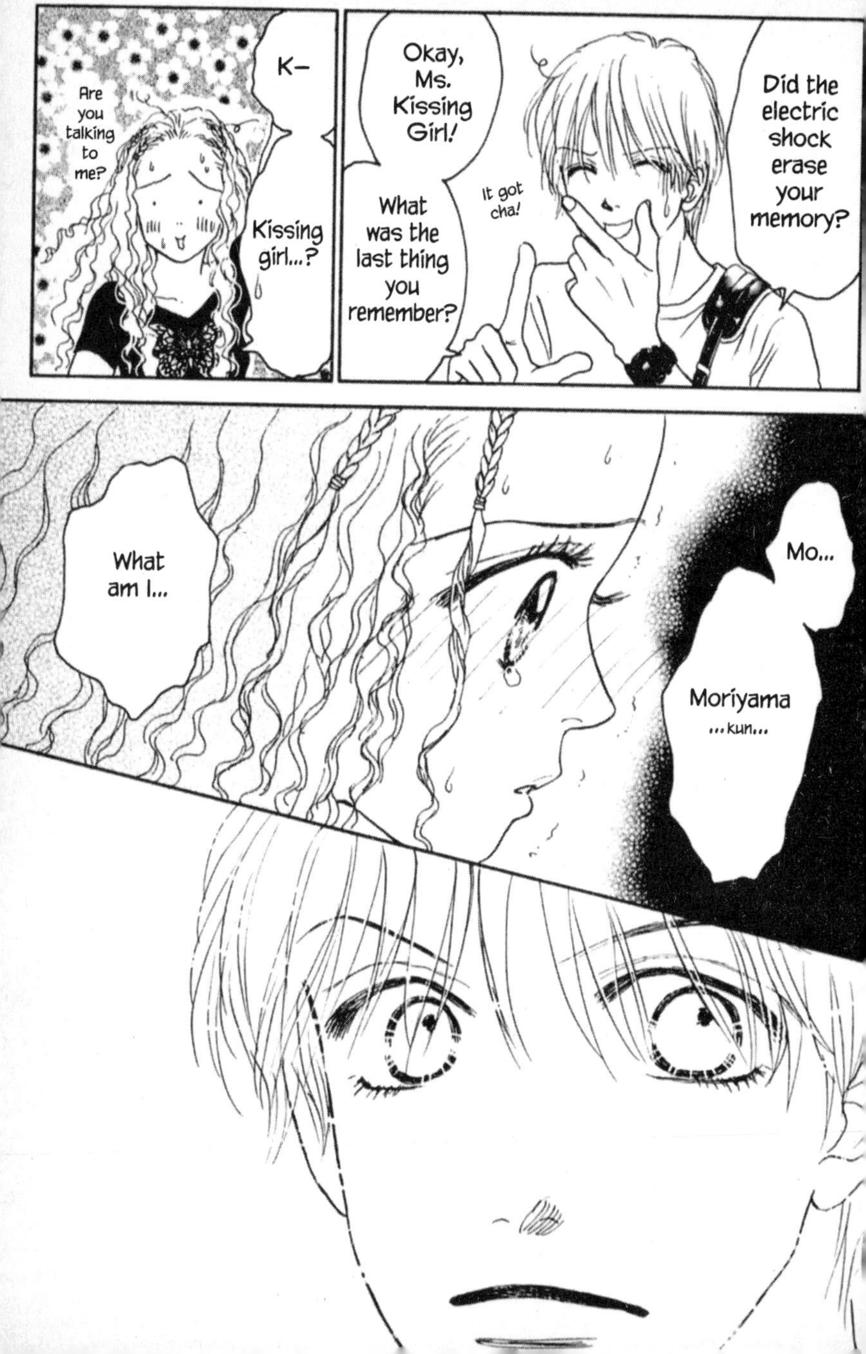
Did the electric shock erase your memory?
It got cha!
Okay, Ms. Kissing Girl!
What was the last thing you remember?
K–
Kissing girl...?
Are you talking to me?
Mo...
Moriyama ...kun...
What am I...

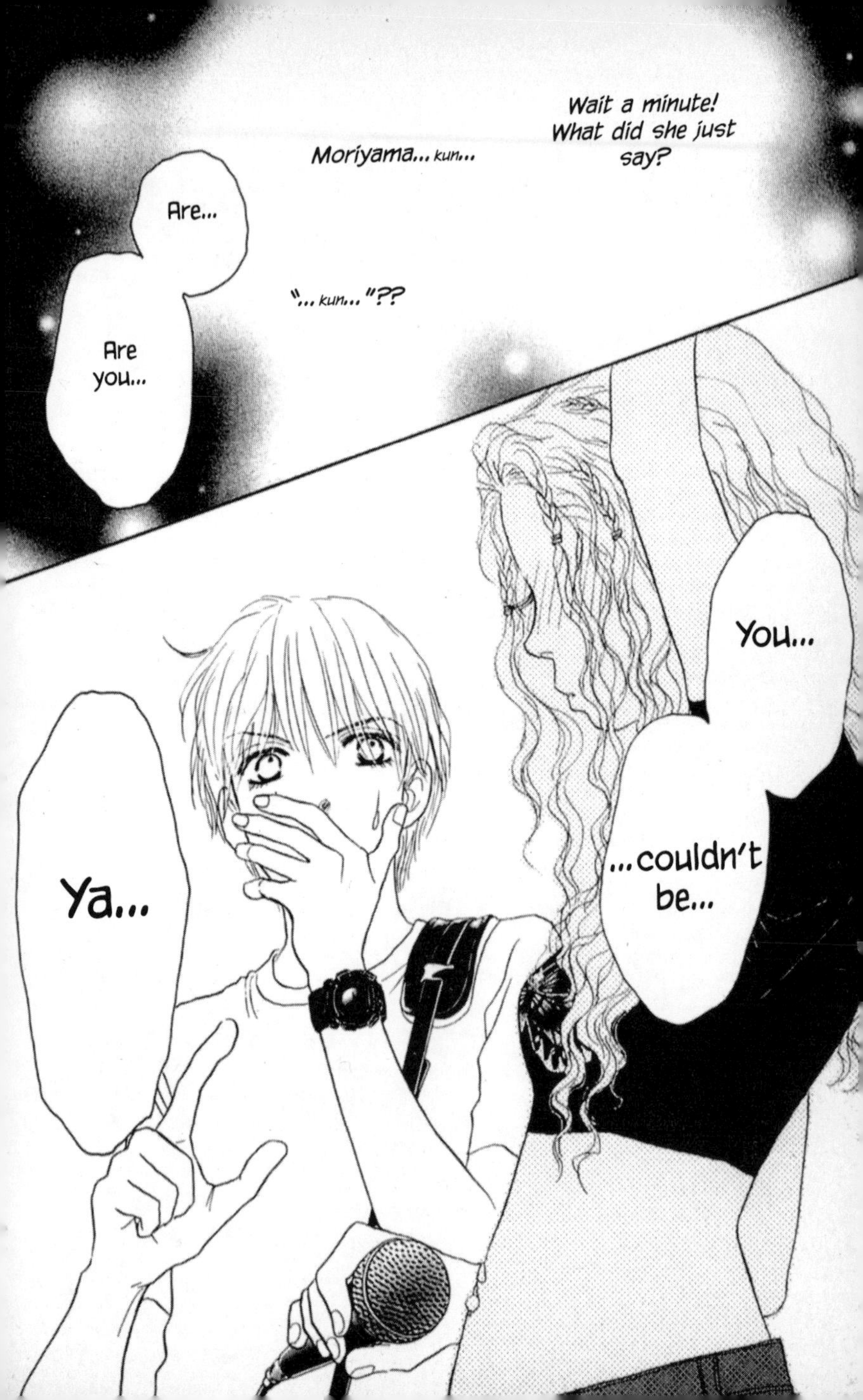
Wait a minute! What did she just say?
Moriyama... kun...
"... kun..."??
Are...
Are you...
You...
...couldn't be...
Ya...

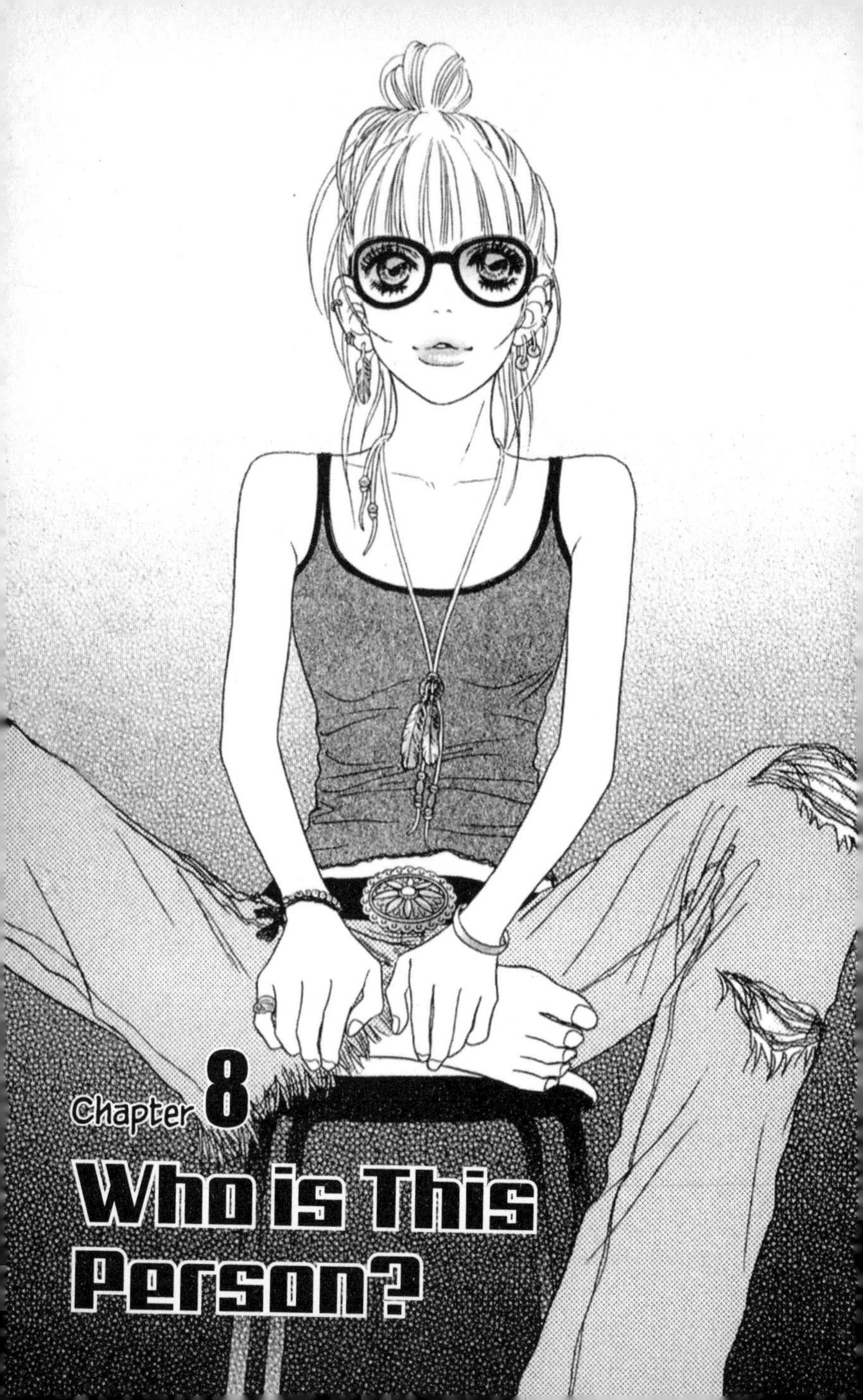
Chapter 8
Who is This Person?

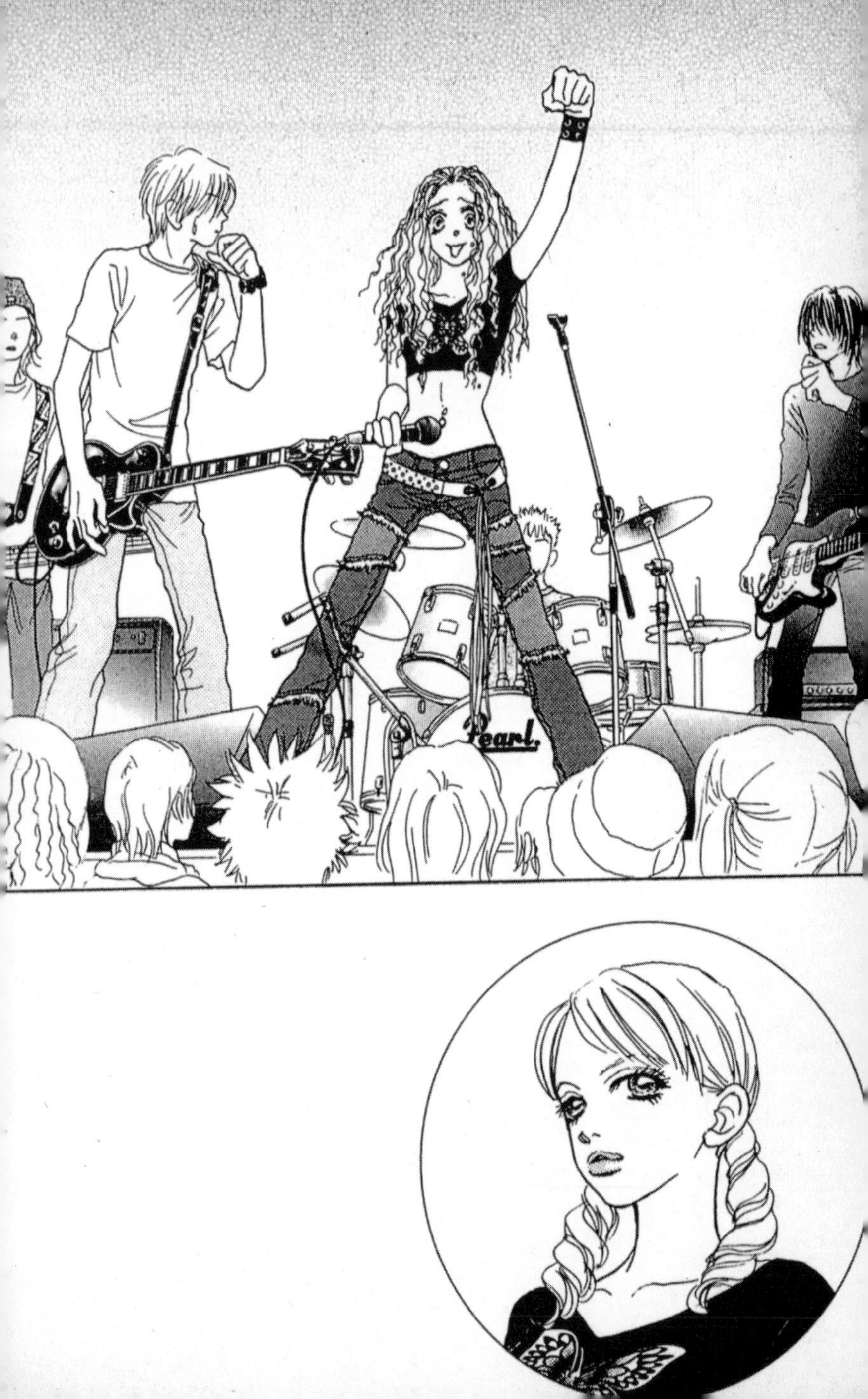
Pearl.

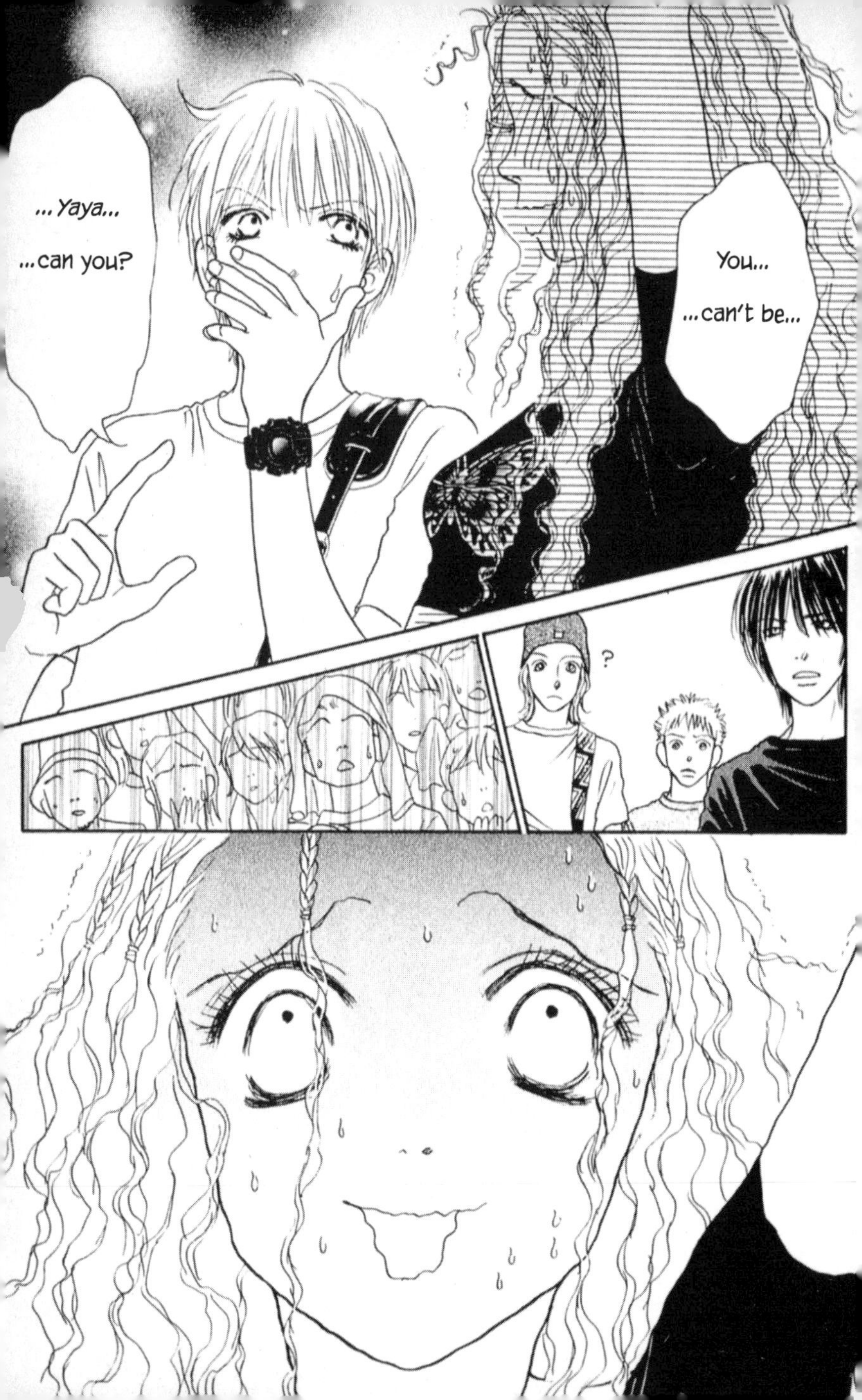

You...
...can't be...
...Yaya...
...can you?
?

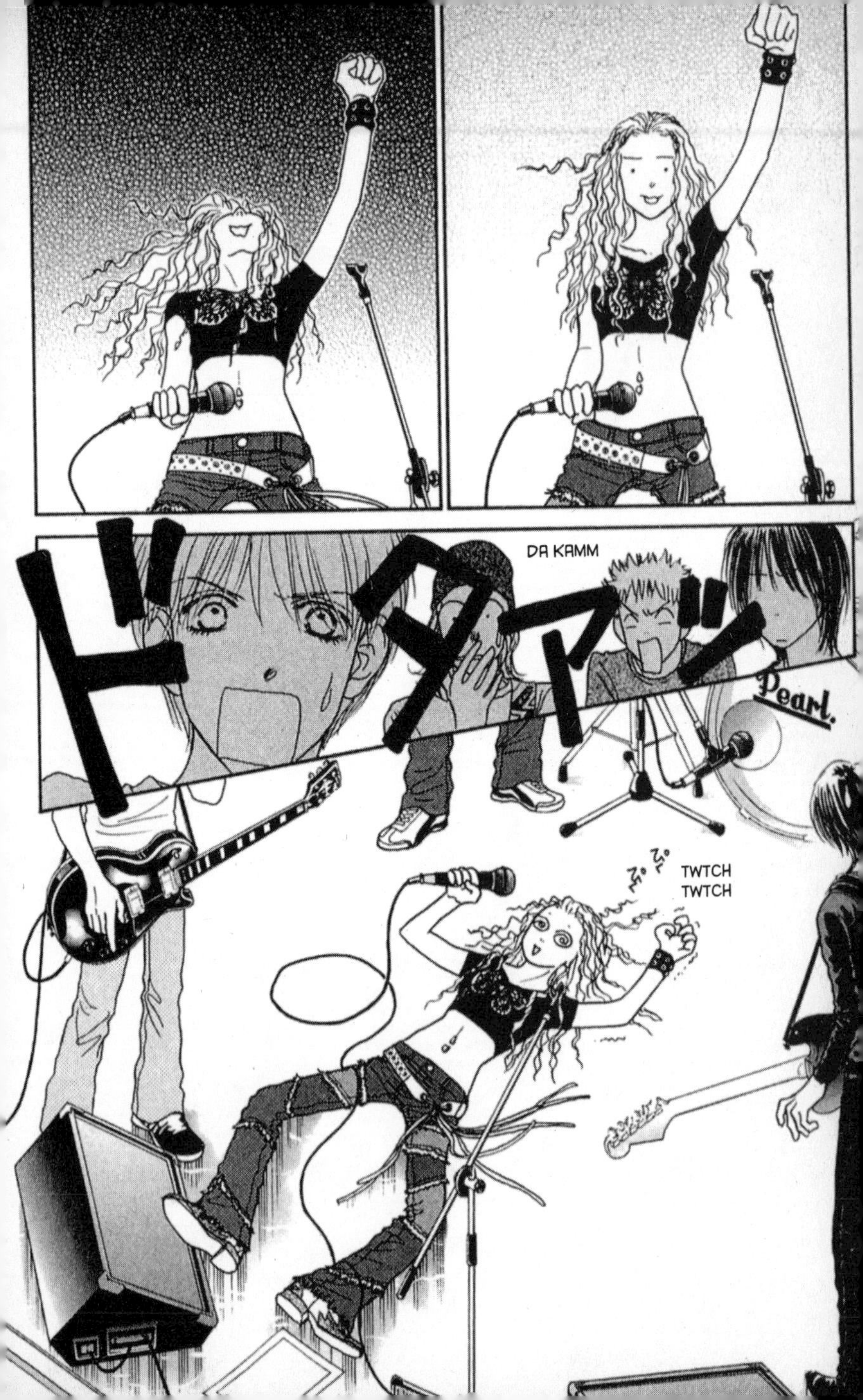
DA KAMM
Pearl.
TWTCH
TWTCH

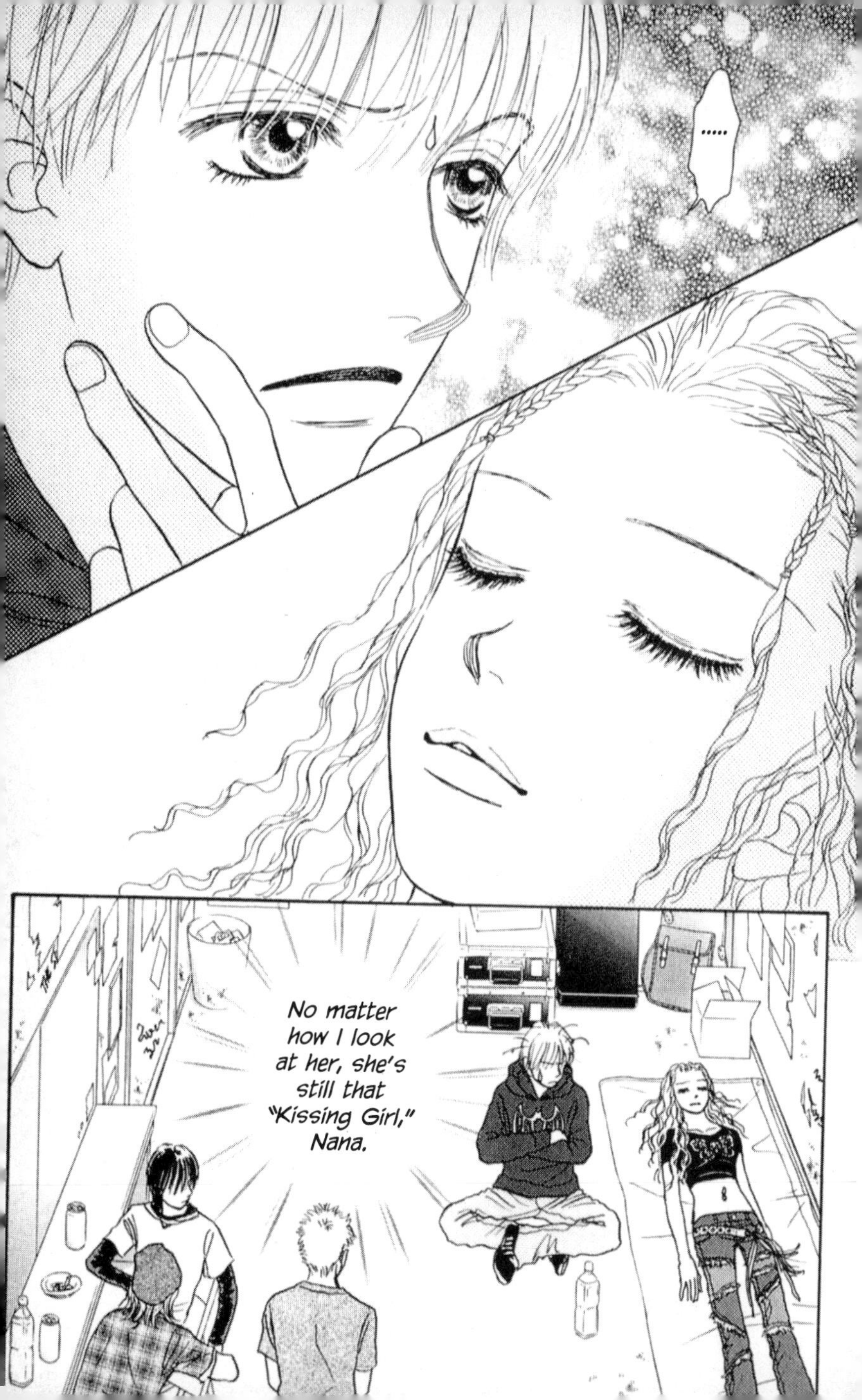
......
No matter how I look at her, she's still that "Kissing Girl," Nana.

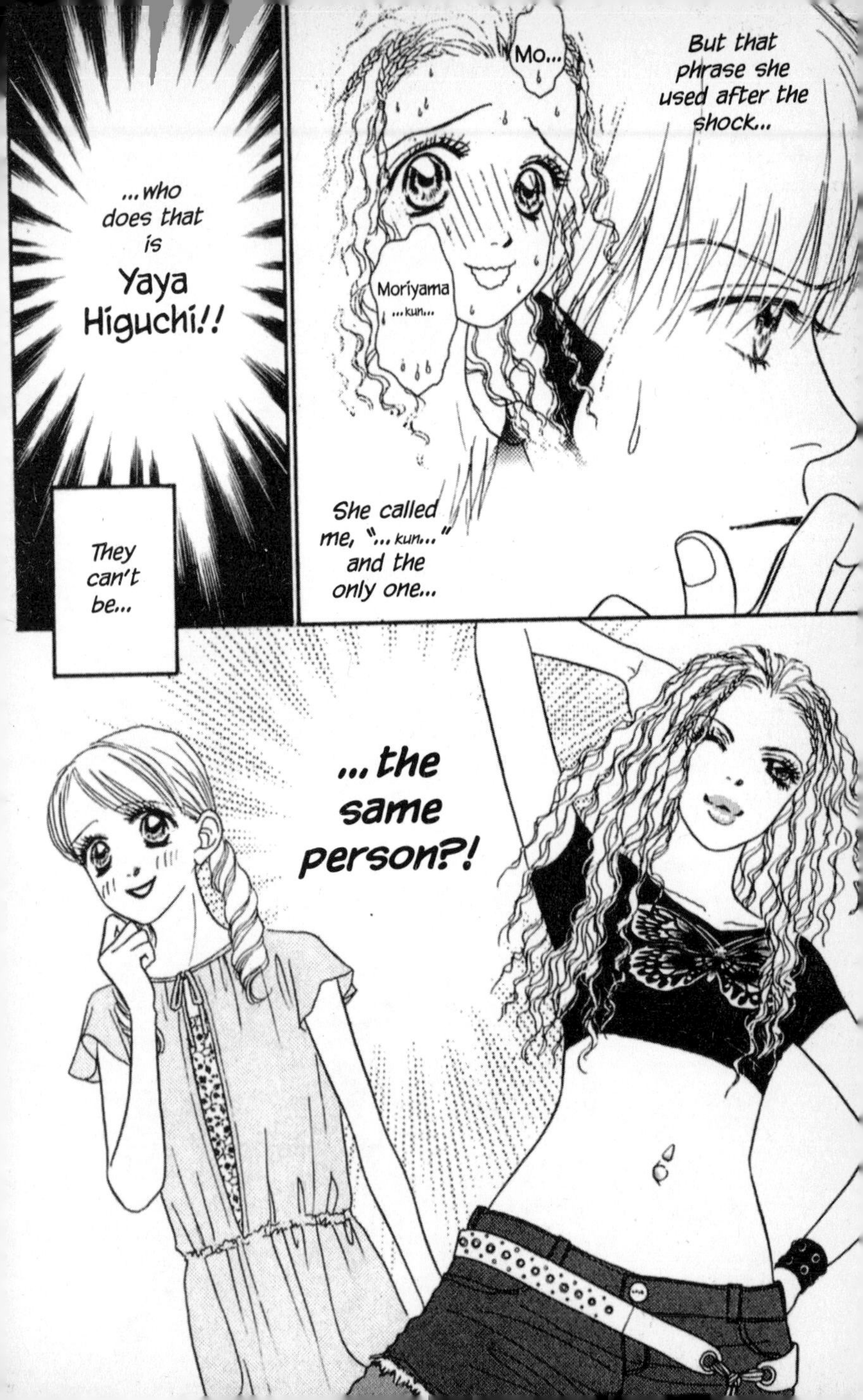
But that phrase she used after the shock...
Mo...
Moriyama ...kun...
She called me, "...kun..." and the only one...
...who does that is Yaya Higuchi!!
They can't be...
...the same person?!

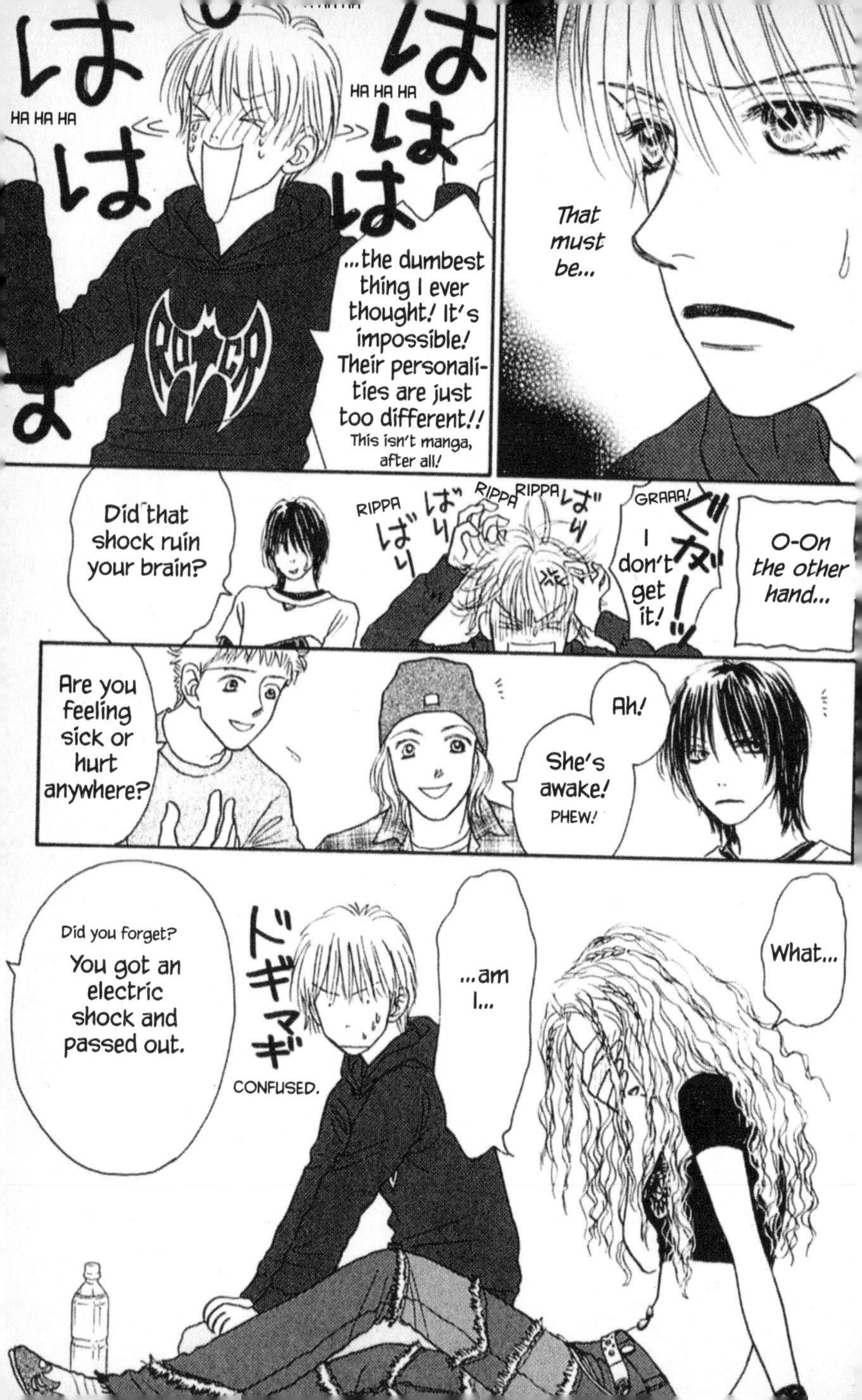
That must be...
ははは
HA HA HA
ははは
HA HA HA
...the dumbest thing I ever thought! It's impossible! Their personalities are just too different!!
This isn't manga, after all!
O-On the other hand...
GRAAA!
I don't get it!
ばり
RIPPA
ばり
RIPPA
ばり
RIPPA
Did that shock ruin your brain?
Ah!
She's awake!
PHEW!
Are you feeling sick or hurt anywhere?
What...
...am I...
ドギマギ
CONFUSED.
Did you forget?
You got an electric shock and passed out.

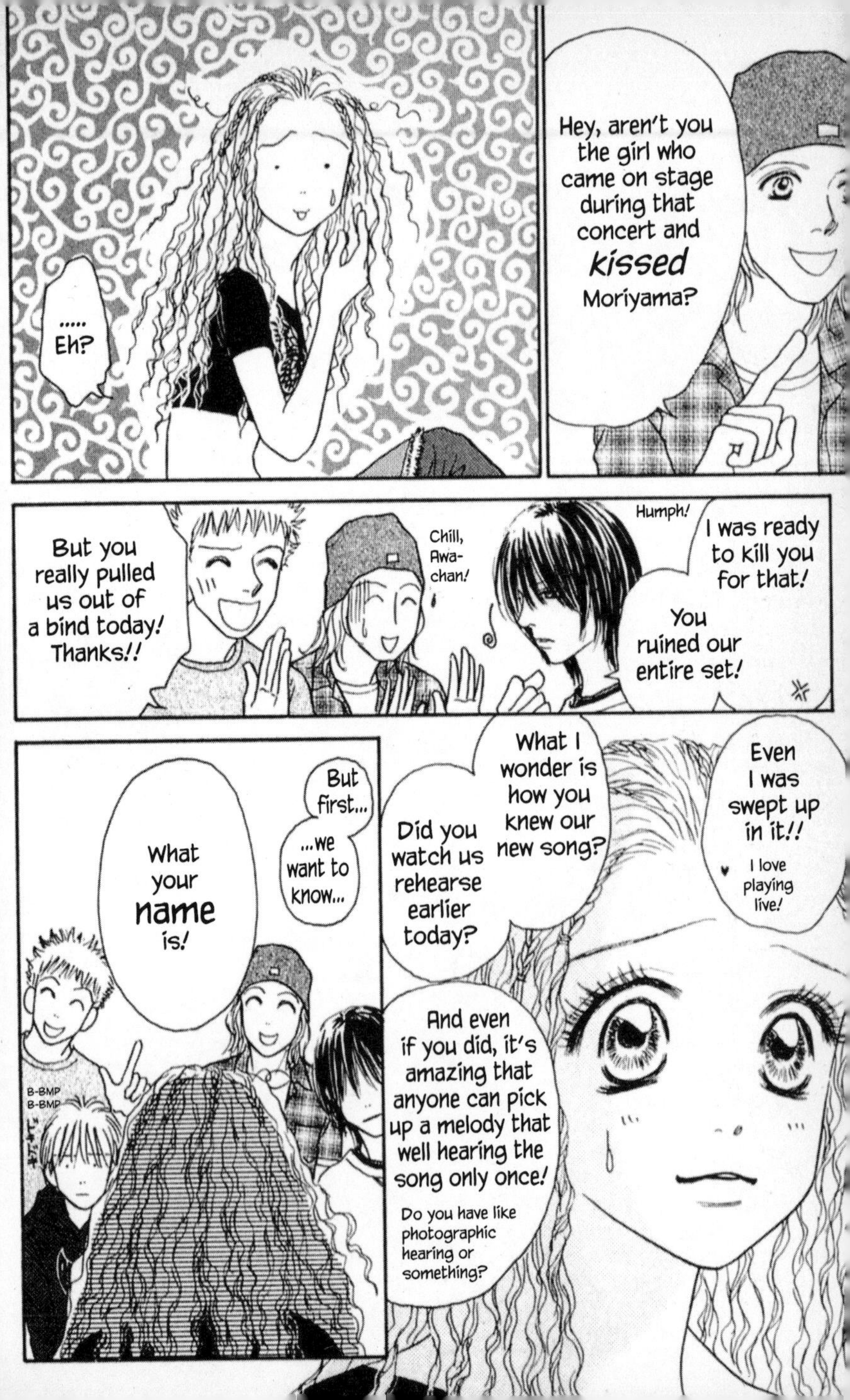

Hey, aren't you the girl who came on stage during that concert and *kissed* Moriyama?
..... Eh?
Humph!
I was ready to kill you for that!
You ruined our entire set!
Chill, Awa-chan!
But you really pulled us out of a bind today! Thanks!!
Even I was swept up in it!!
I love playing live!
What I wonder is how you knew our new song?
Did you watch us rehearse earlier today?
And even if you did, it's amazing that anyone can pick up a melody that well hearing the song only once!
Do you have like photographic hearing or something?
But first...
...we want to know...
What your **name** is!
B-BMP B-BMP

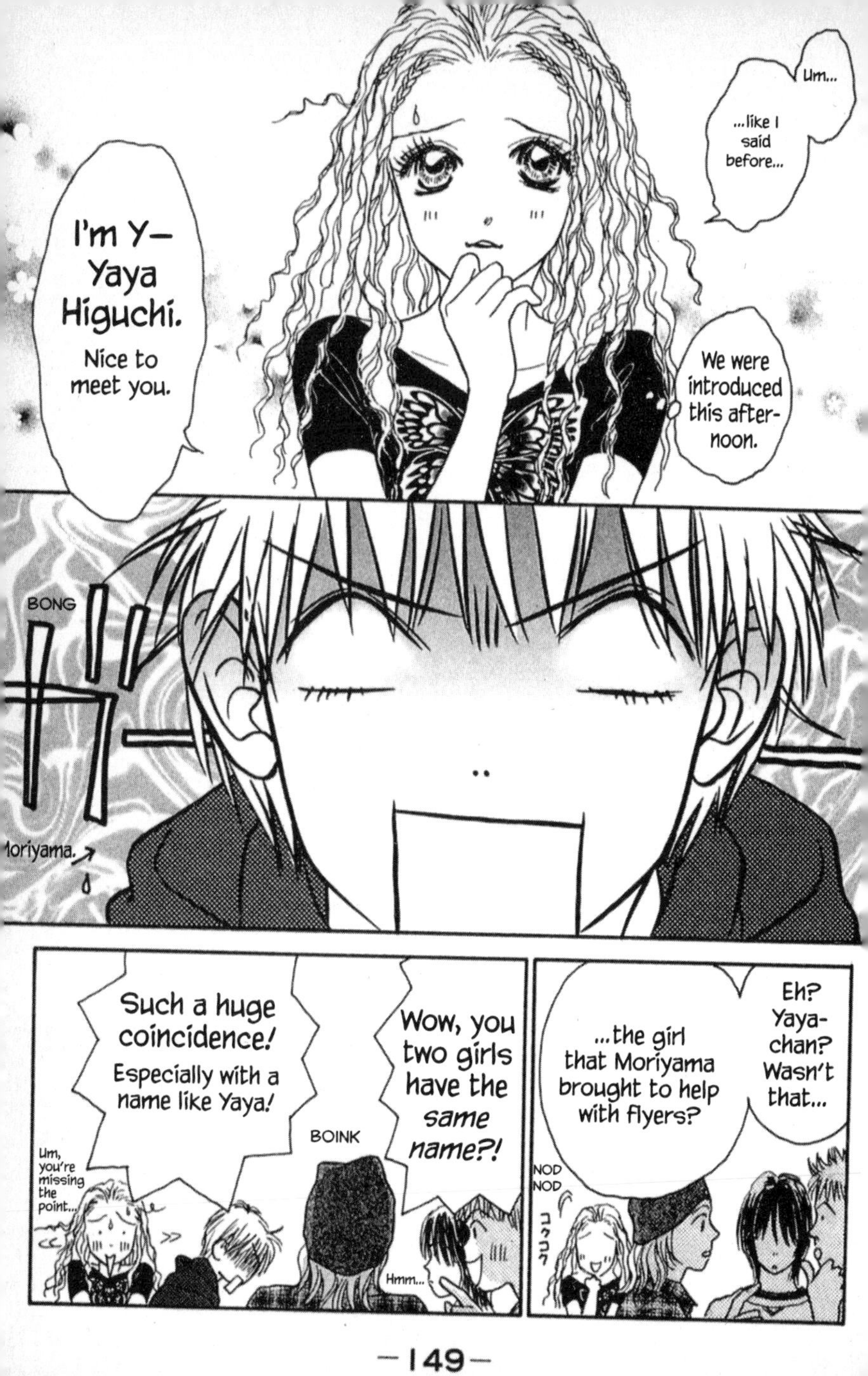
Um...
...like I said before...
We were introduced this afternoon.
I'm Y— Yaya Higuchi.
Nice to meet you.
BONG
oriyama.
Eh? Yaya-chan? Wasn't that...
...the girl that Moriyama brought to help with flyers?
NOD NOD
Wow, you two girls have the same name?!
BOINK
Hmm...
Such a huge coincidence!
Especially with a name like Yaya!
Um, you're missing the point...

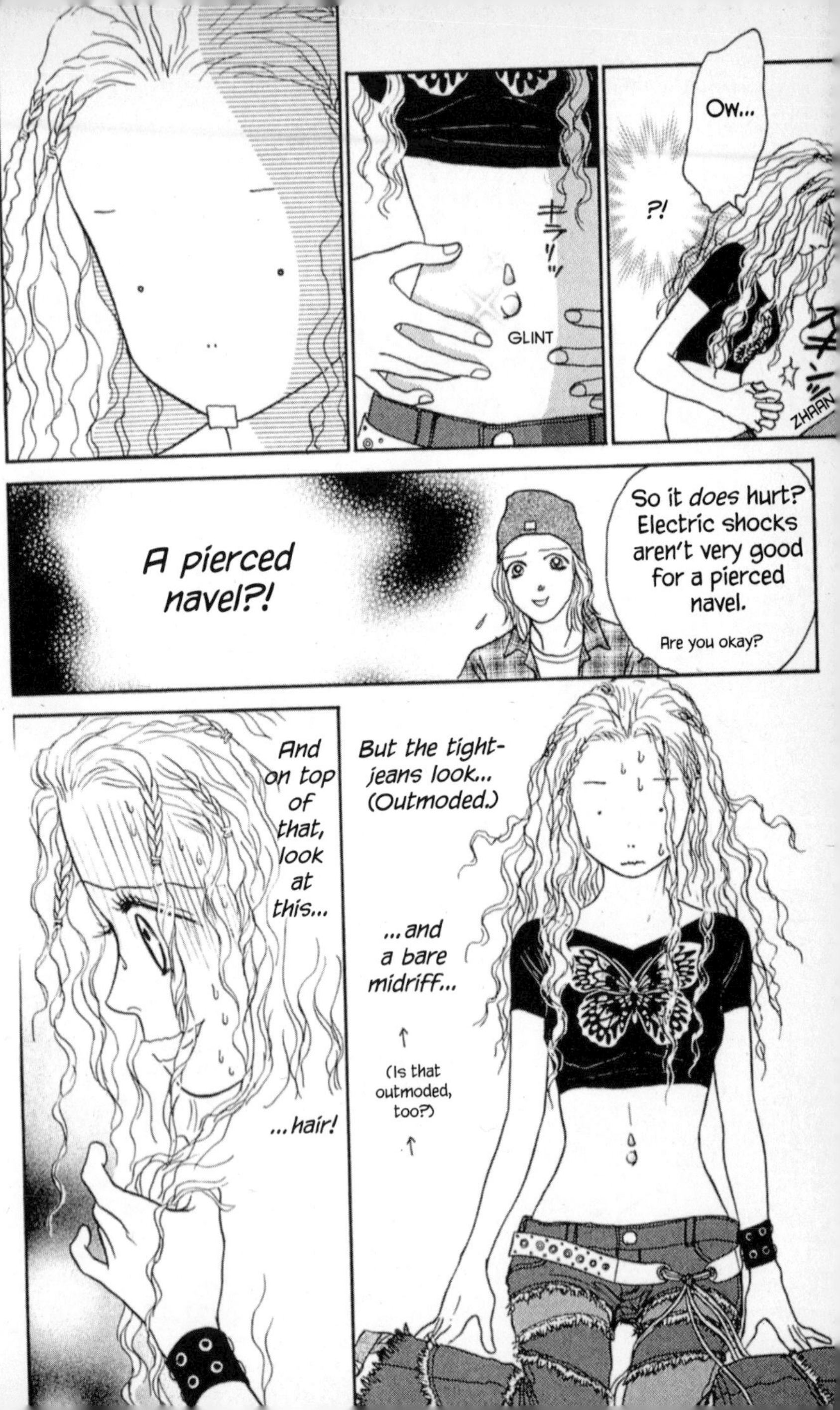
Ow...
?!
ZHAAN
GLINT
A pierced navel?!
So it does hurt? Electric shocks aren't very good for a pierced navel.
Are you okay?
But the tight-jeans look... (Outmoded.)
...and a bare midriff...
(Is that outmoded, too?)
And on top of that, look at this...
...hair!

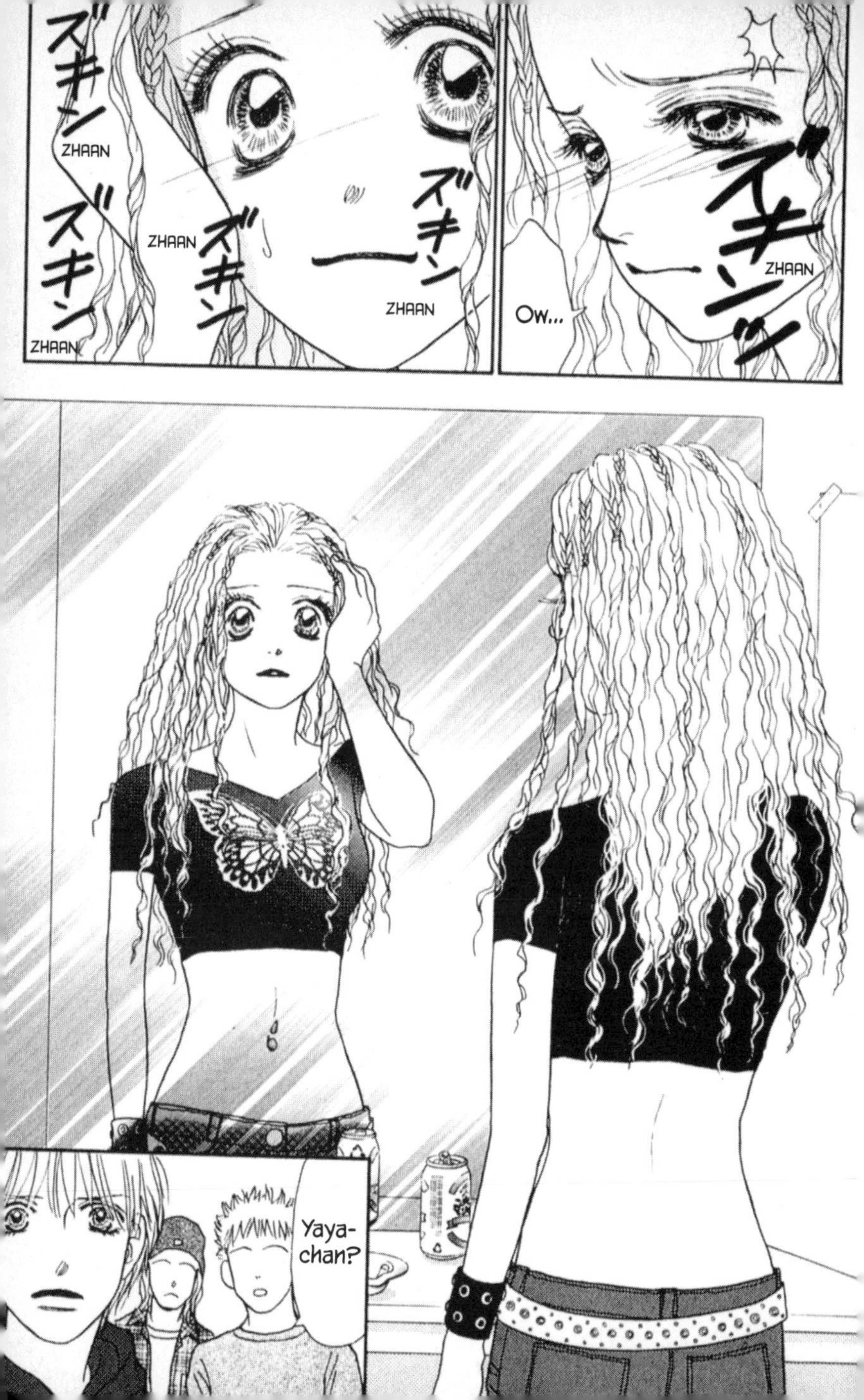
ズキンッ
ZHAAN
Ow...
ズキン
ZHAAN
ズキン
ZHAAN
ズキン
ZHAAN
ズキン
ZHAAN
Yaya-
chan?

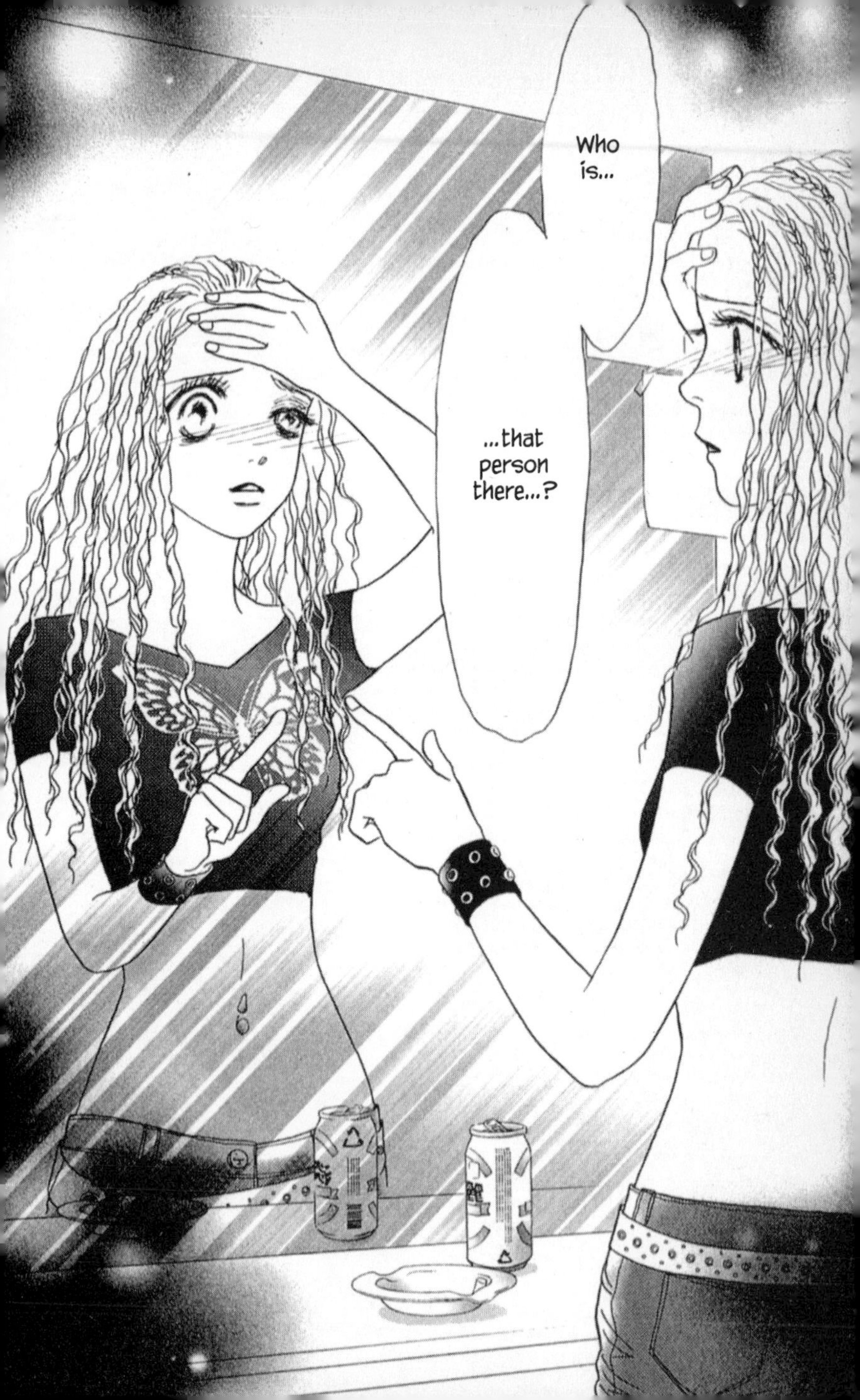
Who is...
...that person there...?

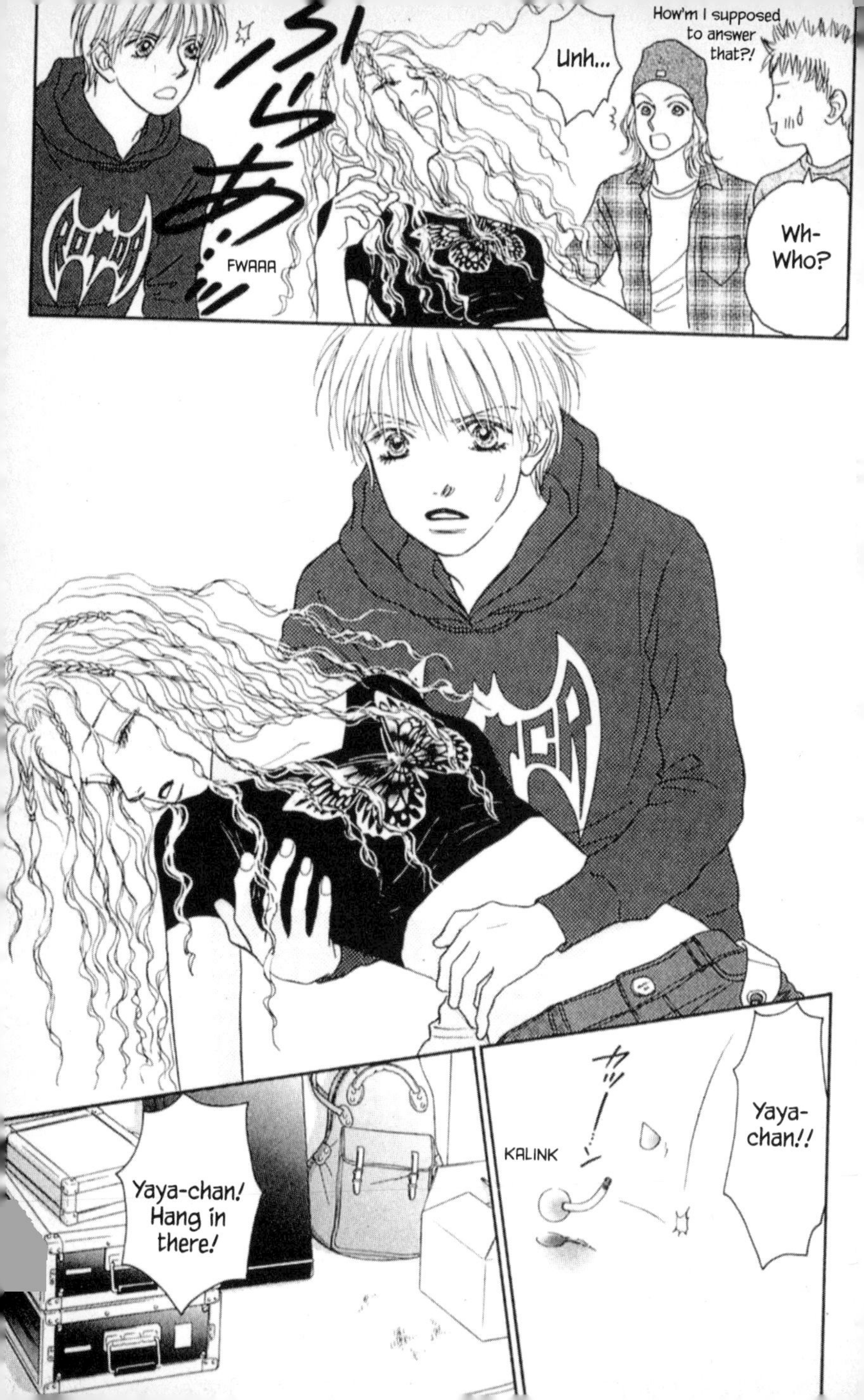

How'm I supposed to answer that?!
Wh- Who?
Unh...
FWAAA
Yaya-chan!!
KALINK
Yaya-chan! Hang in there!

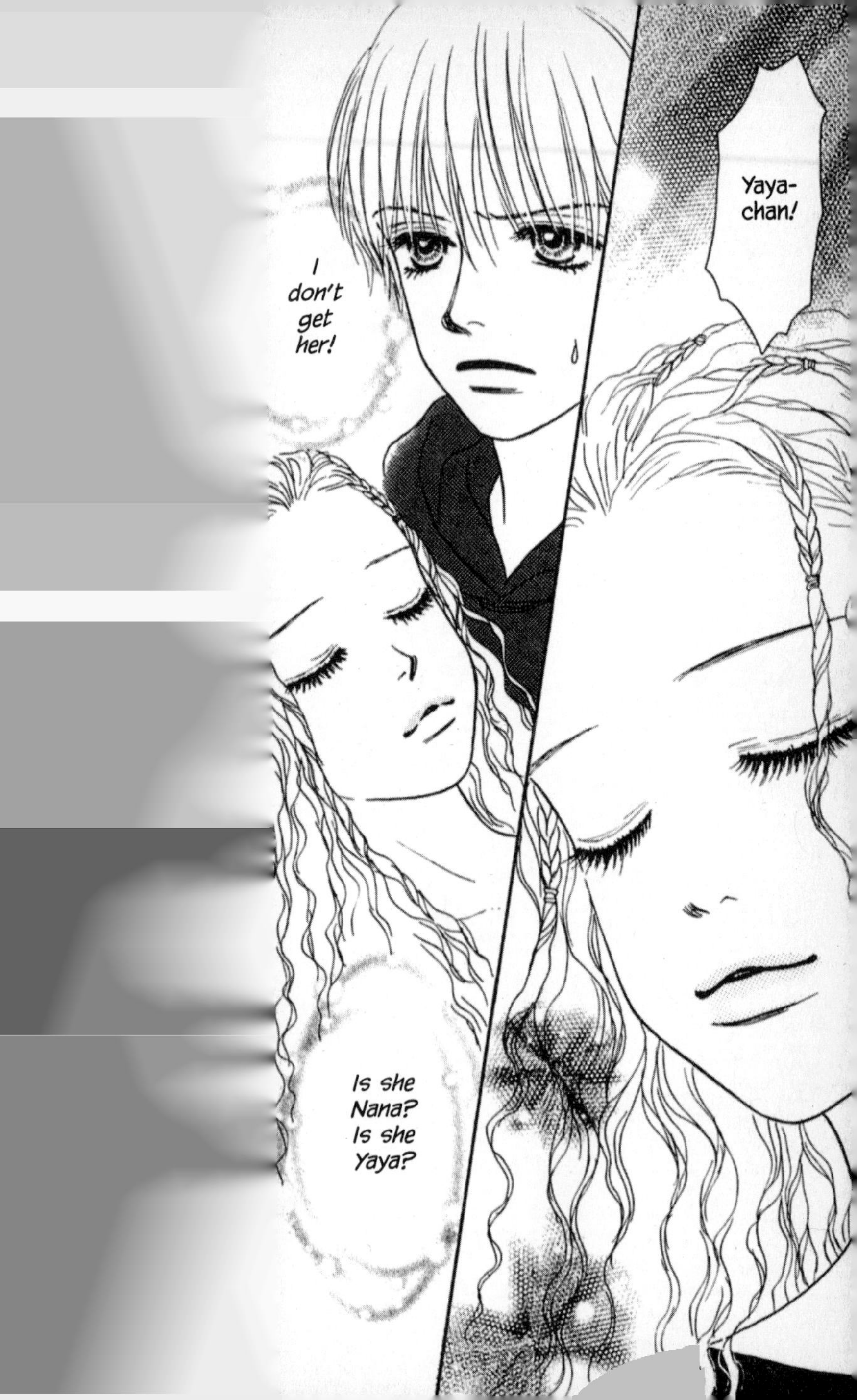
Yaya-chan!
I don't get her!
Is she Nana? Is she Yaya?

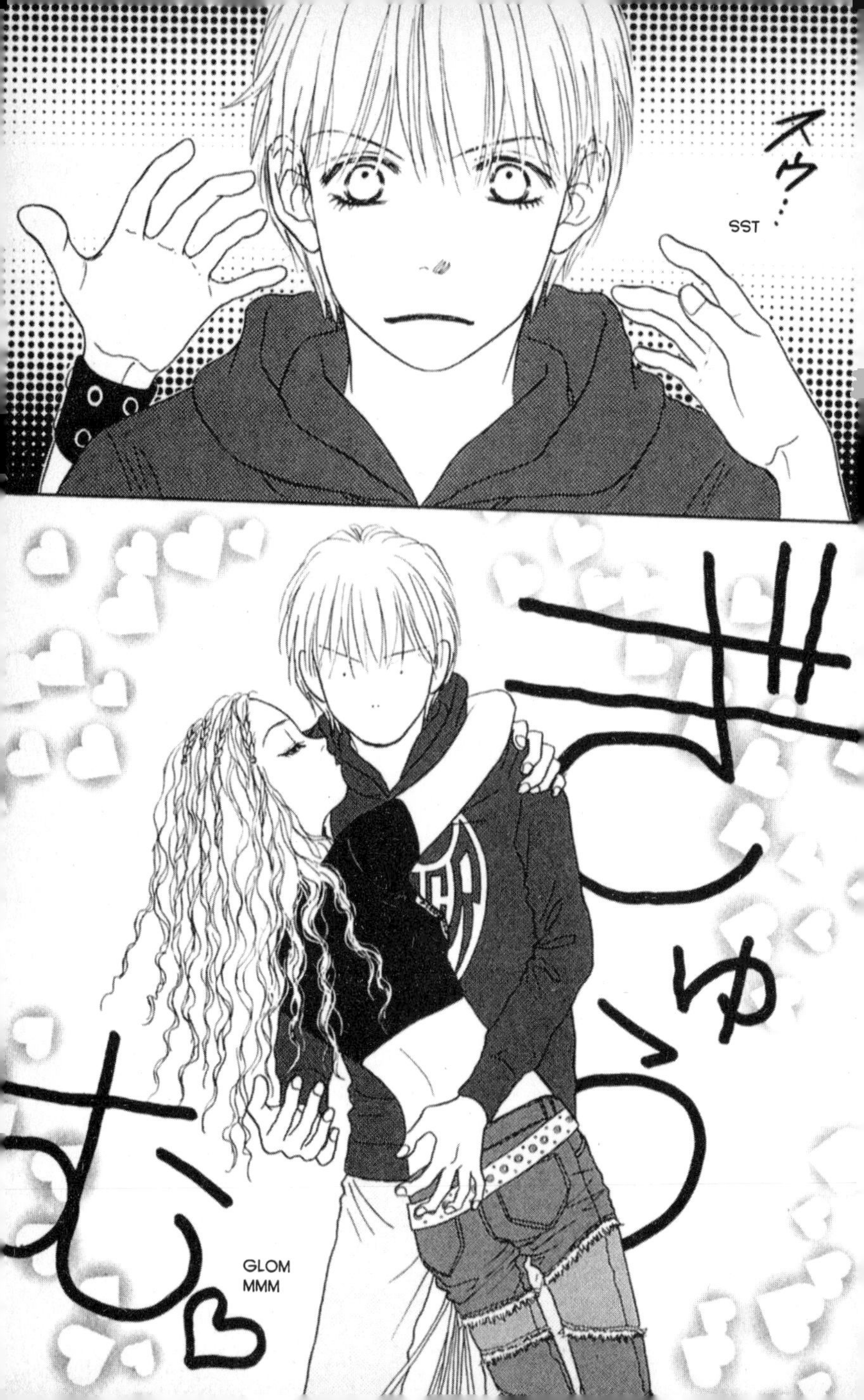
スゥ…
SST
GLOM
MMM

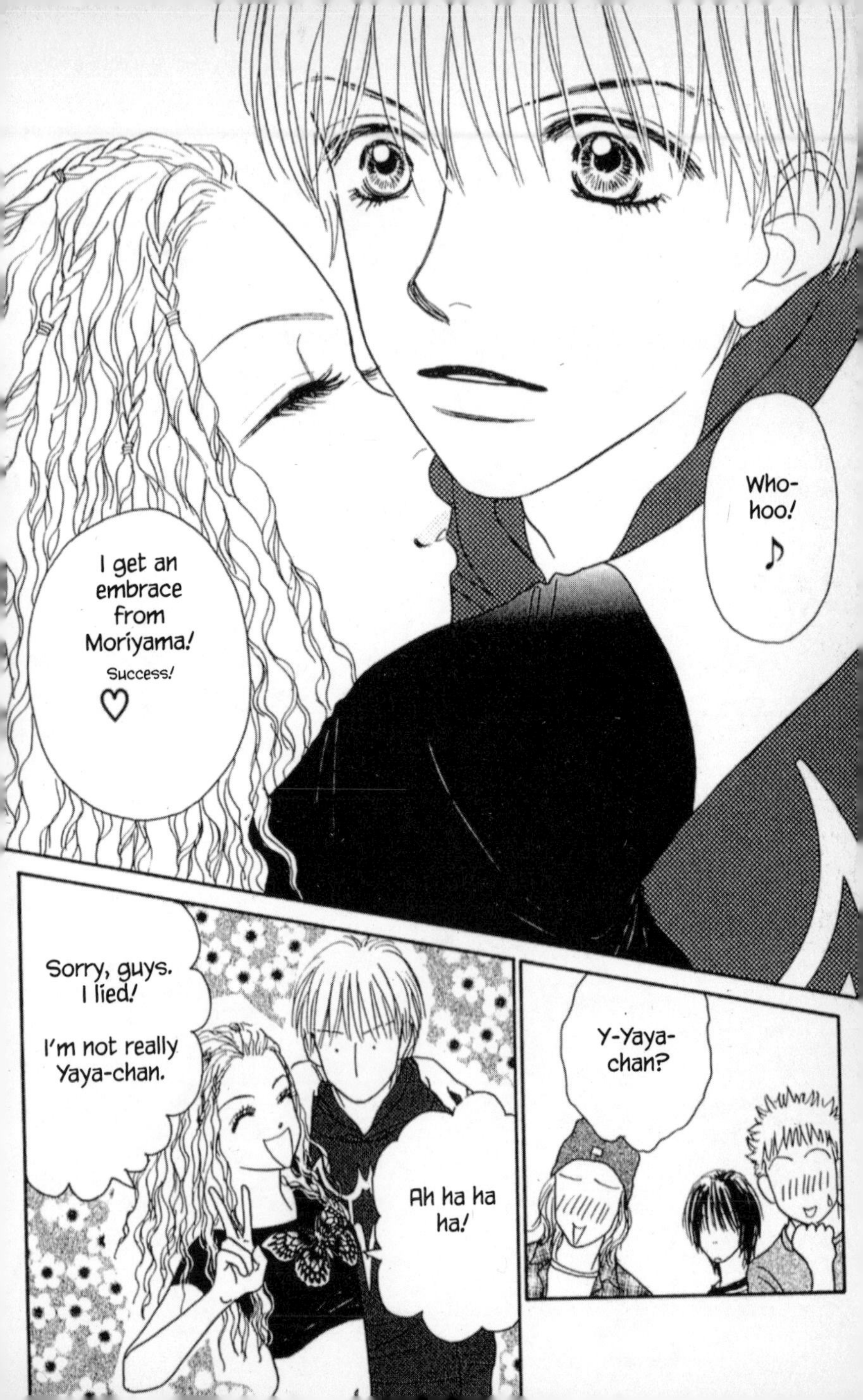
Who-hoo! ♪
I get an embrace from Moriyama! Success! ♡
Y-Yaya-chan?
Sorry, guys. I lied!
I'm not really Yaya-chan.
Ah ha ha ha!

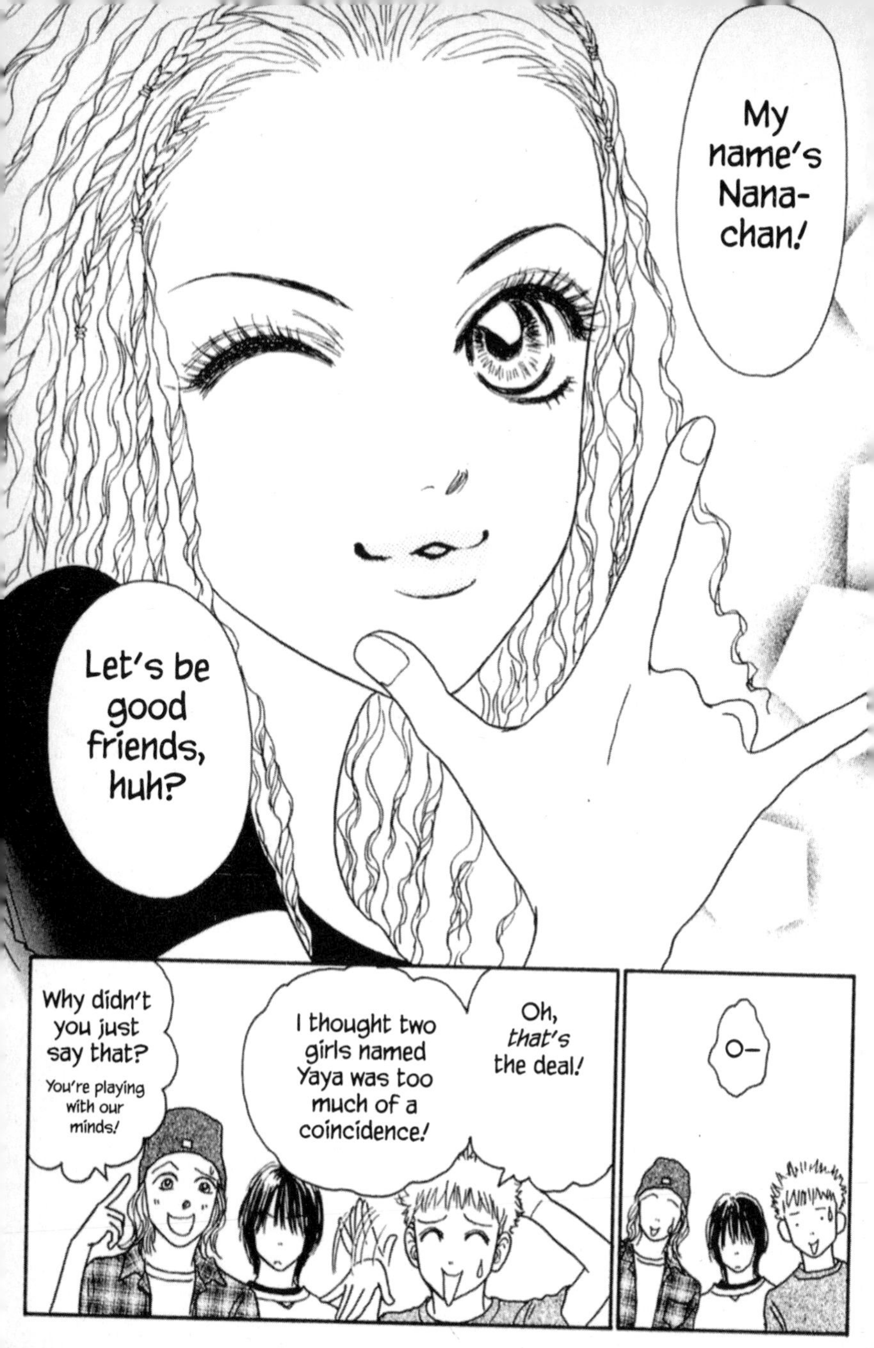

My name's Nana-chan!
Let's be good friends, huh?
O–
Oh, *that's* the deal!
I thought two girls named Yaya was too much of a coincidence!
Why didn't you just say that?
You're playing with our minds!

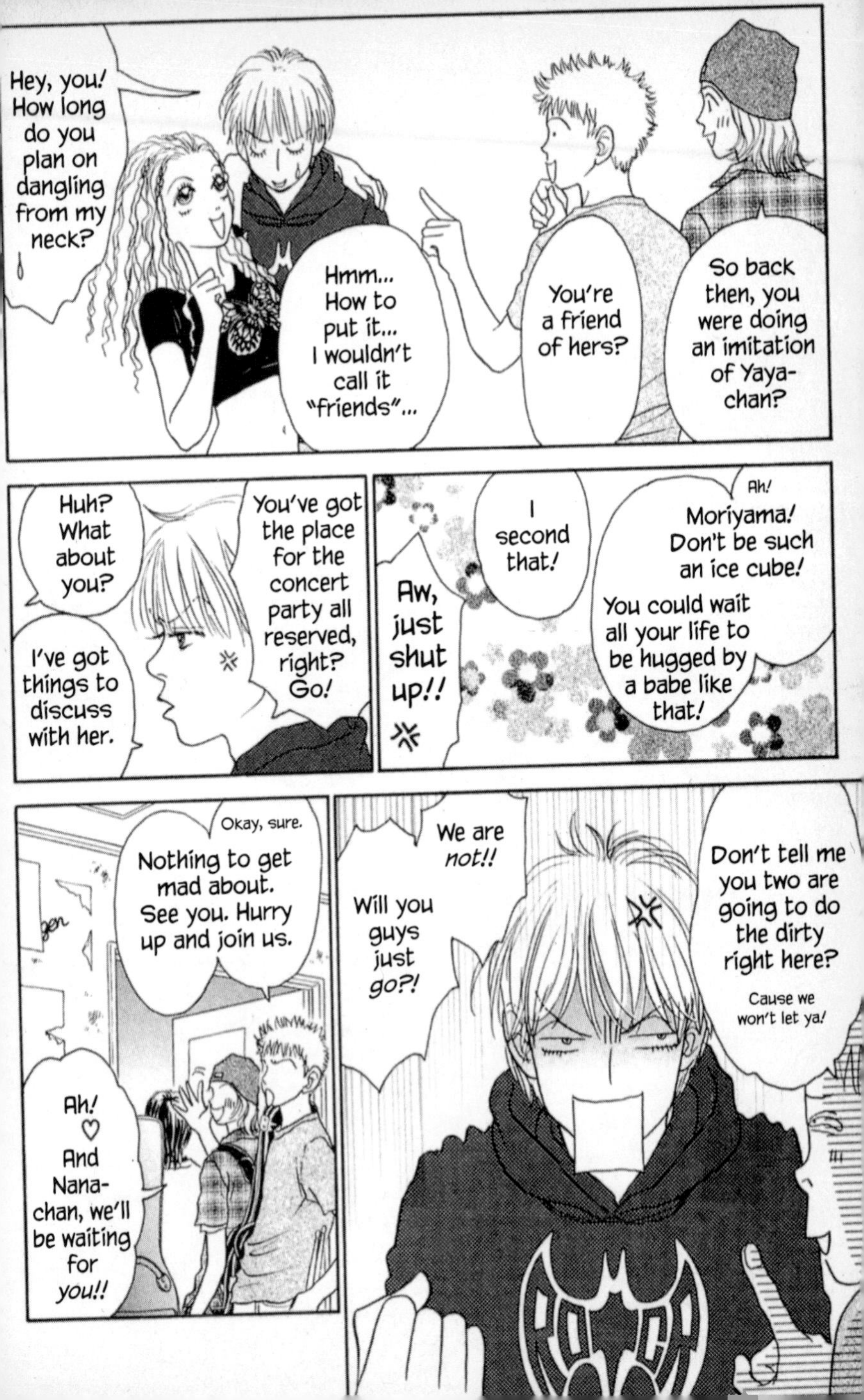
Hey, you! How long do you plan on dangling from my neck?
Hmm... How to put it... I wouldn't call it "friends"...
You're a friend of hers?
So back then, you were doing an imitation of Yaya-chan?
Huh? What about you?
I've got things to discuss with her.
You've got the place for the concert party all reserved, right? Go!
Aw, just shut up!!
I second that!
Ah! Moriyama! Don't be such an ice cube!
You could wait all your life to be hugged by a babe like that!
Okay, sure.
Nothing to get mad about. See you. Hurry up and join us.
Ah! ♡ And Nana-chan, we'll be waiting for *you!!*
We are *not!!*
Will you guys just *go?!*
Don't tell me you two are going to do the dirty right here?
Cause we won't let ya!

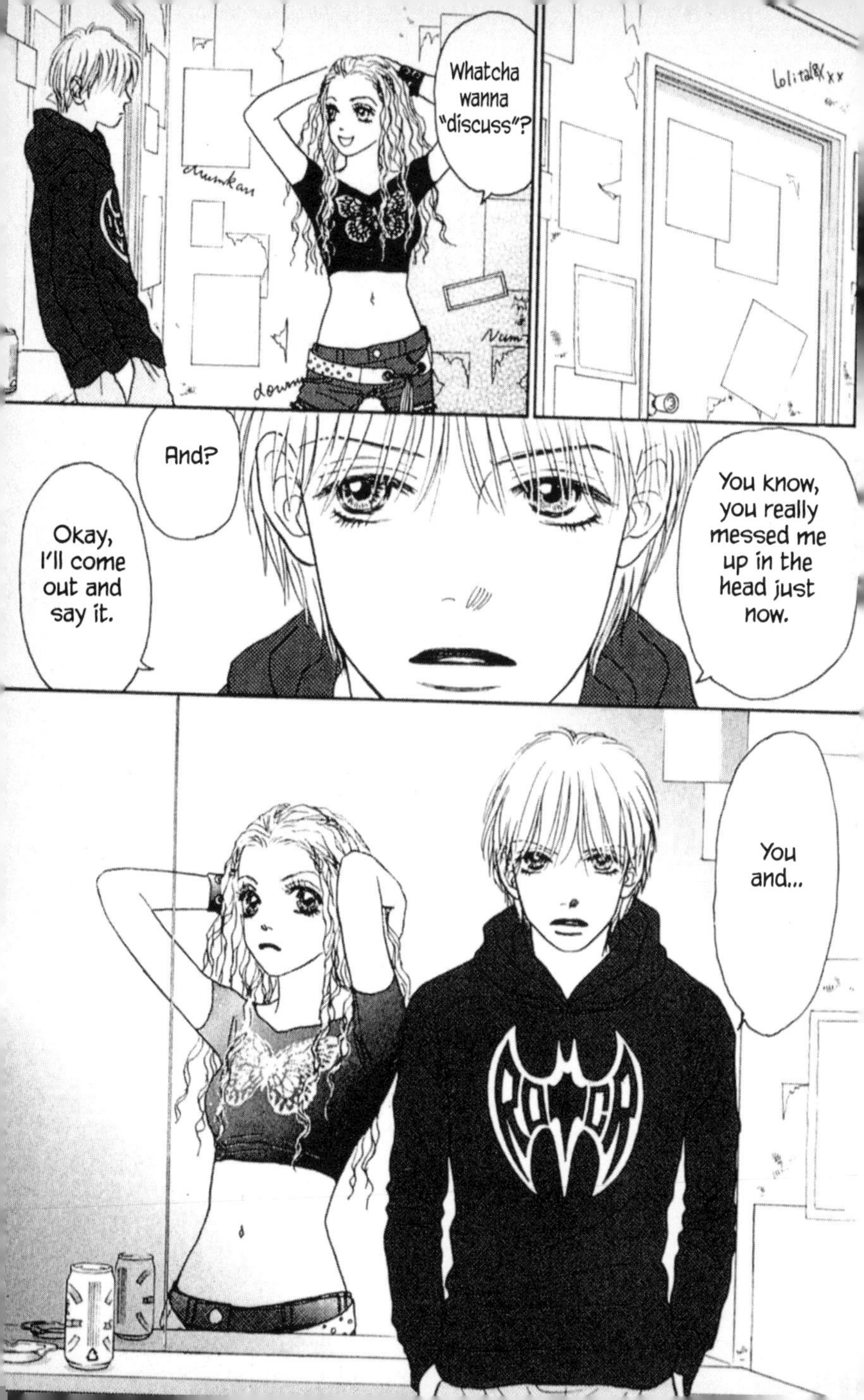
Whatcha wanna "discuss"?
You know, you really messed me up in the head just now.
And?
Okay, I'll come out and say it.
You and...

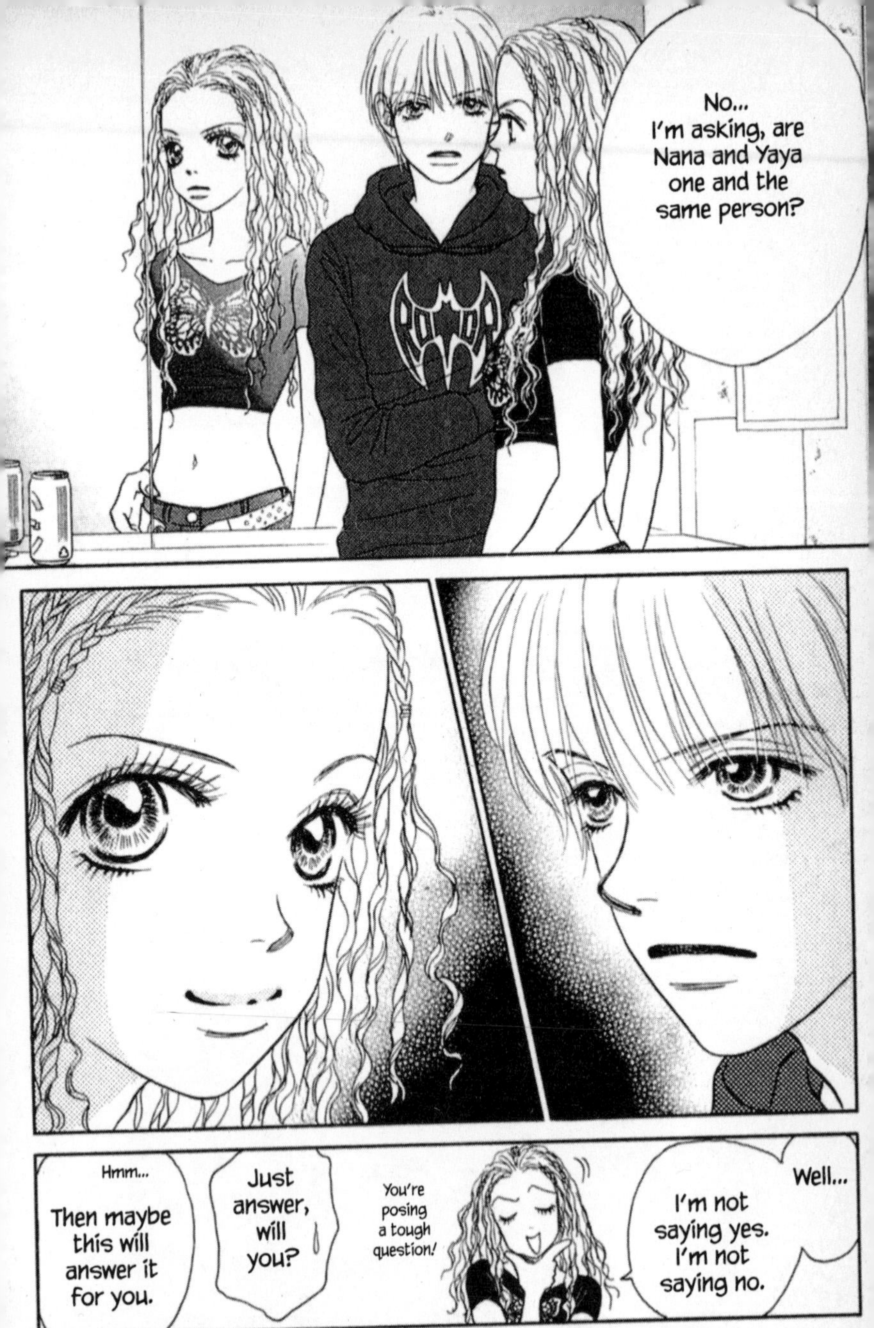
No... I'm asking, are Nana and Yaya one and the same person?
Well...
I'm not saying yes. I'm not saying no.
You're posing a tough question!
Just answer, will you?
Hmm...
Then maybe this will answer it for you.

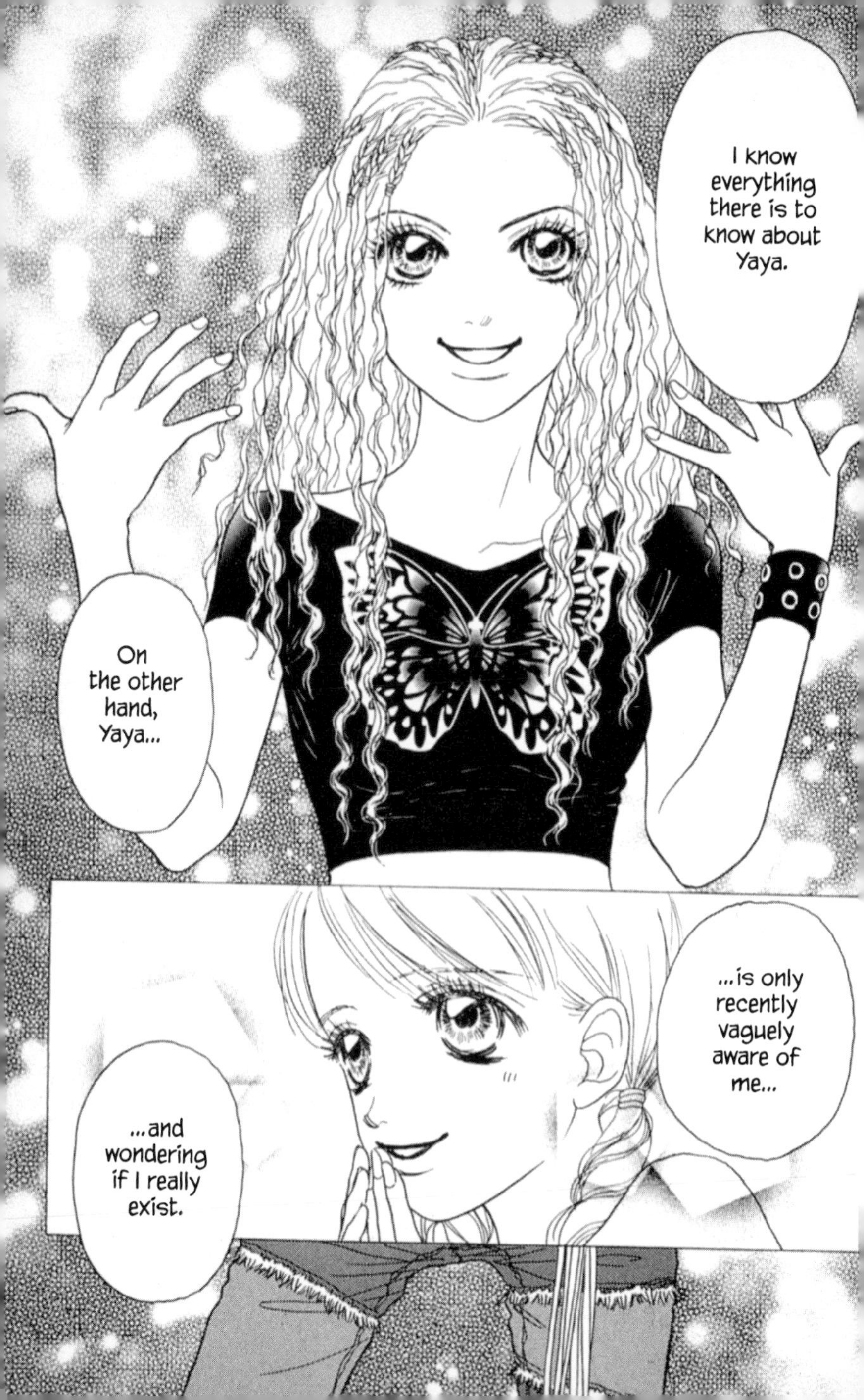
I know everything there is to know about Yaya.
On the other hand, Yaya...
...is only recently vaguely aware of me...
...and wondering if I really exist.

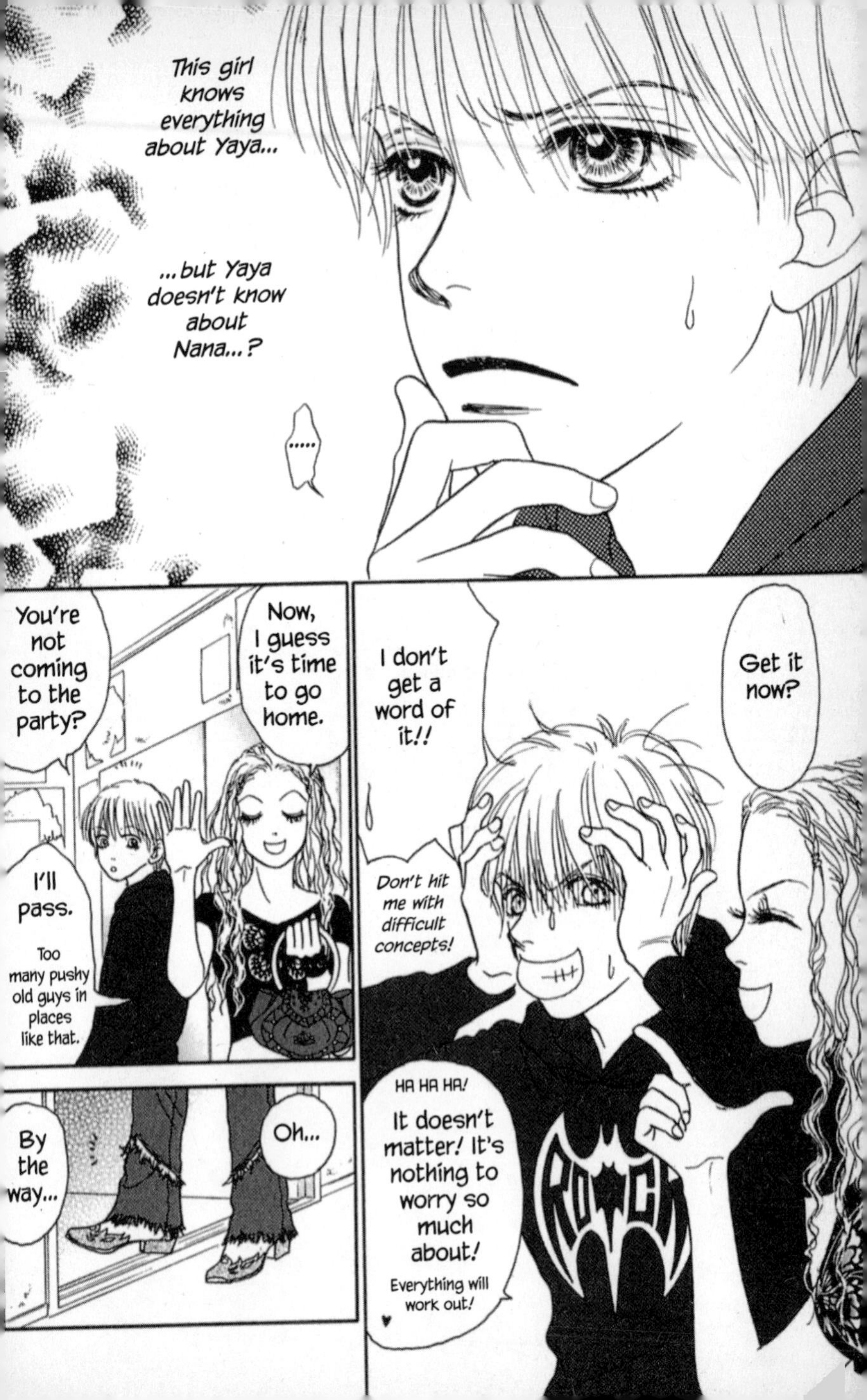
This girl knows everything about Yaya...
...but Yaya doesn't know about Nana...?
......
Get it now?
I don't get a word of it!!
Don't hit me with difficult concepts!
HA HA HA!
It doesn't matter! It's nothing to worry so much about!
Everything will work out!
Now, I guess it's time to go home.
You're not coming to the party?
I'll pass.
Too many pushy old guys in places like that.
Oh...
By the way...

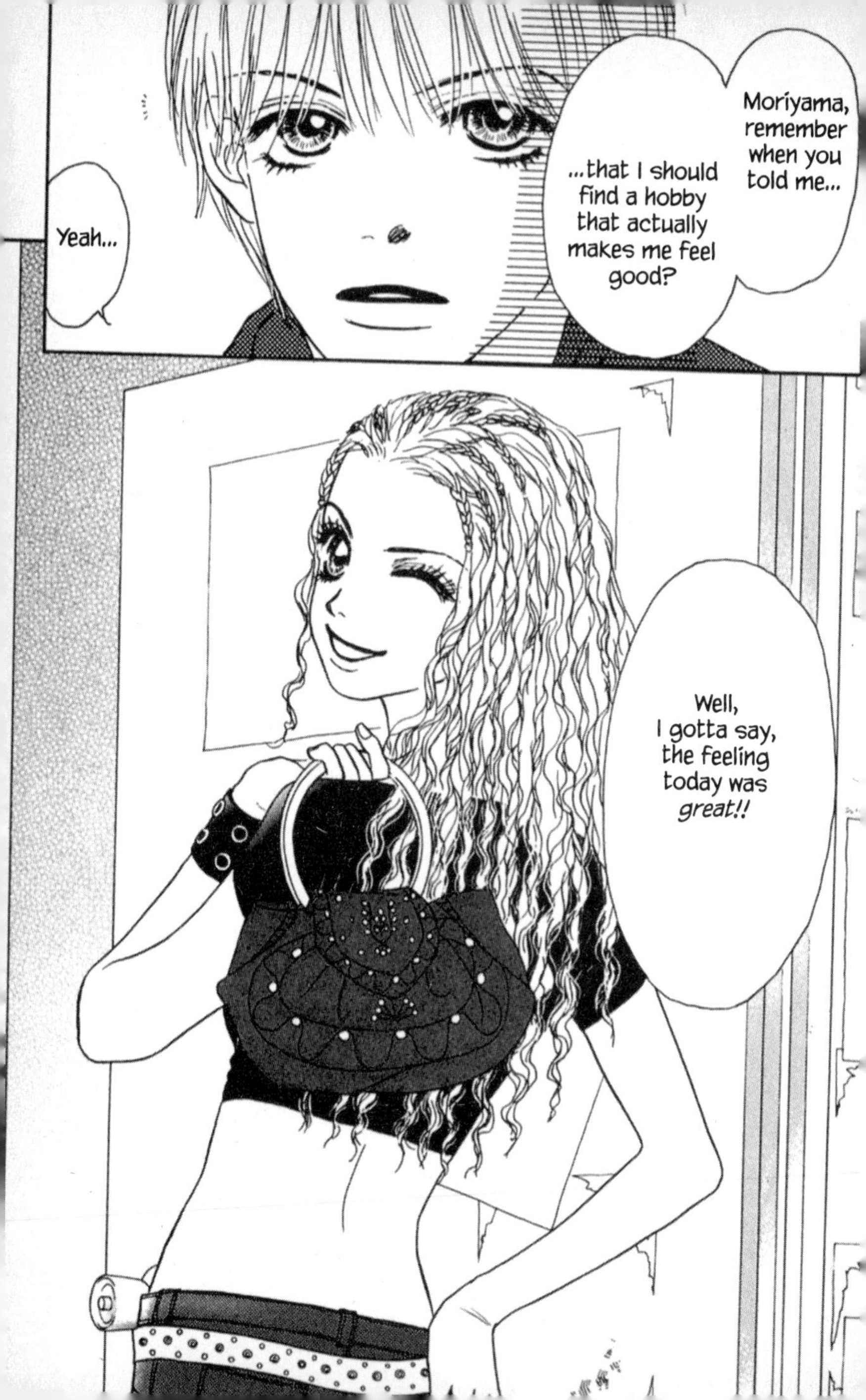
Moriyama, remember when you told me...
...that I should find a hobby that actually makes me feel good?
Yeah...
Well, I gotta say, the feeling today was *great!!*

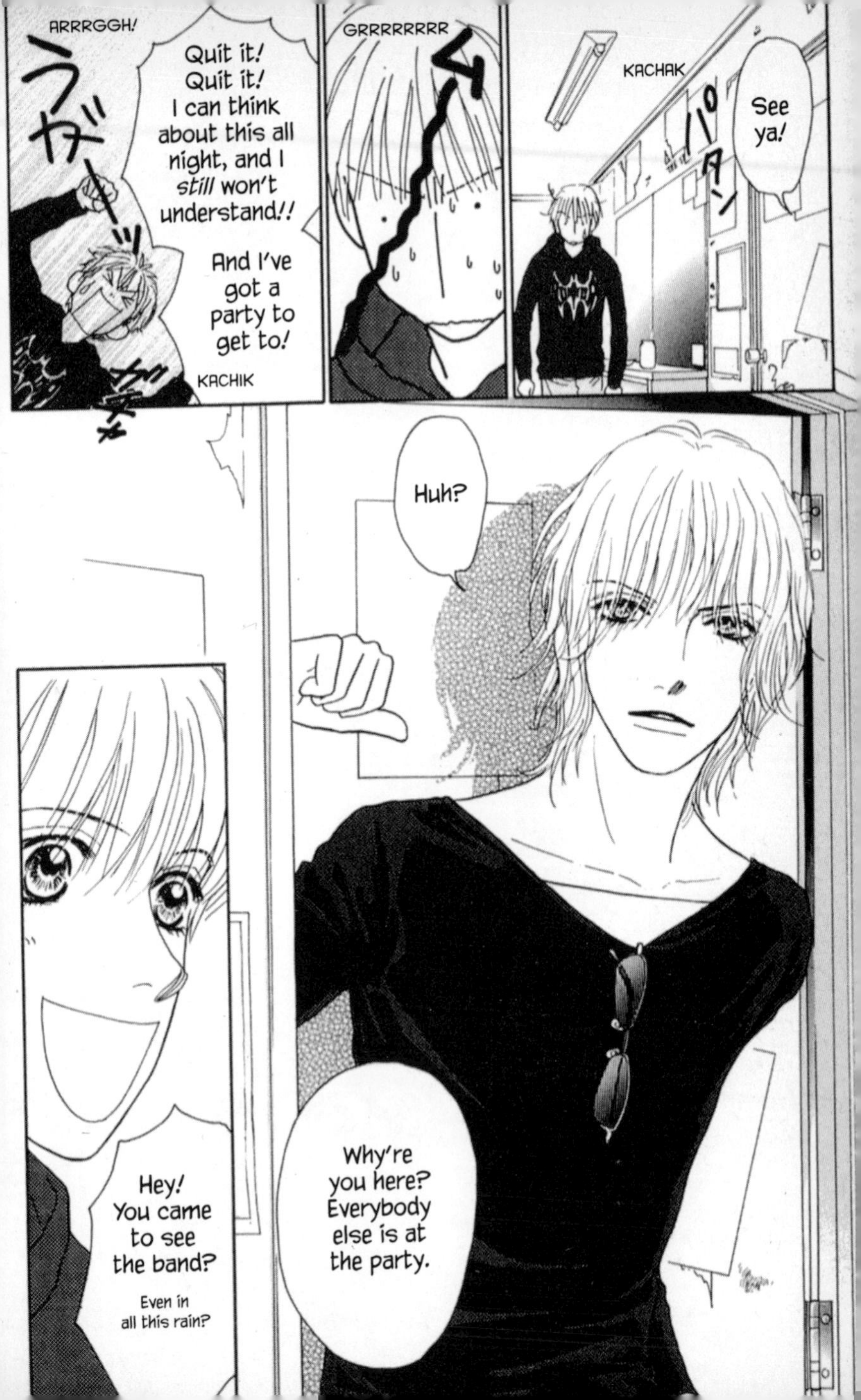
KACHAK
See ya!
GRRRRRRRR
ARRRGGH!
Quit it! Quit it! I can think about this all night, and I *still* won't understand!!
And I've got a party to get to!
KACHIK
Huh?
Why're you here? Everybody else is at the party.
Hey! You came to see the band?
Even in all this rain?

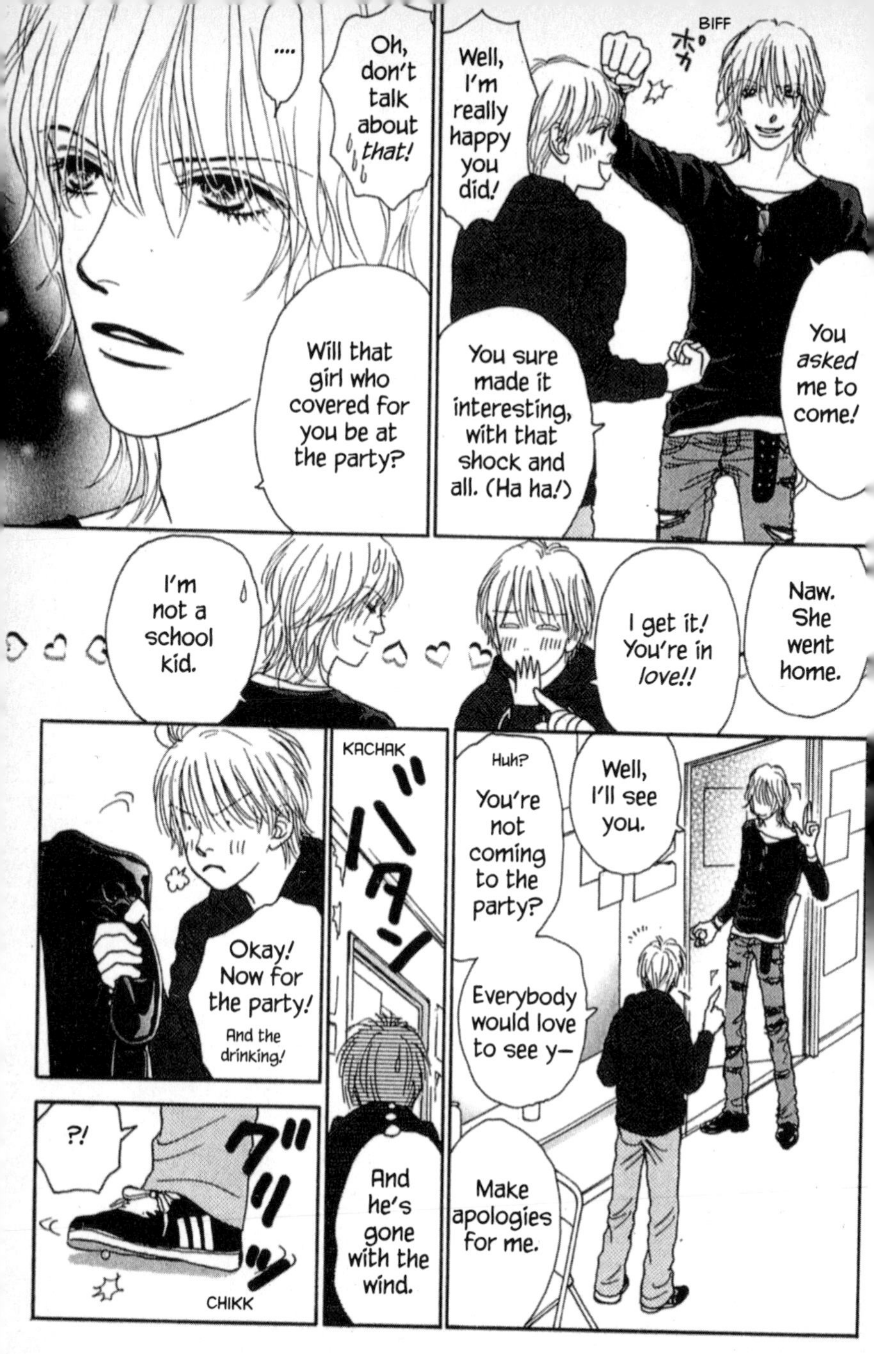
BIFF
You *asked* me to come!
Well, I'm really happy you did!
You sure made it interesting, with that shock and all. (Ha ha!)
Oh, don't talk about *that*!
....
Will that girl who covered for you be at the party?
Naw. She went home.
I get it! You're in *love*!!
I'm not a school kid.
Well, I'll see you.
Huh?
You're not coming to the party?
Everybody would love to see y—
Make apologies for me.
KACHAK
And he's gone with the wind.
Okay! Now for the party!
And the drinking!
?!
CHIKK

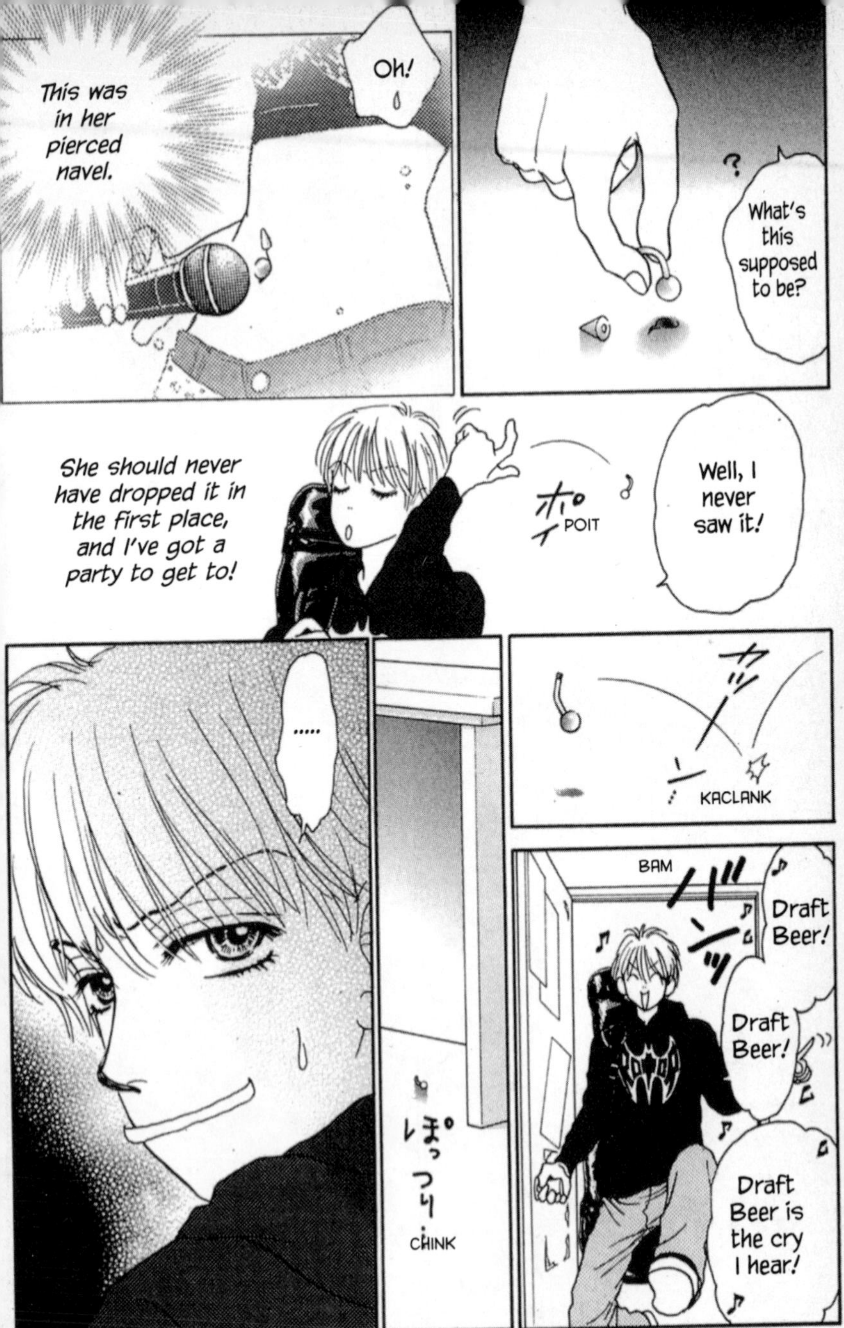
Oh!
This was in her pierced navel.
?
What's this supposed to be?
Well, I never saw it!
ポイ POIT
She should never have dropped it in the first place, and I've got a party to get to!
カツーン KACLANK
.....
ぽっつり CHINK
バーンッ BAM
Draft Beer!
Draft Beer!
Draft Beer is the cry I hear!

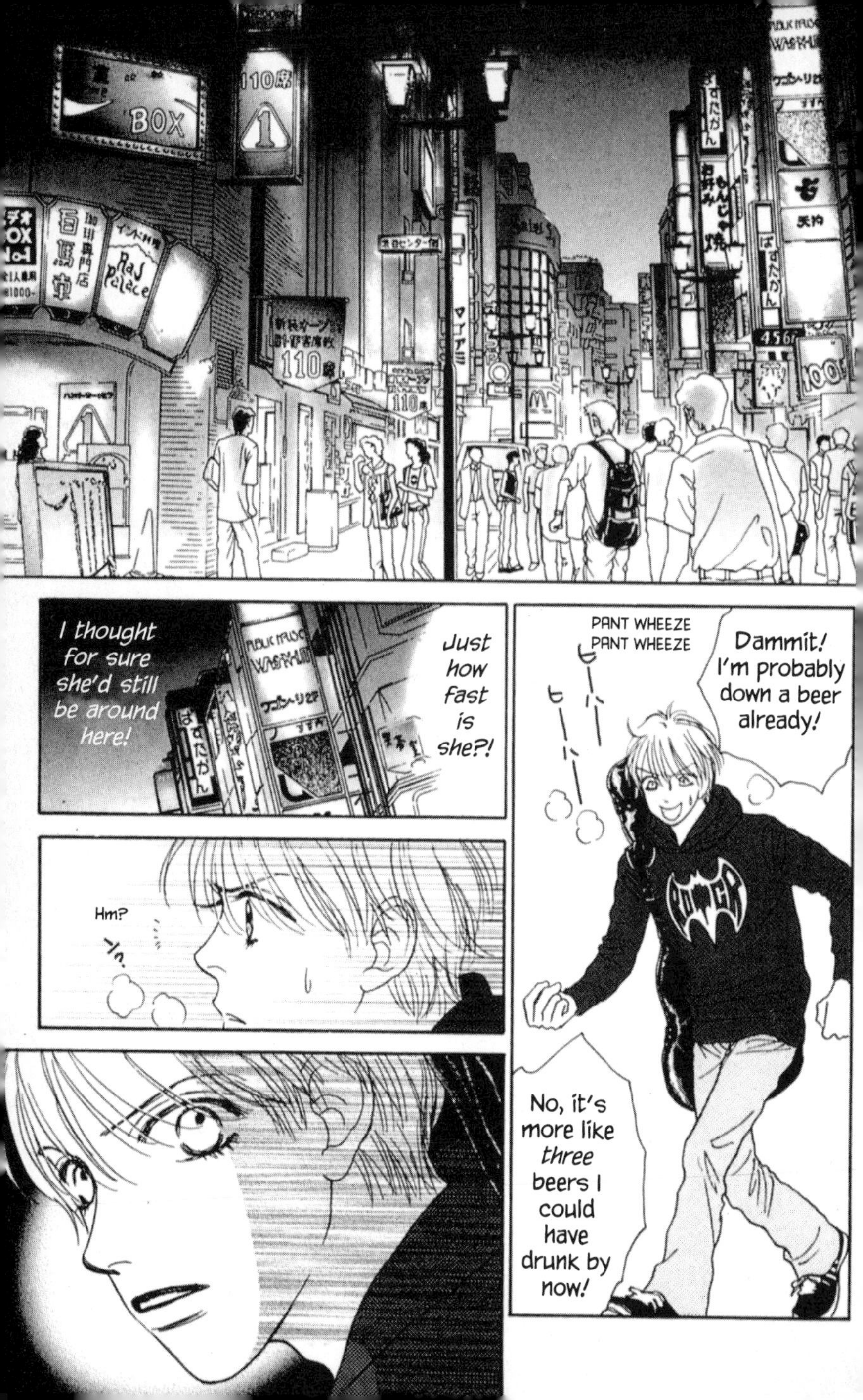
BOX
110席
Raj Palace
110席
110席
I thought for sure she'd still be around here!
Just how fast is she?!
PANT WHEEZE
PANT WHEEZE
Dammit! I'm probably down a beer already!
Hm?
No, it's more like *three* beers I could have drunk by now!

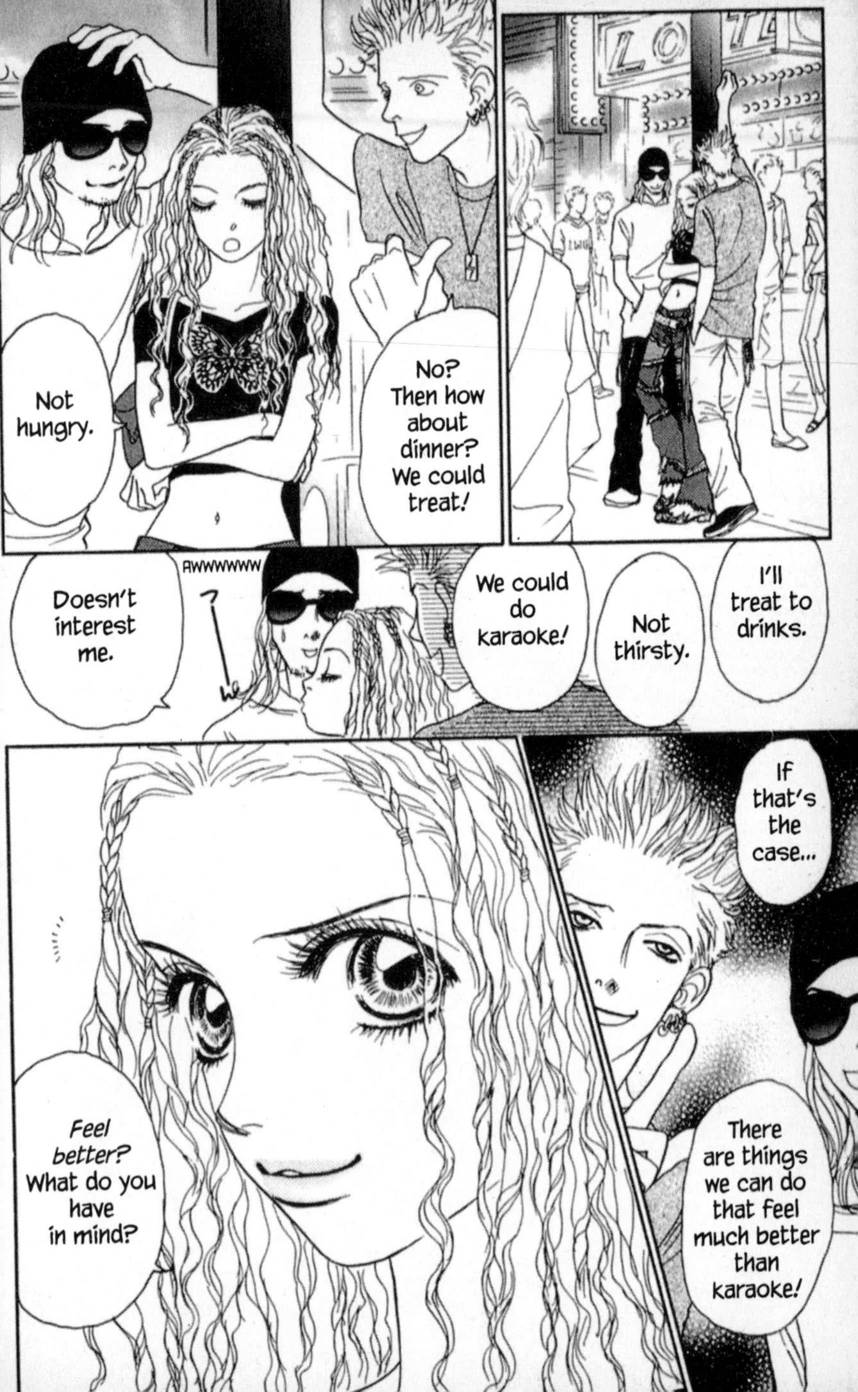
No? Then how about dinner? We could treat!
Not hungry.
I'll treat to drinks.
Not thirsty.
We could do karaoke!
Doesn't interest me.
AWWWWWW
If that's the case...
There are things we can do that feel much better than karaoke!
Feel better? What do you have in mind?

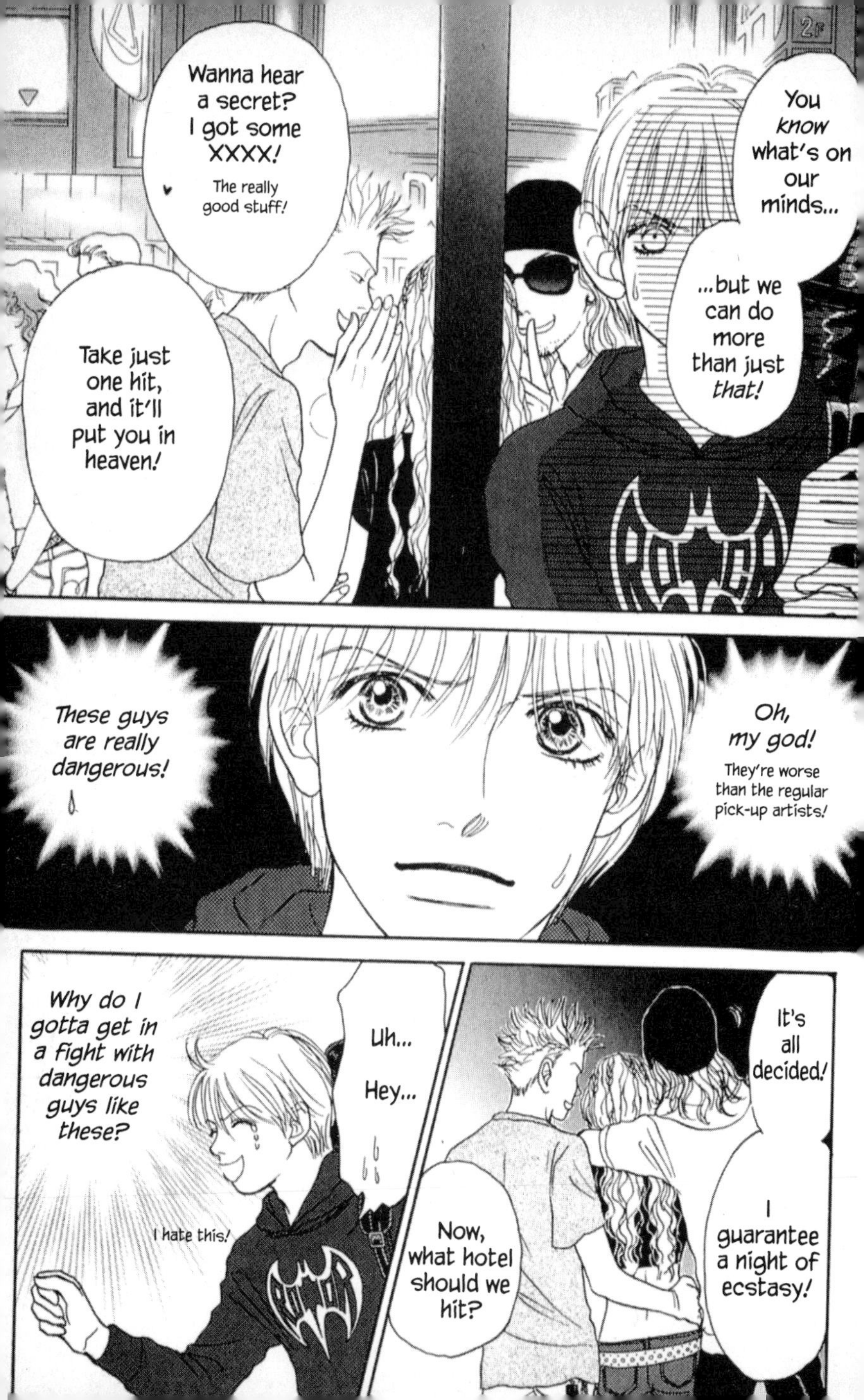
Wanna hear a secret? I got some XXXX!
The really good stuff!
Take just one hit, and it'll put you in heaven!
You know what's on our minds...
...but we can do more than just that!
These guys are really dangerous!
Oh, my god!
They're worse than the regular pick-up artists!
Why do I gotta get in a fight with dangerous guys like these?
I hate this!
Uh...
Hey...
Now, what hotel should we hit?
It's all decided!
I guarantee a night of ecstasy!

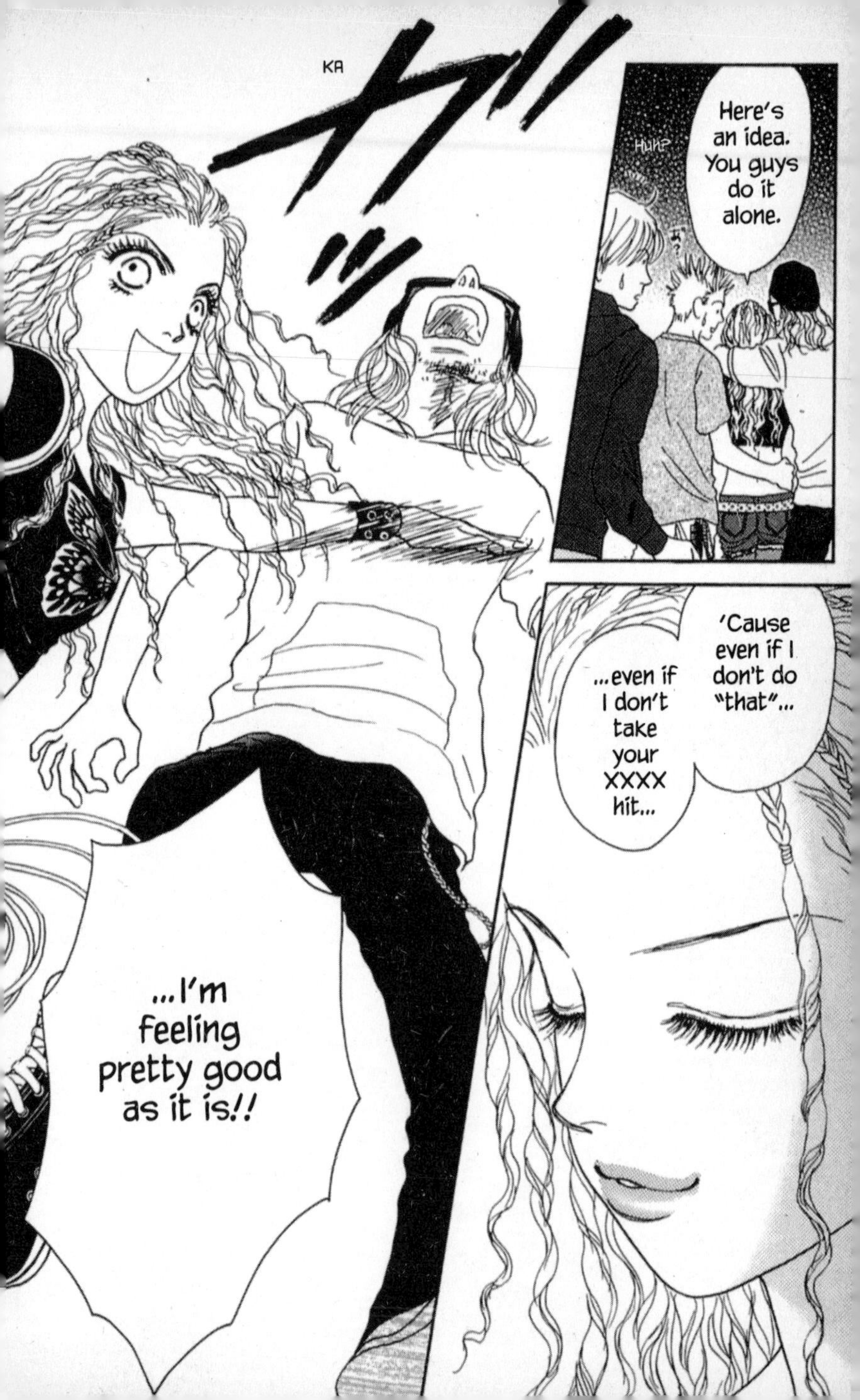
Here's an idea. You guys do it alone.
Huh?
'Cause even if I don't do "that"...
...even if I don't take your XXXX hit...
KA
...I'm feeling pretty good as it is!!

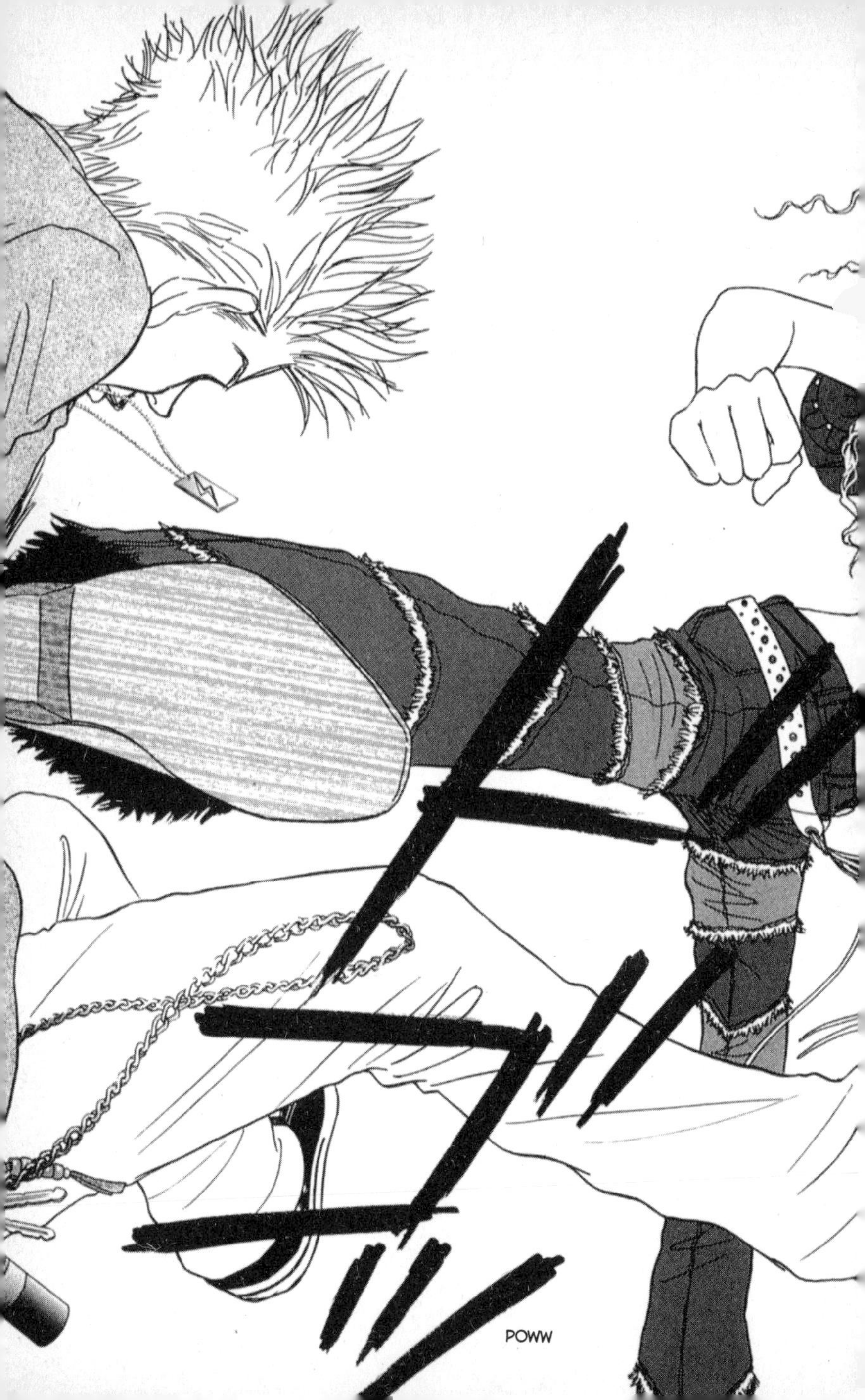
POWW

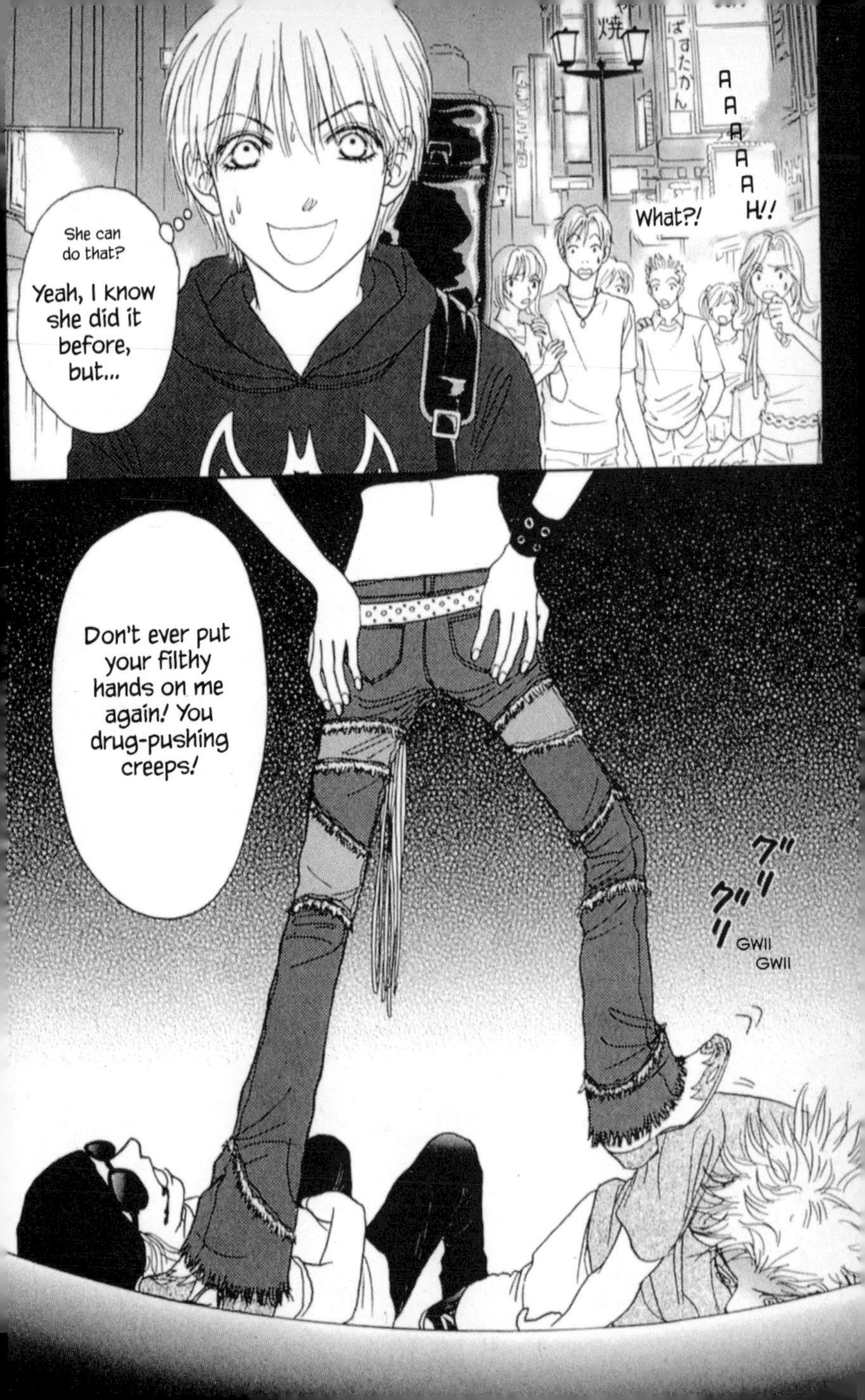

焼
ぱすたかん
AAAAAH!!
What?!
She can do that?
Yeah, I know she did it before, but...
Don't ever put your filthy hands on me again! You drug-pushing creeps!
グリグリ
GWII GWII

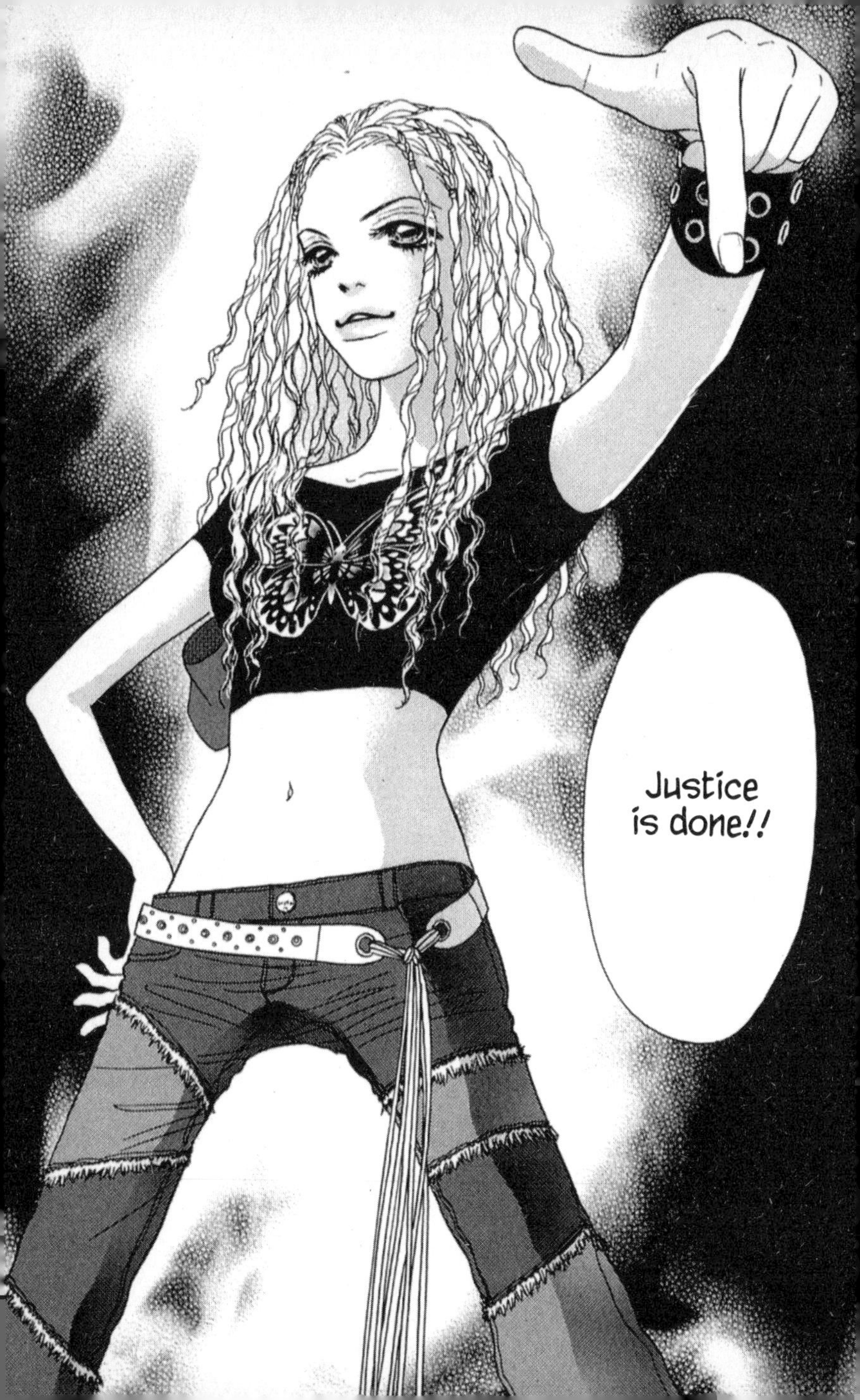
Justice is done!!

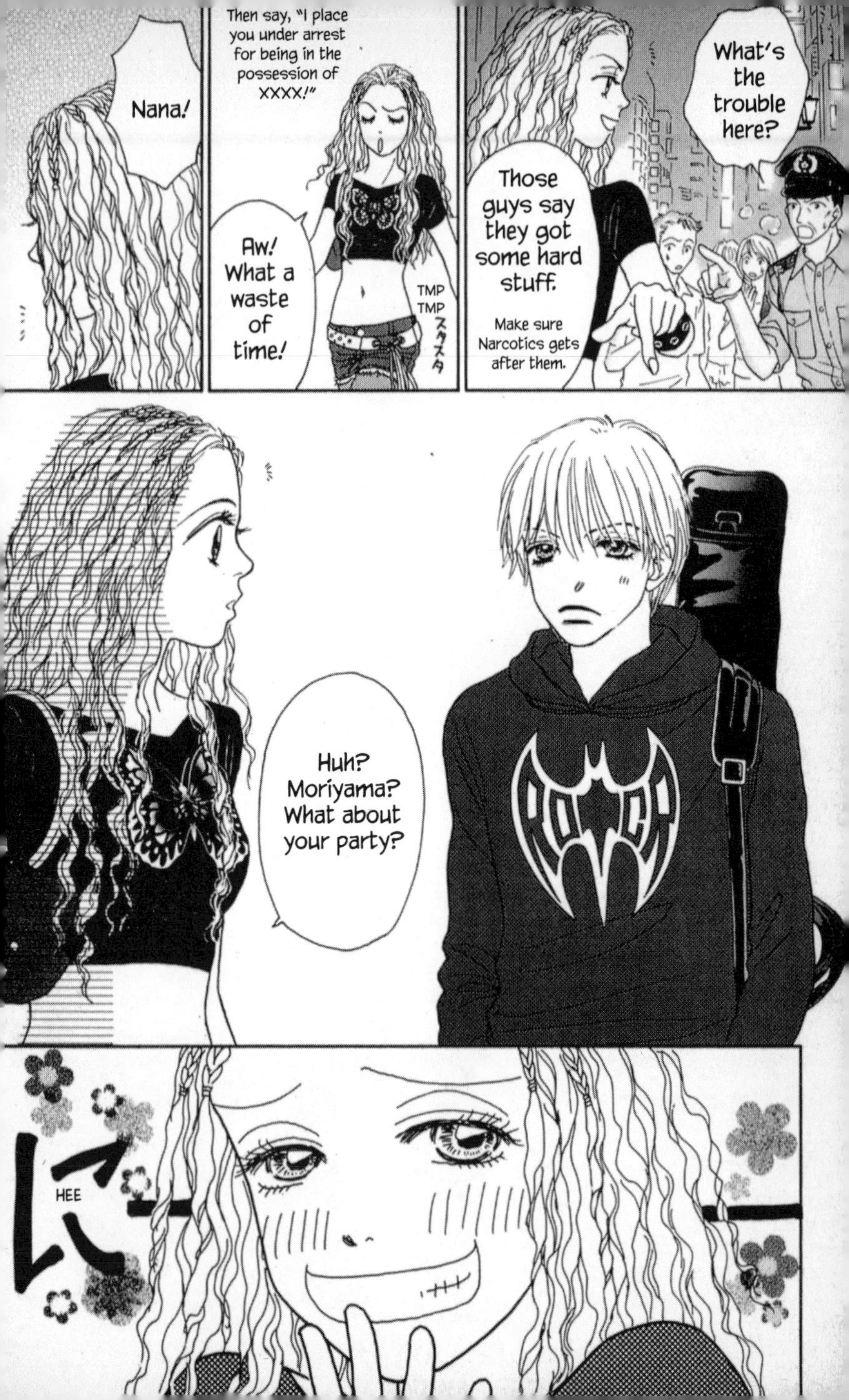
What's the trouble here?
Those guys say they got some hard stuff.
Make sure Narcotics gets after them.
Then say, "I place you under arrest for being in the possession of XXXX!"
Aw! What a waste of time!
TMP TMP
スタスタ
Nana!
Huh? Moriyama? What about your party?
HEE

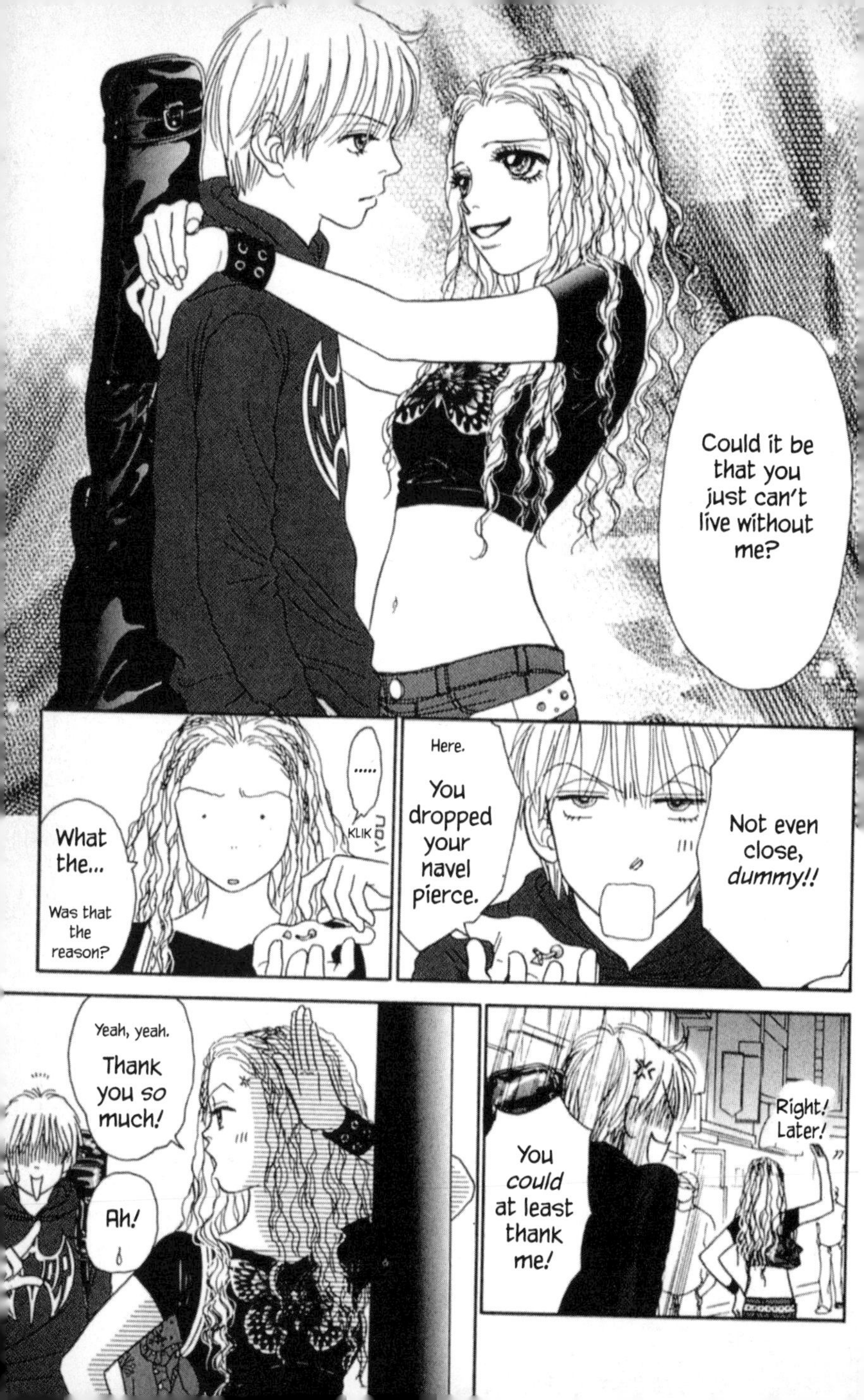
Could it be that you just can't live without me?
.....
KLIK
Here.
You dropped your navel pierce.
What the...
Was that the reason?
Not even close, dummy!!
Yeah, yeah.
Thank you so much!
Ah!
You could at least thank me!
Right! Later!

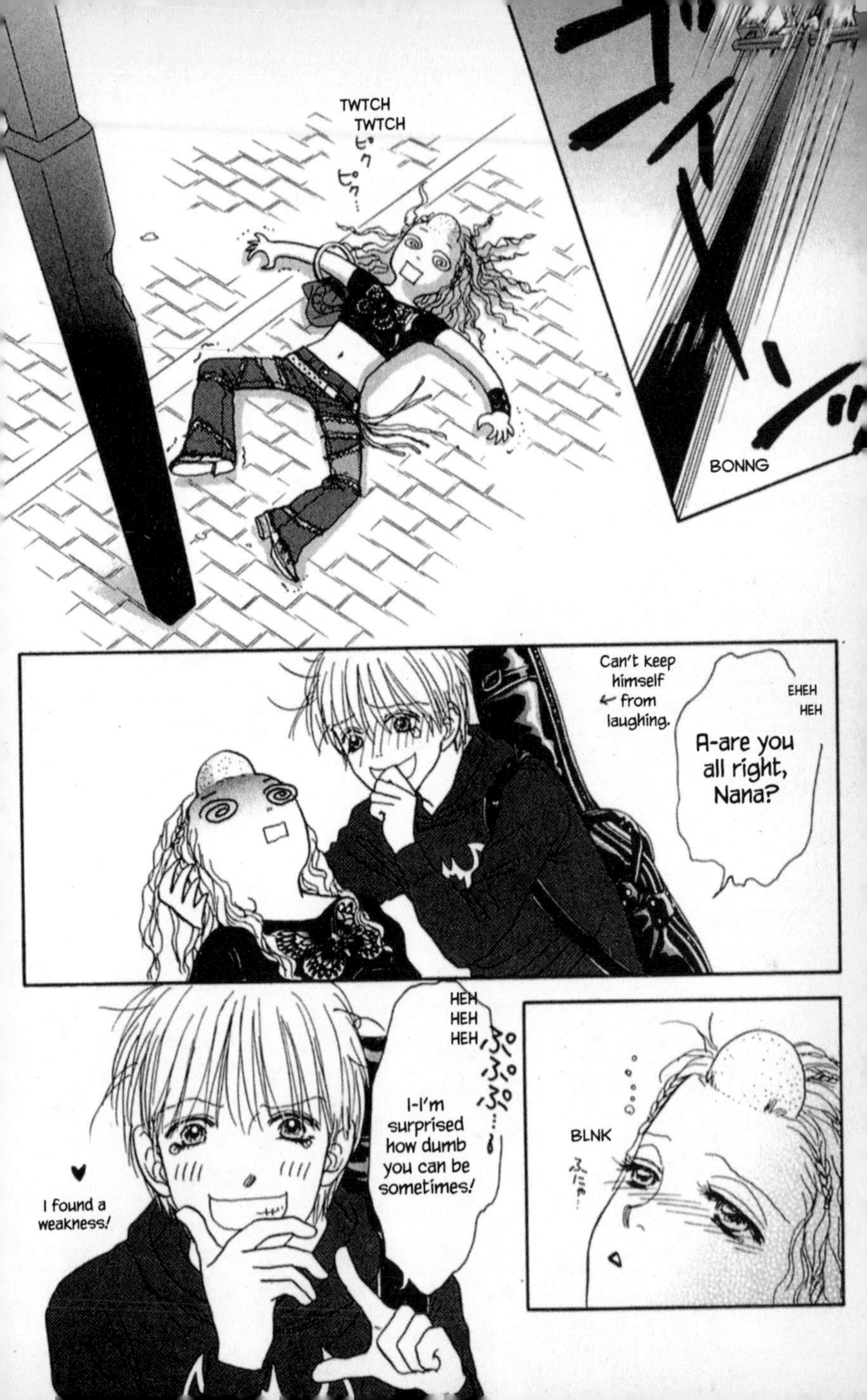
BONNG
TWTCH TWTCH
ピク ピク…
EHEH HEH
A-are you all right, Nana?
Can't keep himself from laughing.
BLNK
ふにゃ…
HEH HEH HEH
ふふふ…
I-I'm surprised how dumb you can be sometimes!
I found a weakness!

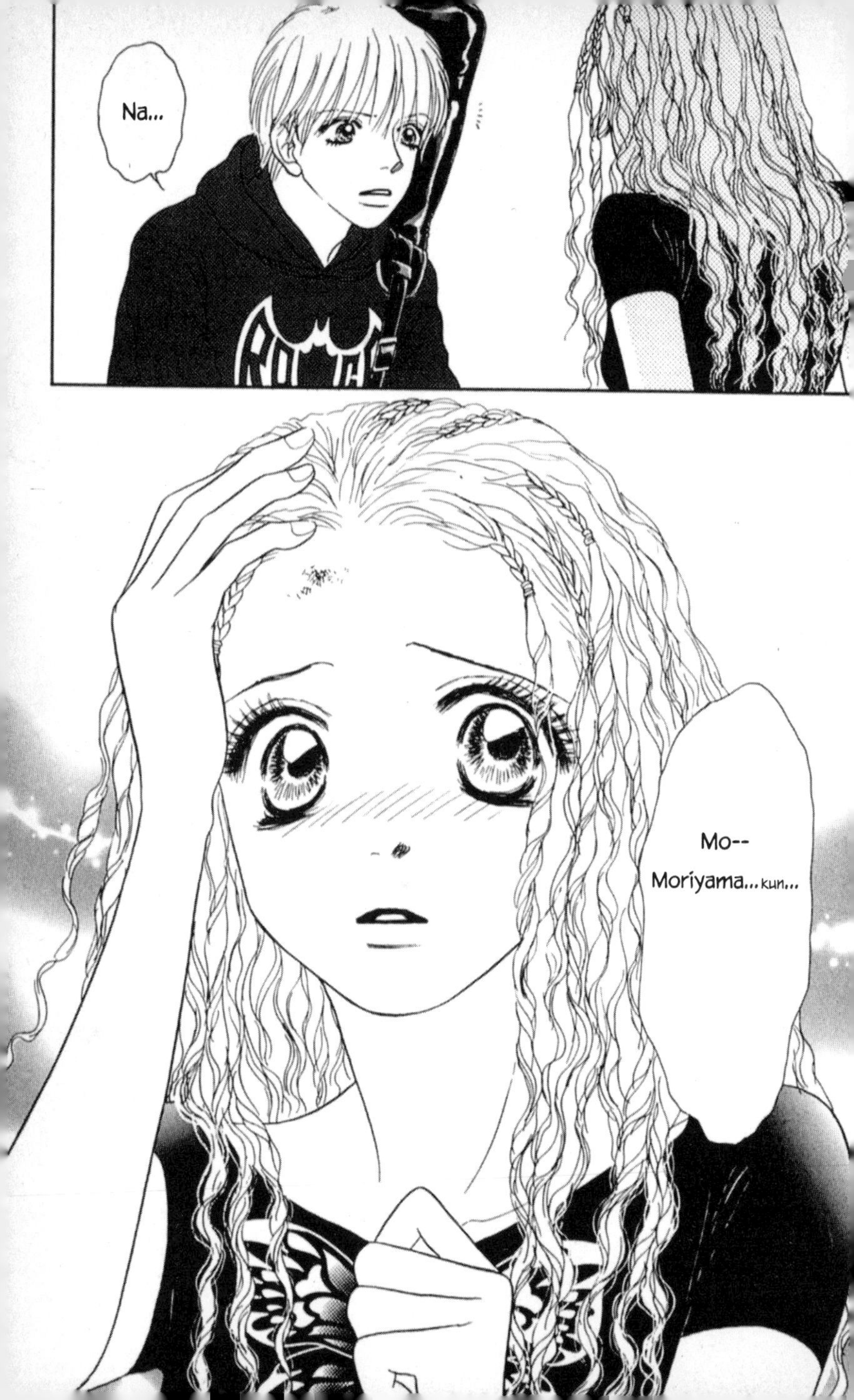
Na...
Mo-- Moriyama...kun...

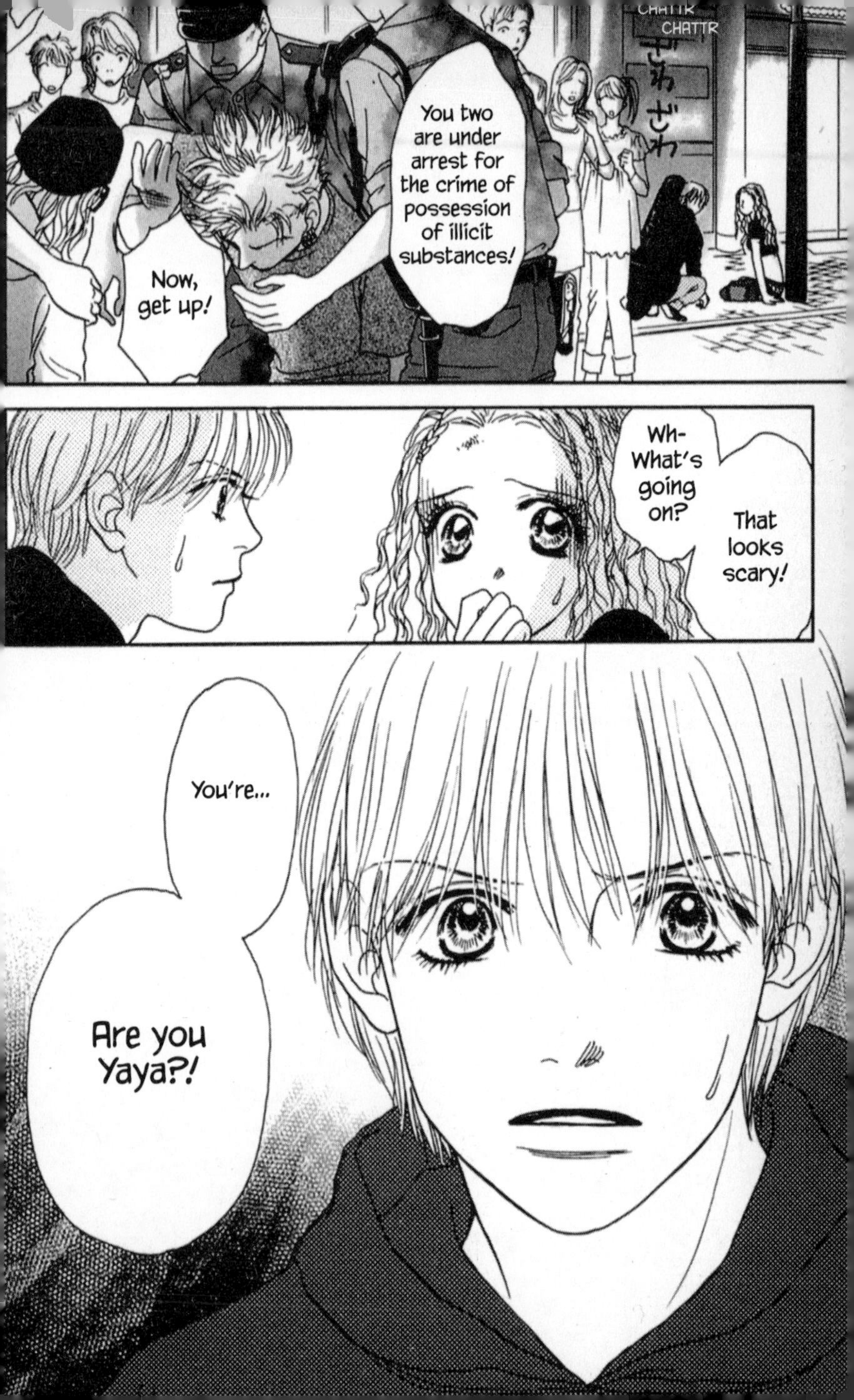
CHATTR
ざわざわ
You two are under arrest for the crime of possession of illicit substances!
Now, get up!
Wh- What's going on?
That looks scary!
You're...
Are you Yaya?!

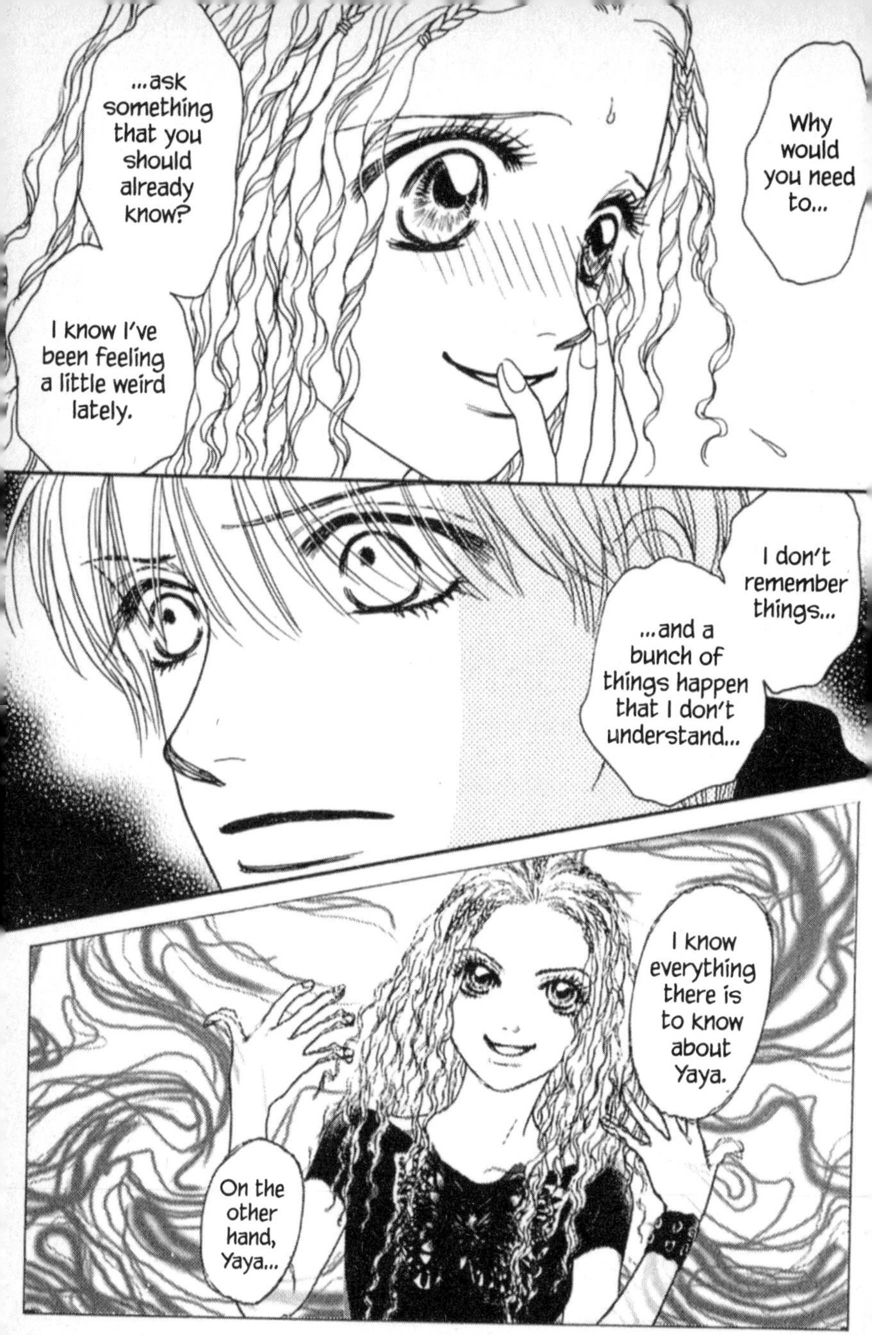
Why would you need to...
...ask something that you should already know?
I know I've been feeling a little weird lately.
I don't remember things...
...and a bunch of things happen that I don't understand...
I know everything there is to know about Yaya.
On the other hand, Yaya...

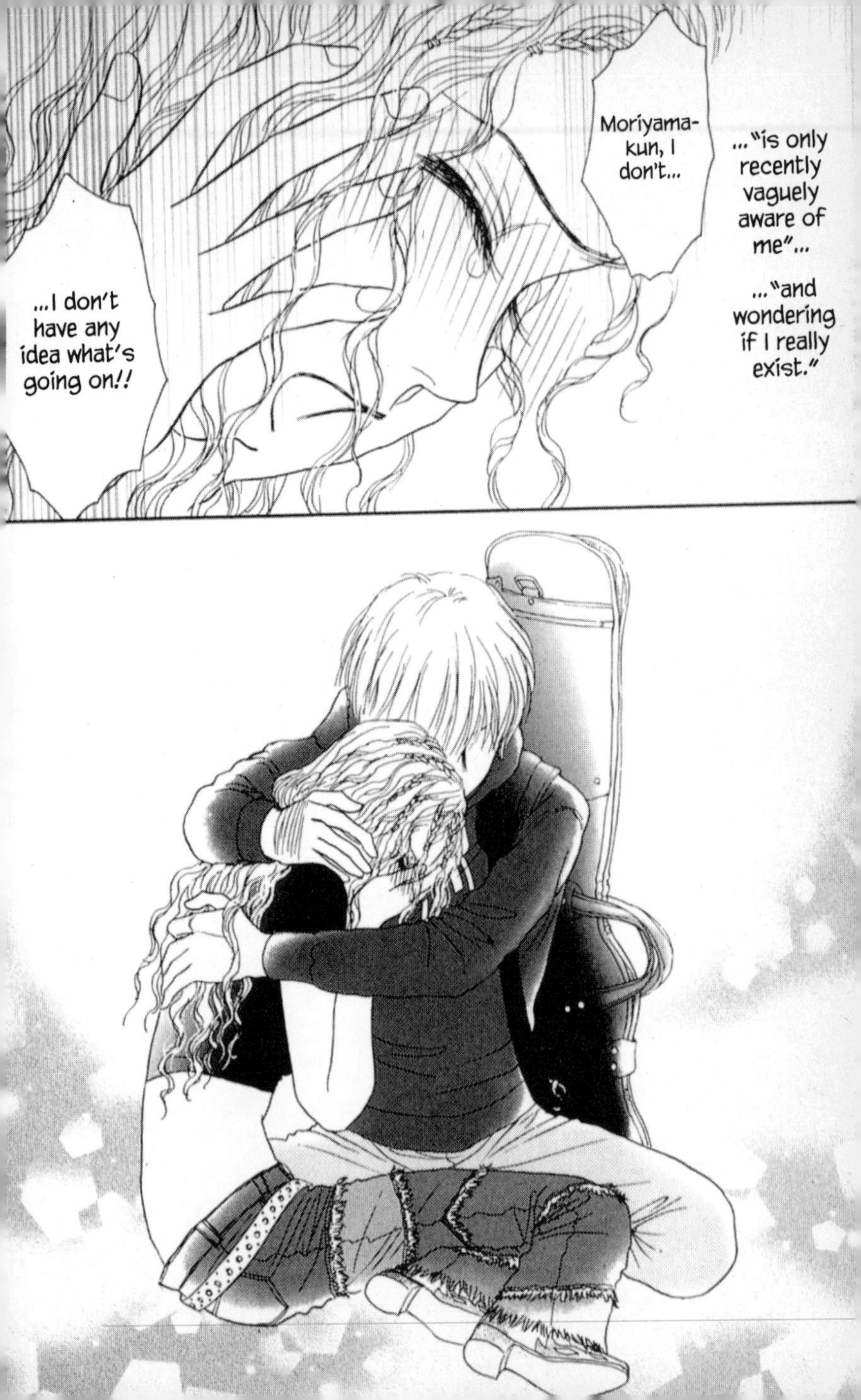
..."is only recently vaguely aware of me"...
..."and wondering if I really exist."
Moriyama-kun, I don't...
...I don't have any idea what's going on!!

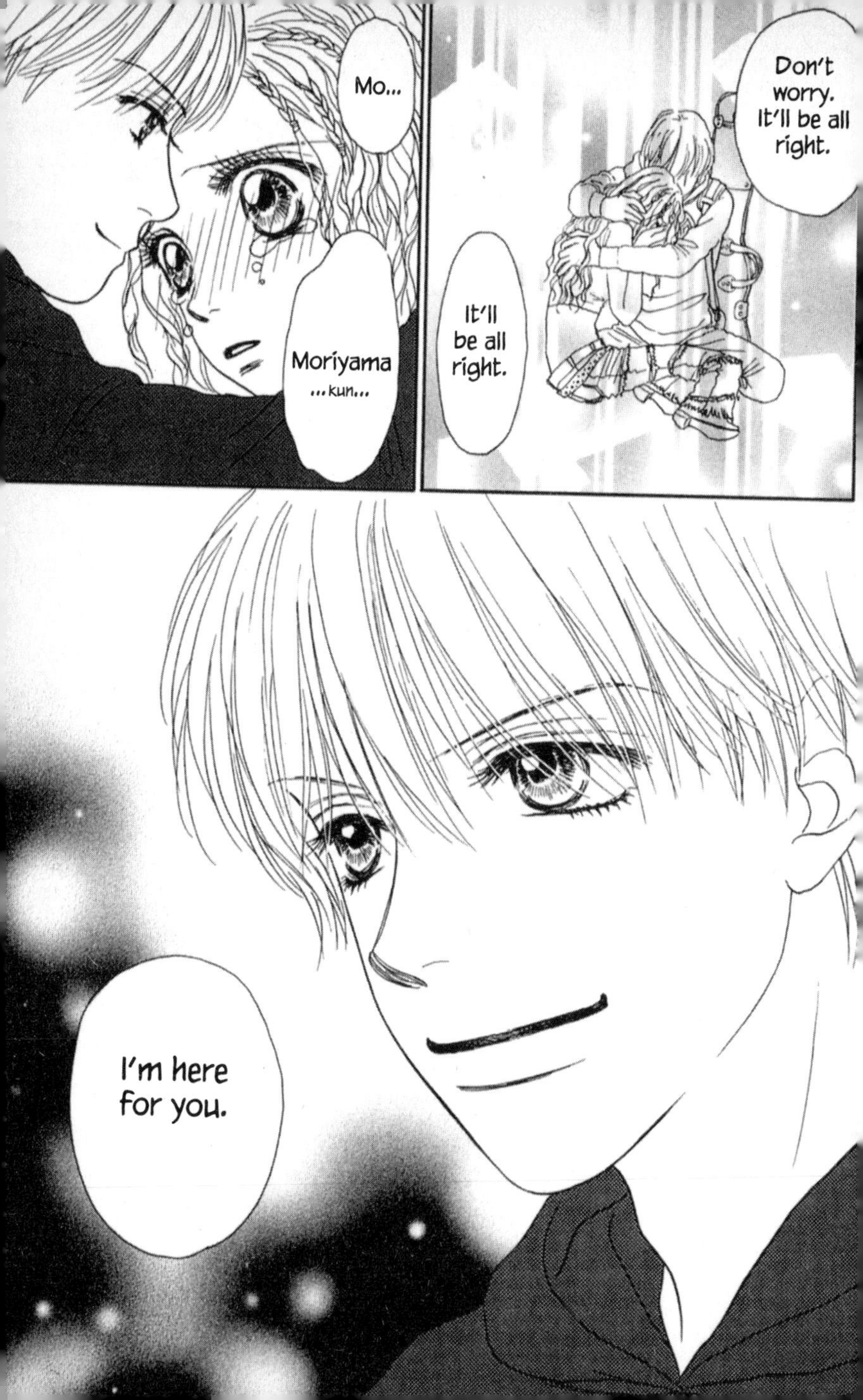
Don't worry. It'll be all right.
It'll be all right.
Mo...
Moriyama ...kun...
I'm here for you.

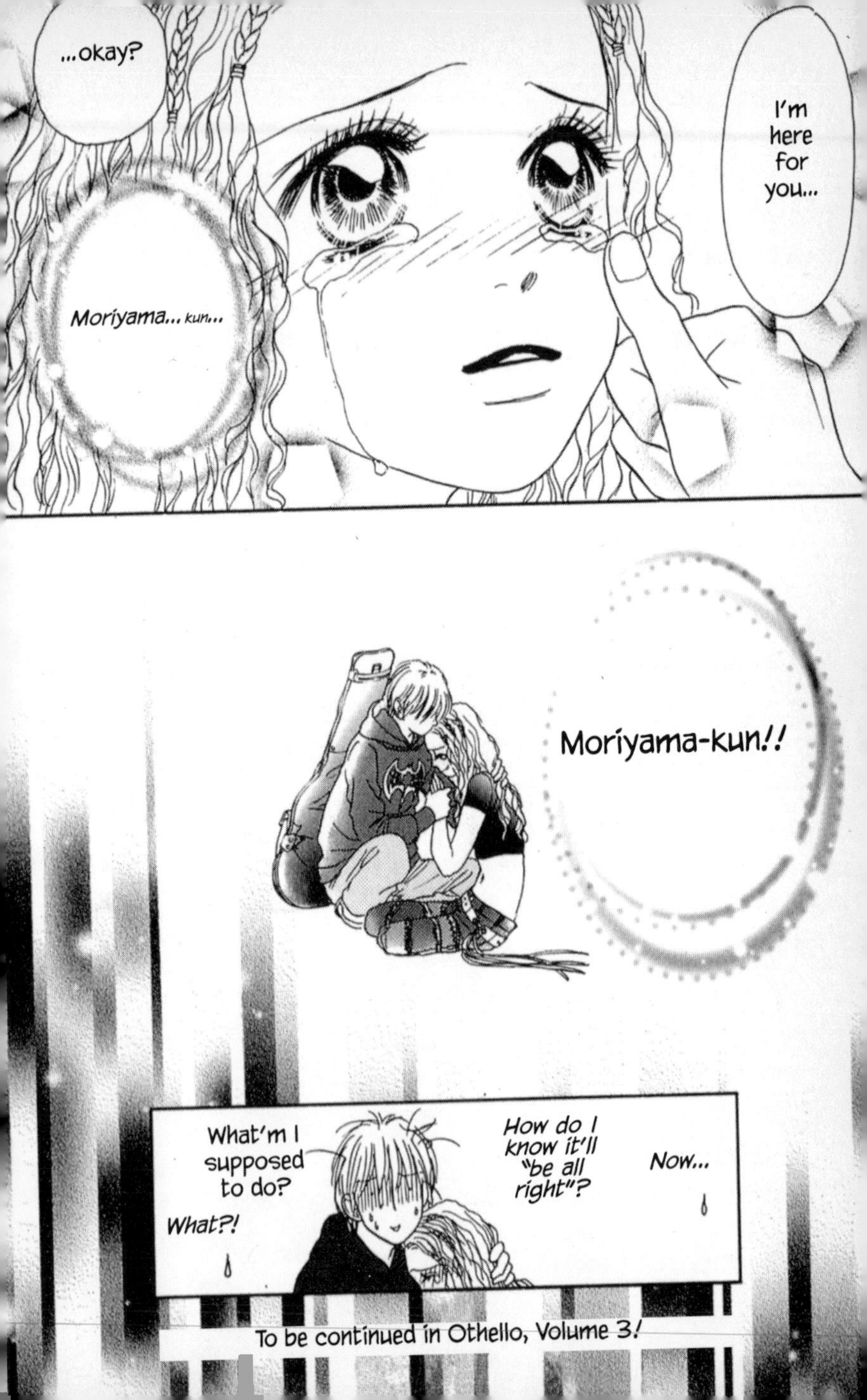
I'm here for you...
...okay?
Moriyama... kun...
Moriyama-kun!!
Now...
How do I know it'll "be all right"?
What'm I supposed to do?
What?!
To be continued in Othello, Volume 3!

+++++STAFF+++++

vol.1~8(2001.2~7/2002.3~6)

+++

Emi-Nishi

Michiyo-Kobori

Mitsuyo-Anzai

Rie-Sekine

Rie-Takeuchi

Eiko-Kobayashi

+++

Editor (Betsu-fure)

Satoru-Matsumoto

+++

My family

Hachiro & Yoshimi

+++

& YOU !

Thank You !!

by Satomi-Ikezawa

2002.8

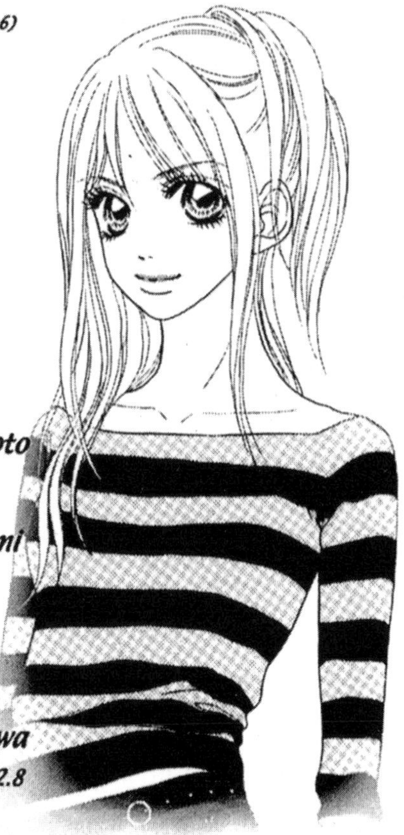

+++Please Access My Home Page+++

http://home.catv.ne.jp/dd/ikezawa/

About the Author

Satomi Ikezawa's previous work before *Othello* is *Guru Guru Pon-chan*. She currently continues to work on *Othello*, which is being serialized in the Kodansha weekly manga magazine, *Bessatsu Friend*.

Ikezawa won the 24th Kodansha Manga Prize in 2000 for *Guru Guru Pon-chan*.

She has two Labradors, named Guts and Ponta.

Translation Notes

Japanese is a tricky language for most Westerners, and translation is often more art than science. For your edification and reading pleasure, here are notes on some of the places where we could have gone in a different direction in our translation of the work, or where a Japanese cultural reference is used.

The New School Year, Page 5

As do many schools, Japan divides up its graduating classes into different homeroom classes. Unlike most Western schools, however, the homeroom students take *all* of their classes together. The people in your homeroom will be the people with whom you spend almost every minute of every school day throughout the entire year. So the class list becomes even more important to Japanese students than it would be in the West.

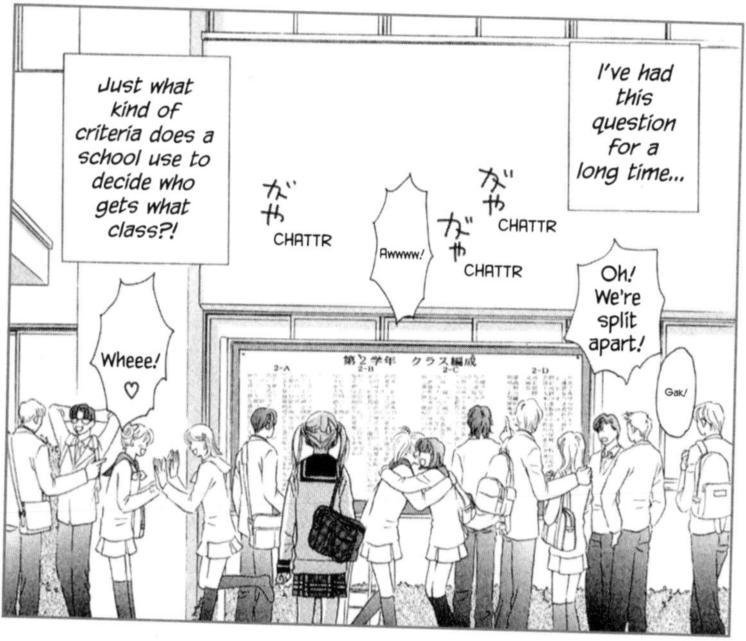
I've had this question for a long time...
Just what kind of criteria does a school use to decide who gets what class?!
CHATTR
CHATTR
Oh! We're split apart!
Gak!
Awwww!
CHATTR
Wheee! ♡
第2学年 クラス編成

Act Studio, Page 28

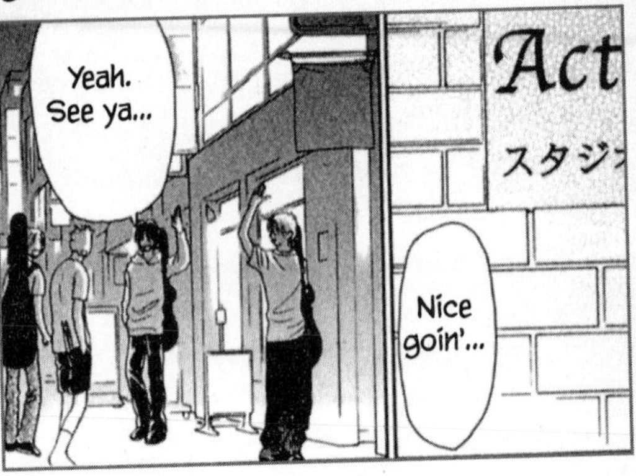
Act
Nice goin'...
Yeah. See ya...

The studio that Moriyama commutes to after school is probably an oblique reference to the Okinawa Actors School in Okinawa, Japan. There are many schools which teach young people how to perform on stage, similar to the New York City High School for the Performing Arts (popularized in the movie *Fame*). However, the Actors School is more specialized, concentrating on what it takes to make it in modern Japanese pop culture ... especially as idols.

Les Paul, Page 35

One of the premier names among guitar manufacturers today.

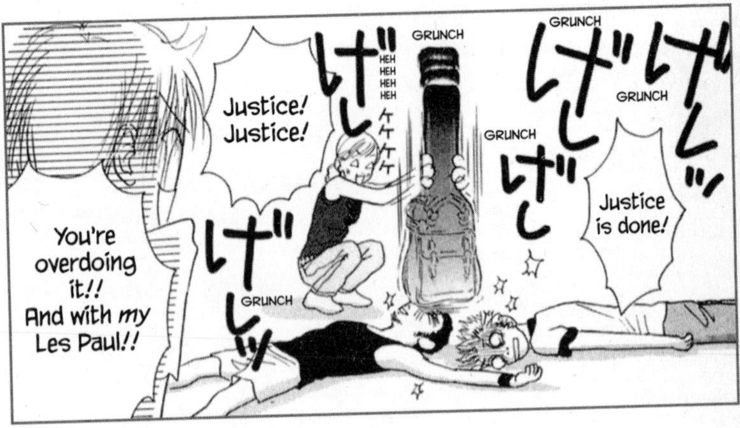
GRUNCH
GRUNCH
Justice is done!
GRUNCH
GRUNCH
HEH HEH HEH HEH
Justice! Justice!
GRUNCH
You're overdoing it!! And with *my* Les Paul!!

Harajuku Station, Page 51

Yaya has her own reasons for loving Harajuku Station, but in truth it is a very pretty place. The open-air platform is situated on the edge of Yoyogi Park and about twenty feet below ground level, so it gives the impression of being surrounded by trees and greenery—unusual for a station sitting between two of Tokyo's busiest urban centers, Shinjuku and Shibuya. The architecture is Tudor-style and conveys the romantic feel of the 1910s or 1920s.

Harajuku! Harajuku Station!
It's like an elixir just arriving at the station!

Assigned Seats, Page 81

In the same way all homerooms stay together (and only the teachers move from room to room), so also does a student stay in one seat for the entire year. Due to the lack of mobility, the importance of getting yourself a good seat becomes paramount.

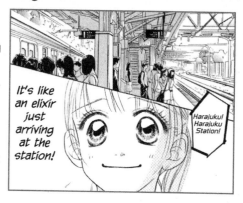

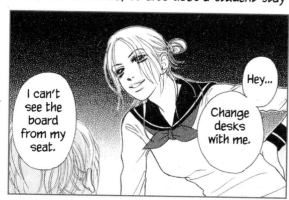

Hey...
Change desks with me.
I can't see the board from my seat.

Open-Air Concerts, Page 95

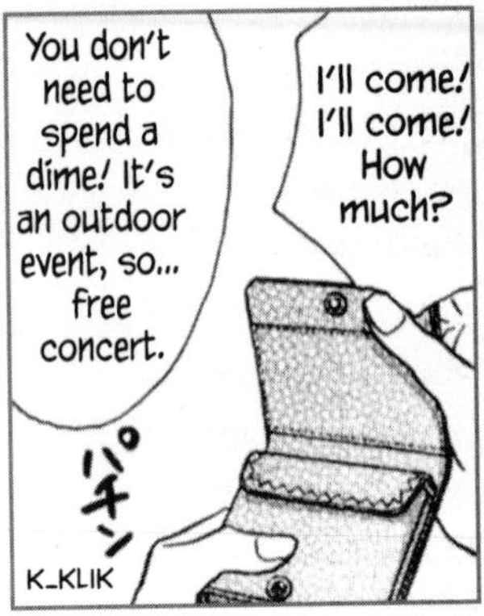
I'll come! I'll come! How much?
You don't need to spend a dime! It's an outdoor event, so... free concert.
K-KLIK

Anyone wanting to hear some free rock music can hightail it to Harajuku on a Sunday afternoon and listen to one of the many bands competing for the attention of fans, passersby, and especially record-label representatives who may be hiding in the crowd. But Harajuku isn't the only place for free music. Many parks and other public areas have bandstands and offer live, free performances to draw people into their facilities. The bands are usually unpaid, but the exposure may bring new fans to their paying gigs in bars and clubs.

Smokestack Women, Page 111

They're everywhere. People sensitive to tobacco smoke have a hard time of it in Japan. Although the trend is downward (declining at about 1% per year), there is still an enormous number of smokers. A recent survey estimated nearly one in four women in their twenties smoke. Not surprisingly, deaths directly attributed to tobacco use are up to more than 50,000 a year.

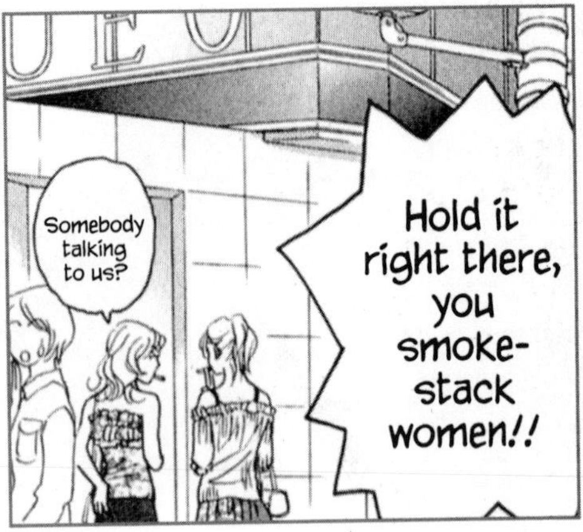
Hold it right there, you smoke-stack women!!
Somebody talking to us?

Outmoded Page 150

Tight jeans (in Japan called *han-ketsu* or half-butt) are more often called hip-hugger jeans.

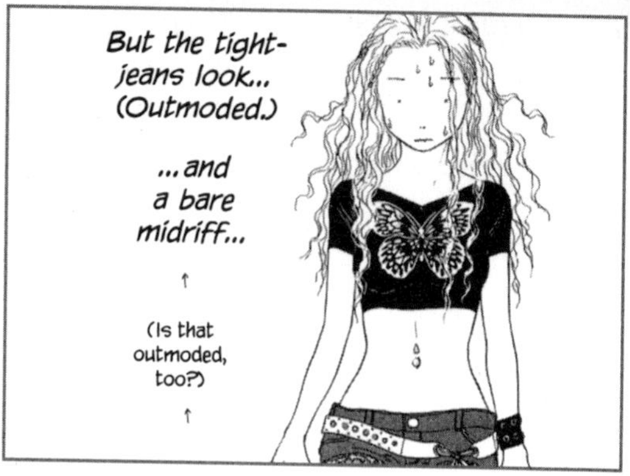
But the tight-jeans look... (Outmoded.)
...and a bare midriff...
(Is that outmoded, too?)

The Dangerous Part of Town, Page 167

There are districts in most urban centers of Japan that are considered more dangerous than other parts of the city. The Kabuki-cho section of Shinjuku, for example, is filled with hostess bars, pachinko and gambling houses, love hotels, and other less-than-upstanding businesses, and is rumored to be infiltrated by Yakuza (the Japanese mob). Still, with the minuscule crime rate in Japan, even these "dangerous" sections are safer than any American city's urban center.

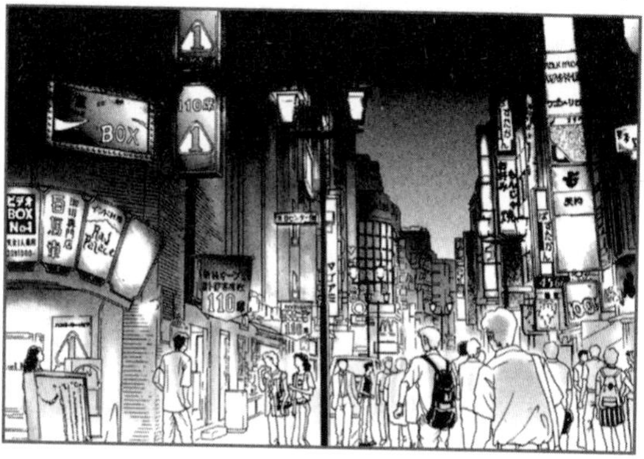
BOX
110番
BOX No.1
Raj Palace

Police Arrest, Page 174

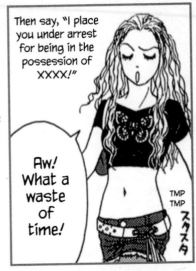

Then say, "I place you under arrest for being in the possession of XXXX!"
Aw! What a waste of time!
TMP TMP
スタスタ

Arrests in Japan usually involve the police officer making a statement that explains precisely what laws the suspect will be charged with breaking. Since, just like in the West, police dramas are very popular, Nana can rattle off a standard arrest speech in the same way that most Americans can recite the Miranda Rights. It's best not to be on the receiving end of that speech, because the conviction rate in Japan is reportedly above 90% (and some reports have it as high as 98%). In other words, if you get arrested in Japan, it's nearly the same as being convicted.

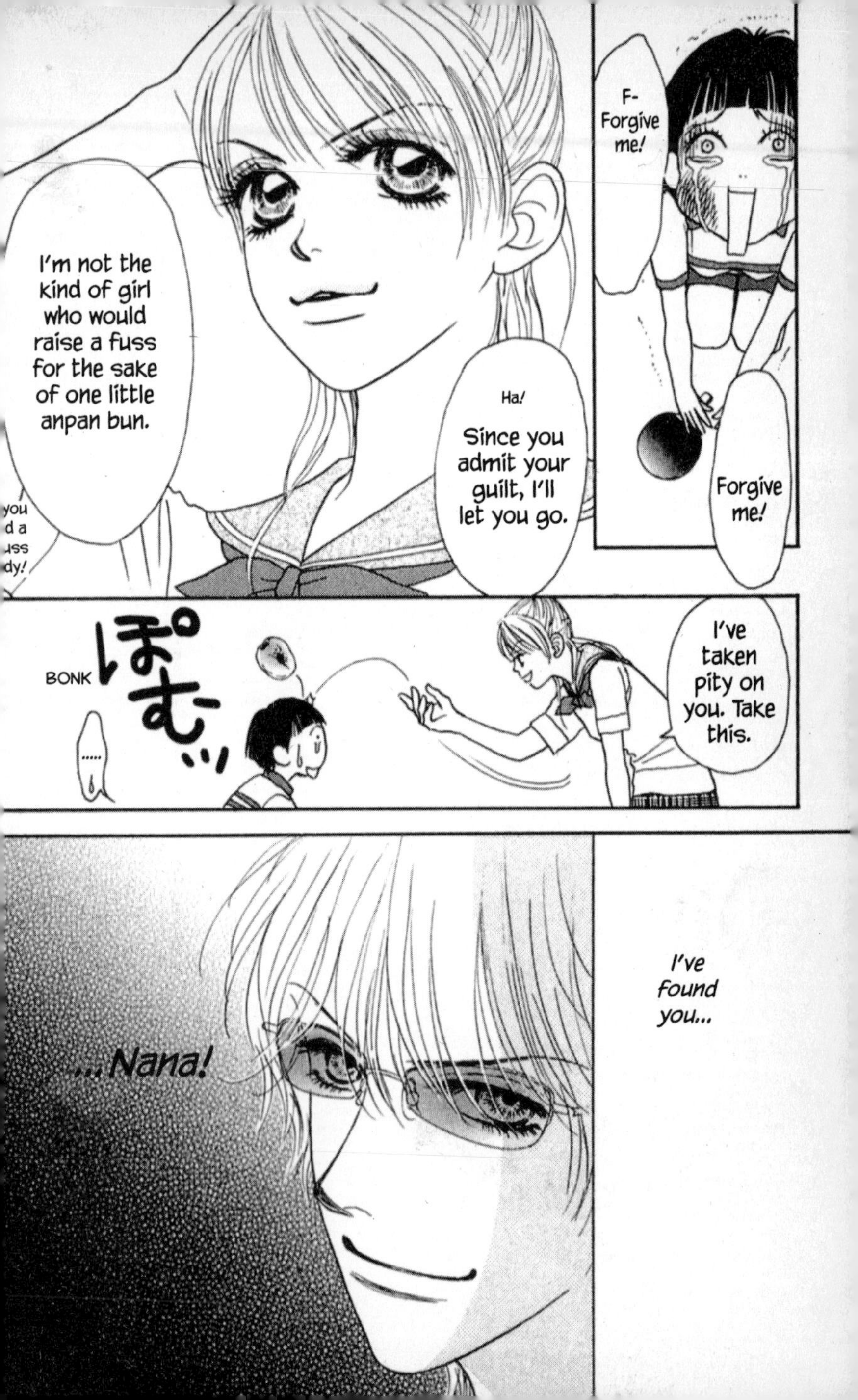

F- Forgive me!
Forgive me!
Ha!
Since you admit your guilt, I'll let you go.
I'm not the kind of girl who would raise a fuss for the sake of one little anpan bun.
I've taken pity on you. Take this.
ぽむっ
BONK
......
I've found you...
...Nana!

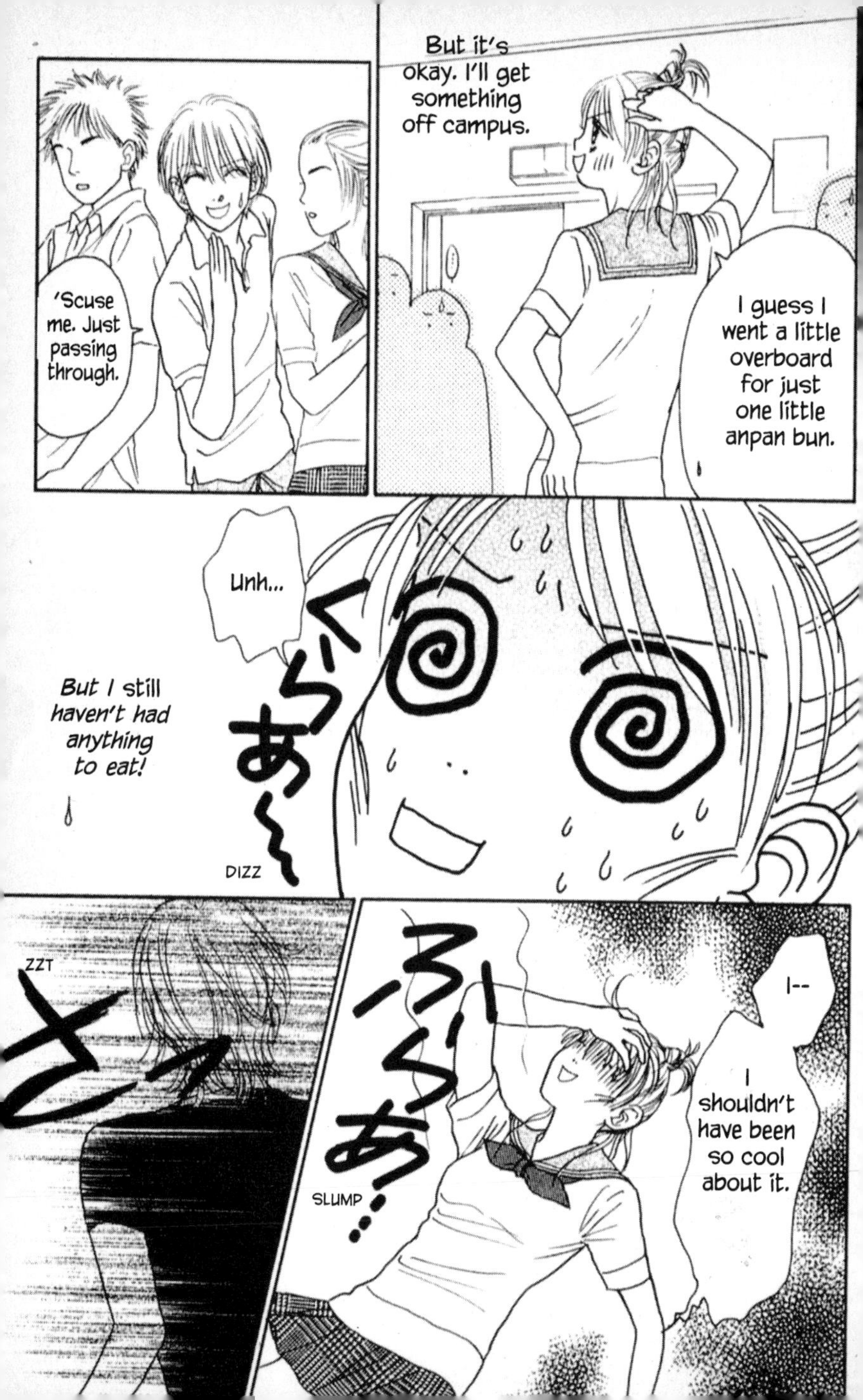
But it's okay. I'll get something off campus.
I guess I went a little overboard for just one little anpan bun.
'Scuse me. Just passing through.
Unh...
くらあ〜
DIZZ
But I still haven't had anything to eat!
I--
I shouldn't have been so cool about it.
ふらあ…
SLUMP
ZZT

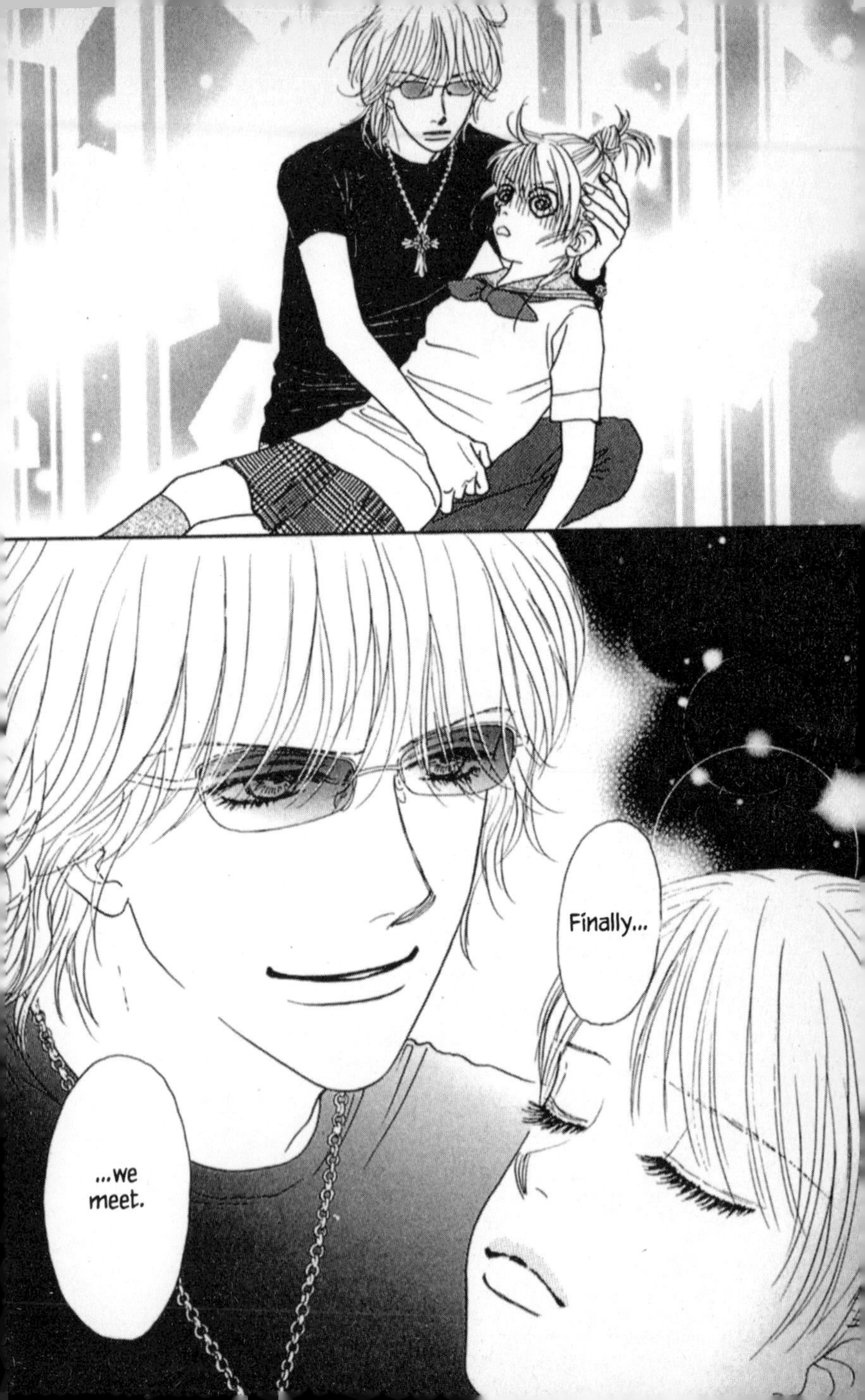
Finally...
...we meet.

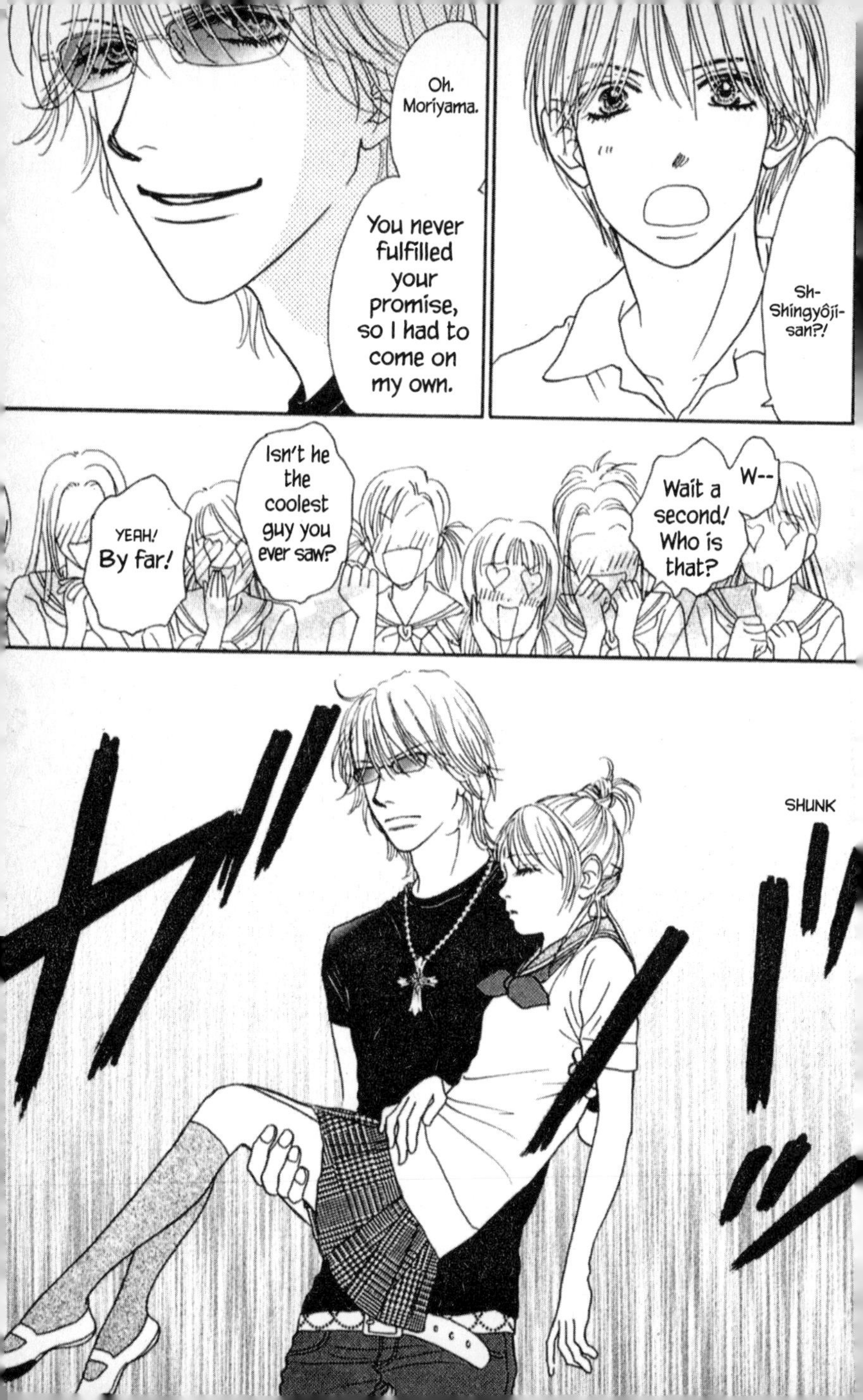
Sh-Shingyôji-san?!
Oh. Moriyama.
You never fulfilled your promise, so I had to come on my own.
W--
Wait a second! Who is that?
Isn't he the coolest guy you ever saw?
YEAH! By far!
SHUNK

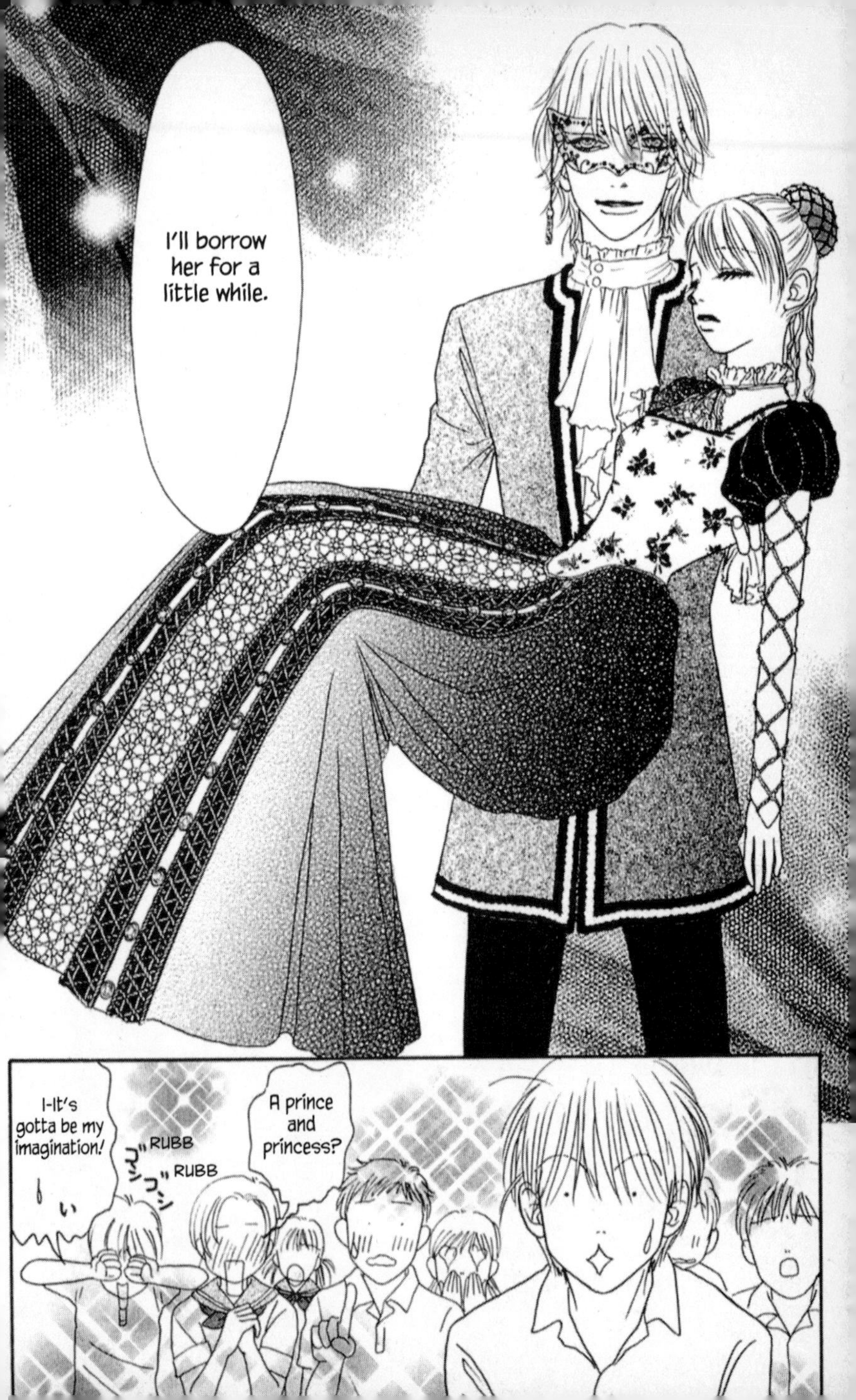
I'll borrow her for a little while.
A prince and princess?
RUBB
RUBB
I-It's gotta be my imagination!

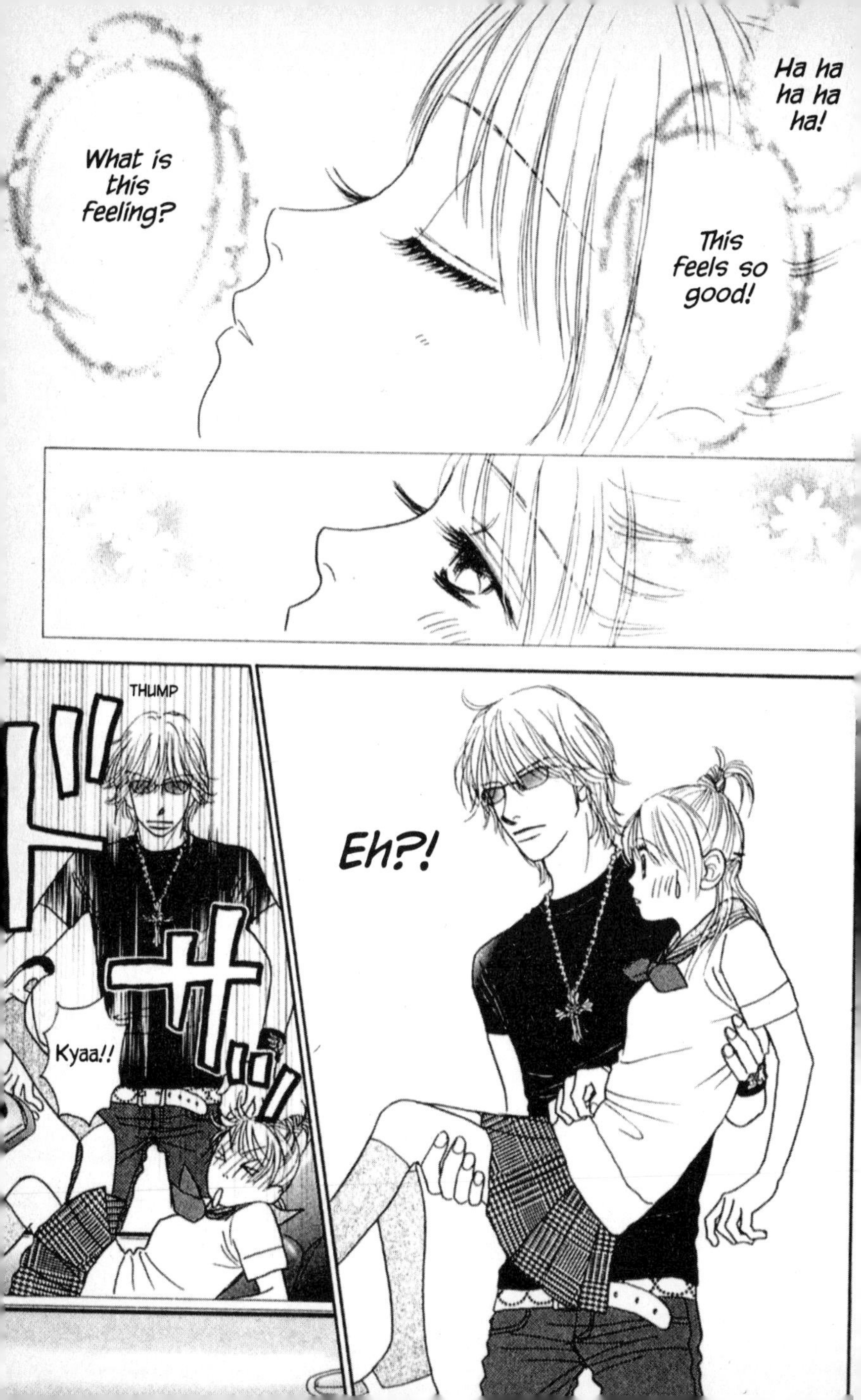
Ha ha ha ha ha!
This feels so good!
What is this feeling?
Eh?!
THUMP
Kyaa!!

FREE COLLARS KINGDOM

フリーカラーズキングダム

TAKUYA FUJIMI

THOSE FEISTY FELINES!

It's hard to resist Cyan: he's an adorable catboy, whose cute ears and tail have made him a beloved pet. But then his family abandons him, leaving the innocent Cyan to fend for himself.

Just when Cyan thinks he's all alone in the world, he meets the Free Collars, a cool gang of stray cats who believe that no feline should allow a human to imprison his Wild Spirit. They invite Cyan to join them, and the reluctant housecat has to decide fast, because a rival gang of cats is threatening the Free Collars' territory! Can Cyan learn to free his Wild Spirit—and help his new friends save their home?

Ages 16+

Special extras in each volume! Read them all!

Guru Guru Pon-Chan

RUFF RUFF LIFE

Ponta is a Labrador retriever puppy, the Koizumi family's pet. She's full of energy and usually up to some kind of mischief. But when Grandpa Koizumi, an amateur inventor, creates the Guru Guru Bone, Ponta's curiosity causes trouble. She nibbles the bone—and turns into a human girl!

Surprised but undaunted, Ponta ventures out of the house and meets Mirai Iwaki, the most popular boy at school. When Mirai saves her from a speeding car, Ponta changes back into her puppy self. Yet much has changed for Ponta during her short adventure as a human. Her heart races and her face flushes when she thinks of Mirai now. She's in love! Using the power of the Guru Guru Bone, Ponta switches back and forth from dog to girl—but can she win Mirai's affections?

1
Guru Guru
Pon-Chan
SATOMI IKEZAWA Creator of Othello!

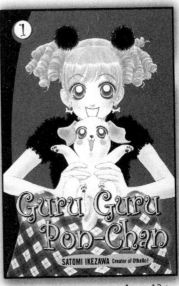

Ages: 13+

Winner of the Kodansha Manga of the Year Award!

Includes special extras after the story!

tanoshimi

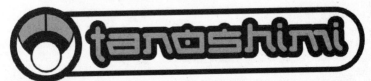

NEGIMA!™

BY KEN AKAMATSU

Negi Springfield is a ten-year-old wizard teaching English at an all-girls Japanese school. He dreams of becoming a master wizard like his legendary father, the Thousand Master. At first his biggest concern was concealing his magic powers, because if he's ever caught using them publicly, he thinks he'll be turned into an ermine! But in a world that gets stranger every day, it turns out that the strangest people of all are Negi's students! From a librarian with a magic book to a centuries-old vampire, from a robot to a ninja, Negi will risk his own life to protect the girls in his care!

Ages: 16+

Special extras in each volume! Read them all!

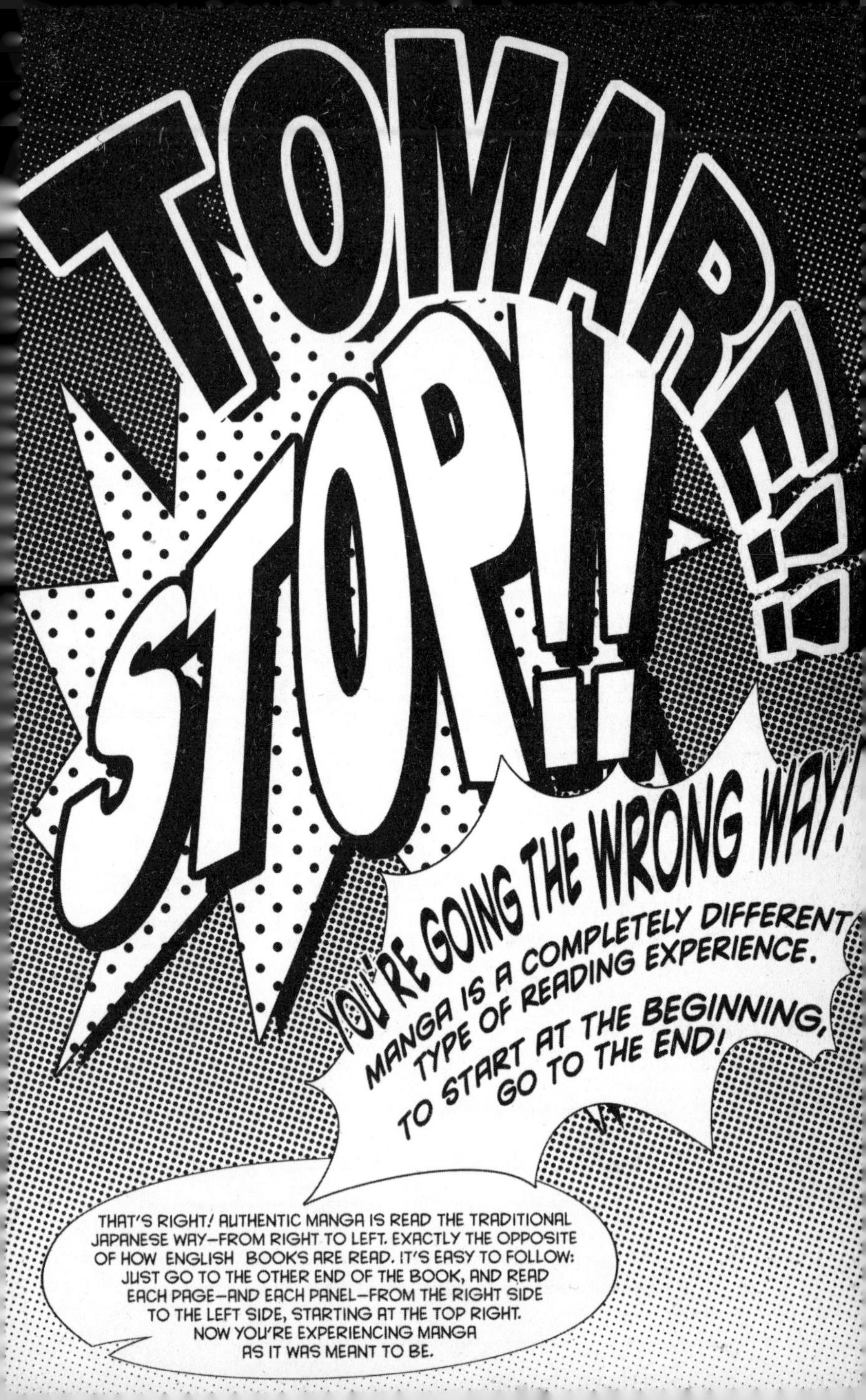
TOMARE!!
STOP!!
YOU'RE GOING THE WRONG WAY!
MANGA IS A COMPLETELY DIFFERENT TYPE OF READING EXPERIENCE.
TO START AT THE BEGINNING, GO TO THE END!
THAT'S RIGHT! AUTHENTIC MANGA IS READ THE TRADITIONAL JAPANESE WAY—FROM RIGHT TO LEFT. EXACTLY THE OPPOSITE OF HOW ENGLISH BOOKS ARE READ. IT'S EASY TO FOLLOW: JUST GO TO THE OTHER END OF THE BOOK, AND READ EACH PAGE—AND EACH PANEL—FROM THE RIGHT SIDE TO THE LEFT SIDE, STARTING AT THE TOP RIGHT. NOW YOU'RE EXPERIENCING MANGA AS IT WAS MEANT TO BE.